# MYTHICAL
# MONSTERS

# MYTHICAL
# MONSTERS

# CHARLES GOULD

**SENATE**

*Mythical Monsters*

This edition published in 1995 by Senate, an imprint of
Studio Editions Ltd, Princess House, 50 Eastcastle Street,
London W1N 7AP, England

ISBN 1 85958 178 1
Printed and bound in Guernsey by
The Guernsey Press Co. Ltd

# PREFACE.

THE Author has to express his great obligations to many gentlemen who have assisted him in the preparation of this volume, either by affording access to their libraries, or by furnishing or revising translations from the Chinese, &c. ; and he must especially tender them to J. Haas, Esq., the Austro-Hungarian Vice-Consul at Shanghai, to Mr. Thomas Kingsmill and the Rev. W. Holt of Shanghai, to Mr. Falconer of Hong-Kong, and to Dr. N. B. Dennys of Singapore.

For the sake of uniformity, the author has endeavoured to reduce all the romanised representations of Chinese sounds to the system adopted by S. W. Williams, whose invaluable dictionary is the most available one for students. No alteration, however, has been made when quotations from eminent sinologues like Legge have been inserted.

Should the present volume prove sufficiently interesting to attract readers, a second one will be issued at a future date, in continuation of the subject.

*June*, 1884.

---

## NOTE BY THE PUBLISHERS.

THE Publishers think it right to state that, owing to the Author's absence in China, the work has not had the advantage of his supervision in its passage through the press. It is also proper to mention that the MS. left the Author's hands eighteen months ago.

13, WATERLOO PLACE. S.W.
*January*, 1886.

# CONTENTS.

# MYTHICAL MONSTERS.

## INTRODUCTION.

It would have been a bold step indeed for anyone, some thirty years ago, to have thought of treating the public to a collection of stories ordinarily reputed fabulous, and of claiming for them the consideration due to genuine realities, or to have advocated tales, time-honoured as fictions, as actual facts; and those of the nursery as being, in many instances, legends, more or less distorted, descriptive of real beings or events.

Now-a-days it is a less hazardous proceeding. The great era of advanced opinion, initiated by Darwin, which has seen, in the course of a few years, a larger progress in knowledge in all departments of science than decades of centuries preceding it, has, among other changes, worked a complete revolution in the estimation of the value of folk-lore; and speculations on it, which in the days of our boyhood would have been considered as puerile, are now admitted to be not merely interesting but necessary to those who endeavour to gather up the skeins of unwritten history, and to trace the antecedents and early migrations from parent sources of nations long since alienated from each other by customs, speech, and space.

I have, therefore, but little hesitation in gravely proposing to submit that many of the so-called mythical animals, which throughout long ages and in all nations have been the fertile subjects of fiction and fable, come legitimately within the scope of plain matter-of-fact Natural History, and that they may be considered, not as the outcome of exuberant fancy, but as creatures which really once existed, and of which, unfortunately, only imperfect and inaccurate descriptions have filtered down to us, probably very much refracted, through the mists of time.

I propose to follow, for a certain distance only, the path which has been pursued in the treatment of myths by mythologists, so far only, in fact, as may be necessary to trace out the homes and origin of those stories which in their later dress are incredible ; deviating from it to dwell upon the possibility of their having preserved to us, through the medium of unwritten Natural History, traditions of creatures once co-existing with man, some of which are so weird and terrible as to appear at first sight to be impossible. I propose stripping them of those supernatural characters with which a mysteriously implanted love of the wonderful has invested them, and to examine them, as at the present day we are fortunately able to do, by the lights of the modern sciences of Geology, Evolution, and Philology.

For me the major part of these creatures are not chimeras but objects of rational study. The dragon, in place of being a creature evolved out of the imagination of Aryan man by the contemplation of lightning flashing through the caverns which he tenanted, as is held by some mythologists, is an animal which once lived and dragged its ponderous coils, and perhaps flew ; which devastated herds, and on occasions swallowed their shepherd ; which, establishing its lair in some cavern overlooking the fertile plain, spread terror and destruction around, and, protected from assault by dread or superstitious feeling, may even have been subsidised by the terror-stricken peasantry, who, failing the power to destroy it, may have preferred tethering offerings of cattle adjacent to its cavern to having it come down to seek supplies from amongst their midst.*

To me the specific existence of the unicorn seems not incredible, and, in fact, more probable than that theory which assigns its origin to a lunar myth.†

Again, believing as I do in the existence of some great undescribed inhabitant of the ocean depths, the much-derided sea-serpent, whose home seems especially to be adjacent to Norway, I recognise this monster as originating the myths of the midgard serpent which the Norse Elder Eddas have collected, this being the contrary view to that taken by mythologists, who invert the derivation, and suppose the stories current among the Norwegian fishermen to be modified versions of this important element of Norse mythology.‡

---

* This tributary offering is a common feature in dragon legends. A good example is that given by El Edrisi in his history of the dragon destroyed by Alexander the Great in the island of Mostachin (one of the Canaries?).

† The latest writer on this point summarizes his views, in his opening remarks, as follows :—" The science of heraldry has faithfully preserved to modern times various phases of some of those remarkable legends which, based upon a study of natural phenomena, exhibit the process whereby the greater part of mythology has come into existence. Thus we find the solar gryphon, the solar phœnix, a demi-eagle displayed issuing from flames of fire; the solar lion and the lunar unicorn, which two latter noble creatures now harmoniously support the royal arms. I propose in the following pages to examine the myth of the unicorn, the wild, white, fierce, chaste, moon, whose two horns, unlike those of mortal creatures, are indissolubly twisted into one; the creature that endlessly fights with the lion to gain the crown or summit of heaven, which neither may retain, and whose brilliant horn drives away the darkness and evil of the night even as we find in the myth, that Venym is defended by the horn of the unicorn."—*The Unicorn; a Mythological Investigation.* Robert Brown, jun., F.S.A. London, 1881.

‡ " The midgard or world-serpent we have already become tolerably well acquainted with, and recognise in him the wild tumultuous sea. Thor contended with him; he got him on his hook, but did not succeed

I must admit that, for my part, I doubt the general derivation of myths from "the contemplation of the visible
workings of external nature."* It seems to me easier to
suppose that the palsy of time has enfeebled the utterance of
these oft-told tales until their original appearance is almost
unrecognisable, than that uncultured savages should possess
powers of imagination and poetical invention far beyond
those enjoyed by the most instructed nations of the present
day ; less hard to believe that these wonderful stories of gods
and demigods, of giants and dwarfs, of dragons and monsters
of all descriptions, are transformations than to believe them
to be inventions.†

The author of *Atlantis*,‡ indeed, claims that the gods and
goddesses of the ancient Greeks, the Phœnicians, the Hindoos, and the Scandinavians were simply the kings, queens,
and heroes of Atlantis, and the acts attributed to them in
mythology a confused recollection of real historical events.
Without conceding the *locus* of the originals, which requires
much greater examination than I am able to make at the

---

in killing him.  We also remember how Thor tried to lift him in the
form of a cat.  The North abounds in stories about the sea-serpent,
which are nothing but variations of the original myths of the Eddas.
Odin cast him into the sea, where he shall remain until he is conquered
by Thor in Ragnarok."—*Norse Mythology*, p. 387.  R. B. Anderson,
Chicago, 1879.

* *Vide* Anderson.

† Just as even the greatest masters of fiction adapt but do not origi-
nate.  Harold Skimpole and Wilkins Micawber sat unconsciously for
their portraits in real life, and the most charming characters and fertile
plots produced by that most prolific of all writers, A. Dumas, are mere
elaborations of people and incidents with which historical memoirs
provided him.

‡ *Atlantis; the Antediluvian World.*  J. Donelly, New York, 1882.
The author has amassed, with untiring labour, a large amount of evidence to prove that the island of Atlantis, in place of being a myth or
fable of Plato, really once existed ; was the source of all modern arts
and civilization ; and was destroyed in a catastrophe which he identifies
with the Biblical Deluge.

present time, I quite agree with him as to the principle. I believe that the mythological deities represent a confused chronology of far-distant times, and that the destruction of the Nemean lion, the Lernean hydra, and the Minotaur are simply the records of acts of unusual bravery in combating ferocious animals.

On the first landing of Pizarro the Mexicans entertained the opinion that man and horse were parts of one strange animal,* and we have thus a clue to the explanation of the origin of the belief in centaurs from a distant view of horsemen, a view possibly followed by the immediate flight of the observer, which rendered a solution of the extraordinary phenomenon impossible.

### ON THE CREDIBILITY OF REMARKABLE STORIES.

Ferdinand Mendez Pinto quaintly observes, in one of his earlier chapters, "I will not speak of the Palace Royal, because I saw it but on the outside, howbeit the Chinese tell such wonders of it as would amaze a man; for it is my intent to relate nothing save what we beheld here with our own eyes, and that was so much as that I am afraid to write it; not that it would seem strange to those who have seen and read the marvels of the kingdom of China, but because I doubt that they which would compare those wondrous things that are in the countries they have not seen, with that little they have seen in their own, will make some question

---

* So also, Father Stanislaus Arlet, of the Society of Jesus, writing to the General of the Society in 1698 respecting a new Mission in Peru, and speaking of a Peruvian tribe calling themselves Canisian, says: "Having never before seen horses, or men resembling us in colour and dress, the astonishment they showed at our first appearance among them was a very pleasing spectacle to us, the sight of us terrifying them to such a degree that the bows and arrows fell from their hand; imagining, as they afterwards owned, that the man, his hat, his clothes, and the horse he rode upon, composed but one animal."

of it, or, it may be, give no credit at all to these truths,
because they are not conformable to their understanding
and small experience."*

---

* *The Voyages and Adventures of Ferdinand Mendez Pinto*, done into
English by H. C. Gent, London, 1653, p. 109. The vindication of
Pinto's reputation for veracity will doubtless one day be, to a great
extent, effected, for although his interesting narrative is undoubtedly
embroidered with a rich tissue of falsity, due apparently to an exaggerated credulity upon his part, and systematic deception upon that of his
Chinese informants, he certainly is undeserving of the wholesale con-
demnation of which Congreve was the reflex when he made Foresight,
addressing Sir Sampson Legend, say : "Thou modern Mandeville,
Ferdinand Mendez Pinto was but a type of thee, thou liar of the first
magnitude."—*Love for Love*, Act. 2, Scene 1. There are many points
in his narrative which are corroborated by history and the accounts of
other voyages ; and it must be remembered that, although the major
part of the names of places and persons which he gives are now unrecognisable, yet this may be due to alterations from the lapse of time,
and from the difficulty of recognising the true original Chinese or
Japanese word under those produced by the foreign mode of translitera-
tion in vogue in those days. Thus the Port Liampoo of Pinto is now
and has been for many years past only known as Ningpo, the first name
being a term of convenience, used by the early Portuguese voyagers,
and long since abandoned. Just as the wonderful Quinsay of Marco
Polo (still known by that name in Pinto's time) has been only success-
fully identified (with Hangchow-fu) through the antiquarian research
of Colonel Yule. So also the titles of Chaems, Tutons, Chumbins,
Aytons, Anchacy's, which Pinto refers to (p. 108), are only with difficulty recognisable in those respectively of Tsi'ang (a Manchu governor),
Tu-tung (Lieutenant-General), Tsung-ping (Brigadier-General), Tao-tai
[? ?] (Intendant of Circuit) and Ngan-ch'a She-sze (Provincial Judge),
as rendered by the modern sinologue Mayers in his Essay on the
Chinese Government, Shanghai, 1878. The incidental references to the
country, people, habits, and products, contained in the chapter describing
his passage in captivity from Nanquin to Pequin are true to nature, and
the apparently obviously untruthful statement which he makes of the
employment by the King of Tartary of thousands of rhinoceri both as
beasts of burthen and articles of food (p. 158) is explicable, I think, on
the supposition that some confusion has arisen, either in translation or
transcription, between rhinoceros and camel. Anyone who has seen the
long strings of camels wending their way to Pekin from the various
northern roads through the passes into Mongolia, would readily believe

Now as some of the creatures whose existence I shall have to contend for in these volumes are objects of derision to a large proportion of mankind, and of reasonable doubt to another, I cannot help fortifying myself with some such out-work of reasoning as the pith of Pinto's remarks affords, and supplementing it by adding that, while the balance between scepticism and credulity is undoubtedly always difficult to hold, yet, as Lord Bacon well remarks, "There is nothing makes a man suspect much more than to know little; and therefore men should remedy suspicion by procuring to know more."

Whately extends Bacon's proposition by adding, "This is equally true of the suspicions that have reference to things as persons"; in other words, ignorance and suspicion go hand-in-hand, and so travellers' tales, even when supported by good evidence, are mostly denied credence or accepted with repugnance, when they offend the experience of those who, remaining at home, are thus only partially educated. Hence it is, not to go too far back for examples, that we have seen Bruce, Mungo Park, Du Chaillu, Gordon Cumming, Schliemann,* and Stanley treated with the most ungenerous criticism and contemptuous disbelief by persons who, however well informed in many subjects, lacked the extended and appreciative views which can only be acquired by travel.

Nor is this incredulity limited to travellers' tales about savage life. It is just as often displayed in reference to the

---

that a large transport corps of them could easily be amassed by a despotic monarch; while the vast numbers of troops to which Pinto makes reference are confirmed by more or less authentic histories.

* "I was myself an eye-witness of two such discoveries and helped to gather the articles together. The slanderers have long since been silenced, who were not ashamed to charge the discoverer with an imposture."—Prof. Virchow, in Appendix I. to Schliemann's *Ilios.* Murray, 1880.

surroundings of uneventful life, provided they are different from those with which we are familiar.

Saladin rebuked the Knight of the Leopard for falsehood when the latter assured him that the waters of lakes in his own country became at times solidified, so that armed and mounted knights could cross them as if on dry land. And the wise Indian who was taken down to see the large American cities, with the expectation that, being convinced of the resources and irresistible power of civilization he would influence his tribe to submission on his return, to the surprise of the commissioners who had conveyed him, spoke in directly contrary terms to those expected of him, privately explaining in reply to their remonstrances, that had he told the truth to his tribe he would have been indelibly branded for the remainder of his life as an outrageous and contemptible liar. Chinese students, despatched for education in American or European capitals, are compelled on their return to make similar reservations, under pain of incurring a like penalty; and officials who, from contact with Europeans at the open ports, get their ideas expanded too quickly, are said to be liable to isolation in distant regions, where their advanced and fantastic opinions may do as little harm to right-thinking people as possible.*

Even scientific men are sometimes as crassly incredulous as the uncultured masses. On this point hear Mr. A. R. Wallace.† "Many now living remember the time (for it is

---

* "But ask them to credit an electric telegram, to understand a steam-engine, to acknowledge the microscopic revelations spread out before their eyes, to put faith in the Atlantic cable or the East India House, and they will tell you that you are a barbarian with blue eyes, a fan kwai, and a sayer of that which is not. The dragon and the phœnix are true, but the rotifer and the message, the sixty miles an hour, the cable, and the captive kings are false."—*Household Words*, October 30th, 1855.

† Address delivered to the Biological Section of the British Association. Glasgow, 1876.

little more than twenty years ago) when the antiquity of man, as now understood, was universally discredited. Not only theologians, but even geologists taught us that man belonged to the existing state of things; that the extinct animals of the tertiary period had finally disappeared, and that the earth's surface had assumed its present condition before the human race first came into existence. So prepossessed were scientific men with this idea, which yet rested on purely negative evidence, and could not be supported by any argument of scientific value, that numerous facts which had been presented at intervals for half a century, all tending to prove the existence of man at very remote epochs, were silently ignored, and, more than this, the detailed statements of three distinct and careful observers confirming each other were rejected by a great scientific society as too improbable for publication, only because they proved (if they were true) the co-existence of man with extinct animals."*

The travels of that faithful historian, Marco Polo, were for a long time considered as fables, and the graphic descriptions of the Abbé Huc even still find detractors continuing the *rôle* of those who maintained that he had never even visited the countries which he described.

Gordon Cumming was disbelieved when he asserted that he had killed an antelope, out of a herd, with a rifle-shot at a distance of eight hundred yards.

Madame Merian† was accused of deliberate falsehood in reference to her description of a bird-eating spider nearly

---

* In 1854 a communication from the Torquay Natural History Society, confirming previous accounts by Mr. Goodwin Austen, Mr. Vivian, and the Rev. Mr. McEnery, "that worked flints occurred in Kents Hole with remains of extinct species," was rejected as too improbable for publication.

† "She is set down a thorough heretic, not at all to be believed, a manufacturer of unsound natural history, an inventor of false facts in science."—Gosse, *Romance of Nat. Hist.*, 2nd Series, p. 227.

two hundred years ago. But now-a-days Mr. Bates and other reliable observers have confirmed it in regard to South America, India, and elsewhere.

Audubon was similarly accused by botanists of having invented the yellow water-lily, which he figured in his *Birds of the South* under the name of Nymphæa lutea, and after having lain under the imputation for years, was confirmed at last by the discovery of the long-lost flower, in Florida, by Mrs. Mary Trent, in the summer of 1876;* and this encourages us to hope that some day or other a fortunate sportsman may rediscover the Haliætus Washingtonii, in regard to which Dr. Cover says: "That famous bird of Washington was a myth; either Audubon was mistaken, or else, as some do not hesitate to affirm, he lied about it."

FIG. 1.—FISHERMAN ATTACKED BY OCTOPUS.
*(Facsimile from a drawing by Hokusai, a celebrated Japanese artist who lived about the beginning of the present century.)*

Victor Hugo was ridiculed for having exceeded the bounds of poetic license when he produced his marvellous word-painting of the devil-fish, and described a man as becoming its helpless victim. The thing was derided as a monstrous

* *Pop. Sci. Monthly*, No. 60, April 1877.

impossibility ; yet within a few years were discovered, on the shores of Newfoundland, cuttle-fishes with arms extending to thirty feet in length, and capable of dragging a good-sized boat beneath the surface ; and their action has been reproduced for centuries past, as the representation of a well-known fact, in *net sukes* (ivory carvings) and illustrations by Japanese artists.*

* "By the kindness of my friend, Mr. Bartlett, I have been enabled to examine a most beautiful Japanese carving in ivory, said to be one hundred and fifty years old, and called by the Japanese *net suke* or *togle*. These togles are handed down from one generation to the next, and they record any remarkable event that happens to any member of a family. This carving is an inch and a half long, and about as big as a walnut. It represents a lady in a quasi-leaning attitude, and at first sight it is difficult to perceive what she is doing ; but after a while the details come out magnificently. The unfortunate lady has been seized by an octopus when bathing—for the lady wears a bathing-dress. One extended arm of the octopus is in the act of coiling round the lady's neck, and she is endeavouring to pull it off with her right hand; another arm of the sea-monster is entwined round the left wrist, while the hand is fiercely tearing at the mouth of the brute. The other arms of the octopus are twined round, grasping the lady's body and waist—in fact, her position reminds one very much of Laocoon in the celebrated statue of the snakes seizing him and his two sons. The sucking discs of the octopus are carved exactly as they are in nature, and the colour of the body of the creature, together with the formidable aspect of the eye, are wonderfully represented. The face of this Japanese lady is most admirably done; it expresses the utmost terror and alarm, and possibly may be a portrait. So carefully is the carving executed that the lady's white teeth can be seen between her lips. The hair is a perfect gem of work; it is jet black, extended down the back, and tied at the end in a knot; in fact, it is so well done that I can hardly bring myself to think that it is not real hair, fastened on in some most ingenious manner ; but by examining it under a powerful magnifying glass I find it is not so—it is the result of extraordinary cleverness in carving. The back of the little white comb fixed into the thick of the black hair adds to the effect of this magnificent carving of the hair. I congratulate Mr. Bartlett on the acquisition of this most beautiful curiosity. There is an inscription in Japanese characters on the underneath part of the carving, and Mr. Bartlett and myself would, of course, only be too glad to get this translated."—Frank Buckland, in *Land and Water.*

Before the days of Darwinism, what courage was requisite in a man who propounded any theory a little bit extravagant! Hark how, even less than twenty years ago, the ghost of the unfortunate Lord Monboddo had bricks of criticism pelted at it, half earnestly, half contemptuously, by one of our greatest thinkers, whose thought happened to run in grooves different from those travelled in by the mind of the unfortunate Scotchman.

" Lord Monboddo* had just finished his great work, by which he derives all mankind from a couple of apes, and all the dialects of the world from a language originally framed by some Egyptian gods, when the discovery of Sanskrit came on him like a thunderbolt. It must be said, however, to his credit, that he at once perceived the immense importance of the discovery. He could not be expected to sacrifice his primordial monkeys or his Egyptian idols, &c."

And again : "It may be of interest to give one other extract in order to show how well, apart from his men with, and his monkeys without, tails, Lord Monboddo could sift and handle the evidence that was placed before him."

Max Müller also furnishes us with an amazing example of scepticism on the part of Dugald Stewart. He says† : "However, if the facts about Sanskrit were true, Dugald Stewart was too wise not to see that the conclusions drawn from them were inevitable. He therefore denied the reality of such a language as Sanskrit altogether, and wrote his famous essay to prove that Sanskrit had been put together, after the model of Greek and Latin, by those archforgers and liars, the Brahmans, and that the whole of Sanskrit literature was an imposition."

So Ctesias attacked Herodotus. The very existence of

---

* Max Müller, *Science of Language*, 4th edition, p. 163–165. London, 1864.

† *Science of Language*, p. 168.

Homer has been denied, and even the authorship of Shake-speare's plays questioned.\*

We are all familiar enough now with the black swan, but Ovid† considered it as so utterly impossible that he clinched, as it were, an affirmation by saying, "If I doubted, O Maximus, of thy approval of these words, I could believe that there are swans of the colour of Memnon" [*i.e.* black]; and even so late as the days of Sir Thomas Browne, we find them classed by him with flying horses, hydras, centaurs, harpies, and satyrs, as monstrosities, rarities, or else poetical fancies.‡

Now that we have all seen the great hippopotamus disport himself in his tank in the gardens of the Zoological Society, we can smile at the grave arguments of the savant who, while admitting the existence of the animal, disputed the possibility of his walking about on the bed of a river, because his great bulk would prevent his rising again.§ But I dare-

---

\* "When a naturalist, either by visiting such spots of earth as are still out of the way, or by his good fortune, finds a very queer plant or animal, he is forthwith accused of inventing his game, the word not being used in its old sense of *discovery* but in its modern of *creation.* As soon as the creature is found to sin against preconception, the great (mis?) guiding spirit, *à priori* by name, who furnishes philosophers with their omniscience *pro re natâ,* whispers that no such thing *can* be, and forthwith there is a charge of hoax. The heavens themselves have been charged with hoaxes. When Leverrier and Adams predicted a planet by calculation, it was gravely asserted in some quarters that the planet which had been calculated was not *the* planet but another which had clandestinely and improperly got into the neighbourhood of the true body. The disposition to suspect hoax is stronger than the disposition to hoax. Who was it that first announced that the classical writings of Greece and Rome were one huge hoax perpetrated by the monks in what the announcer would be as little or less inclined than Dr. Maitland to call the dark ages?"—*Macmillan,* 1860.

† *Poetic Epistles,* Bk. iii., Ep. 3.

‡ *Rara avis in terris, nigroque simillima cygno.*

§ "Having showed the foregoing description of the mountain cow, called by the Spaniards *ante* [*manatee*?], to a person of honour, he was pleased to send it to a learned person in Holland." This learned person

say it passed muster in his days as a very sound and shrewd observation, just as, possibly, but for the inconvenient waggery of Peter Pindar, might have done the intelligent inquiry, which he records, after the seam in the apple-dumpling.

Poor Fray Gaspar de Jan Bernardine who, in 1611, undertook the journey by land from India to Portugal, was unfortunate enough to describe the mode in which the captain of the caravan communicated intelligence to Bagdad by carrier pigeon. "He had pigeons whose young and nests were at his house in that city, and every two days he let fly a pigeon with a letter tied to its foot containing the news of his journey. This account met with but little belief in Europe, and was treated there as a matter of merriment."*

The discredit under which this traveller fell is the more surprising because the same custom had alreadybeen noted by Sir John Mandeville, who, in speaking of Syria and adjacent countries, says : "In that contree, and other contrees beyond, thei have custom, whan thei schulle usen warre, and when men holden sege abouten Cytee or Castelle, and thei withinen dur not senden messagers with lettres frō Lord to Lord for to ask Sokour, thei maken here Lettres and bynden hem to the Nekke of a Colver and leten the Colver flee, and the Colveren ben so taughte, that thei flun with the Lettres to the very place that men wolde send hem to.  For the Col-

---

discusses it and compares it with the hippopotamus, and winds up by saying, in reference to a description of the habits of the hippopotamus, as noticed at Loango by Captain Rogers, to the effect that when they are in the water they will sink to the bottom, and then walk as on dry ground, "but what he says of her sinking to the bottom in deep rivers, and walking there, if he adds, what I think he supposes, that it rises again, and comes on the land, I much question; for that such a huge body should raise itself up again (though I know whales and great fish can do) transcends the faith of J. H."—F. J. Knapton, *Collection of Voyages*, vol. ii., part ii. p. 13.  4 vols., London, 1729.

\* *Historical Account of Discoveries and Travels in Asia.*  Hugh Murray, F.R.S.E., 3 vols. 8vo. Edinburgh, 1820.

veres ben norrysscht in the Places Where thei been sent to,
and thei senden them there, for to beren here Lettres, and
the Colveres retournen agen, where as thei ben norrischt,
and so thei dou commonly."

While, long before, Pliny had referred to it in his *Natural
History** as follows : " In addition to this, pigeons have acted
as messengers in affairs of importance. During the siege of
Mutina, Decimus Brutus, who was in the town, sent
despatches to the camp of the Consuls, fastened to pigeons'
feet. Of what use to Antony, then, were his entrenchments?
and all the vigilance of the besieging army ? his nets, too,
which he had spread in the river, while the messenger of the
besieged was cleaving the air ? "

The pace of railways ; steam communication across the
Atlantic ; the Suez Canal† ; were not all these considered in
former days to be impossible ? With these examples of
failure of judgment before us, it may be fairly asked whether,
in applying our minds to the investigation of the reality of
creatures apparently monstrous, we duly reflect upon the
extraordinary, almost miraculous, events which incessantly
occur in the course of the short existence of all animated
nature ? Supposing the history of insects were unknown to
us, could the wildest imagination conceive such a marvellous
transformation as that which takes place continually around
us in the passage from the larva through the chrysalis to the
butterfly ? or human ingenuity invent one so bizarre as that
recorded by Steenstrup in his theory of the alternation of
generation ?

We accept as nothing marvellous, only because we see
them daily, the organization and the polity of a community

---

* Bk. x., chap. 53.

† A writer in *Macmillan's Magazine* in 1860 concludes a series of ob-
jections to the canal as follows : " And the Emperor must hesitate to
identify himself with an operation which might not impossibly come to
be designated by posterity as ' Napoleon's Folly.' "

of ants ; their collaboration, their wars, and their slaveries
have been so often stated that they cease to astonish.   The
same may be said of the marvellous architecture of birds,
their construction of houses to live in, of bowers to play in,
and even of gardens to gratify their sense of beauty.*

We admire the ingenious imagination of Swift, and
essayists dwell upon his happy conceits and upon the ability
with which, in his celebrated work, he has ordered all things
to harmonise in dimensions with the enlarged and reduced
scales on which he has conceived the men and animals of
Brobdignag and Lilliput.   So much even has this quaint
idea been appreciated, that his story has achieved a small
immortality, and proved one of the numerous springs from
which new words have been imported into our language.
Yet the peculiar and essential singularities of the story are
quite equalled, or even surpassed, by creatures which are, or
have been, found in nature.   The imaginary diminutive cows
which Gulliver brought back from Lilliput, and placed in the
meadows at Dulwich, are not one bit more remarkable, in
respect to relative size, than the pigmy elephant (*E. Falconeri*)
whose remains have been found in the cave-deposits of Malta,
associated with those of pigmy hippopotami, and which was
only two feet six inches high ; or the still existing *Hippopotamus (Chœropsis) liberiensis*, which M. Milne Edwardes†
figures as little more than two feet in height.

The lilliputian forests from which the royal navy was constructed contained even large trees in comparison with the
dwarf oaks of Mexico,‡ or with the allied, even smaller

---

* The Bower Bird, *Ptilonorhyncus holosericeus*, and the Garden-
building Bird of New Guinea, *Amblyornis inornara*.

† *Recherches, &c. des Mammiferes*, plate 1.   Paris, 1868 to 1874.

‡ " This obstacle was a forest of oaks, not giant oaks, but the very
reverse, a forest of dwarf oaks (*Quercus nana*).   Far as the eye could
reach extended the singular wood, in which no tree rose above thirty

species, which crawls like heather about the hill-slopes of China and Japan, and still more so in comparison with that singular pine, the most diminutive known (*Dacrydium taxifolium*), fruiting specimens of which, according to Kirk, are sometimes only two inches high, while the average height is only six to ten inches; while even among the forests of Brobdignag, a very respectable position could be held by the mammoth trees of California (*Sequoia gigantea*), or by the loftier white gums of Australia (*Eucalyptus amygdalina*), which occasionally reach, according to Von Mueller,* the enormous height of 480 feet. Nor could more adequate tenants (in point of size) be found to occupy them than the gigantic reptilian forms lately discovered by Marsh among the deposits of Colorado and Texas.

Surely a profound acquaintance with the different branches of natural history should render a man credulous rather than incredulous, for there is hardly conceivable a creature so monstrous that it may not be paralleled by existing ones in every-day life.†

---

inches in height. Yet was it no thicket, no undergrowth of shrubs, but a true forest of oaks, each tree having its separate stem, its boughs, its lobed leaves, and its bunches of brown acorns."—Capt. Mayne Reid, *The War Trail*, chap. lxiv.

* Respecting the timber trees of this tract, Dr. Ferdinand von Mueller, the Government botanist, thus writes :—" At the desire of the writer of these pages, Mr. D. Bogle measured a fallen tree of *Eucalyptus amygdalina*, in the deep recesses of Dandenong, and obtained for it a length of 420 feet, with proportions of width, indicated in a design of a monumental structure placed in the exhibition; while Mr. G. Klein took the measurement of a *Eucalyptus* on the Black Spur, ten miles distant from Healesville, 480 feet high ! In the State forest of Dandenong, it was found by actual measurement that an acre of ground contained twenty large trees of an apparent average height of about 350 feet."—R. Brough Smyth, *The Gold Fields of Victoria*. Melbourne, 1869.

† " In the next place, we must remember how impossible it is for the mind to invent an entirely new fact. There is nothing in the mind of

Are the composite creatures of Chaldæan mythology so very much more wonderful than the marsupial kangaroo, the duck-billed platypus, and the flying lizard of Malaysia which

Fig. 2.—PTERODACTYLUS.  (*After Figuier.*)

are, or the pterodactylus, rhamphorynchus, and archæopteryx which have been?   Does not geological science, day by day, trace one formation by easy gradation to another, bridge over

Fig. 3.—RHAMPHORYNCHUS.  (*From "Nature."*)

the gaps which formerly separated them, carry the proofs of the existence of man constantly further and further back into remote time, and disclose the previous existence of inter-

man that has not pre-existed in nature.   Can we imagine a person, who never saw or heard of an elephant, drawing a picture of such a two-tailed creature?"—J. Donelly, *Rangarok*, p. 119.   New York, 1883.

mediate types (satisfying the requirements of the Darwinian theory) connecting the great divisions of the animal kingdom, of reptile-like birds and bird-like reptiles ?   Can we suppose that we have at all exhausted the great museum of nature ? Have we, in fact, penetrated yet beyond its ante-chambers ?

FIG. 4.—ARCHÆOPTERYX.

Does the written history of man, comprísing a few thousand years, embrace the whole course of his intelligent existence ? or have we in the long mythical eras, extending over hundreds of thousands of years and recorded in the chronologies of Chaldæa and of China, shadowy mementoes of pre-historic man, handed down by tradition, and perhaps transported by a few survivors to existing lands from others which, like the fabled (?) Atlantis of Plato, may have been submerged, or the scene of some great catastrophe which destroyed them with all their civilization.

The six or eight thousand years which the various interpreters of the Biblical record assign for the creation of the world and the duration of man upon the earth, allow little enough space for the development of his civilization—a civilization which documental evidence carries almost to the verge of the limit—for the expansion and divergence of stocks, or the obliteration of the branches connecting them.

But, fortunately, we are no more compelled to fetter our belief within such limits as regards man than to suppose that his appearance on the globe was coeval with or immediately successive to its own creation at that late date.  For while geological science, on the one hand, carries back the creation of the world and the appearance of life upon its surface to a period so remote that it is impossible to estimate it, and difficult even to faintly approximate to it, so, upon the other, the researches of palæontologists have successively traced back the existence of man to periods variously estimated at from thirty thousand to one million years—to periods when he co-existed with animals which have long since become extinct, and which even excelled in magnitude and ferocity most of those which in savage countries dispute his empire at the present day.   Is it not  reasonable to suppose that his combats with these would  form  the most important topic of conversation, of tradition, and of primitive song, and that graphic accounts of such struggles, and of the terrible nature of the foes encountered, would be handed down from father to son, with a fidelity of description and an accuracy of memory unsuspected by us, who, being acquainted with reading and writing, are led to depend upon their artificial assistance, and thus in a measure fail to cultivate a faculty which, in common with those of keenness of vision and hearing, are essential to the existence of man in a savage or semi-savage condition ?*

The illiterate backwoodsman or trapper (and hence by inference the savage or semi-civilized man), whose mind is

---

* " I conceive that quite a large proportion of the most profound thinkers are satisfied to exert their memory very moderately.  It is, in fact, a distraction from close thought to exert the memory overmuch, and a man engaged in the study of an abstruse subject will commonly rather turn to his book-shelves for the information he requires than tax his memory to supply it."—R. A. Proctor, *Pop. Sci. Monthly*, Jan. 1874.

occupied merely by his surroundings, and whose range of thought, in place of being diffused over an illimitable horizon, is confined within very moderate limits, develops remarkable powers of observation and an accuracy of memory in regard to localities, and the details of his daily life, surprising to the scholar who has mentally to travel over so much more ground, and, receiving daily so many and so far more complex ideas, can naturally grasp each less firmly, and is apt to lose them entirely in the haze of a period of time which would still leave those of the uneducated man distinguishable or even prominent landmarks.*    Variations in traditions must, of course, occur in time, and the same histories, radiating in all directions from centres, vary from the original ones by increments dependent on proportionately altered phases of temperament and character, induced by change of climate, associations and conditions of life; so that the early written history of every country reproduces under its own garb, and with a claim to originality, attenuated, enriched, or deformed versions of traditions common in their origin to many or all.†

---

* " It was through one of these happy chances (so the Brothers Grimm wrote in 1819) that we came to make the acquaintance of a peasant woman of the village of Nieder-Zwehrn, near Cassel, who told us the greater part of the Märchen of the second volume, and the most beautiful of it too. She held the old tales firmly in her memory, and would sometimes say that this gift was not granted to everyone, and that many a one could not keep anything in its proper connection. Anyone inclined to believe that tradition is easily corrupted or carelessly kept, and that therefore it could not possibly last long, should have heard how steadily she always abided by her record, and how she stuck to its accuracy. She never altered anything in repeating it, and if she made a slip, at once righted herself as soon as she became aware of it, in the very midst of her tale. The attachment to tradition among people living on in the same kind of life with unbroken regularity, is stronger than we, who are fond of change, can understand."—*Odinic Songs in Shetland.* Karl Blind, *Nineteenth Century,* June 1879.

† See quotation from Gladstone, *Nineteenth Century,* Oct. 1879.

Stories of divine progenitors, demigods, heroes, mighty hunters, slayers of monsters, giants, dwarfs, gigantic serpents, dragons, frightful beasts of prey, supernatural beings, and myths of all kinds, appear to have been carried into all corners of the world with as much fidelity as the sacred Ark of the Israelites, acquiring a moulding—graceful, weird or uncouth—according to the genius of the people or their capacity for superstitious belief; and these would appear to have been materially affected by the varied nature of their respective countries.  For example, the long-continuing dwellers in the open plains of a semi-tropical region, relieved to a great extent from the cares of watchfulness, and nurtured in the grateful rays of a genial but not oppressive sun, must have a more buoyant disposition and more open temperament than those inhabiting vast forests, the matted overgrowth of which rarely allows the passage of a single ray, bathes all in gloom, and leaves on every side undiscovered depths, filled with shapeless shadows, objects of vigilant dread, from which some ferocious monster may emerge at any moment.  Again, on the one hand, the nomad roaming in isolation over vast solitudes, having much leisure for contemplative reflection, and on the other, the hardy dwellers on storm-beaten coasts, by turns fishermen, mariners, and pirates, must equally develop traits which affect their religion, polity, and customs, and stamp their influences on mythology and tradition.

The Greek, the Celt, and the Viking, descended from the same Aryan ancestors, though all drawing from the same sources their inspirations of religious belief and tradition, quickly diverged, and respectively settled into a generous martial race—martial in support of their independence rather than from any lust of conquest—polite, skilled, and learned; one brave but irritable, suspicious, haughty, impatient of control ; and the last, the berserker, with a ruling passion for maritime adventure, piracy, and hand-to-hand heroic struggles, to be terminated in due course by a hero's death and a welcome to the banqueting halls of Odin in Walhalla.

The beautiful mythology of the Greek nation, comprising a pantheon of gods and demigods, benign for the most part, and often interesting themselves directly in the welfare of individual men, was surely due to, or at least greatly induced by, the plastic influences of a delicious climate, a semi-insular position in a sea comparatively free from stormy weather, and an open mountainous country, moderately fertile. Again, the gloomy and sanguinary religion of the Druids was doubtless moulded by the depressing influences of the seclusion, twilight haze, and dangers of the dense forests in which they hid themselves—forests which, as we know from Cæsar, spread over the greater part of Gaul, Britain, and Spain; while the Viking, having from the chance or choice of his ancestors, inherited a rugged seaboard, lashed by tempestuous waves and swept by howling winds, a seaboard with only a rugged country shrouded with unsubdued forests at its back, exposed during the major portion of the year to great severity of climate, and yielding at the best but a niggard and precarious harvest, became perforce a bold and skilful mariner, and, translating his belief into a language symbolic of his new surroundings, believed that he saw and heard Thor in the midst of the howling tempests, revealed majestic and terrible through rents in the storm-cloud. Pursuing our consideration of the effects produced by climatic conditions, may we not assume, for example, that some at least of the Chaldæans, inhabiting a pastoral country, and being descended from ancestors who had pursued, for hundreds or thousands of years, a nomadic existence in the vast open steppes in the highlands of Central Asia, were indebted to those circumstances for the advance which they are credited with having made in astronomy and kindred sciences. Is it not possible that their acquaintance with climatology was as exact or even more so than our own? The habit of solitude would induce reflection, the subject of which would naturally be the causes influencing the vicissitudes of weather.  The possibilities of rain or sunshine, wind or storm, would be with them a prominent object of solicitude ; and the necessity, in an unfenced country, of extending their watch over their flocks and herds throughout the night, would perforce more or less rivet their attention upon the glorious constellations of the heavens above, and lead to habits of observation which, systematized and long continued by the priesthood, might have produced deductions accurate in the result even if faulty in the process.

The vast treasures of ancient knowledge tombed in the ruins of Babylon and Assyria, of which the recovery and deciphering is as yet only initiated, may, to our surprise, reveal that certain secrets of philosophy were known to the ancients equally with ourselves, but lost through intervening ages by the destruction of the empire, and the fact of their conservancy having been entrusted to a privileged and limited order, with which it perished.*

* Mr. C. P. Daly, President of the American Geographical Society, informs us, in his Annual Address [for 1880], that in one book found in the royal library at Nineveh, of the date 2000 B.C., there is—

1. A catalogue of stars.
2. Enumeration of twelve constellations forming our present zodiac.
3. The intimation of a Sabbath.
4. A connection indicated (according to Mr. Perville) between the weather and the changes of the moon.
5. A notice of the spots on the sun: a fact they could only have known by the aid of telescopes, which it is supposed they possessed from observations that they have noted down of the rising of Venus, and the fact that Layard found a crystal lens in the ruins of Nineveh. (N.B.—As to the above, I must say that telescopes are not always necessary to see the spots on the sun : these were distinctly visible with the naked eye, in the early mornings, to myself and the officers of the S.S. *Scotia*, in the Red Sea, in the month of August of 1883, after the great volcanic disturbances near Batavia.  The resulting atmospheric effects were very marked in the Red Sea, as elsewhere, the sun, when near the horizon, appearing of a pale green colour, and exhibiting the spots distinctly.)

We hail as a new discovery the knowledge of the existence of the so-called spots upon the surface of the sun, and scientists, from long-continued observations, profess to distinguish a connection between the character of these and atmospheric phenomena ; they even venture to predict floods and droughts, and that for some years in anticipation ; while pestilences or some great disturbance are supposed to be likely to follow the period when three or four planets attain their apogee within one year, a supposition based on the observations extended over numerous years, that similar events had accompanied the occurrence of even one only of those positions at previous periods.

May we not speculate on the possibility of similar or parallel knowledge having been possessed by the old Chaldæan and Egyptian priesthood ; and may not Joseph have been able, by superior ability in its exercise, to have anticipated the seven years' drought, or Noah, from an acquaintance with meteorological science, to have made an accurate forecast of the great disturbances which resulted in the Deluge and the destruction of a large portion of mankind ? *

---

* Ammianus Marcellinus (bk. xxii., ch. xv., s. 20), in speaking of the Pyramids, says: "There are also subterranean passages and winding retreats, which, it is said, men skilful in the ancient mysteries, by means of which they divined the coming of a flood, constructed in different places lest the memory of all their sacred ceremonies should be lost."

As affording a minor example of prophesy, I quote a correspondent's communication, relating to Siam, to the *North China Daily News* of July 28th, 1881 :—" Singularly enough the prevalence of cholera in Siam this season has been predicted for some months. The blossoming of the bamboo (which in India is considered the invariable forerunner of an epidemic) was looked upon as ominous, while the enormous quantity and high quality of the fruit produced was cited as pointing out the overcharge of the earth with matter which, though tending to the development of vegetable life, is deleterious to human. From these and other sources of knowledge open to those accustomed to read the book of nature, the prevalence of cholera, which, since 1873, has been almost unknown in Siam, was predicted and looked for ; and, unlike most modern predic-

Without further digression in a path which opens the most pleasing speculations, and could be pursued into endless ramifications, I will merely, in conclusion, suggest that the same influences which, as I have shown above, affect so largely the very nature of a people, must similarly affect its traditions and myths, and that due consideration will have to be given to such influences, in the case of some at least of the remarkable animals which I propose to discuss in this and future volumes.

tions, it has been certainly fulfilled. So common was the belief, that when, some months since, a foreign official in Siamese employ applied for leave of absence, it was opposed by some of the native officials on the ground that he ought to stay and take his chance of the cholera with the rest of them."

CHRONOLOGICAL LIST OF SOME AUTHORS WRITING ON, AND
WORKS RELATING TO NATURAL HISTORY, TO WHICH
REFERENCES ARE MADE IN THE PRESENT VOLUME;
EXTRACTED TO A GREAT EXTENT, AS TO THE WESTERN
AUTHORS, FROM KNIGHT'S " CYCLOPÆDIA OF BIOGRAPHY."

*The Shan Hai King*—According to the commentator Kwoh
P'oh (A.D. 276–324), this work was compiled three
thousand years before this time, or at seven dynasties' distance. Yang Sun of the Ming dynasty
(commencing A.D. 1368), states that it was compiled by Kung Chia (and Chung Ku ?) from engravings on nine urns made by the Emperor Yü,
B.C. 2255. Chung Ku was an historiographer,
and at the time of the last Emperor of the Hia
dynasty (B.C. 1818), fearing that the Emperor
might destroy the books treating of the ancient
and present time, carried them in flight to Yin.

*The 'Rh Ya*—Initiated according to tradition, by Chow Kung;
uncle of Wu Wang, the first Emperor of the Chow
dynasty, B.C. 1122. Ascribed also to Tsze Hea,
the disciple of Confucius.

*The Bamboo Books*—Containing the Ancient Annals of China,
said to have been found A.D. 279, on opening the
grave of King Seang of· Wei [died B.C. 295]. Age
prior to last date, undetermined. Authenticity disputed, favoured by Legge.

*Confucius*—Author of Spring and Autumn Classics, &c.,
  B.C. (551–479).

*Ctesias*—Historian, physician to Artaxerxes, B.C. 401.

*Herodotus*—B.C. 484.

*Aristotle*—B.C. 384.

*Megasthenes*—About B.C. 300.   In time of Seleucus Nicator.
  His work entitled *Indica* is only known by extracts
  in those of Strabo, Arrian, and Ælian.

*Eratosthenes*—Born B.C. 276.   Mathematician, Astronomer,
  and Geographer.

*Posidonius*—Born about B.C. 140.   Besides philosophical
  treatises, wrote works on geography, history, and
  astronomy, fragments of which are preserved in
  the works of Cicero, Strabo, and others.

*Nicander*—About B.C. 135.   Wrote the *Theriaca*, a poem
  of 1,000 lines, in hexameter, on the wounds caused
  by venomous animals, and the treatment.   Is followed in many of his errors by Pliny.   Plutarch
  says the *Theriaca* cannot be called a poem, because
  there is in it nothing of fable or falsehood.

*Strabo*—Just before the Christian era.   Geographer.

*Cicero*—Born B.C. 106.

*Propertius* (*Sextus Aurelius*)—Born probably about B.C. 56.

*Diodorus Siculus*—Wrote the *Bibliotheca Historica* (in Greek),
  after the death of Julius Cæsar (B.C. 44).   Of the
  40 books composing it only 15 remain, viz. Books
  1 to 5 and 11 to 20.

*Juba*—Died A.D. 17.   Son of Juba I., King of Numidia.
  Wrote on Natural History.

*Pliny*—Born A.D. 23.

*Lucan*—A.D. 38.   The only work of his extant is the *Pharsalia*, a poem on the civil war between Cæsar and
  Pompey.

*Ignatius*—Either an early Patriarch, A.D. 50, or Patriarch of Constantinople, 799.

*Isidorus*—Isidorus of Charaux lived probably in the first century of our era. He wrote an account of the Parthian empire.

*Arrian*—Born about A.D. 100. His work on the Natural History, &c. of India is founded on the authority of Eratosthenes and Megasthenes.

*Pausanias*—Author of the Description or Itinerary of Greece. In the 2nd century.

*Philostratus*—Born about A.D. 182.

*Solinus, Caius Julius*—Did not write in the Augustan age, for his work entitled *Polyhistor* is merely a compilation from Pliny's *Natural History*. According to Salmasius, he lived about two hundred years after Pliny.

*Ælian*—Probably middle of the 3rd century A.D. *De Naturâ Animalium.* In Greek.

*Ammianus Marcellinus*—Lived in 4th century.

*Cardan, Jerome A.*—About the end of 4th century A.D.

Printing invented in China, according to Du Halde, A.D. 924. Block-printing used in A.D. 593.

*Marco Polo*—Reached the Court of Kublai Khan in A.D. 1275.

*Mandeville, Sir John de*—Travelled for thirty-three years in Asia dating from A.D. 1327. As he resided for three years in Peking, it is probable that many of his fables are derived from Chinese sources.

Printing invented in Europe by John Koster of Haarlem, A.D. 1438.

*Scaliger, Julius Cæsar*—Born April 23rd, 1484. Wrote *Aristotelis Hist. Anim. liber decimus cum vers. et comment.* 8vo. Lyon, 1584, &c.

*Gesner*—Born 1516.   *Historiæ Animalium*, &c.

*Ambrose Paré*—Born 1517.    Surgeon.

*Belon, Pierre.*—Born 1518.   Zoologist, Geographer, &c.

*Aldrovandus*—Born 1552.   Naturalist.

*Tavernier, J. B.*—Born 1605.

*Păn Ts'ao Kang Muh.*—By Li Shê-chin of the Ming dynasty
        (A.D. 1368–1628).

*Yuen Kien Léi Han.*   A.D. 1718.

# CHAPTER I.

## ON SOME REMARKABLE ANIMAL FORMS.

THE reasoning upon the question whether dragons, winged snakes, sea-serpents, unicorns, and other so-called fabulous monsters have in reality existed, and at dates coeval with man, diverges in several independent directions.

We have to consider : —

1.—Whether the characters attributed to these creatures are or are not so abnormal in comparison with those of known types, as to render a belief in their existence impossible or the reverse.

2.—Whether it is rational to suppose that creatures so formidable, and apparently so capable of self-protection, should disappear entirely, while much more defenceless species continue to survive them.

3.—The myths, traditions, and historical allusions from which their reality may be inferred require to be classified and annotated, and full weight given to the evidence which has accumulated of the presence of man upon the earth during ages long prior to the historic period, and which may have been ages of slowly progressive civilization, or perhaps cycles of alternate light and darkness, of knowledge and barbarism.

4.—Lastly, some inquiry may be made into the geographical conditions obtaining at the time of their possible existence.

It is immaterial which of these investigations is first entered upon, and it will, in fact, be more convenient to defer a portion of them until we arrive at the sections of this volume treating specifically of the different objects to which it is devoted, and to confine our attention for the present to those subjects which, from their nature, are common and in a sense prefatory to the whole subject.

I shall therefore commence with a short examination of some of the most remarkable reptilian forms which are known to have existed, and for that purpose, and to show their general relations, annex the accompanying tables, compiled from the anatomy of vertebrated animals by Professor Huxley :—

*Amphibia.*

### REPTILES CLASSIFIED BY HUXLEY.

| ORDER. | — | SUB-ORDER. | GROUPS. | ILLUSTRATIVE GENERA. | RANGE OF THE ORDER. |
|---|---|---|---|---|---|
| Chelonia. | Land tortoises | 1. Testudinea | | Pyxis, Cinyxis | The Chelonia are first known to occur in the Lias. |
| ,, | River and marsh do. | 2. Emydea | a Terrapenes b Chelodines | Emys, Cistudo / Chelys, Chelodina | |
| ,, | Mud tortoises Turtles | 3. Trionychoidea 4. Euereta | | Gymnopus Cryptopus Sphargis, Chelone | To recent. |
| Plesiosauria. | | 5. . . . | Post Triassic | Plesiosaurus Pliosaurus | Trias to Chalk inclusive. |
| ,, | | 6. . . . | Triassic | Nothosaurus Simosaurus Pistosaurus | |
| Lacertilia. | Geckos | 7. Ascalabota | | | recent |
| ,, | | 8. Rhynchocephala | | Sphenodon or Rhyncocephalus | |
| ,, | | 9. Homœosauria | ' . . . | | Solenhofen slates to Trias |
| ,, | | 10. Protosauria | | | Permian |
| ,, | Monitor | 11. Platynota | | | recent |
| ,, | | 12. Eunota | | | ,, |
| ,, | | 13. Lacertina | | | ,, |
| ' | | 14. Chalcidea | | | ,, |

Permian to recent.

## REPTILES CLASSIFIED BY HUXLEY.—*cont.*

| ORDER. | — | SUB-ORDER. | GROUPS. | ILLUSTRATIVE GENERA. | RANGE OF THE ORDER. |
|---|---|---|---|---|---|
| Lacertilia. | | 15. Scincoidea | | | Recent |
| „ | | 16. Dolichosauria | | Dolichosaurus | Chalk |
| „ | | 17. Mosasauria | | Mososaurus | Chalk |
| „ | | 18. Amphisbænoida | | Chirotes Amphis-bæna | |
| „ | | 19. Chamæleonida | | | }Permian to recent. |
| Ophidia. | Non-vene-mous con-stricting | 20. Aglyphodontia | | Python, Tortrix | |
| „ | | 21. Opisthoglyphia | | | |
| „ | | 22. Proteroglyphia | | | }Older Tertiary to recent. |
| „ | Vipers and Rattle-snakes | 23. Solenoglyphia | | Crotalus | |
| „ | | 24. Typhlopidæ | | | |
| Icthyo-sauria. | . . . | | | Icthyosaurus | Trias(?) to chalk inclusive. |
| Crocodile. | Alligator | 26. Alligatoridæ | | Alligator Caiman Jacare | |
| „ | Crocodiles | 27. Crocodilidæ | | Crocodilus Mecistops | |
| „ | Gavials | 28. Gavialidæ | | Rhynchosuchus Gavialis | }Trias to recent |
| „ | | 29. Teleosauridæ | | Teleosaurus | |
| „ | | 30. Belodontidæ | | Belodon | |
| Dicyno-dontia. | | 31. . . . | | Dicynodon Oudenodon | }Trias. |
| Ornitho-scelida | | 32. Dinosauria | | Thecodontosaurus Scelidosaurus | Trias Lias Middle & Upper Mesozoic Solenho-fen slates }Mesozoic formations. |
| | | | | Megalosaurus Iguanodon | |
| | | 33. Compsognatha | | . . . | |
| Ptero-sauria. | Flying reptile | 34. Pterodactylidæ | | Ornithopterus Pterodactylus Rhamphorynchus Dimorphodon | Lias to Chalk inclusive. |

*Aves.*

The most bird-like of reptiles, the Pterosauria, appear to have possessed true powers of flight; they were provided with wings formed by an expansion of the integument, and supported by an enormous elongation of the ulnar finger of the anterior limb. The generic differences are based upon the comparative lengths of the tail, and upon the dentition. In *Pterodactylus* (see Fig. 2, p. 18), the tail is very short, and the jaws strong, pointed, and toothed to their anterior extremities. In *Rhamphorynchus* (see Fig. 3, p. 18), the tail is very long and the teeth are not continuous to the extremities of the jaws, which are produced into toothless beaks. The majority of the species are small, and they are generally considered to have been inoffensive creatures, having much the habits and insectivorous mode of living of bats. One British species, however, from the white chalk of Maidstone, measures more than sixteen feet across the outstretched wings; and other forms recently discovered by Professor Marsh in the Upper Cretaceous deposits of Kansas, attain the gigantic proportions of nearly twenty-five feet for the same measurements; and although these were devoid of teeth (thus approaching the class Aves still more closely), they could hardly fail, from their magnitude and powers of flight, to have been formidable, and must, with their weird aspects, and long outstretched necks and pointed heads, have been at least sufficiently alarming.

We need go no farther than these in search of creatures which would realise the popular notion of the winged dragon.

The harmless little flying lizards, belonging to the genus Draco, abounding in the East Indian archipelago, which have many of their posterior ribs prolonged into an expansion of the integument, unconnected with the limbs, and have a limited and parachute-like flight, need only the element of size, to render them also sufficiently to be dreaded, and capable of rivalling the Pterodactyls in suggesting the general idea of the same monster.

It is, however, when we pass to some of the other groups, that we find ourselves in the presence of forms so vast and terrible, as to more than realise the most exaggerated impression of reptilian power and ferocity which the florid imagination of man can conceive.

We have long been acquainted with numerous gigantic terrestrial Saurians, ranging throughout the whole of the Mesozoic formations, such as *Iguanodon* (characteristic of the Wealden), *Megalosaurus* (Great Saurian), and *Hylæosaurus* (Forest Saurian), huge bulky creatures, the last of which, at least, was protected by dermal armour partially produced into prodigious spines; as well as with remarkable forms essentially marine, such as *Icthyosaurus* (Fish-like Saurian), *Plesiosaurus*, &c., adapted to an oceanic existence and propelling themselves by means of paddles. The latter, it may be remarked, was furnished with a long slender swan-like neck, which, carried above the surface of the water, would present the appearance of the anterior portion of a serpent.

To the related land forms the collective term Dinosauria (from δεινός " terrible ") has been applied, in signification of the power which their structure and magnitude imply that they possessed; and to the others that of Enaliosauria, as expressive of their adaptation to a maritime existence. Yet, wonderful to relate, those creatures which have for so many years commanded our admiration fade into insignificance in comparison with others which are proved, by the discoveries of the last few years, to have existed abundantly upon, or near to, the American continent during the Cretaceous and Jurassic periods, by which they are surpassed, in point of magnitude, as much as they themselves exceed the mass of the larger Vertebrata.

Take, for example, those referred to by Professor Marsh in the course of an address to the American Association for the Advancement of Science, in 1877, in the following terms :—
" The reptiles most characteristic of our American cretaceous strata are the Mososauria, a group with very few representatives in other parts of the world. In our cretaceous seas

they rule supreme, as their numbers, size, and carnivorous habits enabled them to easily vanquish all rivals. Some were at least sixty feet in length, and the smallest ten or twelve. In the inland cretaceous sea from which the Rocky Mountains were beginning to emerge, these ancient ' sea-serpents' abounded, and many were entombed in its muddy bottom ; on one occasion, as I rode through a valley washed out of this old ocean-bed, I saw no less than seven different skeletons of these monsters in sight at once. The Moso-sauria were essentially swimming lizards with four well-developed paddles, and they had little affinity with modern serpents, to which they have been compared."

Or, again, notice the specimens of the genus Cidastes, which are also described as veritable sea-serpents of those ancient seas, whose huge bones and almost incredible number of vertebræ show them to have attained a length of nearly two hundred feet. The remains of no less than ten of these monsters were seen by Professor Mudge, while riding through the Mauvaise Terres of Colorado, strewn upon the plains, their whitened bones bleached in the suns of centuries, and their gaping jaws armed with ferocious teeth, telling a wonderful tale of their power when alive.

The same deposits have been equally fertile in the remains of terrestrial animals of gigantic size. The *Titanosaurus montanus,* believed to have been herbivorous, is estimated to have reached fifty or sixty feet in length ; while other Dino-saurians of still more gigantic proportions, from the Jurassic beds of the Rocky Mountains, have been described by Pro-fessor Marsh. Among the discovered remains of *Atlantosaurus immanis* is a femur over six feet in length, and it is estimated from a comparison of this specimen with the same bone in living reptiles that this species, if similar in proportions to the crocodile, would have been over one hundred feet in length.

But even yet the limit has not been reached, and we hear

of the discovery of the remains of another form, of such Titanic proportions as to possess a thigh-bone over twelve feet in length.

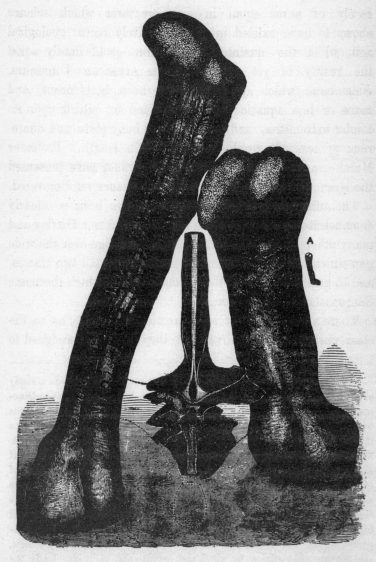

FIG. 5.—MONSTER BONES OF EXTINCT GIGANTIC SAURIANS FROM COLORADO, SHOWING RELATIVE PROPORTIONS TO CORRESPONDING BONE IN THE CROCODILE (A). (*From the " Scientific American."*)

From these considerations it is evident that, on account of the dimensions usually assigned to them, no discredit can be attached to the existence of the fabulous monsters of which we shall speak hereafter; for these, in the various myths, rarely or never equal in size creatures which science shows to have existed in a comparatively recent geological age, while the quaintest conception could hardly equal the reality of yet another of the American Dinosaurs, *Stegosaurus*, which appears to have been herbivorous, and more or less aquatic in habit, adapted for sitting upon its hinder extremities, and protected by bony plate and numerous spines. It reached thirty feet in length. Professor Marsh considers that this, when alive, must have presented the strangest appearance of all the Dinosaurs yet discovered.

The affinities of birds and reptiles have been so clearly demonstrated of late years, as to cause Professor Huxley and many other comparative anatomists to bridge over the wide gap which was formerly considered to divide the two classes, and to bracket them together in one class, to which the name Sauropsidæ has been given.*

There are, indeed, not a few remarkable forms, as to the class position of which, whether they should be assigned to

---

* "It is now generally admitted by biologists who have made a study of the Vertebrata that birds have come down to us through the Dinosaurs, and the close affinity of the latter with recent struthious birds will hardly be questioned. The case amounts almost to a demonstration if we compare with Dinosaurs their contemporaries, the Mesozoic birds. The classes of birds and reptiles as now living are separated by a gulf so profound that a few years since it was cited by the opponents of evolution as the most important break in the animal series, and one which that doctrine could not bridge over. Since then, as Huxley has clearly shown, this gap has been virtually filled by the discoveries of bird-like reptiles and reptilian birds. Compsognathus and Archæopteryx of the old world, and Icthyornis and Hesperornis of the new, are the stepping-stones by which the evolutionist of to-day leads the doubting brother across the shallow remnant of the gulf, once thought impassable."—*Marsh.*

birds or reptiles, opinion was for a long time, and is in a few instances still, divided. It is, for example, only of late years that the fossil form Archæopteryx* (Fig. 4, p. 19) from the Solenhofen slates, has been definitely relegated to the former, but arguments against this disposal of it have been based upon the beak or jaws being furnished with true teeth, and the feather of the tail attached to

FIG. 6.—SIVATHERIUM (RESTORED), FROM THE UPPER MIOCENE DEPOSITS OF THE SIWALIK HILLS. (*After Figuier.*)

a series of vertebræ, instead of a single flattened one as in birds. It appears to have been entirely plumed, and to have had a moderate power of flight.

On the other hand, the Ornithopterus is only provisionally

---

* Professor Carl Vogt regards the Archæopteryx "as neither reptile nor bird, but as constituting an intermediate type. He points out that there is complete homology between the scales or spines of reptiles and the feathers of birds. The feather of the bird is only a reptile's scale further developed, and the reptile's scale is a feather which has remained in the embryonic condition. He considers the reptilian homologies to preponderate."

classed with reptiles, while the connection between the two classes is drawn still closer by the copious discovery of the birds from the Cretaceous formations of America, for which we are indebted to Professor Marsh.

The Lepidosiren, also, is placed mid-way between reptiles and fishes. Professor Owen and other eminent physiologists consider it a fish ; Professor Bischoff and others, an amphibian reptile. It has a two-fold apparatus for respiration, partly aquatic, consisting of gills, and partly aerial, of true lungs.

So far, then, as abnormality of type is concerned, we have here instances quite as remarkable as those presented by most of the strange monsters with the creation of which mythological fancy has been credited.

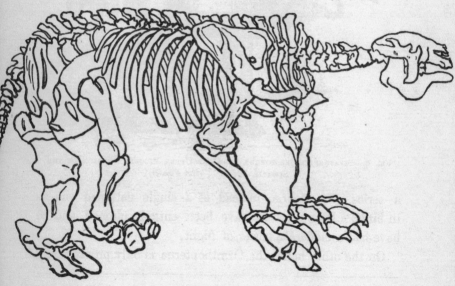

Fig. 7.—Skeleton of Megatherium. (After Figuier.)

Among mammals I shall only refer to the Megatherium, which appears to have been created to burrow in the earth and to feed upon the roots of trees and shrubs, for which purpose every organ of its heavy frame was adapted. This

Hercules among animals was as large as an elephant or rhinoceros of the largest species, and might well, as it has existed until a late date, have originated the myths, current among the Indians of South America, of a gigantic tunnelling or burrowing creature, incapable of supporting the light of day.*

---

\* A similar habit is ascribed by the Chinese to the mammoth and to the gigantic Sivatherium (Fig. 6, p. 39), a four-horned stag, which had the bulk of an elephant, and exceeded it in height. It was remarkable for being in some respects between the stags and the pachyderms. The Dinotherium (Fig. 8), which had a trunk like an elephant, and two inverted tusks, presented in its skull a mixture of the characteristics of the elephant, hippopotamus, tapir, and dugong. Its remains occur in the Miocene of Europe.

FIG. 8.—DINOTHERIUM. *(After Figuier.)*

# CHAPTER II.

### EXTINCTION OF SPECIES.

In reviewing the past succession of different forms of ancient life upon the globe, we are reminded of a series of dissolving views, in which each species evolves itself by an imperceptible gradation from some pre-existing one, arrives at its maximum of individuality, and then slowly fades away, while another type, either higher or lower, evolved in turn from it, emerges from obscurity, and succeeds it on the field of view.

Specific individuality has in all cases a natural term, dependent on physical causes, but that term is in many cases abruptly anticipated by a combination of unfavourable conditions.

Alteration of climate, isolation by geological changes, such as the submergence of continents and islands, and the competition of other species, are among the causes which have at all times operated towards its destruction; while, since the evolution of man, his agency, so far as we can judge by what we know of his later history, has been especially active in the same direction.

The limited distribution of many species, even when not enforced by insular conditions, is remarkable, and, of course, highly favourable to their destruction. A multiplicity of examples are familiar to naturalists, and possibly not a few may have attracted the attention of the ordinary observer.

For instance, it is probably generally known, that in our own island, the red grouse (which, by the way, is a species peculiar to Great Britain) is confined to certain moorlands, the ruffs and reeves to fen districts, and the nightingale,* chough, and other species to a few counties ; while Ireland is devoid of almost all the species of reptiles common to Great Britain. In the former cases, the need of or predilection for certain foods probably determines the favourite locality, and there are few countries which would not furnish similar examples. In the latter, the explanation depends on biological conditions dating prior to the separation of Ireland from the main continent. Among birds, it might fairly be presumed that the power of flight would produce unlimited territorial expansion, but in many instances the reverse is found to be the case : a remarkable example being afforded by the island of Tasmania, a portion of which is called the unsettled waste lands, or Western Country. This district, which comprises about one-third of the island upon the western side, and is mainly composed of mountain chains of granites, quartzite, and mica schists, is entirely devoid of the numerous species of garrulous and gay-plumaged birds, such as the Mynah mocking-bird, white cockatoo, wattle bird, and Rosella parrot, though these abundantly enliven the eastern districts, which are fertilized by rich soils due to the presence of ranges of basalt, greenstone, and other trappean rocks.

Another equally striking instance is given by my late father, Mr. J. Gould, in his work on the humming-birds. Of two species, inhabiting respectively the adjacent moun-

---

* "It enters Europe early in April, spreads over France, Britain, Denmark, and the south of Sweden, which it reaches by the beginning of May. It does not enter Brittany, the Channel Islands, or the western part of England, never visiting Wales, except the extreme south of Glamorganshire, and rarely extending farther north than Yorkshire."— A. R. Wallace, *Geographical Distribution of Animals*, vol. i. p. 21. London, 1876.

tains of Pichincha and Chimborazo at certain elevations, each
is strictly confined to its own mountain ; and, if my memory
serves me correctly, he mentions similar instances of species
peculiar to different peaks of the Andes.

Limitation by insular isolation is intelligible, especially in
the case of mammals and reptiles, and of birds possessing
but small power of flight ; and we are, therefore, not surprised to find Mr. Gosse indicating, among other examples,
that even the smallest of the Antilles has each a fauna of its
own, while the humming-birds, some of the parrots, cuckoos,
and pigeons, and many of the smaller birds are peculiar to
Jamaica.  He states still further, that in the latter instance
many of the animals are not distributed over the whole
island, but confined to a single small district.

Continental limitation is effected by mountain barriers.
Thus, according to Mr. Wallace, almost all the mammalia,
birds, and insects on one side of the Andes and Rocky
Mountains are distinct in species from those on the
other ; while a similar difference, but smaller in degree,
exists with reference to regions adjacent to the Alps and
Pyrenees.

Climate, broad rivers, seas, oceans, forests, and even large
desert wastes, like the Sahara or the great desert of Gobi,
also act more or less effectively as girdles which confine
species within certain limits.

Dependence on each other or on supplies of appropriate
food also form minor yet practical factors in the sum of
limitation ; and a curious example of the first is given by
Dr. Van Lennep with reference to the small migratory birds
that are unable to perform the flight of three hundred and
fifty miles across the Mediterranean.  He states that these
are carried across on the backs of cranes.*

* *Bible Customs in Bible Lands.*  By H. J. Van Lennep, D.D.  1875.
Quoted in *Nature*, March 24, 1881.

In the autumn many flocks of cranes may be seen coming from the North, with the first cold blast from that quarter, flying low, and uttering a peculiar cry, as if of alarm, as they circle over the cultivated plains. Little birds of every species may be seen flying up to them, while the twittering cries of those already comfortably settled upon their backs may be distinctly heard. On their return in the spring they fly high, apparently considering that their little passengers can easily find their way down to the earth.

The question of food-supply is involved in the more extended subject of geological structure, as controlling the flora and the insect life dependent on it. As an example we may cite the disappearance of the capercailzie from Denmark with the decay of the pine forests abundant during late Tertiary periods.

Collision, direct or indirect, with inimical species often has a fatal ending. Thus the dodo was exterminated by the swine which the early visitors introduced to the Mauritius and permitted to run wild there ; while the indigenous insects, mollusca, and perhaps some of the birds of St. Helena, disappeared as soon as the introduction of goats caused the destruction of the whole flora of forest trees.

The Tsetse fly extirpates all horses, dogs, and cattle, from certain districts of South Africa, and a representative species in Paraguay is equally fatal to new-born cattle and horses.

Mr. Darwin * shows that the struggle is more severe between species of the same genus, when they come into competition with each other, than between species of distinct genera. Thus one species of swallow has recently expelled another from part of the United States; and the misselthrush has driven the song-thrush from part of Scotland. In Australia the imported hive-bee is rapidly exterminating the small stingless native bee, and similar cases might be found in any number.

Mr. Wallace, in quoting Mr. Darwin as to these facts, points the conclusion that " any slight change, therefore,

---

* *Origin of Species*, C. Darwin. 5th edit. 1869.

of physical geography or of climate, which allows allied species hitherto inhabiting distinct areas to come into contact, will often lead to the extermination of one of them."

It is the province of the palæontologist to enumerate the many remarkable forms which have passed away since man's first appearance upon the globe, and to trace their fluctuations over both hemispheres as determined by the advance and retreat of glacial conditions, and by the protean forms assumed by past and existing continents under oscillations of elevation and depression. Many interesting points, such as the dates of the successive separation of Ireland and Great Britain from the main continent, can be determined with accuracy from the record furnished by the fossil remains of animals of those times; and many interesting associations of animals with man at various dates, in our present island home and in other countries, have been traced by the discovery of their remains in connection with his, in bone deposits in caverns and elsewhere.

Conversely, most valuable deductions are drawn by the zoologist from the review which he is enabled to take, through the connected labours of his colleagues in all departments, of the distinct life regions now mapped out upon the face of the globe. These, after the application of the necessary corrections for various disturbing or controlling influences referred to above, afford proof reaching far back into past periods, of successive alterations in the disposition of continents and oceans, and of connections long since obliterated between distant lands.

The palæontologist reasons from the past to the present, the zoologist from the present to the past; and their mutual labours explain the evolution of existing forms, and the causes of the disparity or connection between those at present characterizing the different portions of the surface of the globe.

The palæontologist, for example, traces the descent of the

horse, which, until its reintroduction by the Spaniards was unknown in the New World, through a variety of intermediate forms, to the genus Orohippus occurring in Eocene deposits in Utah and Wyoming. This animal was no larger than a fox, and possessed four separated toes in front, and three behind. Domestic cattle he refers to the Bos primigenius, and many existing Carnivora to Tertiary forms such as the cave-bear, cave-lion, sabre-tiger, and the like.

The zoologist groups the existing fauna into distinct provinces, and demands, in explanation of the anomalies which these exhibit, the reconstruction of large areas, of which only small outlying districts remain at the present date, in many instances widely separated by oceans, though once forming parts of the same continent; and so, for the simile readily suggests itself, the workers in another branch of science, Philology, argue from words and roots scattered like fossils through the various dialects of very distant countries, a mutual descent from a common Aryan language: the language of a race of which no historical record exists, though in regard to its habits, customs, and distribution much may be affirmed from the large collection of word specimens stored in philological museums.

Thus Mr. Sclater, on zoological grounds, claims the late existence of a continent which he calls Lemuria, extending from Madagascar to Ceylon and Sumatra; and for similar reasons Mr. Wallace extends the Australia of Tertiary periods to New Guinea and the Solomon Islands, and perhaps to Fiji, and from its marsupial types infers a connection with the northern continent during the Secondary period.

Again, the connection of Europe with North Africa during a late geological period is inferred by many zoologists from the number of identical species of mammalia inhabiting the opposite sides of the Mediterranean, and palæontologists confirm this by the discovery of the remains of elephants in cave-deposits in Malta, and of hippopotami in

Gibraltar; while hydrographers furnish the supplemental suggestive evidence that an elevation of only fifteen hundred feet would be sufficient to establish two broad connections between the two continents—so as to unite Italy with Tripoli and Spain with Morocco, and to convert the Mediterranean Sea into two great lakes, which appears, in fact, to have been its condition during the Pliocene and Post Pliocene periods.

It was by means of these causeways that the large pachyderms entered Britain, then united to the continent; and it was over them they retreated when driven back by glacial conditions, their migration northward being effectually prevented by the destruction of the connecting arms of land.

Some difference of opinion exists among naturalists as to the extent to which zoological regions should be subdivided, and as to their respective limitations.

But Mr. A. R. Wallace, who has most recently written on the subject, is of opinion that the original division proposed by Mr. Sclater in 1857 is the most tenable, and he therefore adopts it in the very exhaustive work upon the geographical distribution of animals which he has recently issued. Mr. Sclater's Six Regions are as follows:—

1.—*The Palœarctic Region*, including Europe, Temperate Asia, and North Africa to the Atlas mountains.
2.—*The Ethiopian Region*, Africa south of the Atlas, Madagascar, and the Mascarene islands, with Southern Arabia.
3.—*The Indian Region*, including India south of the Himalayas, to South China, and to Borneo and Java.
4.—*The Australian Region*, including Celebes and Lombok, Eastward to Australia and the Pacific islands.
5.—*The Nearctic Region*, including Greenland, and North America, to Northern Mexico.
6.—*The Neotropical Region*, including South America, the Antilles, and Southern Mexico.

This arrangement is based upon a detailed examination of the chief genera and families of birds, and also very nearly represents the distribution of mammals and of reptiles. Its regions are not, as in other subsequently proposed and more artificial systems, controlled by climate; for they range, in some instances, from the pole to the tropics. It probably approaches more nearly than any other yet proposed to that desideratum, a division of the earth into regions, founded on a collation of the groups of forms indigenous to or typical of them, and upon a selection of those peculiar to them; with a disregard of, or only admitting with caution, any which, though common to and apparently establishing connection between two or more regions, may have in fact but little value for the purpose of such comparison; from the fact of its being possible to account for their extended range by their capability of easy transport from one region to another by common natural agencies.*

Such an arrangement should be consistent with the retrospective information afforded by palæontology; and, taking an extended view of the subject, be not merely a catalogue

---

* Thus Mr. Wallace considers that the identity of the small fish, *Galaxias attenuatus*, which occurs in the mountain streams of Tasmania, with one found in those of New Zealand, the Falkland Islands, and the temperate regions of South America, cannot be considered as demonstrating a land connection between these places within the period of its specific existence. For there is a possibility that its ova have been transported from one point to another on floating ice; and for similar reasons fresh-water fish generally are unsafe guides to a classification of zoological regions. Mr. Darwin has shown (*Origin of Species*, and *Nature*, vol. xviii. p. 120 and vol. xxv. p. 529) that mollusca can be conveyed attached to or entangled in the claws of migratory birds. Birds themselves are liable to be blown great distances by gales of wind. Beetles and other flying insects may be similarly transferred. Reptiles are occasionally conveyed on floating logs and uprooted trees. Mammals alone appear to be really trustworthy guides towards such a classification, from their being less liable than the other classes to accidental dispersion.

of the present, but also an index of the past. It should
afford an illustration of an existing phase of the distribution
of animal life, considered as the last of a long series of similar
phases which have successively resulted from changes in the
disposition of land and water, and from other controlling
agencies, throughout all time. A reconstruction of the areas
respectively occupied by the sea and the land at different
geological periods will be possible, or at least greatly facili-
tated, when a complete system of similar groupings, illustrative of each successive period, has been compiled.

It is obvious that any great cosmical change, affecting to
a wide extent any of the regions, might determine a destruction of specific existence ; and this on a large scale, in comparison with the change which is always progressing in a
smaller degree in the different and isolated divisions.

The brief remarks which I have made on this subject are
intended to suggest, rather than to demonstrate—which could
only be done by a lengthy series of examples—the causes
influencing specific existence and its in many cases extreme
frailty of tenure. And I shall now conclude by citing from
the works of Lyell and Wallace a short list of notable
species, now extinct, whose remains have been collected
from late Tertiary, and Post Tertiary deposits—that is to
say, at a time subsequent to the appearance of man. From
other authors I have extracted an enumeration of species
which have become locally or entirely extinct within the
historic period.

These instances will, I think, be sufficient to show that,
as similar destructive causes must have been in action
during pre-historic times, it is probable that, besides those
remarkable animals of which remains have been discovered,
many others which then existed may have perished without
leaving any trace of their existence. There is, consequently,
a possibility that some at least of the so-called *myths*
respecting extraordinary creatures, hitherto considered fabu-

lous, may merely be distorted accounts—*traditions*—of species as yet unrecognised by Science, which have actually existed, and that not remotely, as man's congener.

FIG. 9.—THE MAMMOTH. (*After Jukes.*)

## Extinct Post Tertiary Mammalia.

THE MAMMOTH.—Among other remarkable forms whose remains have been discovered in those later deposits, in which geologists are generally agreed that remains of man or traces of his handicraft have also been recognised, there is one which stands out prominently both for its magnitude and extensive range in time and space. Although the animal itself is now entirely extinct, delineations by the hand of Palæolithic man have been preserved, and even frozen carcases, with the flesh uncorrupted and fit for food, have been occasionally discovered.

This is the mammoth, the *Elephas primigenius* of Blumenbach, a gigantic elephant nearly a third taller than the largest modern species, and twice its weight. Its body was protected from the severity of the semi-arctic conditions under which it flourished by a dense covering of reddish wool, and long black hair, and its head was armed or ornamented with tusks exceeding twelve feet in length, and curiously curved into three parts of a circle. Its ivory has long been, and still is, a valuable article of commerce, more especially in North-eastern Asia, and in Eschscholtz Bay in North America, near Behring's straits, where entire skeletons are occasionally discovered, and where even the nature of its food has been ascertained from the undigested contents of its stomach.

There is a well-known case recorded of a specimen found (1799), frozen and encased in ice, at the mouth of the Lena. It was sixteen feet long, and the flesh was so well preserved that the Yakuts used it as food for their dogs. But similar instances occurred previously, for we find the illustrious savant and Emperor Kang Hi [A.D. 1662 to 1723] penning the following note* upon what could only have been this species :—

"The cold is extreme, and nearly continuous on the coasts of the northern sea beyond Tai-Tong-Kiang. It is on this coast that the animal called Fen Chou is found, the form of which resembles that of a rat, but which equals an elephant in size. It lives in obscure caverns, and flies from the light. There is obtained from it an ivory as white as that of the elephant, but easier to work, and which will not split. Its flesh is very cold and excellent for refreshing the blood. The ancient work Chin-y-king speaks of this animal in these terms : 'There is in the depths of the north a rat which weighs as much as a thousand pounds ; its flesh is very good for those who are heated.' The Tsée-Chou calls it Tai-Chou and speaks of another species which is not so large. It

---

* *Mémoires concernant l'histoire, &c. des Chinois, par les Missionaires de Pekin,* vol. iv. p. 481.

says that this is as big as a buffalo, buries itself like a mole, flies the light, and remains nearly always under ground ; it is said that it would die if it saw the light of the sun or even that of the moon."

Fig. 10.—Tooth of the Mammoth. (*After Figuier.*)

It seems probable that discoveries of mammoth tusks formed in part the basis for the story which Pliny tells in reference to fossil ivory. He says * :— "These animals [elephants] are well aware that the only spoil that we are anxious to procure of them is the part which forms their weapon of defence, by Juba called their horns, but by Herodotus, a much older writer, as well as by general usage, and more appropriately, their teeth. Hence it is that, when these tusks have fallen off, either from accident or old age, they bury them in the earth."

Nordenskjöld † states that the savages with whom he came in contact frequently offered to him very fine mammoth tusks, and tools made of mammoth ivory. He computes that since the conquest of Siberia, useful tusks from more than twenty thousand animals have been collected.

Mr. Boyd Dawkins,‡ in a very exhaustive memoir on this animal, quotes an interesting notice of its fossil ivory having

---

* *The Natural History of Pliny*, J. Bostock and H. T. Riley, book viii. chap iv.

† *The Voyage of the Vega*, A. E. Nordenskjöld. London, 1881.

‡ *On the Range of the Mammoth in Space and Time*, by W. B. Dawkins, *Quart. Journ. Geol. Soc.*, 1879, p. 138.

been brought for sale to Khiva. He derives [*] this account from an Arabian traveller, Abou-el-Cassim, who lived in the middle of the tenth century.

Figuier [†] says : "New Siberia and the Isle of Lachon are for the most part only an agglomeration of sand, of ice, and of elephants' teeth. At every tempest the sea casts ashore new quantities of mammoth's tusks, and the inhabitants of New Siberia carry on a profitable commerce in this fossil ivory. Every year during the summer innumerable fisher- men's barks direct their course to this isle of bones, and during winter immense caravans take the same route, all the convoys drawn by dogs, returning charged with the tusks of the mammoth, weighing each from one hundred and fifty to two hundred pounds. The fossil ivory thus with- drawn from the frozen north is imported into China and Europe."

In addition to its elimination by the thawing of the frozen grounds of the north, remains of the mammoth are procured from bogs, alluvial deposits, and from the destruction of submarine beds.[‡] They are also found in cave deposits, associated with the remains of other mammals, and with

---

[*] The notice is taken from *Les Peuples du Caucause, ou Voyage d'Abou-el-Cassim*, par M. C. D'Ohsson, p. 80, as follows :—" On trouve souvent dans la Boulgarie des os (fossils) d'une grandeur prodigieuse. J'ai vu une dent qui avait deux palmes de large sur quatre de long, et un crâne qui ressemblait à une hutte (Arabe). On y déterre des dents semblables aux défenses d'éléphants, blanche comme la neige et pesant jusqu' à deux cents menns. On ne sait pas à quel animal elles ont appartenu, mais on les transporte dans le Khoragur (Kiva), où elles se vendent à grand prix. On en fait des peignes, des vases, et d'autres objets, comme on façonne l'ivoire; toute fois cette substance est plus dure que l'ivoire ; jamais elle ne se brise."

[†] *The World before the Deluge*, L. Figuier. London, 1865.

[‡] According to Woodward, over two thousand grinders were dredged up by the fishermen of Happisburgh in the space of thirteen years ; and other localities in and about England are also noted. — Dana's *Manual of Geology*, p. 564.

flint implements. This creature appears to have been an object of the chase with Palæolithic man.

Mr. Dawkins, reviewing all the discoveries, considers that its range, at various periods, extended over the whole of Northern Europe, and as far south as Spain; over Northern Asia, and North America down to the Isthmus of Darien. Dr. Falconer believes it to have had an elastic constitution, which enabled it to adapt itself to great change of climate.

Murchison, De Verneuil, and Keyserling believed that this species, as well as the woolly rhinoceros, belonged to the Tertiary fauna of Northern Asia, though not appearing until the Quaternary period in Europe.

Mr. Dawkins shows it to have been pre-glacial, glacial, and post-glacial in Britain and in Europe, and, from its relation to the intermediate species *Elephas armeniacus*, accepts it as the ancestor of the existing Indian elephant. Its disappearance was rapid, but not in the opinion of most geologists cataclysmic, as suggested by Mr. Howorth.

Another widely distributed species was the *Rhinoceros ticho-rhinus*—the smooth-skinned rhinoceros—also called the woolly rhinoceros and the Siberian rhinoceros, which had two horns, and, like the mammoth, was covered with woolly hair. It attained a great size; a specimen, the carcase of which was found by Pallas imbedded in frozen soil near Wilui, in Siberia (1772), was eleven and a half feet in length. Its horns are considered by some of the native tribes of northern Asia to have been the talons of gigantic birds; and Ermann and Middendorf suppose that their discovery may have originated the accounts by Herodotus of the gold-bearing griffons and the arimaspi.

Its food, ascertained by Von Brandt, and others, from portions remaining in the hollows of its teeth, consisted of leaves and needles of trees still existing in Siberia. The range of this species northwards was as extensive as that of

the mammoth, but its remains have not yet been discovered
south of the Alps and Pyrenees.

The investigation,* made by M. E. Lartet in 1860, of the
contents of the Grotto of Aurignac, in the department of the
Haute Garonne, from which numerous human skeletons had
been previously removed in 1852, shows that this animal was
included among the species used as ordinary articles of food,
or as exceptional items at the funeral feasts of the Palæolithic
troglodytes. In the layers of charcoal and ashes immediately
outside the entrance to the grotto, and surrounding what is
supposed to have been the hearth, the bones of a young
*Rhinoceros tichorhinus* were found, which had been split open
for the extraction of the marrow. Numerous other species
had been dealt with in the same manner; and all these
having received this treatment, and showing marks of the
action of fire, had evidently been carried to the cave for
banqueting purposes. The remains of Herbivora associated
with those of this rhinoceros, consisted of bones of the
mammoth, the horse (*Equus caballus*), stag (*Cervus elaphus*),
elk (*Megaceros hibernicus*), roebuck (*C. capreolus*), reindeer
(*C. tarandus*), auroch (*Bison europæus*.) Among carnivora
were found remains of *Ursus spelæus* (cave-bear), *Ursus
arctos?* (brown bear), *Meles taxus* (badger), *Putorius vulgaris*
(polecat), *Hyæna spelæa* (cave-hyæna), *Felis spelæa* (cave-lion),
*Felis catus ferus* (wild cat), *Canis lupus* (wolf), *Canis vulpis*
(fox). Within the grotto were also found remains of *Felis
spelæa* (cave-lion) and *Sus scrofa* (pig). The cave-bear, the
fox, and indeed most of these, probably also formed articles
of diet, but the hyæna seems to have been a post attendant
at the feast, and to have rooted out and gnawed off the
spongy parts of the thrown-away bones after the departure
of the company.

In the Pleistocene deposits at Würzburg, in Franconia,

---

* Lyell, *Antiquity of Man*, p. 185, 2nd edit., 1863.

a human finger-bone occurs with bones of this species, and also of other large mammalia, such as the mammoth, cave-bear, and the like.

And flint implements, and pointed javelin-heads made of reindeer horn, are found associated with it in the vicinity of the old hearths established by Palæolithic man in the cave called the Trou du Sureau, on the river Malignée in Belgium.

In the cavern of Goyet, also in Belgium, there are five bone layers, alternating with six beds of alluvial deposits, showing that the cave had been inhabited by different species at various periods. The lion was succeeded by the cave-bear, and this by hyænas; then Palæolithic man became a tenant and has left his bones there, together with flint implements and remains of numerous species, including those already enumerated as his contemporaries.

THE SABRE-TOOTHED TIGER OR LION. — This species, *Machairodus\* latifrons* of Owen, was remarkable for having long sabre-shaped canines. It belongs to an extinct genus, of which four other species are known, characterised by the possession of serrated teeth. The genus is known to be represented in the Auvergne beds between the Eocene and Miocene, in the Miocene of Greece and India, in the Pliocene of South America and Europe, and in the Pleistocene. Mr. Dawkins believes that this species survived to post-glacial times. It is one of the numerous animals whose remains have been found with traces of man and flint implements in cave deposits at Kent's Hole, near Torquay, and elsewhere.

THE CAVE-BEAR, *Ursus spelœus*, of Rosenmüller.—The appearance of this species has been preserved to us in the drawing by Palæolithic man found in the cave of Massat (Arieze).

---

\* Fr. μάχαιρα " a sword," and ὀδούς " a tooth."

It occurs in the Cromer Forest Bed, a deposit referred by
Mr. Boyd Dawkins to the early part of the Glacial period,
and generally regarded as transitional between the Pliocene
and Quaternary.    It is also found in the caves of Perigaud,
which are considered to belong to the reindeer era of
M. Lartet or the opening part of the Recent period, and
numerous discoveries of its remains at dates intermediate to
these have been made in Britain and in Europe.    Carl
Vogt, indeed, is of opinion that this species is the progenitor
of our living brown bear, *Ursus arctos*, and Mr. Boyd Dawkins also says that those " who have compared the French,
German, and British specimens, gradually realize the fact
that the fossil remains of the bears form a graduated series,
in which all the variations that at first sight appear specific
vanish away."

It has been identified by Mr. Busk among the associated
mammalian bones of the Brixham cave.    Its remains are
very abundant in the bone deposit of the Trou de Sureau in
Belgium, and in the cavern of Goyet, which it tenanted
alternately with the lion and hyæna, and, like them, appears
to have preyed on man and the larger mammalia.

Mr. Prestwich has obtained it in low-level deposits of river
gravels in the valleys of the north of France and south of
England, and it has been obtained from the Löss, a loamy,
usually unstratified deposit, which is extensively distributed
over central Europe, in the valleys of the Rhine, Rhone,
Danube, and other great rivers.    This deposit is considered
by Mr. Prestwich to be equivalent to other high-level gravels
of the Pleistocene period.

THE MASTODON.—The generic title Mastodon has been
applied to a number of species allied to the elephants, but
distinguished from them by a peculiar structure of the molar
teeth ; these are rectangular, and in their upper surfaces
exhibit a number of great conical tuberosities with rounded
points disposed in pairs, to the number of four or five,

according to the species; whereas in the elephants they are broad and uniform, and regularly marked with furrows of large curvature. The mastodons, in addition to large tusks in the premaxillæ, like those of the elephant, had also in most instances, a pair of shorter ones in the mandible.

FIG. 11.—MASTODON'S TOOTH (WORN). (*After Figuier.*)

Cuvier established the name Mastodon,* or teat-like toothed animals, for the gigantic species from America which Buffon had already described under the name of the animal or elephant of the Ohio.

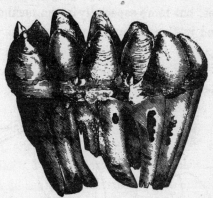

FIG. 12.—MASTODON'S TOOTH. (*After Figuier.*)

The form first appears in the Upper Miocene of Europe, five species being known, two of them from Pikermi, near Athens, and one, *M. angustidens*, from the Miocene beds of

* From μαστός " a teat," and ὀδούς " a tooth."

Malta. Mastodon remains have also been found in the beds of the Sivalik hills, and four species of mastodon in all are known to have ranged over India during those periods.

In Pliocene deposits we have abundant remains of *M. arvernensis*, and *M. longirostris* from the Val d'Arno in Italy, and the *M. Borsoni* from central France.

The *M. arvernensis* may be considered as a characteristic Pliocene species in Italy, France, and Europe generally. In Britain it occurs in the Norwich Crag and the Red Crag of Suffolk.

Species of mastodon occur in the Pliocene of La Plata, and of the temperate regions of South America; on the Pampas, and in the Andes of Chili.

The *Mastodon mirificus* of Leidy is the earliest known species in America; this occurs in Pliocene deposits on the Niobrara and the Loup fork, west of the Mississippi.

The remains of the *Mastodon americanus* of Cuvier occur abundantly in the Post Pliocene deposits throughout the United States, but more especially in the northern half; they are also found in Canada and Nova Scotia.

FIG. 13.—THE MASTODON.

Perfect skeletons are occasionally procured from marshes, where the animals had become mired. In life this species appears to have measured from twelve to thirteen feet in height and twenty-four to twenty-five feet in length, including seven feet for the tusks. Undigested food found with its remains show that it lived partly on spruce and fir-trees. A distinct species characterised the Quaternary deposits of South America.

THE IRISH ELK.—The species (*Megaceros hibernicus*), commonly but erroneously called the Irish Elk, was, as professor Owen* has pointed out, a true deer, whose place is between the fallow and reindeer.

Though now extinct, it survived the Palæolithic period, and may possibly have existed down to historic times. Mr. Gosse adduces some very strong testimony on this point, and is of opinion that its extinction cannot have taken place more than a thousand years ago.

It had a flattened and expanded form of antler, with peculiarities unknown among existing deer, and was, in comparison with these, of gigantic size ; the height to the summit of the antlers being from ten to eleven feet in the largest individuals, and the span of the antlers, in one case, over twelve feet.

Although its remains have been found most abundantly in Ireland, it was widely distributed over Britain and middle Europe. It has been found in peat swamps, lacustrine marls, bone caverns, fen deposits, and the Cornish gravels. It has been obtained from the cavern of Goyet in Belgium, and from the burial-place at Aurignac, in the department of the Haute Garonne. Its known range in time is from the early part of the Glacial period down to, possibly, historic periods.

The CAVE-HYÆNA—*Hyæna spelæa* of Goldfuss—is, like the cave-bear, characteristic of Europe during the Palæolithic age. It has been found in numerous caves in Britain, such as Kent's Hole, the Brixham cave, and one near Wells in

---

* *Palæontology*, R. Owen. Edinburgh, 1860.

Somersetshire, explored by Dawkins in 1859 ; in all of these the remains are associated with those of man, or with his implements. This species is closely related to the *H. crocuta* of Zimm, at present existing in South Africa, and is by some geologists considered identical with it. It is, however, larger.

It appears to have to some extent replaced the cave-bear in Britain ; we are also, doubtless, greatly indebted to it for some of the extensive collections of bones in caverns, resulting from the carcases which it had dragged thither, and imperfectly destroyed.

In a cave at Kirkdale, in the vale of Pickering, the bones of about three hundred individuals—hyænas—were found mingled with the remains of the mammoth, bear, rhinoceros, deer, cave-lion, brown bear, horse, hare, and other species. Mr. Dawkins,* in describing it, says : " The pack of hyænas fell upon reindeer in the winter, and at other times on horses and bisons, and were able to master the hippopotamus, the lion, the slender-nosed rhinoceros, or the straight-tusked elephant, and to carry their bones to their den, where they were found by Dr. Buckland. The hyænas also inhabiting the ' Dukeries,' dragged back to their dens fragments of lion."

Notable Quaternary forms (now extinct) on the American continent are the gigantic sloth-like animals *Megatherium*, which reached eighteen feet in length, and *Mylodon*, one species of which (*M. robustus*) was eleven feet in length ; Armadillos, such as *Glyptodon*, with a total length of nine feet ; *Chlamydotherium*, as big as a rhinoceros ; and *Pachytherium*, equalling an ox.

In Australia we find marsupial forms as at the present day ; but they were gigantic in comparison with the latter. As for example, the *Diprotodon*, which equalled in size a hippopotamus, and the *Nototherium*, as large as a bullock.

---

* *The British Lion*, W. Boyd Dawkins, *Contemporary Review*, 1882.

I may mention a few other species, the remains of which are associated with some of those commented on in the last few pages; but which, as they have undoubtedly continued in existence down to the present period, are external to the present portion of my argument, and are either treated of elsewhere, or need only to be referred to in a few words.

FIG. 14.—MYLODON ROBUSTUS. (*After Figuier.*)

It must also be borne in mind that the linking together of species by the discovery of intermediate graduated forms, is daily proceeding; so that some even of those spoken of in greater detail may shortly be generally recognised, as at present they are held by a few, to be identical with existing forms.

The HIPPOPOTAMUS.—The *Hippopotamus major,* now considered identical with the larger of the two African species— *H. amphibia,* has been found associated with *E. antiquus* and *R. hemitœchus* of Falc in Durdham Down and Kirkdale caves, and in those at Kent's Hole and Ravenscliff. It has also been found in river gravels at Grays, Ilford, and elsewhere, in the lower part of the river-border deposits of Amiens with flint implements, and in Quaternary deposits on the continent of Europe.

THE CAVE-LION—*Felis spelœa*—is now considered to be merely a variety of the African lion (*Felis leo*), although of larger size; it had a very wide range over Britain and Europe during the Post Pliocene period, as also did the leopard (*F. pardus*) and probably the lynx (*Lyncus*).

The REINDEER or CARIBOO—*Cervus tarandus*—which still exists, both domesticated and wild, in northern Europe and America, is adapted for northern latitudes. It formerly extended over Europe, and in the British Isles probably survived in the north of Scotland until the twelfth century.

Its remains have been found in Pleistocene deposits in numerous localities, but most abundantly in those which M. Lartet has assigned to the period which he calls the Reindeer age.

Other Pleistocene mammals still existing, but whose range is much restricted, are the musk ox (*Ovibos moschatus*), familiar to us, from the accounts of arctic expeditions, as occurring in the circumpolar regions of North America; the glutton (*Gulo luscus*), the auroch (*Bison europœus*), the wild horse (*E. fossilis*), the arctic fox (*Canis lagopus*), the bison (*Bison priscus*), the elk or moose (*Alces malchis*), found in Norway and North America, the lemming, the lagomys or tail-less hare, &c.

As examples of total extinction in late years, we may mention the dodo, the solitaire, and species allied to them, in the islands of Mauritius, Bourbon, and Reunion; the moa in New Zealand; the *Æpiornis* in Madagascar; the great auk, *Alca impennis*, in northern seas, and the *Rhytina Stelleri*, common once in the latitude of Behring's Straits, and described by Steller in 1742.

The Dodo, a native of the island of Mauritius, was about 50 lbs. in weight, and covered with loose downy plumage, it

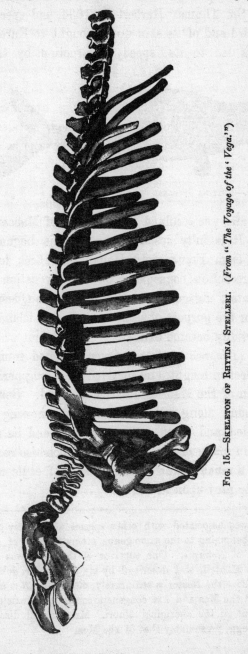

FIG. 15.—SKELETON OF RHYTINA STELLERI. (*From "The Voyage of the 'Vega.'"*)

was unable to rise from the ground in consequence of the imperfect development of its wings; it was minutely described by Sir Thomas Herbert in 1634, and specimens of the living bird and of its skin were brought to Europe. Its unwieldiness led to its speedy destruction by the early voyagers.

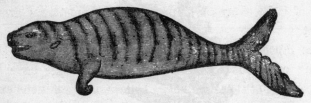

FIG. 16.—RHYTINA STELLERI.   (*From " The Voyage of the ' Vega.' "*)

The Solitaire was confined to the island of Mascaregue or Bourbon.   It is fully described by Francis Leguat, who, having fled from France into Holland in 1689, to escape religious persecution consequent on the revocation of the Edict of Nantes, engaged under the Marquis de Quesne in an expedition for the purpose of settlement on that island.   This bird also speedily became extinct.

The Moa (*Dinornis giganteus,* Owen) reached from twelve to fourteen feet in height, and survived for a long period after the migration of the Maories to New Zealand.   Bones of it have been found along with charred wood, showing that it had been killed and eaten by the natives; and its memory is preserved in many of their traditions, which also record the existence of a much larger bird, a species of eagle or hawk, which used to prey upon it.*

---

* The Moa was associated with other species also nearly or totally extinct: some belonging to the same genus, others to those of *Papteryx,* of *Nestor,* and of *Notornis.*   One survivor of the latter was obtained by Mr. Gideon Mantell, and described by my father, Mr. John Gould, in 1850.   I believe the Nestor is still, rarely, met with.   Mr. Mantell is of opinion that the Moa and his congeners continued in existence long after the advent of the aboriginal Maori.   Mr. Mantell discovered a gigantic fossil egg, presumably that of the Moa.

Rapidly approaching total extinction are the several species of *Apteryx* in the same country—remarkable birds with merely rudimentary wings : as also the *Notornis*, a large Rail—at first, and for a long time, only known in the fossil state, but of which a living specimen was secured by Mr. Walter Mantell in 1849 : and the *Kapapo* (*Strigops habroptilus*) of G. R. Gray—a strange owl-faced nocturnal ground-parrot.

The *Æpyornis maximus* was almost as large as the Moa ; of this numerous fossil bones and a few eggs have been discovered, but there are not, I believe, any traditions extant among the natives of Madagascar of its having survived to a late period.

The Great Auk (*Alca impennis*) is now believed to be extinct. It formerly occurred in the British Isles, but more abundantly in high latitudes ; and its remains occur in great numbers on the shores of Iceland, Greenland, and Denmark, as also of Labrador and Newfoundland.

FIG. 17.—RHYTINA STELLERI. (*After J. Fr. Brandt.*)

Steller's Sea-cow (*Rhytina Stelleri* of Cuvier) was a mammal allied to the Manatees and Dugongs ; it was discovered by Behring in 1768 on a small island lying off the Kamtchatkan coast. It measured as much as from twenty-eight to thirty-five feet in length, and was soon nearly exterminated by Behring's party and other voyagers who visited the island. The last one of which there is any record was killed in 1854.*

---

* A. E. Nordenskiöld, *The Voyage of the ' Vega,'* vol. i. p. 272, *et seq.* London, 1881.

To the above may be added the *Didunculus,* a species of
ground-pigeon peculiar to the Samoa Islands, and the *Nestor
productus,* a parrot of Norfolk Island.   An extended list might
be prepared, from fossil evidences, of other species which
were at one time associated with those I have enumerated.

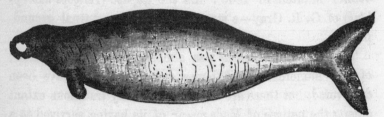

FIG. 18.—RHYTINA STELLERI.   (*From " The Voyage of the ' Vega.' "*)

In conclusion, I may point out that that excellent naturalist
Pliny* records the disappearance, in his days, of certain species
formerly known.   He mentions the Incendiary, the Clivia,
and the Subis (species of birds), and states that there were
many other birds mentioned in the Etruscan ritual, which
were no longer to be found in his time.   He also says that
there had been a bird in Sardinia resembling the crane, and
called the Gromphæna, which was no longer known even by
the people of the country.

## Local Extinction.

Of local extinction we may note in our own island the cases
of the beaver, the bear, the wolf, the wild cattle, the elk,
the wild boar, the bustard, and the capercailzie; of these
the beaver survived in Wales and Scotland until the time
of Giraldus Cambrensis in 1188, and Pennant notes indications of its former existence in the names of several streams
and lakes in Wales.   It was not uncommon throughout the
greater part of Europe down to the Middle Ages.

* Pliny, *Nat. Hist.,* Bk. x., chap. xvii., and Bk. xxx., chap. liii,

The bear, still common in Norway and the Pyrenees, is alluded to, as Mr. Gosse points out, in the Welsh Triads,* which are supposed to have been compiled in the seventh century. They say that "the Kymri, a Celtic tribe, first inhabited Britain; before them were no men here, but only bears, wolves, beavers, and oxen with high prominences." Mr. Gosse adds, "The Roman poets knew of its existence here. Martial speaks of the robber Laureolis being exposed on the cross to the fangs of the Caledonian bear; and Claudian alludes to British bears. The Emperor Claudius, on his return to Rome after the conquest of this island, exhibited, as trophies, combats of British bears in the Arena. In the Penitential of Archbishop Egbert, said to have been compiled about A.D. 750, bears are mentioned as inhabiting the English forests, and the city of Norwich is said to have been required to furnish a bear annually to Edward the Confessor, together with six dogs, no doubt for baiting him."

The wolf, though greatly reduced in numbers during the Heptarchy, when Edgar laid an annual tribute of three hundred wolf-skins upon the Welsh, still occurred in formidable numbers in England in 1281, and not unfrequently until the reign of Henry VII. The last wolf was killed in Scotland in the year 1743, and in Ireland in 1770.†

The wild cattle are now only represented by the small herds in Chartley Castle, Chillingham, and Cadgow parks; the spare survivors probably of the species referred to by Herodotus when he speaks of "large ferocious and fleet white bulls" which abounded in the country south of Thrace, and continued in Poland, Lithuania, and Muscovy until the fifteenth century, or perhaps of the Urus described by Cæsar as little inferior to the elephant in size, and inhabiting the

* *The Romance of Natural History*, by P. H. Gosse, 2nd Series, London 1875.
† *Pop. Sci. Monthly*, October 1878.

Hercynian forest, and believed to be identical with the *Bos primigenius* found in a fossil state in Britain.

The wild boar was once abundant in Scotland and England. The family of Baird derives its heraldic crest from a grant of David I. of Scotland, in recognition of his being saved from an infuriated boar which had turned on him. In England only nobles and gentry were allowed to hunt it, and the slaughter of one by an unauthorized person within the demesnes of William the Conqueror was punished by the loss of both eyes.*

The bustard, once abundant, is now extinct in Britain, so far as the indigenous race is concerned. Occasionally a chance visitant from the continent is seen ; but there, also, its numbers have been greatly diminished. It was common in Buffon's time in the plains of Poitou and Champagne, though now extremely rare, and is still common in Eastern Asia.

The capercailzie, or cock of the woods, after complete extinction, has been reintroduced from Norway, and, under protection, is moderately abundant in parts of Scotland.

In America, the process of extermination marches with the settlement of the various states. W. J. J. Allen records the absolute disappearance of the walrus from the Gulf of St. Lawrence, and of the moose, the elk, and the Virginian deer, from many of the states in which they formerly abounded. This also is true, to some extent, of the bear, the beaver, the grey wolf, the panther, and the lynx.

The buffalo (*Bos americanus*) is being destroyed at the rate of two hundred and fifty thousand annually, and it is estimated that the number slain by hunters for their hides during the last forty years amounts to four millions. It has disappeared in the eastern part of the continent from many extensive tracts which it formerly inhabited.

Among the ocean whales, both the right and the sperm

* *Excelsior*, vol. iii. London, 1855.

have only been preserved from extinction by the fortunate discovery of petroleum, which has reduced the value of their oil, and thus lessened considerably the number of vessels equipped for the whale fishery.

In South Africa, elephants and all other large game are being steadily exterminated within the several colonies.

In Australia, we find that the seals which thronged the islands of Bass's Straits in countless thousands, at the period when Bass made his explorations there, have utterly disappeared. The bulk of them were destroyed by seal-hunters from Sydney within a few years after his discovery. The lamentable records of the *Sydney Gazette* of that period show this, for they detail the return to port, after a short cruise, of schooners laden with from twelve to sixteen thousand skins each. The result of this has been that for many years past the number of seals has been limited to a few individuals, to be found on one or two isolated rocks off Clarke's Island, and on Hogan's group.

The great sea-elephant, which, in Peron's time, still migrated for breeding purposes from antarctic regions to the shores of King's Island, where it is described by him as lining the long sandy beaches by hundreds, has been almost unseen there since the date of his visit, and its memory is only preserved in the names of Sea-Elephant Bay, Elephant Rock, &c. which are still inscribed on our charts.

The introduction of the Dingo, by the Australian blacks in their southward migration, is supposed to have caused the extinction of the Thylacinus (*T. cynocephalus*), or striped Australian wolf, on the main land of Australia, where it was once abundant ; it is now only to be found in the remote portions of the island of Tasmania. This destruction of one species by another is paralleled in our own country by the approaching extinction of the indigenous and now very rare black rat, which has been almost entirely displaced by the fierce grey rat from Norway.

We learn from incidental passages in the *Bamboo Books**
that the rhinoceros, which is now unknown in China, formerly
extended throughout that country. We read of King Ch'aou,
named Hĕa (B.C. 980), that "in his sixteenth year [of reign]
the king attacked Ts'oo, and in crossing the river Han met
with a large rhinoceros." And, again, of King E, named
Sĕĕ (B.C. 860), that "in his sixth year, when hunting in the
forest of Shay, he captured a rhinoceros and carried it
home." There is also mention made—though this is less
conclusive—that in the time of King Yiu, named Yeu
(B.C. 313), the King of Yueh sent Kung-sze Yu with a
present of three hundred boats, five million arrows, together
with rhinoceros' horns and elephants' teeth.

Elephants are now unknown in China except in a domesticated state, but they probably disputed its thick forest and
jungly plains with the Miaotsz, Lolos, and other tribes which
held the country before its present occupants. This may be
inferred from the incidental references to them in the *Shan
Hai King*, a work reputed to be of great antiquity, of which
more mention will be made hereafter, and from evidence
contained in other ancient Chinese works which has been
summarized by Mr. Kingsmill† as follows:—

"The rhinoceros and elephant certainly lived in Honan
B.C. 600. The *Tso-chuen*, commenting on the C'hun T'siu
of the second year of the Duke Siuen (B.C. 605), describes
the former as being in sufficient abundance to supply skins
for armour. The want, according to the popular saying,
was not of rhinoceroses to supply skins, but of courage to
animate the wearers. From the same authority (Duke Hi
XIII., B.C. 636) we learn that while T'soo (Hukwang) produced ivory and rhinoceros' skins in abundance, Tsin, lying

---

* *The Chinese Classics*, vol. iii. p. 1, by James Legge, B.D.

† Inaugural Address by President, T. W. Kingsmill, North China
Branch of the Royal Asiatic Society, 1877.

north of the Yellow River, on the most elevated part of the
Loess, was dependent on the other for its supplies of those
commodities. The *Tribute of Yu* tells the same tale. Yang-
chow and King (Kiangpeh and Hukwang), we are told, sent
tribute of ivory and rhinoceros' hide, while Liang (Shensi)
sent the skins of foxes and bears. Going back to mythical
times, we find Mencius (III. ii. 9) telling how Chow Kung
expelled from Lu (Shantung) the elephants and rhinoceroses,
the tigers and leopards."

Mr. Kingsmill even suggests that the species referred to
were the mammoth and the Siberian rhinoceros (*R. ticho-
rhinus*).

M. Chabas* publishes an Egyptian inscription showing
that the elephant existed in a feral state in the Euphrates
Valley in the time of Thothmes III. (16th century B.C.).
The inscription records a great hunting of elephants in the
neighbourhood of Nineveh.

Tigers still abound in Manchuria and Corea, their skins
forming a regular article of commerce in Vladivostock, New-
chwang, and Seoul. They are said to attain larger dimensions in these northern latitudes than their southern congener,
the better-known Bengal tiger. They are generally extinct
in China Proper; but Père David states that he has seen
them in the neighbourhood of Pekin, in Mongolia, and at
Moupin, and they are reported to have been seen near Amoy.
Within the last few years† a large specimen was killed by
Chinese soldiery within a few miles of the city of Ningpo;
and it is probable that at no distant date they ranged over
the whole country from Hindostan to Eastern Siberia, as
they are incidentally referred to in various Chinese works—
the *Urh Yah* specially recording the capture of a white tiger

* Chabas, *Études sur l'Antiquité Historique, d'apres les sources Égyp-
tiennes.*

† Subsequently to 1874.

in the time of the Emperor Süen of the Han dynasty, and of a black one, in the fourth year of the reign of Yung Kia, in a netted surround in Kien Ping Fu in the district of Tsz Kwei.

The tailed deer or Mi-lu (*Cervus Davidianus* of Milne Edwardes), which Chinese literature* indicates as having once been of common occurrence throughout China, is now only to be found in the Imperial hunting grounds south of Peking, where it is restricted to an enclosure of fifty miles in circumference. It is believed to exist no longer in a wild state, as no trace of it has been found in any of the recent explorations of Asia. The *Ch'un ts'iu* (B.C. 676) states that this species appeared in the winter of that year, in such numbers that it was chronicled in the records of Lu (Shantung), and that in the following autumn it was followed by an inroad of " Yih," which Mr. Kingsmill believes to be the wolf.

There also appears reason to suppose that the ostrich had a much more extended range than at present ; for we find references in the *Shi-Ki*,† or book of history of Szema Tsien, to " large birds with eggs as big as water-jars " as inhabiting T'iaou-chi, identified by Mr. Kingsmill as Sarangia or Drangia ; and, in speaking of Parthia, it says, " On the return of the mission he sent envoys with it that they might see the extent and power of China. He sent with them, as presents to the Emperor, eggs of the great bird of the country, and a curiously deformed man from Samarkand."

The gigantic Chelonians which once abounded in India

---

* O. F. von Mollendorf, *Journal* of North China Branch of the Royal Asiatic Society, New Series, No. 2, and T. W. Kingsmill, " The Border Lands of Geology and History," *Journal* of North China Branch of the Royal Asiatic Society, 1877.

† " Intercourse of China with Eastern Turkestan and the adjacent country in the second century B.C.," T. W. Kingsmill, *Journal* of North China Branch of the Royal Asiatic Society, New Series, No. 14.

and the Indian seas are now entirely extinct; but we have had little difficulty in believing the accounts of their actual and late existence contained in the works of Pliny and Ælian since the discovery of the Colossochelys, described by Dr. Falconer, in the Upper Miocene deposits of the Siwalik Hills in North-Western India. The shell of *Colossochelys Atlas* (Falconer and Cautley) measured twelve feet, and the whole animal nearly twenty.

Pliny,* who published his work on Natural History about A.D. 77, states that the turtles of the Indian Sea are of such vast size that a single shell is sufficient to roof a habitable cottage, and that among the islands of the Red Sea the navigation is mostly carried on in boats formed from this shell.

Ælian,† about the middle of the third century of our era, is more specific in his statement, and says that the Indian river-tortoise is very large, and in size not less than a boat of fair magnitude; also, in speaking of the Great Sea, in which is Taprobana (Ceylon), he says: "There are very large tortoises generated in this sea, the shell of which is large enough to make an entire roof; for a single one reaches the length of fifteen cubits, so that not a few people are able to live beneath it, and certainly secure themselves from the vehement rays of the sun; they make a broad shade, and so resist rain that they are preferable for this purpose to tiles, nor does the rain beating against them sound otherwise than if it were falling on tiles. Nor, indeed, do those who inhabit them have any necessity for repairing them, as in the case of broken tiles, for the whole roof is made out of a solid shell so that it has the appearance of a cavernous or under-mined rock, and of a natural roof."

---

* *The Natural History of Pliny.* Translated by J. Bostock and H. T. Biley, 6 vols. Bohn, London, 1857.
† *Æliani de Natura Animalium*, F. Jacobs. Jenæ, 1832.

El Edrisi, in his great geographical work,* completed
A.D. 1154, speaks of them as existing down to his day, but
as his book is admitted to be a compilation from all preceding
geographical works, he may have been simply quoting, without special acknowledgment, the statements given above.
He says, speaking of the Sea of Herkend (the Indian Ocean
west of Ceylon), "It contains turtles twenty cubits long,
containing within them as many as one thousand eggs."
Large tortoises formerly inhabited the Mascarene islands, but
have been destroyed on all of them, with the exception of
the small uninhabited Aldabra islands, north of the Seychelle
group; and those formerly abundant on the Galapagos islands
are now represented by only a few survivors, and the species
rapidly approaches extinction.

I shall close this chapter with a reference to a creature
which, if it may not be entitled to be called "the dragon,"
may at least be considered as first cousin to it. This is a
lacertilian of large size, at least twenty feet in length, pano-
plied with the most horrifying armour, which roamed over
the Australian continent during Pleistocene times, and probably until the introduction of the aborigines.

Its remains have been described by Professor Owen in
several communications to the Royal Society,† under the
name of *Megalania prisca*. They were procured by Mr. G.
F. Bennett from the drift-beds of King's Creek, a tributary
of the Condamine River in Australia. It was associated with
correspondingly large marsupial mammals, now also extinct.

From the portions transmitted to him Professor Owen
determined that it presented in some respects a magnified
resemblance of the miniature existing lizard, *Moloch horridus*,

---

* *Géographie d'Edrisi, traduite de l'Arabe en Français*, P. Amédée
Jaubert, 2 vols. Paris, 1836.

† *Phil. Trans.*, vol. cxlix. p. 43, 1859; vol. clxxi. p. 1,037, 1880;
vol. clxxii. p. 547, 1881.

found in Western Australia,* of which Dr. Gray remarks, " The external appearance of this lizard is the most ferocious of any that I know." In Megalania the head was rendered horrible and menacing by horns projecting from its sides, and from the tip of the nose, which would be " as available against the attacks of Thylacoleo as the buffalo's horns are against those of the South African lion." The tail consisted of a series of annular segments armed with horny spikes, represented by the less perfectly developed ones in the existing species *Uromastix princeps* from Zanzibar, or in the above-mentioned moloch. In regard to these the Professor says, " That the horny sheaths of the above-described supports or cores arming the end of the tail may have been applied to deliver blows upon an assailant, seems not improbable, and this part of the organization of the great extinct Australian dragon may be regarded, with the cranial horn, as parts of both an offensive and defensive apparatus."

The gavial of the Ganges is reported to be a fish-eater only, and is considered harmless to man. The Indian museums, however, have large specimens, which are said to have been captured after they had destroyed several human beings; and so we may imagine that this structurally herbivorous lizard (the Megalania having a horny edentate upper jaw) may have occasionally varied his diet, and have proved an importunate neighbour to aboriginal encampments in which toothsome children abounded, and that it may, in fact, have been one of the sources from which the myth of the Bunyip, of which I shall speak hereafter, has been derived.

---

* Description of some New Species and Genera of Reptiles from Western Australia, discovered by John Gould, Esq., *Annals and Magazine of Natural History*, vol. vii. p. 88, 1841.

# CHAPTER III.

## ANTIQUITY OF MAN.

I DO not propose to bestow any large amount of space upon the enumeration of the palæontological evidence of the antiquity of man. The works of the various eminent authors who have devoted themselves to the special consideration of this subject exhaust all that can be said upon it with our present data, and to these I must refer the reader who is desirous of acquainting himself critically with its details, confining myself to a few general statements based on these labours.

In the early days of geological science when observers were few, great groups of strata were arranged under an artificial classification, which, while it has lost to a certain extent the specific value which it then assumed to possess, is still retained for purposes of convenient reference. Masters of the science acquired, so to say, a possessive interest in certain regions of it, and the names of Sedgwick, Murchison, Jukes, Phillips, Lyell, and others became, and will remain, inseparably associated with the history of those great divisions of the materials of the earth's crust, which, under the names of the Cambrian, Silurian, Devonian, Carboniferous, and Tertiary formations, have become familiar to us.

In those days, when observations were limited to a comparatively small area, the lines separating most of these formations were supposed to be hard and definite; forms of life which characterized one, were presumed to have become

entirely extinct before the inauguration of those which succeeded them, and breaks in the stratigraphical succession
appeared to justify the opinion, held by a large and influential
section, that great cataclysms or catastrophes had marked the
time when one age or formation terminated and another
commenced to succeed it.

By degrees, and with the increase of observers, both in
England and in every portion of the world, modifications of
these views obtained; passage beds were discovered, connecting by insensible gradations formations which had
hitherto been supposed to present the most abrupt separa-
tions; transitional forms of life connecting them were
unearthed; and an opinion was advanced, and steadily confirmed, which at the present day it is probable no one would
be found to dispute, that not all in one place or country, but
discoverable in some part or other of the world, a perfect
sequence exists, from the very earliest formations of which
we have any cognizance, up to the alluvial and marine
deposits in process of formation at the present day.*

---

* " We shall, I think, eventually more fully recognise that, as is the
case with the periods of the day, each of the larger geological divisions
follows the other, without any actual break or boundary; and that the
minor subdivisions are like the hours on the clock, useful and conventional rather than absolutely fixed by any general cause in Nature."—
Annual Address, President of Geological Society, 1875.

" With regard to stratigraphical geology, the main foundations are
already laid, and a great part of the details filled in. The tendency of
modern discoveries has already been, and will probably still be, to fill
up those breaks, which, according to the view of many, though by no
means all geologists, are so frequently assumed to exist between different
geological periods and to bring about a more full recognition of the
continuity of geological time. As knowledge increases, it will, I think,
become more and more apparent that all existing divisions of time are
to a considerable extent local and arbitrary. But, even when this is
fully recognised, it will still be found desirable to retain them, if only
for the sake of convenience and approximate precision."—Annual
Address, President of Geological Society, 1876.

Correlatively it was deduced that the same phenomena of
nature have been in action since the earliest period when
organic existence can be affirmed.  The gradual degradation
of pre-existing continents by normal destructive agencies,
the upheaval and subsidence of large areas, the effusion from
volcanic vents, into the air or sea, of ashes and lavas, the
action of frost and ice, of heat, rain, and sunshine—all these
have acted in the past as they are still acting before our
eyes.

In earlier days, arguing from limited data, a progressive
creation was claimed which confined the appearance of the
higher form of vertebrate life to a successive and widely-
stepped gradation.

Hugh Miller, and other able thinkers, noted with satisfac-
tion the appearance, first of fish, then of reptiles, next of
birds and mammals, and finally, as the crowning work of all,
both geologically and actually, quite recently of man.

This wonderful confirmation of the Biblical history of
creation appealed so gratefully to many, that it caused for a
time a disposition to cramp discovery, and even to warp the
facts of science, in order to make them harmonize with the
statements of Revelation.  The alleged proofs of the existence
of pre-historic man were for a long time jealously disputed,
and it was only by slow degrees that they were admitted,
that the tenets of the Darwinian school gained ground, and
that the full meaning was appreciated of such anomalies as
the existence at the present day of Ganoid fishes both in
America and Europe, of true Palæozoic type, or of Oolitic
forms on the Australian continent and in the adjacent seas.

But step by step marvellous palæontological discoveries
were made, and the pillars which mark the advent of each
great form of life have had to be set back, until now no one
would, I think, be entirely safe in affirming that even in the
Cambrian, the oldest of all fossiliferous formations, vestiges
of mammals, that is to say, of the highest forms of life, may

not at a future day be found, or that the records contained between the Cambrian and the present day, may not in fact be but a few pages as compared with the whole volume of the world's history.*

* "It was not until January 1832, that the second volume of the *Principles* was published, when it was received with as much favour as the first had been. It related more especially to the changes in the organic world, while the former volume had treated mainly of the inorganic forces of nature. Singularly enough, some of the points which were seized on by his great fellow-labourer Murchison for his presidential address to this Society in 1832, as subjects for felicitation, are precisely those which the candid mind of Lyell, ever ready to attach the full value to discoveries or arguments from time to time brought forward, even when in opposition to his own views, ultimately found reason to modify. We can never, I think, more highly appreciate Sir Charles Lyell's freshness of mind, his candour and love of truth, than when we compare certain portions of the first edition of the *Principles* with those which occupy the same place in the last, and trace the manner in which his judicial intellect was eventually led to conclusions diametrically opposed to those which he originally held. To those acquainted only with the latest editions of the *Principles*, and with his *Antiquity of Man*, it may sound almost ironical in Murchison to have written, 'I cannot avoid noticing the clear and impartial manner in which the untenable parts of the dogmas concerning the alteration and transmutation of species and genera are refuted, and how satisfactorily the author confirms the great truth of the recent appearance of man upon our planet.'

"By the work (*Principles of Geology*, vol. iii.), as a whole, was dealt the most telling blow that had ever fallen upon those to whom it appears 'more philosophical to speculate on the possibilities of the past than patiently to explore the realities of the present,' while the earnest and careful endeavour to reconcile the former indications of change with the evidence of gradual mutation now in progress, or *which may be* in progress, received its greatest encouragement. The doctrines which Hutton and Playfair had held and taught assumed new and more vigorous life as better principles were explained by their eminent successor, and were supported by arguments which, as a whole, were incontrovertible."—Annual Address, President of Geological Society, 1876.

"But, as Sir Roderick Murchison has long ago proved, there are parts of the record which are singularly complete, and in those parts we have the proof of creation without any indication of development. The Silurian rocks, as regards oceanic life, are perfect and abundant in

It is with the later of these records that we have to deal, in which discoveries have been made sufficiently progressive to justify the expectation that they have by no means reached their limit, and sufficiently ample in themselves to open the widest fields for philosophic speculation and deduction.

Before stating these, it may be premised that estimates have been attempted by various geologists of the collective age of the different groups of formations. These are based on reasonings which for the most part it is unnecessary to give in detail, in so much as these can scarcely yet be considered to have passed the bounds of speculation, and very different results can be arrived at by theorists according to the relative importance which they attach to the data employed in the calculation.

Thus Mr. T. Mellard Reade, in a paper communicated to the Royal Society in 1878, concludes that the formation of the sedimentary strata must have occupied at least six hundred million years : which he divides in round numbers as follows :—

|  | Millions of Years. |
|---|---|
| Laurentian, Cambrian, and Silurian . . . . | 200 |
| Old Red, Carboniferous, Permian, and New Red . | 200 |
| Jurassic, Wealden, Cretaceous, Eocene, Miocene, Pliocene, and Post Pliocene . . . . . | 200 |
|  | 600 |

He estimates the average thickness of the sedimentary crust of the earth to be at least one mile, and from a compu-

---

the forms they have preserved. *Yet there are no fish.* The Devonian age followed tranquilly and without a break, and in the Devonian sea, suddenly, fish appear, appear in shoals, and in form of the highest and most perfect type."—The Duke of Argyll, *Primeval Man*, p. 45, London, 1869.

* T. Mellard Reade, " Limestone as an Index of Geological Time," *Proceedings*, Royal Society, London, vol. xxviii., p. 281.

tation of the proportion of carbonate and sulphate of lime
to materials held in suspension in various river-waters from
a variety of formations, infers that one-tenth of this crust is
calcareous.

He estimates the annual flow of water in all the great
river-basins, the proportion of rain-water running off the
granitic and trappean rocks, the percentage of lime in solution which they carry down, and arrives at the conclusion
that the minimum time requisite for the elimination of the
calcareous matter contained in the sedimentary crust of the
earth, is at least six hundred millions of years.

A writer in the *Gentleman's Magazine** (Professor Huxley ?),
whose article I am only able to quote at second-hand, makes
an estimate which, though much lower than the above, is still
of enormous magnitude, as follows :—

|  | Feet. | Years. |
|---|---|---|
| Laurentian . . . . | 30,000 | 30,000,000 |
| Cambrian . . . . . | 25,000 | 25,000,000 |
| Silurian . . . . . | 6,000 | 6,000,000 |
| Old Red and Devonian . . | 10,000 | 10,000,000 |
| Carboniferous . . . . | 12,000 | 12,000,000 |
| Secondary . . . . . | 10,000 | 10,000,000 |
| Tertiary and Post Tertiary . | 1,000 | 1,000,000 |
| Gaps and unrepresented strata . | 6,000 | 6,000,000 |
|  | Total . | 100,000,000 |

Mr. Darwin, arguing upon Sir W. Thompson's estimate of
a minimum of ninety-eight and maximum of two hundred
millions of years since the consolidation of the crust, and on
Mr. Croll's estimate of sixty millions, as the time elapsed
since the Cambrian period, considers that the latter is quite
insufficient to permit of the many and great mutations of
life which have certainly occurred since then. He judges

* *Scientific American*, Supplement, February 1881.

from the small amount of organic change since the commencement of the glacial epoch, and adds that the previous one hundred and forty million years can hardly be considered as sufficient for the development of the varied forms of life which certainly existed towards the close of the Cambrian period.

On the other hand, Mr. Croll considers that it is utterly impossible that the existing order of things, as regards our globe, can date so far back as anything like five hundred millions of years, and, starting with referring the commencement of the Glacial epoch to two hundred and fifty thousand years ago, allows fifteen millions since the beginning of the Eocene period, and sixty millions of years in all since the beginning of the Cambrian period. He bases his arguments ᴗⁿ the limit to the age of the sun's heat as detailed by Sir William Thompson.

Sir Charles Lyell and Professor Haughton respectively estimated the expiration of time from the commencement of the Cambrian at two hundred and forty and two hundred millions of years, basing their calculations on the rate of modification of the species of mollusca, in the one case, and on the rate of formation of rocks and their maximum thickness, in the other.

This, moreover, is irrespective of the vast periods during which life must have existed, which on the development theory necessarily preceded the Cambrian, and, according to Mr. Darwin, should not be less than in the proportion of five to two.

In fine, one school of geologists and zoologists demand the maximum periods quoted above, to account for the amount of sedimentary deposit, and the specific developments which have occurred ; the other considers the periods claimed as requisite for these actions to be unnecessary, and to be in excess of the limits which, according to their views, the physical elements of the case permit.

Mr. Wallace, in reviewing the question, dwells on the probability of the rate of geological changes having been greater in very remote times than it is at present, and thus opens a way to the reconciliation of the opposing views so far as one half the question is concerned.

Having thus adverted to the principles upon which various theorists have in part based their attacks on the problem of the estimation of the duration of geological ages, I may now make a few more detailed observations upon those later periods during which man is, now, generally admitted to have existed, and refer lightly to the earlier times which some, but not all, geologists consider to have furnished evidences of his presence.

I omit discussing the doubtful assertions of the extreme antiquity of man, which come to us from American observers, such as are based on supposed footprints in rocks of secondary age, figured in a semi-scientific and exceedingly valuable popular journal. There are other theories which I omit, both because they need further confirmation by scientific investigators, and because they deal with periods so remote as to be totally devoid of significance for the argument of this work.

Nor, up to the present time, are the evidences of the existence of man during Miocene and Pliocene times admitted as conclusive. Professor Capellini has discovered, in deposits recognised by Italian geologists as of Pliocene age, cetacean bones, which are marked with incisions such as only a sharp instrument could have produced, and which, in his opinion, must be ascribed to human agency. To this view it is objected that the incisions might have been made by the teeth of fishes, and further evidence is waited for.

Not a few discoveries have been made, apparently extending the existence of man to a much more remote antiquity, that of Miocene times. M. l'Abbé Bourgeois has collected, from undoubted Miocene strata at Thenay, supposed flint implements which he conceives to exhibit evidences of having been fashioned by man, as well as stones showing in some cases traces of the action of fire, and which he supposes to have been used as pot-boilers. M. Carlos Ribeiro has made similar discoveries of worked flints and quartzites in the Pliocene and Miocene of the Tagus; worked flint has been found in the Miocene of Aurillac (Auvergne) by M. Tardy, and a cut rib of *Halitherium fossile*, a Miocene species, by M. Delaunay at Pouancé.

Very divided opinions are entertained as to the interpretation of the supposed implements discovered by M. l'Abbé Bourgeois. M. Quatrefages, after a period of doubt, has espoused the view of their being of human origin, and of Miocene age. " Since then," he says, " fresh specimens discovered have removed my last doubts. A small knife or scraper, among others, which shows a fine regular finish, can, in my opinion, only have been shaped by man. Nevertheless, I do not blame those of my colleagues who deny or still doubt. In such a matter there is no very great urgency, and, doubtless, the existence of Miocene man will be proved, as that of Glacial and Pliocene has been, by facts." Mr. Geikie, from whose work—*Prehistoric Europe*—I have summarized the above statements, says, in reference to this question: " There is unquestionably much force in what M. Quatrefages says; nevertheless, most geologists will agree with him that the question of man's Miocene age still remains to be demonstrated by unequivocal evidence. At present, all that we can safely say is, that man was probably living in Europe near the close of the Pliocene period, and that he was certainly an occupant of our continent during glacial and interglacial times."

Professor Marsh considers that the evidence, as it stands to-day, although not conclusive, " seems to place the first appearance of man [in America] in the Pliocene, and that the best proofs of this are to be found on the Pacific coast."

He adds : " During several visits to that region many facts were brought to my knowledge which render this more than probable. Man, at this time, was a savage, and was doubtless forced by the great volcanic outbreaks to continue his migration. This was at first to the south, since mountain chains were barriers on the east," and " he doubtless first came across Behring's Straits."

I have hitherto assumed a certain acquaintance, upon the part of the general reader, with the terms Eocene, Miocene, and Pliocene, happily invented by Sir Charles Lyell to designate three of the four great divisions of the Tertiary age. These, from their universal acceptation and constant use, have " become familiar in our mouths as household words." But it will be well, before further elaborating points in the history of these groups, bearing upon our argument, to take into consideration their subdivisions, and the equivalent or contemporary deposits composing them in various countries. This can be most conveniently done by displaying these, in descending order, in a tabular form, which I accordingly annex below. This is the more desirable as there are few departments in geological science which have received more attention than this; or in which greater returns, in the shape of important and interesting discoveries relative to man's existence, have been made.

Comparatively recent—comparatively, that is to say, with regard to the vast æons that preceded them, but extending back over enormous spaces of time when contrasted with the limited duration of written history,—they embrace the period during which the mainly existing distribution of land and ocean has obtained, and the present forms of life have appeared by evolution from preceding species, or, as some few still maintain, by separate and special creation.

## THE TERTIARY OR CAINOZOIC AGE.

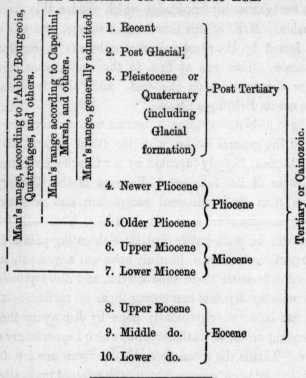

| Man's range, according to l'Abbé Bourgeois, Quatrefages, and others. | Man's range according to Capellini, Marsh, and others. | Man's range, generally admitted. | | | |
|---|---|---|---|---|---|
| | | | 1. Recent | | |
| | | | 2. Post Glacial | | Post Tertiary |
| | | | 3. Pleistocene or Quaternary (including Glacial formation) | | |
| | | | 4. Newer Pliocene | Pliocene | Tertiary or Cainozoic. |
| | | | 5. Older Pliocene | | |
| | | | 6. Upper Miocene | Miocene | |
| | | | 7. Lower Miocene | | |
| | | | 8. Upper Eocene | Eocene | |
| | | | 9. Middle do. | | |
| | | | 10. Lower do. | | |

## PLIOCENE.
### BRITAIN.

| | | Norwich |
|---|---|---|
| Newer Pliocene. | | *Sand loam and gravel* |
| | | Marine, land, and fresh-water shells |
| | Many shells abundant, such as | Fusus striatus |
| | | „ antiquus |
| | | Tunitella communis |
| | | Cardium edule, still existing in adjacent sea. |
| | | Norwich Crag. |
| Older Pliocene. | Crag | Red, |
| | | White, or |
| | | Coralline |

## MIOCENE.

| | BRITAIN. | FRANCE. | OTHER COUNTRIES OF EUROPE. | | INDIA. | AMERICA. |
|---|---|---|---|---|---|---|
| **UPPER MIOCENE.** | Ferruginous sands of the North downs. | Faluns of Touraine and Bordeaux. | Edgehem beds / Diest sands / Boldeberg beds } | Belgium | Fresh-water deposits of Siwalik hills with *Mastodon* *Sivatherium* *Colossochelys* *Rhinoceros* *Felis* *Machairodus* *Equus* *Hippotherium* *Camelopardalis* | Fresh-water deposits in Oregon |
| | Terebratula grandis. | *Dinotherium.* | Superga beds } | Italy | | White river group in the Upper Missouri Regions |
| | | *Mastodon.* | Deposits of Pikermé } | Greece | | *Oreodont* |
| | | *Lamantine.* | with *Mastodon* *Dinotherium* *Hipparion* *Antelope* *Camelopardalis* | | | *Brontetherium.* |
| | Astarte pyrula with other shells common to the Crag. | Marine shells such as *Cypræa, Oliva, Mitra, Conus,* indicative of an elevated temperature. | | | | Wind river group (Fresh-water deposit). |
| | | Fresh-water deposits of Gers near the base of the Pyrenees. | Beds above the brown coal with Marine shells } | Croatia | | |
| | | *Dinotherium giganteum.* | | | | |
| | | *Mastodon angustidens.* | | | | |
| **LOWER MIOCENE.** | Hempstead beds, Isle of Wight. | Calcaire de la Beauce, fresh-water deposits of Auvergne, Sandstone, indusial limestone of Cantal. | Fresh-water Molasse at Oeningen / *Abundant flora* / Marine Molasse } | Switzerland | | Miocene deposits over a large part of the Atlantic Tertiary border. |
| | Marine and fresh water *Voluta* *Oyrena* *Cerithium* &c. &c. | Fluvio-marine strata of Merignac and Bazas? | Kleyn Spawn beds and Limburg beds } | Belgium | | In California Miocene marine deposits reach from 4,000 to 5,000 feet in thickness. |
| | | *Cerithium, Pyrula,* &c. | Marine and Fluvialite shells | | | |
| | Lignite deposits of Bovey Tracey. | Asterias limestone. | Most of the Lignites are Lower Miocene } | Germany | | |
| | Numerous plants, such as *Sequoia Nysa, Annona,* indicating a sub-tropical climate. | *Nummulites.* Fresh-water strata of Fontainebleau. Grès de Fontainebleau (Marine). | Lower (fresh-water) Molasse | | | |

## EOCENE.

The subdivisions of the Eocene have been worked out in great detail in Britain, France, and America. Those of most other countries have either not yet been fully studied or their exact equivalence remains undetermined.

| | BRITAIN. | FRANCE. | CONTINENT OF EUROPE AND ASIA. | INDIA. | N. AMERICA. East of the Rocky Mts. | N. AMERICA. West of the Rocky Mts. | S. AMERICA. |
|---|---|---|---|---|---|---|---|
| UPPER EOCENE. | A1 Bembridge Series { Palæotherium, Anoplotherium, Charropotamus &c. } | Gypseous Series of Montmatre — Land and fresh-water shells. Many quadrupeds (4/5ths of them Perrissodactyls), Trionyx, Emys. | | | | Uinta group. Uintatherium | Deposits believed to be of Tertiary age, in the Pampas, contain Palæotherium and Anoplotherium, and other forms presenting a resemblance to the fauna of that period in Europe. |
| | A2 Osborne Series { Fresh-water & brackish genera, Do., Emys, Trionyx, Alligator, Crocodilus, Lepidosteus } | Calcaire Siliceux | | | | Bridger group: Orohippus, Dinoceras, Uintatherium, Tinoceras, Tillotherium | |
| | A3 Headon Series { Voluta, Mitra } | Grès de Beauchamp | | | Vicksburg beds | Green River group | |
| | A4 Barton Clay — Cerithium, Voluta, Cowries, Marine Serpents, Nummulites | Calcaire Grossier — Nummulites, Miliolite limestone of minute Foraminifera, Nummulites Cerithium, &c. &c. | Nummulitic Limestone of the Alps, Carpathians N. Africa Asia Minor Western Thibet. | Nummulitic formation of Cutch, portions of the Himalaya, and frontiers of China. | Claiborne beds, Zeuglodon cetoides [The Alabama Period] Marine deposits | | |
| MIDDLE EOCENE. | B1 Bagshot and Bracklesham Sands and Clays — indicating a warm climate with a vegetation reminding the botanist of the types of tropical India and Australia | Soissonnais Sands — Nummulites Nerita, &c. &c. | | | | | |
| | B2 Wanting | Argile de Londres | | | The Claiborne beds are considered by Lyell as the equivalent of the Middle Eocene of Britain; the parallelism of the other American deposits has not yet been completed. | | |
| LOWER EOCENE. | C1 London Clay and Bognor beds — Palms, Turtles, Sea Snakes, Crocodiles, Conus, Voluta, Cyprina, Nautilus, and other shells indicating a semi-tropical climate | Argile plastique and lignite — Fluviatile shells, Large bird Gastornis Parisiensis | | | | Wahsatch | |
| | C2 Plastic and Mottled Clays and Sands | | | | | Coryphodon, Eohippus | |
| | C3 Thanet Sands — Pholadomya, Cyprina, &c. | Sables de Bracheux | | | | Laramic or Lignitic Period. | |

We learn, both from the nature of these deposits and from
their organic contents, that climatic oscillations have been
passing during the whole period of their deposition over the
surface of the globe, and inducing corresponding fluctuations
in the character of the vegetable and animal life abounding
on it. A complete collation of these varying conditions at
synchronous periods remains to be achieved, but the study
of our own country, and those adjacent to it, shows that
alternations of tropical, boreal, and temperate climate have
occurred in it; a remarkable series of conditions which has
only lately been thoroughly and satisfactorily accounted for.

Thus, during a portion of the Eocene period a tropical
climate prevailed, as is evidenced by deposits containing
remains of palms of an equatorial type, crocodiles, turtles,
tropical shells, and other remains attesting the existence of
a high temperature. The converse is proved of the Pleistocene by the existence of a boreal fauna, and the widespread
evidences of glacial action. The gradations of climate during
the Miocene and Pliocene, and the amelioration subsequent
to the glacial period, have resulted in the gradual development or appearance of specific life as it exists at present.

Corresponding indications of secular variability of climate
are derived from all quarters: during the Miocene age,
Greenland (in N. Lat. 70°) developed an abundance of trees,
such as the yew, the Redwood, a Sequoia allied to the Californian species, beeches, planes, willows, oaks, poplars, and
walnuts, as well as a Magnolia and a Zamia. In Spitzbergen
(N. Lat. 78° 56′) flourished yews, hazels, poplars, alders,
beeches, and limes. At the present day, a dwarf willow and
a few herbaceous plants form the only vegetation, and the
ground is covered with almost perpetual ice and snow.

Many similar fluctuations of climate have been traced right
back through the geological record; but this fact, though
interesting in relation to the general solution of the causes,
has little bearing on the present purpose.

Sir Charles Lyell conceived that all cosmical changes of climate in the past might be accounted for by the varying preponderance of land in the vicinity of the equator or near the poles, supplemented, of course, in a subordinate degree by alteration of level and the influence of ocean currents. When, for example, at any geological period the excess of land was equatorial, the ascent and passage northwards of currents of heated air would, according to his view, render the poles habitable; while, *per contrâ*, the excessive massing of land around the pole, and absence of it from the equator, would cause an arctic climate to spread far over the now temperate latitudes.

The correctness of these inferences has been objected to by Mr. James Geikie and Dr. Croll, who doubt whether the northward currents of air would act as successful carriers of heat to the polar regions, or whether they would not rather dissipate it into space upon the road.   On the other hand, Mr. Geikie, though admitting that the temperature of a large *unbroken* arctic continent would be low, suggests that, as the winds would be stripped of all moisture on its fringes, the interior would therefore be without accumulations of snow and ice; and in the more probable event of its being deeply indented by fjords and bays, warm sea-currents (the representatives of our present Gulf and Japan streams, but possessing a higher temperature than either, from the greater extent of equatorial sea-surface originating them, and exposed to the sun's influence) would flow northward, and, ramifying, carry with them warm and heated atmospheres far into its interior, though even these, he thinks, would be insufficient in their effects under any circumstances to produce the sub-tropical climates which are known to have existed in high latitudes.

Mr. John Evans* has thrown out the idea that possibly a

---

* *Proceedings*, Royal Society, vol. xv. No. 82, 1866.

complete translation of geographical position with respect to polar axes may have been produced by a sliding of the whole surface crust of the globe about a fluid nucleus. This, he considers, would be induced by disturbances of equilibrium of the whole mass from geological causes. He further points out that the difference between the polar and equatorial diameters of the globe, which constitutes an important objection to his theory, is materially reduced when we take into consideration the enormous depth of the ocean over a large portion of the equator, and the great tracts of land elevated considerably above the sea-level in higher latitudes. He also speculates on the general average of the surface having in bygone geological epochs approached much more nearly to that of a sphere than it does at the present time.

Sir John Lubbock favoured the idea of a change in the position of the axis of rotation, and this view has been supported by Sir H. James* and many later geologists.† If I apprehend their arguments correctly, this change could only have been produced by what may be termed geological revolutions. These are great outbursts of volcanic matter, elevations, subsidences, and the like. These having probably been almost continuous throughout geological time, incessant changes, small or great, would be demanded in the position of the axis, and the world must be considered as a globe rolling over in space with every alteration of its centre of gravity. The possibility of this view must be left for mathematicians and astronomers to determine.

Sounder arguments sustain the theory propounded by Dr. Croll (though this, again, is not universally accepted), that all these alterations of climate can be accounted for by the effects of nutation, and the precession of the equinoxes.

---

* *Athenæum*, August 25, 1860, &c.

† The mass of astronomers, however, deny that this is possible to any very great extent.

From these changes, combined with the eccentricity of the
ecliptic from the first, it results that at intervals of ten
thousand five hundred years, the northern and southern
hemispheres are alternately in aphelion during the winter,
and in perihelion during the summer months, and *vice versâ* ;
or, in other words, that if at any given period the inclination
of the earth's axis produces winter in the northern hemisphere, while the earth is at a maximum distance from that
focus of its orbit in which the sun is situated, then, after
an interval of ten thousand five hundred years, and as a
result of the sum of the backward motion of the equinoxes
along the ecliptic, at the rate of 50′ annually, the converse
will obtain, and it will be winter in the northern hemisphere
while the earth is at a minimum distance from the sun.

The amount of eccentricity of the ecliptic varies greatly
during long periods, and has been calculated for several
million years back.   Mr. Croll* has demonstrated a theory
explaining all great secular variations of climate as indirectly
the result of this, through the action of sundry physical
agencies, such as the accumulation of snow and ice, and
especially the deflection of ocean currents.   From a consideration of the tables which he has computed of the eccentricity and longitude of the earth's orbit, he refers the glacial
epoch to a period commencing about two hundred and forty
thousand years back, and extending down to about eighty
thousand years ago, and he describes it as " consisting of
a long succession of cold and warm periods ;  the warm
periods of the one hemisphere corresponding in time with
the cold periods of the other, and *vice versâ.*"

Having thus spoken of the processes adopted for estimating
the duration of geological ages, and the results which have
been arrived at, with great probability of accuracy, in regard

* James Croll, F.R.S., &c., *Climate and Time in their Geological Relations.*

to some of the more recent, it now only remains to briefly state the facts from which the existence of man, during these latter periods, has been demonstrated. The literature of this subject already extends to volumes, and it is therefore obviously impossible, in the course of the few pages which the limits of this work admit, to give anything but the shortest abstract, or to assign the credit relatively due to the numerous progressive workers in this rich field of research. I therefore content myself with taking as my text-book Mr. James Geikie's *Prehistoric Europe*, the latest and most exhaustive work upon the subject, and summarizing from it the statements essential to my purpose.

From it we learn that, long prior to the ages when men were acquainted with the uses of bronze and iron, there existed nations or tribes, ignorant of the means by which these metals are utilized, whose weapons and implements were formed of stone, horn, bone, and wood.

These, again, may be divided into an earlier and a later race, strongly characterized by the marked differences in the nature of the stone implements which they respectively manufactured, both in respect to the material employed and the amount of finish bestowed upon it. To the two periods in which these people lived the terms Palæolithic and Neolithic have been respectively applied, and a vast era is supposed to have intervened between the retiring from Europe of the one and the appearance there of the other.

Palæolithic man was contemporaneous with the mammoth (*Elephas primigenius*), the woolly rhinoceros (*Rhinoceros primigenius*), the *Hippopotamus major*, and a variety of other species, now quite extinct, as well as with many which, though still existing in other regions, are no longer found in Europe; whereas the animals contemporaneous with Neolithic man were essentially the same as those still occupying it.

The stone implements of Palæolithic man had but little variety of form, were very rudely fashioned, being merely

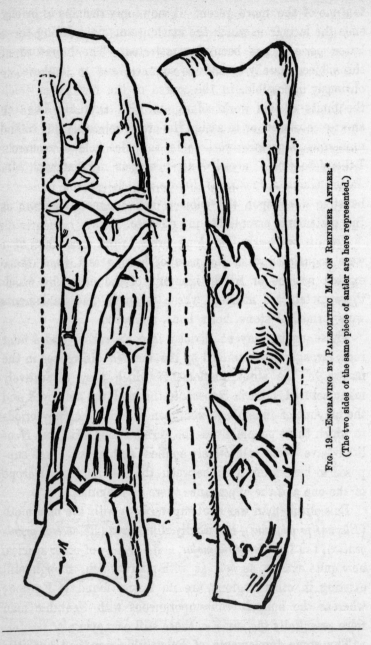

FIG. 19.—ENGRAVING BY PALÆOLITHIC MAN ON REINDEER ANTLER.*

(The two sides of the same piece of antler are here represented.)

* Figs. 19 and 21 are taken, by permission of Edmund Christy, Esq., from *Reliquiæ Aquitanicæ*, &c., London, 1875.

chipped into shape, and never ground or polished ; they were worked nearly entirely out of flint and chert. Those of Neolithic man were made of many varieties of hard stone, often beautifully finished, frequently ground to a sharp point or edge, and polished all over.

Palæolithic men were unacquainted with pottery and the art of weaving, and apparently had no domesticated animals or system of cultivation ; but the Neolithic lake dwellers of Switzerland had looms, pottery, cereals, and domesticated animals, such as swine, sheep, horses, dogs, &c.

Implements of horn, bone, and wood were in common use among both races, but those of the older are frequently distinguished by their being sculptured with great ability or ornamented with life-like engravings of the various animals living at the period ; whereas there appears to have been a marked absence of any similar artistic ability on the part of Neolithic man.

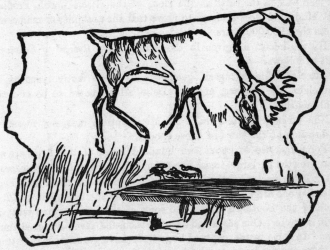

FIG. 20.—REINDEER ENGRAVED ON ANTLER BY PALÆOLITHIC MAN
(*After Geikie.*)

Again, it is noticeable that, while the passage from the Neolithic age into the succeeding bronze age was gradual, and, indeed, that the use of stone implements and, in some

parts, weapons, was contemporaneous with that of bronze in
other places, no evidence exists of a transition from Palæolithic into Neolithic times.  On the contrary, the examination
of bone deposits, such as those of Kent's Cave and Victoria
Cave in England, and numerous others in Belgium and
France, attest " beyond doubt that a considerable period
must have supervened after the departure of Palæolithic man
and before the arrival of his Neolithic successor."  The
discovery of remains of Palæolithic man and animals in river
deposits in England and on the Continent, often at considerable elevations* above the existing valley bottoms, and in
Löss, and the identification of the Pleistocene or Quaternary
period with Preglacial and Glacial times, offer a means of
estimating what that lapse of time must have been.†

---

* In some cases as much as 150 feet.

† "Starting from the opinion generally accepted among geologists,
that man was on the earth at the close of the Glacial epoch, Professor
B. F. Mudge adduces evidence to prove that the antiquity of man cannot
be less than 200,000 years.

"His argument, as given in the *Kansas City Review of Science,* is
about as follows :—

"After the Glacial epoch, geologists fix three distinct epochs, the
Champlain, the Terrace, and the Delta, all supposed to be of nearly
equal lengths.

"Now we have in the delta of the Mississippi a means of measuring
the duration of the third of these epochs.

"For a distance of about two hundred miles of this delta are seen
forest growths of large trees, one after the other, with interspaces of
sand.  There are ten of these distinct forest growths, which have begun
and ended one after the other.  The trees are the bald cypress (*Taxo-
dium*) of the Southern States, and some of them were over twenty-five
feet in diameter.  One contained over five thousand seven hundred annual
rings.  In some instances these huge trees have grown over the stumps
of others equally large, and such instances occur in all, or nearly all, of
the ten forest beds.  This gives to each forest a period of 10,000 years.

"Ten such periods give 100,000 years, to say nothing of the time
covered by the interval between the ending of one forest and the beginning of another, an interval which in most cases was considerable.

"'Such evidence,' writes Professor Mudge, 'would be received in any

Skeletons or portions of the skeletons of human beings, of admitted Palæolithic age, have been found in caverns in the vicinity of Liege in Belgium, by Schmerling, and probably the same date may be assigned those from the Neanderthal Cave near Düsseldorf. A complete skeleton, of tall stature, of probable but not unquestioned Palæolithic age, has also been discovered in the Cave of Mentone on the Riviera.

These positive remains yield us further inferences than can be drawn from the mere discovery of implements or fragmentary bones associated with remains of extinct animals.

The Mentone man, according to M. Rivière, had a rather long but large head, a high and well-made forehead, and the very large facial angle of 85°. In the Liege man the cranium was high and short, and of good Caucasian type; " a fair average human skull," according to Huxley.

Other remains, such as the jaw-bone from the cave of the Naulette in Belgium, and the Neanderthal skeleton, show marks of inferiority; but even in the latter, which was the lowest in grade, the cranial capacity is seventy-five cubic inches or " nearly on a level with the mean between the two human extremes."

We may, therefore, sum up by saying that evidences have been accumulated of the existence of man, and intelligent man, from a period which even the most conservative among geologists are unable to place at less than thirty thousand

---

court of law as sound and satisfactory. We do not see how such proof is to be discarded when applied to the antiquity of our race.

" 'There is satisfactory evidence that man lived in the Champlain epoch. But the Terrace epoch, or the greater part of it, intervenes between the Champlain and the Delta epochs, thus adding to my 100,000 years.

" 'If only as much time is given to both those epochs as to the Delta period, 200,000 years is the total result.' "—*Popular Science Monthly*, No. 91, vol. xvi. No. 1, p. 140, November 1878.

years ; while most of them are convinced both of his existence from at least later Pliocene times, and of the long
duration of ages which has necessarily elapsed since his
appearance—a duration to be numbered, not by tens, but by
hundreds of thousands of years.

FIG. 21.—ENGRAVING BY PALÆOLITHIC MAN ON REINDEER ANTLER.

# CHAPTER IV.

### THE DELUGE NOT A MYTH.

IF we assume that the antiquity of man is as great, or even approximately as great, as Sir Charles Lyell and his followers affirm, the question naturally arises, what has he been doing during those countless ages, prior to historic times ? what evidences has he afforded of the possession of an intelligence superior to that of the brute creation by which he has been surrounded ? what great monuments of his fancy and skill remain ? or has the sea of time engulphed any that he erected, in abysses so deep that not even the bleached masts project from the surface, to testify to the existence of the good craft buried below ?

These questions have been only partially asked, and but slightly answered. They will, however, assume greater proportions as the science of archæology extends itself, and perhaps receive more definite replies when fresh fields for investigation are thrown open in those portions of the old world which Asiatic reserve has hitherto maintained inviolable against scientific prospectors.

If man has existed for fifty thousand years, as some demand, or for two hundred thousand, as others imagine, has his intelligence gone on increasing thoughout the period ? and if so, in what ratio ? Are the terms of the series which involve the unknown quantity stated with sufficient precision to enable us to determine whether his development has been slow, gradual, and more or less uniform, as in arithmetical, or gaining at a rapidly increasing rate, as in geometric progression. Or, to pursue the simile, could it be more

accurately expressed by the equation to a curve which traces
an ascending and descending path, and, though controlled in
reality by an absolute law, appears to exhibit an unaccount-
able and capricious variety of positive and negative phases,
of *points d'arrêt*, nodes, and cusps.

These questions cannot yet be definitely answered ; they
may be proposed and argued on, but for a time the result
will doubtless be a variety of opinions, without the possibility
of solution by a competent arbiter.

For example, it is a matter of opinion whether the intelligence of the present day is or is not of a higher order than
that which animated the *savans* of ancient Greece.    It is
probable that most would answer in the affirmative, so far as
the question pertains to the culture of the masses only, but
how will scholars decide, who are competent to compare the
works of our present poets, sculptors, dramatists, logicians,
philosophers, historians, and statesmen, with those of Homer,
Pindar, Œschylus, Euripides, Herodotus, Aristotle, Euclid,
Phidias, Plato, Solon, and the like ?   Will they, in a word,
consider the champions of intellect of the present day so
much more robust than their competitors of three thousand
years ago as to render them easy victors ?   This would
demonstrate a decided advance in human intelligence during
that period ; but, if this is the case, how is it that all the
great schools and universities still cling to the reverential
study of the old masters, and have, until quite recently,
almost ignored modern arts, sciences, and languages.

We must remember that the ravages of time have put out
of court many of the witnesses for the one party to the suit,
and that natural decay, calamity, and wanton destruction*

---

* Such as the destruction of the Alexandrine Library on three distinct
occasions, (1) upon the conquest of Alexandria by Julius Cæsar, B.C. 48 ;
(2) in A.D. 390 ; and, (3) by Amrou, the general of the Caliph Omar, in
640, who ordered it to be burnt, and so supplied the baths with fuel for

have obliterated the bulk of the philosophy of past ages. With the exceptions of the application of steam, the employment of moveable type in printing,* and the utilization of electricity, there are few arts and inventions which have not descended to us from remote antiquity, lost, many of them, for a time, some of them for ages, and then re-discovered and paraded as being, really and truly, something new under the sun.

Neither must we forget the oratory and poetry, the masterpieces of logical argument, the unequalled sculptures, and the exquisitely proportioned architecture of Greece, or the thorough acquaintance with mechanical principles and engineering skill evinced by the Egyptians, in the construction of the pyramids, vast temples, canals† and hydraulic works.‡

Notice, also, the high condition of civilization possessed

---

six months.  Again, the destruction of all Chinese books by order of Tsin Shi Hwang-ti, the founder of the Imperial branch of the Tsin dynasty, and the first Emperor of United China ; the only exceptions allowed being those relating to medicine, divination, and husbandry. This took place in the year 213 B.C.

* The Chinese have used composite blocks (wood engraved blocks with many characters, analogous to our stereotype plates) from an early period.  May not the brick-clay tablets preserved in the Imperial Library at Babylon have been used for striking off impressions on some plastic material, just as rubbings may be taken from the stone drums in China : may not the cylinders with inscribed characters have been used in some way or other as printing-rollers for propagating knowledge or proclamations?

† As, for example, the old canal from the Nile to the Red Sea, in reference to which Herodotus says (*Euterpe*, 158), " Neco was the son of Psammitichus, and became King of Egypt: he first set about the canal that leads to the Red Sea, which Darius the Persian afterwards completed.  Its length is a voyage of four days, and in width it was dug so that two triremes might sail rowed abreast.  The water is drawn into it from the Nile, and it enters it a little above the city Bubastis, passes near the Arabian city Patumos, and reaches to the Red Sea." In the digging of which one hundred and twenty thousand Egyptians perished in the reign of Neco.

‡ The co-called tanks at Aden, reservoirs constructed one below the

by the Chinese four thousand years ago, their enlightened and humane polity, their engineering works,* their provision for the proper administration of different departments of the State, and their clear and intelligent documents.†

In looking back upon these, I think we can hardly distinguish any such deficiency of intellect, in comparison with ours, on the part of these our historical predecessors as to indicate so rapid a change of intelligence as would, if we were able to carry our comparison back for another similar period, inevitably land us among a lot of savages similar to

other, in a gorge near the cantonments, are as perfect now as they were when they left the hand of the contractor or royal engineer in the time of Moses.

FIG. 22.—ROYAL DIADEM OF THE CHEN DYNASTY. (*From the San Li T'u.*)

* In the 29th year of the Emperor Kwei [B.C. 1559] they chiselled through mountains and tunnelled hills, according to the Bamboo Books.

† An interesting line of investigation might be opened up as to the origin of inventions and the date of their migrations. The Chinese claim the priority of many discoveries, such as chess, printing, issue of bank-notes, sinking of artesian wells, gunpowder, suspension bridges, the mariner's compass, &c. &c. I extract two remarkable wood-cuts from the *San Li T'u*, one appended here showing the origin of our college cap; the other, in the chapter on the Unicorn, appearing to illustrate the fable of the Sphynx.

I also give a series of engravings, reduced facsimiles of those contained in a celebrated Chinese work on antiquities, showing the gradual evolution of the so-called Grecian pattern or scroll ornamentation, and origination of some of the Greek forms of tripods.

益

FIG. 23.—VASE. HAN DYNASTY
B.C. 206 *to* A.D. 23.
(*From the Poh Ku T'u.*)

漢輕重雷紋豆一

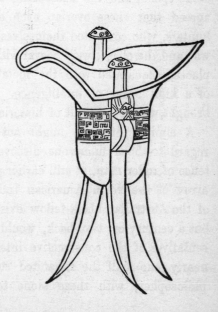

FIG. 24.—CYATHUS OR CUP FOR
LIBATIONS. SHANG DYNASTY,
B.C. 1766 *to* B.C. 1122.
(*From the Poh Ku T'u.*)

those who fringe the civilization of the present period.
Intellectually measured, the civilized men of eight or ten
thousand years ago must, I think, have been but little
inferior to ourselves, and we should have to peer very far
back indeed before we reached a status or condition in which
the highest type of humanity was the congener of the cave
lion, disputing with him a miserable existence, shielded only
from the elements by an overhanging rock, or the fortuitous
discovery of some convenient cavern.

If this be so, we are forced back again to the consideration
of the questions with which this section opened ; where are
the evidences of man's early intellectual superiority ? are they
limited to those deduced from the discovery of certain stone
implements of the early rude, and later polished ages ? and,
if so, can we offer any feasible explanation either of their
non-existence or disappearance ?

In the first place, it may be considered as admitted by
archæologists that no exact line can be drawn between the
later of the two stone-weapon epochs, the polished Neolithic
stone epoch, and the succeeding age of bronze. They are
agreed that these overlap each other, and that the rude
hunters, who contented themselves with stone implements of
war and the chase, were coeval with people existing in other
places, acquainted with the metallurgical art, and therefore
of a high order of intelligence. The former are, in fact,
brought within the limit of historic times.

A similar inference might not unfairly be drawn with
regard to those numerous discoveries of proofs of the existence of ruder man, at still earlier periods. The flint-headed
arrow of the North American Indian, and the stone hatchet
of the Australian black-fellow exist to the present day ; and
but a century or two back, would have been the sole representatives of the constructive intelligence of humanity over
nearly one half the inhabited surface of the world. No
philosopher, with these alone to reason on, could have

FIG. 25.—INCENSE BURNER (?). CHEN DYNASTY, B.C. 1122 *to* B.C. 255.
*(From the Poh Ku T'u.)*

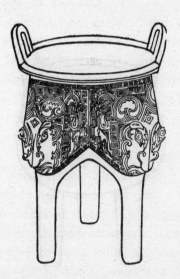

FIG. 26.—TRIPOD OF THE SHANG DYNASTY. *Probable date*, B.C. 1649.
*(From the Poh Ku T'u.)*

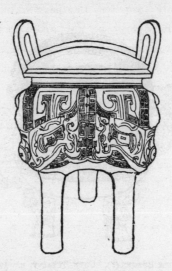

FIG. 27.—TRIPOD OF FU YIH, SHANG DYNASTY.   (*From the Poh Ku T'u.*)

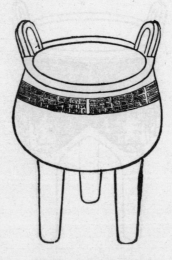

FIG. 28.—TRIPOD OF KWAI WAN, CHEN DYNASTY, B.C. 1122 *to* B.C. 255
(*From the Poh Ku T'u.*)

imagined the settled existence, busy industry, and superior
intelligence which animated the other half; and a parallel
suggestive argument may be supported by the discovery of
human relics, implements, and artistic delineations such as
those of the hairy mammoth or the cave-bear. These may
possibly be the traces of an outlying savage who co-existed
with a far more highly-organized people elsewhere,* just as
at the present day the Esquimaux, who are by some geologists considered as the descendants of Palæolithic man,
co-exist with ourselves. They, like their reputed ancestors,
have great ability in carving on bone, &c.; and as an example
of their capacity not only to conceive in their own minds a

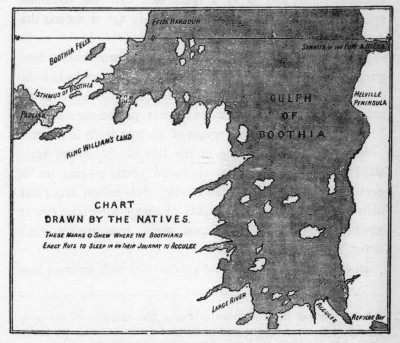

FIG. 29.   (*From Sir John Ross' Second Voyage to the Arctic Regions.*)

* "The old Troglodytes, pile villagers, and bog people, prove to be
quite a respectable society. They have heads so large that many a
living person would be only too happy to possess such."—A. Mitchell,
*The Past in the Present*, Edinburgh, 1880.

correct notion of the relative bearings of localities, but also
to impart the idea lucidly to others, I annex a wood-cut of a
chart drawn by them, impromptu, at the request of Sir J.
Ross, who, inferentially, vouches for its accuracy.

There is but a little step between carving the figure of a
mammoth or horse, and using them as symbols. Multiply
them, and you have the early hieroglyphic written language
of the Chinese and Egyptians. It is not an unfair presumption that at no great distance, in time or space, either some
generations later among his own descendants, or so many
nations' distance among his coevals, the initiative faculty of
the Palæolithic savage was usefully applied to the communication of ideas, just as at a much later date the Kououen
symbolic language was developed or made use of among the
early Chinese.*

Such is, necessarily, the first stage of any written language, and it may, as I think, perhaps have occurred, been
developed into higher stages, culminated, and perished at many
successive epochs during man's existence, presuming it to have
been so extended as the progress of geology tends to affirm.

May not the meandering of the tide of civilization westward during the last three thousand years, bearing on its
crest fortune and empire, and leaving in its hollow decay and
oblivion, possibly be the sequel of many successive waves
which have preceded it in the past, rising, some higher, some
lower, as waves will.

In comparison with the vast epochs of which we treat how

---

* I have given in the annexed plates a few examples of the early
hieroglyphics on which the modern Chinese system of writing is based,
selected from a limited number collected by the early Jesuit fathers in
China, and contained in the *Mémoirs concernant l'Histoire, &c. des Chinois,
par les Missionaires de Pekin*, vol. i., Paris, 1776. The modern Chinese
characters conveying the same idea are attached, and their derivation
from the pictorial hieroglyphics, by modification or contraction, is in
nearly all cases obvious.

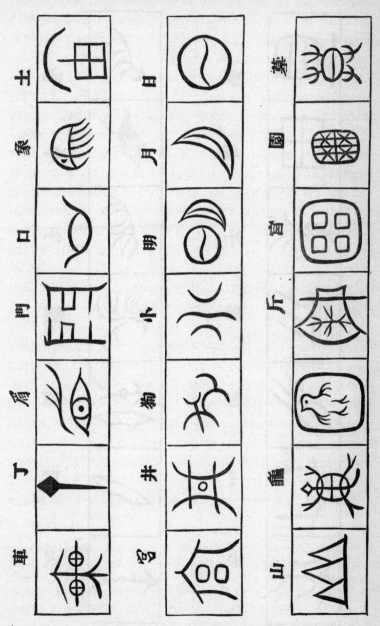

FIG. 30.—EARLY CHINESE HIEROGLYPHICS.

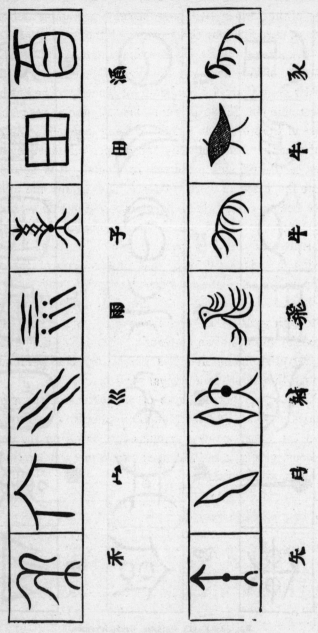

FIG. 31.—EARLY CHINESE HIEROGLYPHICS.

near to us are Nineveh, Babylon, and Carthage! Yet the very
sites of the former two have become uncertain, and of the
last we only know by the presence of the few scattered ruins
on the shores of the Mediterranean Sea. Tyre, the vast
entrepôt of commerce in the days of Solomon, was stated,
rightly or wrongly, by Benjamin of Tudela, to be but barely
discernible (in 1173) in ruins beneath the waves; and the
glory of the world, the temple of King Solomon, was represented at the same date by two copper columns which had
been carried off and preserved in Rome. It is needless to
quote the cases of Persia, Greece, and Rome, and of many
once famous cities, which have dissolved in ruin ; except as
assisting to point the moral that conquest, which is always
recurring, means to a great extent obliteration, the victor
having no sympathy with the preservation of the time-
honoured relics of the vanquished.

When decay and neglect are once initiated, the hand
of man largely assists the ravages of time. The peasant
carts the marbles of an emperor's palace to his lime-kiln,* or
an Egyptian monarch strips the casing of a pyramid† to
furnish the material for a royal residence.

Nor is it beyond the limits of possibility that the arrogant
caprice of some, perhaps Mongol, invader in the future, may
level the imperishable pyramids themselves for the purpose
of constructing some defensive work, or the gratification
of an inordinate vanity.

---

* " The Porcelain Tower of Nankin, once one of the seven wonders
of the world, can now only be found piecemeal in walls of peasants'
huts."—Gutzlaff, *Hist. China*, vol. i. p. 372.

† The outer casing of the pyramid of Cheops, which Herodotus
(*Euterpe*, 125) states to have still exhibited in his time an inscription,
telling how much was expended (one thousand six hundred talents
of silver) in radishes, onions, and garlic for the workmen, has entirely
disappeared ; as also, almost completely, the marble casing of the adjacent
pyramid of Sen-Saophis. According to tradition the missing marbles
in each instance were taken to build palaces with in Cairo.

In later dates how many comfortable modern residences have been erected from the pillage of mediæval abbey, keep, or castle? and how many fair cities* must have fallen to decay, in Central and Eastern Asia, and how many numerous populations dwindled to insignificance since the days when Ghenghis and Timour led forth their conquering hordes, and Nadun could raise four hundred thousand horsemen† to contest the victory with Kublai Khan.

The unconscious ploughman in Britain has for centuries guided his share above the remains of Roman villas, and the inhabitants of the later city of Hissarlik were probably as ignorant that a series of lost and buried cities lay below them, as they would have been incredulous that within a thousand years their own existence would have passed from the memory of man, and their re-discovery been due only to the tentative researches of an enthusiastic admirer of Homer. Men live by books and bards longer than by the works of their hands, and impalpable tradition often survives the material vehicle which was destined to perpetuate it. The name of Priam was still a household word when the site of his palace had been long forgotten.

The vaster a city is, the more likely is it to be constructed upon the site of its own grave, or, in other words, to occupy the broad valley of some important river beneath whose gravels it is destined to be buried.

Perched on an eminence, and based on solid rock, it may escape entombment, but more swiftly and more certainly will

---

* "The work of destruction was carried on methodically. From the Caspian Sea to the Indus, the Mongols ruined, within four years, more than four centuries of continuous labour have since restored. The most flourishing cities became a mass of ruins: Samarkand, Bokhara, Nizabour, Balkh, and Kandahar shared in the same destruction."—Gutzlaff, *Hist. China*, vol. i. p. 358.

† "An army of 700,000 Mongols met half the number of Mahommedans."—*Ibid.* p. 357.

it be destroyed by the elements,\* and by the decomposition of its own material furnish the shroud for its envelopment.† It is not altogether surprising then that no older discoveries than those already quoted have yet been made, for these would probably never have resulted if tradition had not both stimulated and guided the fortunate explorer.

It is, therefore, no unfair inference that the remains of equally important, but very much more ancient cities and memorials of civilization may have hitherto entirely escaped our observation, presuming that we can show some reasonable grounds for belief that, subsequent to their completion, a catastrophe has occurred of sufficiently universal a character to have obliterated entirely the annals of the past, and to have left in the possession of its few survivors but meagre and fragmentary recollections of all that had preceded them.

Now this is precisely what the history and traditions of all nations affirm to have occurred. However, as a variance of opinion exists as to the credence which should be attached to these traditions, I shall, before expressing my own views upon the subject, briefly epitomize those entertained by two authors of sufficient eminence to warrant their being selected as representatives of two widely opposite schools.

These gentlemen, to whom we are indebted for exhaustive papers,‡ embracing the pith of all the information extant

---

\* Those interested in the subject may read with great advantage the section on dynamical geology in Dana's valuable manual. He points out the large amount of wear accomplished by wind carrying sand in arid regions, by seeds falling in some crevice, and bursting rocks open through the action of the roots developed from their sprouting, to say nothing of the more ordinarily recognized destructive agencies of frost and rain, carbonic acid resulting from vegetable decomposition, &c.

† Darwin, in *Vegetable Mould and Earth-worms*, has shown that earthworms play a considerable part in burying old buildings, even to a depth of several feet.

‡ Rev. T. K. Cheyne, Article "Deluge," *Encyclopædia Britannica*, 1877. François Lenormant, "The Deluge, its Traditions in Ancient Histories," *Contemporary Review*, Nov., 1879.

upon the subject, have tapped the same sources of information, consulted the same authorities, ranged their information in almost identical order, argued from the same data, and arrived at diametrically opposite conclusions.

Mr. Cheyne, following the lead of Continental mythologists, deduces that the Deluge stories were on the whole propagated from several independent centres, and adopts the theory of Schirrer and Gerland that they are ether myths, without any historical foundation, which have been transferred from the sky to the earth.

M. Lenormant, upon the other hand, eliminating from the inquiry the great inundation of China in the reign of Yao, and some others, as purely local events, concludes as the result of his researches that the story of the Deluge "is a universal tradition among all branches of the human race," with the one exception of the black. He further argues: "Now a recollection thus precise and concordant cannot be a myth voluntarily invented. No religious or cosmogenic myth presents this character of universality. It must arise from the reminiscences of a real and terrible event, so powerfully impressing the imagination of the first ancestors of our race, as never to have been forgotten by their descendants. This cataclysm must have occurred near the first cradle of mankind and before the dispersion of families from which the different races of men were to spring."

Lord Arundel of Wardour adopts a similar view in many respects to that of M. Lenormant, but argues for the existence of a Deluge tradition in Egypt, and the identity of the Deluge of Yu (in China) with the general catastrophe of which the tradition is current in other countries.

The subject is in itself so inviting, and has so direct a bearing upon the argument of this work that I propose to re-examine the same materials and endeavour to show from them that the possible solutions of the question have not yet been exhausted.

We have as data :—
1. *The Biblical account.*
2. *That of Josephus.*
3. *The Babylonian.*
4. *The Hindu.*
5. *The Chinese.*
6. *The traditions of all nations in the northern hemisphere, and of certain in the southern.*

It is unnecessary to travel in detail over the well-worn ground of the myths and traditions prevalent among European nations, the presumed identity of Noah with Saturn, Janus, and the like, or the Grecian stories of Ogyges and Deucalion. Nor is anyone, I think, disposed to dispute the identity of the cause originating the Deluge legends in Persia and in India. How far these may have descended from independent sources it is now difficult to determine, though it is more than probable that their vitality is due to the written Semitic records. Nor is it necessary to discuss any unimportant differences which may exist between the text of Josephus and that of the Bible, which agree sufficiently closely, but are mere abstracts (with the omission of many important details) in comparison with the Chaldæan account. This may be accounted for by their having been only derived from oral tradition through the hands of Abraham. The Biblical narrative shows us that Abraham left Chaldæa on a nomadic enterprise, just as a squatter leaves the settled districts of Australia or America at the present day, and strikes out with a small following and scanty herd to search for, discover, and occupy new country ; his destiny leading him, may be for a few hundred, may be for a thousand miles. In such a train there is no room for heavy baggage, and the stone tablets containing the detailed history of the Deluge would equally with all the rest of such heavy literature be left behind.

The tradition, however reverenced and faithfully preserved at first, would, under such circumstances, soon get mutilated and dwarfed.   We may, therefore, pass at once to the much more detailed accounts presented in the text of Berosus, and in the more ancient Chaldæan tablets deciphered by the late Mr. G. Smith from the collation of three separate copies.

The account by Berosus (see Appendix) was taken from the sacred books of Babylon, and is, therefore, of less value than the last-mentioned as being second-hand.   The leading incidents in his narrative are similar to those contained in that of Genesis, but it terminates with the vanishing of Xisuthros (Noah) with his wife, daughter, and the pilot, after they had descended from the vessel and sacrificed to the gods, and with the return of his followers to Babylon. They restored it, and disinterred the writings left (by the pious obedience of Xisuthros) in Shurippak, the city of the Sun.

The great majority of mythologists appear to agree in assigning a much earlier date to the Deluge, than that which has hitherto been generally accepted as the soundest interpretation of the chronological evidence afforded by the Bible.

I have never had  the advantage of finding the arguments on which this opinion is based, formulated in association, although, as incidentally referred to  by various authors, they appear to be mainly deduced from the references made, both by sacred and profane writers, to large populations and important cities existing subsequently to the Deluge, but at so early a date, as to imply the necessity of a very long interval indeed between the general annihilation caused by the catastrophe, and the attainment of so high a pitch of civilization and so numerous a population as their existence implies.

Philologists at the same time declare that a similar inference may be drawn from the vast periods requisite for the divergence of different languages from the parent stock,* while the testimony of the monuments and sculptures of ancient Egypt assures us that race distinction of as marked a type as occurs at the present day existed at so early a date† as to preclude the possibility of the derivation of present nations from the descendants of Noah within the limited period usually allowed.

These difficulties vanish, if we consider the Biblical and Chaldean narratives as records of a local catastrophe, of vast extent perhaps, and resulting in general but not total destruction, whose sphere may have embraced the greater portion of Western Asia, and perhaps Europe; but which, while wrecking the great centres of northern civilization, did not extend southwards to Africa and Egypt.‡ The Deluge legends indigenous in Mexico at the date of the Spanish conquest, combining the Biblical incidents of the despatch of birds from a vessel with the conception of four consecutive ages terminating in general destruction, and corresponding with the four ages or Yugas of India, supply in themselves the testimony of their probable origin from Asia. The cataclysm which caused what is called the Deluge may or may not have extended to America, probably not. In a future page

---

* Bunsen estimates that 20,000 years were requisite for the formation of the Chinese language. This, however, is not conceded by other philologists.

† Rawlinson quotes the African type on the Egyptian sculptures as being identical with that of the negro of the present day.

‡ "While the tradition of the Deluge holds so considerable a place in the legendary memories of all branches of the Aryan race, the monuments and original texts of Egypt, with their many cosmogenic speculations, have not afforded one, even distant, allusion to this cataclysm. When the Greeks told the Egyptian priests of the Deluge of Deucalion, their reply was that they had been preserved from it as well as from the conflagration produced by Phaeton; they even added that the Hellenes were childish in attaching so much importance to that event, as there had been several local catastrophes resembling it."—Lenormant, *Contemporary Review*, November 1879.

I shall enumerate a few of the resemblances between the inhabitants of the New World and of the Old indicative of their community of origin.

I refer the reader to M. Lenormant's valuable essay* for his critical notice on the dual composition of the account in Genesis, derived as it appears to be from two documents, one of which has been called the Elohistic and the other the Jehovistic account, and for his comparison of it with the Chaldean narrative exhumed by the late Mr. George Smith from the Royal Library of Nineveh, the original of which is probably of anterior date to Moses, and nearly contemporaneous with Abraham.

I transcribe from M. Lenormant the text of the Chaldean narrative, because there are points in it which have not yet been commented on, and which, as it appears to me, assist in the solution of the Deluge story:—

I will reveal to thee, O Izdhubar, the history of my preservation—and tell to thee the decision of the gods.

The town of Shurippak, a town which thou knowest, is situated on the Euphrates. It was ancient, and in it [men did not honour] the gods. [I alone, I was] their servant, to the great gods — [The gods took counsel on the appeal of] Anu—[a deluge was proposed by] Bel—[and approved by Nabon, Nergal and] Adar.

And the god [Êa,] the immutable lord,—repeated this command in a dream.—I listened to the decree of fate that he announced, and he said to me:—"Man of Shurippak, son of Ubaratutu—thou, build a vessel and finish it [quickly].—By a [deluge] I will destroy substance and life.—Cause thou to go up into the vessel the substance of all that has life.—The vessel thou shalt build—600 cubits shall be the measure of its length—and 60 cubits the amount of its breadth and of its height.— [Launch it] thus on the ocean and cover it with a roof."—I understood, and I said to Êa, my lord:—"[The vessel] that thou commandest me to build thus,—[when] I shall do it—young and old [shall laugh at me]."—[Êa opened his mouth and] spoke.—He said to me, his servant: —"[If they laugh at thee] thou shalt say to them: [Shall be punished] he who has insulted me, [for the protection of the gods] is over me.— . . . . like to caverns . . . . ——— . . . . I will exercise my judgment

---

on that which is on high and that which is below . . . . —— . . . .
Close the vessel . . . . —— . . . . At a given moment that I shall
cause thee to know,—enter into it, and draw the door of the ship towards
thee.—Within it, thy grains, thy furniture, thy provisions,—thy riches,
thy men-servants, and thy maid-servants, and thy young people—the
cattle of the field and the wild beasts of the plain that I will assemble
—and that I will send thee, shall be kept behind thy door."—Khasisatra opened his mouth and spoke;—he said to Êa, his lord :—"No one
has made [such a] ship.—On the prow I will fix . . . . —I shall see
. . . . and the vessel . . . . —the vessel thou commandest me to build
[thus]—which in . . . .*

On the fifth day [the two sides of the bark] were raised.—In its
covering fourteen in all were its rafters—fourteen in all did it count
above.—I placed its roof and I covered it.—I embarked in it on the
sixth day; I divided its floors on the seventh;—I divided the interior
compartments on the eighth. I stopped up the chinks through which
the water entered in;—I visited the chinks and added what was wanting.
—I poured on the exterior three times 3,600 measures of asphalte,—
and three times 3,600 measures of asphalte within.—Three times 3,600
men, porters, brought on their heads the chests of provisions.—I kept
8,600 chests for the nourishment of my family,—and the mariners
divided amongst themselves twice 3,600 chests.—For [provisioning] I
had oxen slain;—I instituted [rations] for each day.—In [anticipation
of the need of] drinks, of barrels and of wine—[I collected in quan-
tity] like to the waters of a river, [of provisions] in quantity like to the
dust of the earth.—[To arrange them in] the chests I set my hand to.—
. . . . of the sun . . . . the vessel was completed.— . . . . strong and
—I had carried above and below the furniture of the ship.—[This
lading filled the two-thirds.]

All that I possessed I gathered together; all I possessed of silver I
gathered together; all that I possessed of gold I gathered—all that
I possessed of the substance of life of every kind I gathered together.
—I made all ascend into the vessel; my servants male and female,—the
cattle of the fields, the wild beasts of the plains, and the sons of the
people, I made them all ascend.

Shamash (the sun) made the moment determined, and—he announced it in these terms:—"In the evening I will cause it to rain
abundantly from heaven; enter into the vessel and close the door."—
The fixed moment had arrived, which he announced in these terms:
"In the evening I will cause it to rain abundantly from heaven."—
When the evening of that day arrived, I was afraid,—I entered into
the vessel and shut my door.—In shutting the vessel, to Buzurshadi-
rabi, the pilot,—I confided this dwelling with all that it contained.

* Here several verses are wanting.

Mu-sheri-ina-namari*—rose from the foundations of heaven in a
black cloud;—Ramman† thundered in the midst of the cloud—and
Nabon and Sharru marched before;—they marched, devastating the
mountain and the plain;—Nergal‡ the powerful, dragged chastisements
after him;—Adar§ advanced, overthrowing before him;—the archangels
of the abyss brought destruction,—in their terrors they agitated the
earth.—The inundation of Ramman swelled up to the sky,—and [the
earth] became without lustre, was changed into a desert.

They broke . . . . of the surface of the [earth like . . . . ;—[they
destroyed] the living beings of the surface of the earth.—The terrible
[Deluge] on men swelled up to [heaven].—The brother no longer saw his
brother; men no longer knew each other.    In heaven—the gods became
afraid of the waterspout, and—sought a refuge; they mounted up to
the heaven of Anu.∥—The gods were stretched out motionless, pressing
one against another like dogs.—Ishtar wailed like a child,—the great
goddess pronounced her discourse:—" Here is humanity returned into
mud, and—this is the misfortune that I have announced in the presence
of the gods.   So I announced the misfortune in the presence of the
gods,—for the evil I announced the terrible [chastisement] of men who
are mine.—I am the mother who gave birth to men, and—like to the
race of fishes, there they are filling the sea;—and the gods by reason of
that—which the archangels of the abyss are doing, weep with me."—
The gods on their seats were seated in tears,—and they held their lips
closed, [revolving] future things.

Six days and as many nights passed; the wind, the waterspout, and
the diluvian rain were in all their strength.    At the approach of the
seventh day the diluvian rain grew weaker, the terrible waterspout—
which had assailed after the fashion of an earthquake—grew calm, the
sea inclined to dry up, and the wind and the waterspout came to an end.
I looked at the sea, attentively observing—and the whole of humanity
had returned to mud; like unto sea-weeds the corpses floated.   I
opened the window, and the light smote on my face.   I was seized with
sadness; I sat down and I wept;—and my tears came over my face.

I looked at the regions bounding the sea; towards the twelve points
of the horizon; not any continent.—The vessel was borne above the
land of Nizir,—the mountain of Nizir arrested the vessel, and did not
permit it to pass over.—A day and a second day the mountain of Nizir
arrested the vessel, and did not permit it to pass over;—the third and

---

* " The water of the twilight at break of day," one of the personifi-
cations of rain.

† The god of thunder.

‡ The god of war and death.

§ The Chaldæo-Assyrian Hercules.

∥ The superior heaven of the fixed stars.

fourth day the mountain of Nizir arrested the vessel, and did not permit it to pass over;—the fifth and sixth day the mountain of Nizir arrested the vessel, and did not permit it to pass over.—At the approach of the seventh day, I sent out and loosed a dove. The dove went, turned, and —found no place to light on, and it came back. I sent out and loosed a swallow; the swallow went, turned, and—found no place to light on, and it came back. I sent out and loosed a raven; the raven went, and saw the corpses on the waters; it ate, rested, turned, and came not back.

I then sent out (what was in the vessel) towards the four winds, and I offered a sacrifice. I raised the pile of my burnt-offering on the peak of the mountain; seven by seven I disposed the measured vases,*—and beneath I spread rushes, cedar, and juniper wood. The gods were seized with the desire of it,—the gods were seized with a benevolent desire of it;—and the gods assembled like flies above the master of the sacrifice. From afar, in approaching, the great goddess raised the great zones that Anu has made for their glory (the gods').† These gods, luminous crystal before me, I will never leave them; in that day I prayed that I might never leave them. "Let the gods come to my sacrificial pile!— but never may Bel come to my sacrificial pile! for he did not master himself, and he has made the waterspout for the Deluge, and he has numbered my men for the pit."

From far, in drawing near, Bel—saw the vessel, and Bel stopped;— he was filled with anger against the gods and the celestial archangels:— "No one shall come out alive! No man shall be preserved from the abyss!"—Adar opened his mouth and said; he said to the warrior Bel:—"What other than Êa should have formed this resolution?—for Ea possesses knowledge and [he foresees] all."—Ea opened his mouth and spake; he said to the warrior Bel:—"O thou, herald of the gods, warrior,—as thou didst not master thyself, thou hast made the water- spout of the deluge.—Let the sinner carry the weight of his sins, the blasphemer the weight of his blasphemy.—Please thyself with this good pleasure, and it shall never be infringed; faith in it never [shall be violated].—Instead of thy making a new deluge, let hyænas appear and reduce the number of men; instead of thy making a new deluge, let there be famine, and let the earth be [devastated];--instead of thy making a new deluge, let Dibbara‡ appear, and let men be [mown down].—I have not revealed the decision of the great gods;—it is Khasisatra who interpreted a dream and comprehended what the gods had decided."

Then, when his resolve was arrested, Bel entered into the vessel.—He

---

* Vases of the measure called in Hebrew *Seäh*. This relates to a detail of the ritualistic prescriptions for sacrifice.

† These metaphorical expressions appear to designate the rainbow.

‡ The god of epidemics.

took my hand and made me rise.—He made my wife rise, and made her place herself at my side.—He turned around us and stopped short; he approached our group.—" Until now Khasisatra has made part of perishable humanity ;—but lo, now, Khasisatra and his wife are going to be carried away to live like the gods,—and Khasisatra will reside afar at the mouth of the rivers."—They carried me away and established me in a remote place at the mouth of the streams.

This narrative agrees with the Biblical one in ascribing the inundation to a deluge of rain ; but adds further details which connect it with intense atmospheric disturbance, similar to that which would be produced by a series of cyclones, or typhoons, of unusual severity and duration.

The intense gloom, the deluge of rain, terrific violence of wind, and the havoc both on sea and land, which accompany the normal cyclones occurring annually on the eastern coast of China, and elsewhere, and lasting but a few hours in any one locality, can hardly be credited, except by those who have experienced them. They are, however, sufficient to render explicable the general devastation and loss of life which would result from the duration of typhoons, or analogous tempests, of abnormal intensity, for even the limited period of six days and nights allotted in the text above, and much more so for that of one hundred and fifty days assigned to it in the Biblical account.

As illustrating this I may refer to a few calamities of recent date, which, though of trivial importance in comparison with the stupendous event under our consideration, bring home to us the terribly devastating power latent in the elements.

In Bengal, a cyclone on October 31, 1876, laid under water three thousand and ninety-three square miles, and destroyed two hundred and fifteen thousand lives.

A typhoon which raged in Canton, Hongkong, and Macao on September 22, 1874, besides much other destruction, destroyed several thousand people in Macao and the adjacent villages, the number of corpses in the town being so numerous that they had to be gathered in heaps and burnt with kerosene, the population, without the Chinese who refused to lend assistance, being insufficient to bury them.

A tornado in Canton, on April 11, 1878, destroyed, in the course of a few minutes, two thousand houses and ten thousand lives.

In view of these few historical facts, which might be greatly supplemented, there appears to my mind to be no difficulty in believing that the continuance, during even only six days and six nights, of extraordinarily violent circular storms over a given area, would, especially if accompanied by so-called tidal or earthquake waves, be sufficient to wreck all sea-going and coasting craft, all river boats, inundate every country embraced within it to a very great extent, submerge each metropolis, city, or village, situate either in the deltas of rivers, or higher up their course, sap, unroof, batter down, and destroy all dwellings on the highlands, level forests, destroy all domestic animals, sweep away all cultivated soil, or bury it beneath an enormous thickness of *débris*, tear away the soil from the declivities of hills and mountains, destroy all shelter, and hence, by exposure, most of those wretched human beings who might have escaped drowning on the lower levels. The few survivors would with difficulty escape starvation, or death from subsequent exposure to the deadly malaria which would be liberated by the rooting up of the accumulated *débris* of centuries. This latter supposition appears to me to be directly indicated by the passage towards the end of the extract referring to famine, and to the devastation of the earth by Dibbara (the god of epidemics).

It is noticeable that in this account there is no suggestion of complete immersion, Khasisatra simply says there is not any continent (*i.e.* all the hill ranges within sight would stand out from the inundation like islands), while he speaks of his vessel being arrested by the mountain of Nizir, which must consequently have been above the surface of the water.

Neither is there any such close limitation of the number

of persons preserved, as in the Biblical story, for Khasisatra took with him his men-servants, maid-servants, and his young people, while the version transmitted by Berosus (see Appendix to this Chapter), states that Xisuthros embarked his wife, children, and his intimate friends, and that these latter subsequently founded numerous cities, built temples, and restored Babylon.

We have thus a fair nucleus for starting a fresh population in the Euphrates valley, which may have received accessions from the gradual concentration of scattered survivors, and from the enterprise of maritime adventurers from the African coast and elsewhere, possibly also nomads from the north, east, and west may have swelled the numbers, and a polyglot community have been established, which subsequently, through race distinctions, jealousies, and incompatibility of language, became again dismembered, as recorded in the history of the attempted erection of the Tower of Babel.

Confining our attention for the moment to this one locality, we may imagine that the young population would not be deterred by any apprehension of physical danger from re-inhabiting such of the old cities as remained recognizable ; since we see that men do not hesitate to recommence the building of cities overthrown by earthquake shocks almost before the last tremblings are over ; or, as in the case of Herculaneum and Pompeii, within the range of volcanoes which may have already repeatedly vomited destroying floods of lava. Yet, in this instance, they would probably invest the calamity with a supernatural horror, and regard it, as the text expresses it, as a chastisement from the gods for their impiety. If this were so, the very memory of such cities would soon be lost, and with it all the treasures of art and literature which they contained.*

---

* It is probably as much from a superstitious sentiment as upon merely physical grounds that many of the deserted cities in Asia have

The Hindu account is taken from the *S'atapatha-Brâhmana,* a work of considerable antiquity, being one of a series which Professor Max Müller believes to have been written eight hundred years before Christ. A literal translation of the legend, as given in this venerable work, is as follows :—

" To Manu in the morning they brought water for washing, just as they bring it for washing the hands. As he was using the water, a fish came into his hand. This (fish) said to him, 'Preserve me, and I will save thee.' (Manu said), 'From what wilt thou preserve me ?' (The fish replied), 'A flood will carry away all these creatures; from that I will preserve thee.' (Manu said), 'How is thy preservation (to be effected) ?' (The fish replied), 'As long as we are small, there is great danger of our destruction; fish even devours fish : at first preserve me in a jar. When I grow too big for that, cut a trench, and preserve me in that. When I outgrow that, carry me to the sea; then I shall be beyond (the reach of) danger.' Soon it became a great fish; it increased greatly. (The fish said), 'In so many years the flood will come ; make a ship and worship me. On the rising of the flood enter the ship, then I will preserve thee.' Having preserved the fish he brought it to the sea. In the same year indicated by the fish (Manu) made a ship and worshipped the fish. When the flood rose he entered the ship ; the fish swam near him : he attached the cable of the ship to his (the fish's) horn. By this means the fish carried him over the northern mountain (Himalayas). (The fish said),

been abandoned ; while, as a noticeable instance, we may quote Gour, the ruined capital of Bengal, which is computed to have extended from fifteen to twenty miles along the bank of the river, and three in depth. The native tradition is that it was struck by the wrath of the gods in the form of an epidemic which slew the whole population. Another case is the reputed presence of a ruined city, in the vicinity of the populous city of Nanking, and at some distance from the right bank of the river Yangtsze, of which the walls only remain, and of the history of which those in the vicinity profess to have lost all record.

'I have preserved thee : fasten the ship to a tree. But lest the water cut thee off whilst thou art on the mountain, as fast as the water subsides thou wilt descend with it.' Accordingly he descended (with the water); hence this became 'Manu's Descent' from the northern mountain. The flood had carried away all those creatures, Manu alone was left. He being desirous of offspring performed a sacred rite ; there also he offered a *pâka*-sacrifice. With clarified butter, coagulated milk, whey, and curds, he made an offering to the waters. In a year a female was produced; and she arose unctuous from the moisture, with clarified butter under her feet. Mitra and Varuna came to her; and said to her, 'Who art thou?' (She said), 'The daughter of Manu.' (They said), 'Say (thou art) our (daughter).' 'No,' she replied, 'I am verily (the daughter) of him who begot me.' They desired a share in her ; she agreed and did not agree. She went on and came to Manu. Manu said to her, 'Who art thou?' 'Thy daughter,' she replied. 'How, revered one, art thou my daughter?' (She replied), 'The offerings which thou hast cast upon the waters,—clarified butter, coagulated milk, whey, and curds,—from them thou hast generated me. I am a blessing. Do thou introduce me into the sacrifice. If thou wilt introduce me into the sacrifice, thou wilt be (blessed) with abundance of offspring and cattle. Whatever blessing thou shalt ask through me, will all be given to thee.' Thus he introduced her in the middle of the sacrifice; for the middle of the sacrifice is that which comes between the final and the introductory prayers. He, desirous of offspring, meditating and toiling, went with her. By her he begot this (offspring), which is (called) 'The offspring of Manu.'"

The correspondence of this legend with the Biblical and the other accounts is remarkable. We have the announcement of the Deluge, the construction of a ship, the preservation therein of a representative man, the settlement of the vessel on a mountain, the gradual subsidence of the water, and the subsequent re-peopling of the world by the man thus preserved. The very scene of the cataclysm is in singular agreement with the other accounts ; for the flood is said to carry Manu " over the northern mountain." This places the scene of the Deluge in Central Asia, beyond the Himalaya mountains, and it proves that the legend embodies a genuine tradition brought by the progenitors of the Hindus from their primæval home, whence also radiated the Semitic and Sinitic branches of mankind.

There has been much discussion as to whether the great inundation which occurred in China during the reign of Yao is identical with that of Genesis or not. The close proximity of date lends a strong support to the assumption, and the supposition that the scene of the Biblical Deluge was local in its origin, but possibly widespread in its results, further favours the view.

As the rise of the Nile at Cairo is the only intimation which the inhabitants of Lower Egypt have of the tropical rains of Central Africa, so the inundation of the countries adjacent to the head waters of the great rivers of China may alone have informed the inhabitants of that country of serious elemental disturbances, only reaching, and in a modified form, their western frontier ; and it may well have been that the deluge which caused a national annihilation in Western Asia was only a national calamity in the eastern portion of it.

This view is strengthened if we consider that Chinese history has no record of any deluge prior to this, which could hardly have been the case had the Chinese migrated from their parent stock subsequent to an event of such importance ; assuming that it had occurred, as there seems valid reason to suppose, within the limits of written history. The anachronism between the two dates assigned by Chinese authors (2297 B.C.)

and the Jewish historian's calculation (2104 B.C.) is only one hundred and ninety-three years, and this is not so great but that we may anticipate its being explained at some future date. Strauchius' computation of 2293 B.C. for the date of the Biblical deluge is within four years, and Ussher's (2349– 2348) within fifty-one of the Chinese one. The reason for supposing the deluge of Yao to be historically true, will be inferred from the arguments borrowed from Mr. Legge on the subject of the *Shu-king*, in another portion of this volume. It is detailed in the great Chinese work on history, the *T'ung-këen-kang-muh*, by Choo He, of which De Mailla's *History of China* professes to be a translation.

This states that the inundation happened in the sixty-first year of the reign of Yao (2297 B.C.), and that the waters of the Yellow River mingled with those of the Ho-hi-ho and the Yangtsze, ruining all the agricultural country, which was converted into one vast sea.

But neither in the Bamboo Books nor in the *Shu-king* do we find that any local phenomena of importance occurred, with the exception of the inundation. In fact, the first work is singularly silent on the subject, and simply says that in his sixty-first year Yao ordered K'wan of Ts'ung to regulate the Ho, and degraded him in his sixty-ninth for being unable to effect it, as we learn elsewhere.

The *Shu* is more explicit. The Emperor, consulting one of his chief officials on the calamity, says: "O chief of the four mountains, destructive in their overflow are the waters of the inundation. In their vast extent they embrace the mountains and overtop the hills, threatening the heavens with their floods, so that the inferior people groan and murmur."

According to De Mailla's translation, K'wan laboured uselessly for nine years, the whole country was overrun with briars and brushwood, the people had almost forgotten the art of cultivating the ground—they were without the necessary seeds—and wild animals and birds destroyed all their attempts at agriculture.

In this extremity Yao consulted Shun, his subsequent successor, who recommended the appointment of Yu, the son of K'wan, in his father's place.

Yu was more successful, and describes his labours as follows :—

"The inundating waters seemed to assail the heavens, and in their vast extent embraced the mountains and over-topped the hills, so that people were bewildered and over-whelmed. I mounted my four conveyances,* and all along the hills hewed down the woods, at the same time, along with Yih, showing the multitudes how to get flesh to eat.

"I also opened passages for the streams throughout the nine provinces, and conducted them to the sea. I deepened, moreover, the channels and canals, and conducted them to the streams, at the same time, along with Tseih, sowing *grain*, and showing the multitudes how to procure the food of toil *in addition* to flesh meat."

Yu's success is simply chronicled in the Bamboo Books as, "In his seventy-fifth year Yu, the Superintendent of Works, regulated the Ho."

There was a legend extant in China in the times of Pinto, which he gives in his book, of the original Chinese having migrated from a region in the West, and, following the course of the Ho in boats, finally settling in the country adjacent to Pekin. That some such event took place is not unlikely. Its acceptance would explain much that is difficult.

The pioneers, pushing through a country infested with

---

* *i.e.* (according to the Historical Records) a carriage to travel along the dry land, a boat to travel along the water, a sledge to travel through miry places, and, by using spikes, to travel on the hills.

hostile aborigines, who would immediately after their passage close up the road of communication behind them—pioneers who may have been fugitives from their kindred through political commotions, or expelled by successful enemies—would have a further barrier against return, even were they disposed to attempt it, in the strong opposing current which had borne them safely to their new homes.

It is probable that such a journey would form an entirely new departure for their history, and that a few generations later it would resemble a nebulous chronological zone, on the far side of which could be dimly seen myths of persons and events representing in reality the history of the not very remote ancestors from whom they had become separated. The early arrivals would have been too much occupied with establishing themselves in their new dominions to be able to give much attention to keeping records or preserving other than the most utilitarian branches of knowledge which they had brought with them. The volumes of their ancestors were probably, like the clay tablets of the royal library of Babylon, not of a portable nature, at all events to fugitives, whose knowledge would, therefore, be rather of a practical than of a cultivated nature, and this would soon become limited for a while to their chiefs and religious instructors, the exigencies of a colony menaced with danger prohibiting any general acquisition or extension of learning.

In this way we can account for the community of the fables relating 'to the remote antiquity of the Chinese with those of Chaldean and Indian mythology, and with the highly civilized administration and astrological knowledge possessed by Yao and Shun as herediton of Fuh Hi, &c.

We can account for their possession of accurate delineations of the dragon, which would form an important decoration of the standards and robes of ceremony which were companions of their flight, while their descriptions of the animal and its qualities would have already entered into the realms of fanciful exaggeration and myth.

The dragon of Yao and Shun's time, and of Yu's time was, in my opinion, an aquatic creature, an alligator; but the dragon of their ancestors was a land lizard, which may even have existed down to the time of the great cataclysm which we call the Deluge, and the memory of which is best preserved in the Chinese drawings which have been handed down from remote antiquity, and have travelled from the great Central Asian centre, which was once alike its habitat and that of their ancestors. Its history may perhaps become evolved when the great store of book knowledge contained in the cuneiform tablets, representing the culture of the other branch of their great ethnological family, has been more extensively explored.

Geologists of the present day have a great objection to the bringing in of cataclysms to account for any considerable natural changes, but this one I conceive to have been of so stupendous a nature as to have been quite capable of both extinguishing a species and confusing the recollection of it. The mere fact of the story of the dragon having survived such a period argues greatly, in my mind, for the reality of its previous existence.

Extending our consideration, we are brought face to face with another very important fact, namely, that a large proportion of the human race content themselves with ephemeral structures. Thus, for example, the Chinese neither have now, nor at any time have had, any great architectural works. "The finest building in China is a reproduction, on a large scale, of the tent; and the wooden construction is always imitated where the materials are stone or marble. The supports, often magnificent logs, brought, at great expense, specially from the Straits, represent tent-poles; and the roof has always the peaked ends and the curves that recall the drooping canvas of the marquee. Architecture evidently died early; it never had life enough to assimilate the new material which it found when it migrated into China Proper. The yamen is a slightly glorified cottage; the temple is an improved yamen. Sculpture is equally neglected in this (æsthetically) benighted country. The human form is as dignified and sightly, to Chinese eyes at least, in China as in the West; but it never seems to have occurred, throughout so many hundreds of years, to any Chinaman to perpetuate it in marble or bronze, or to beautify a city with statues of its deities or great men."*

What holds good of the Chinese now, probably holds good of their ancestors and the race from which they parted company in Central Asia five thousand years ago, when they pierced their way eastwards through the savage aborigines of Thibet and Mongolia, pushing aside tribes which closed in again behind them, so as to intercept their return or communication with their mother country—a country which may have been equally careless of elaborating stupendous and permanent works of architecture such as other nations glory in possessing, and which, like the pyramids of Egypt and of Central America, stand forth for thousands of years as landmarks of the past.

We must, therefore, not be surprised if we do not immediately discover the vestiges of the people of ten, fifteen, or twenty thousand years ago. With an ephemeral architecture (which, as we have seen, is all that a highly populous and long civilized race actually possess), the sites of vast cities may have become entirely lost to recollection in a few thousands of years from natural decay, and how much more so would this be the case if, as we may reasonably argue, minor cataclysms have intervened, such as local inundations, earthquakes, deposition of volcanic ashes from even distant

* Balfour, *North China Daily News*, Feb. 11, 1881.

sources, the spread of sandy deserts, destruction of life by exceptionally deadly pestilence, by miasma, or by the outpour of sulphurous fumes.

We have shown in another chapter how the process of extinction of species continues to the present day, and from the nature of this process we may deduce that the number of species which became extinct during the four or five thousand years preceding the era of exact history must have been considerable.

The less remarkable of these would expire unnoticed; and only those distinguished by their size, ferocity, and dangerous qualities, or by some striking peculiarity, would leave their impress on the mythology of their habitat. Their exact history would be lost as the cities of their epoch crumbled away, and during the passage through dark ages of the people of their period and their descendants, and by conquest or catastrophes such as we have referred to elsewhere; while the slow dispersion which appears to have obtained among all nations would render the record of their qualities the more confused as the myth which embalmed it spread in circling waves farther and farther from its original centre.

Amongst the most fell destroyer both of species and of their history must have been the widespread, although not universal, inundation known as the Biblical Deluge; a deluge which we think the evidence given in the foregoing pages, and gathered from divers nations, justifies us in believing to have really taken place, and not to be, as mythologists claim, a mere ether myth. As to its date, allowance being made for trifling errors, there is no reason for disputing the computation of Jewish chronology, especially as that is closely confirmed by the entirely independent testimony of Chinese history.

This interposes a vast barrier between us and the knowledge of the past, a barrier round which we pass for a short

distance at either end when we study the history of the two
great streams of nations which have diverged from a common
centre, the Chinese towards the East, the Accadian Chaldæans and Semites towards the West; a barrier which we
may hope to surmount when we are able to discover and
explore the lost cities of that common centre, with the
treasures of art and literature which they must undoubtedly
possess.

# CHAPTER V.

## ON THE TRANSLATION OF MYTHS BETWEEN THE OLD AND THE NEW WORLD.

INTERCOURSE between various parts of the old world and the new was probably much more intimate even three or four thousand years ago than we, or at all events our immediate ancestors, have credited. The Deluge Tablets referred to in another chapter contain items from which we gather that sea-going vessels, well equipped and with skilled pilots, were in vogue in the time of Noah, and there is wanting no better proof of their seaworthiness than the fact that his particular craft was able to weather a long-continued tempest which would probably have sunk the greater part of those which keep the seas at the present time. The older Chinese classics make constant allusions to maritime adventure, and the discovery by Schliemann in ancient Troy* of vases with

---

* Dr. Schliemann found a vase in the lowest strata of his excavations at Hissarlik with an inscription in an unknown language.

Six years ago the Orientalist E. Burnouf declared it to be in Chinese, for which he was generally laughed at at the time.

The Chinese ambassador at Berlin, Li Fang-pau, has read and translated the inscription, which states that three pieces of linen gauze are packed in the vase for inspection.

The Chinese ambassador fixes the date of the inscription at about 1200 B.C., and further states that the unknown characters so frequently occurring on the terra cotta are also in the Chinese language, which would show that at this remote period commercial intercourse existed between China and the eastern shores of Asia Minor and Greece.—
*Pop. Sci. Monthly*, No. 98, p. 176, June 1880.

Chinese inscriptions confirms the notion that, at that date at least, commercial exchange was effected between these two widely-distant countries, either directly or by transfer through different entrepôts.

A more striking example, and one which carries us back to a still earlier epoch, will be afforded if the reported discovery of Chinese vestigia in Egyptian tombs is confirmed by further investigation.

The fleets of King Solomon penetrated at least to India, and detached squadrons* probably coasted from island to island along the Malay archipelago; while to descend by gradation to modern times, we may quote the circumnavigation of Africa by Hanno the Carthaginian,† the discovery

---

* Pierre Bergeron suggests that Solomon's fleets, starting from Ezion-geber (subsequently Berenice and now Alcacu), arrived at Babel-mandeb, and then divided, one portion going to Malacca, Sumatra, or Java, the other to Sofala, round Africa, and returning by way of Cadiz and the Mediterranean to Joppa.

† There are various accounts of the circumnavigation of Africa in old times. For example, Herodotus (*Melpomene*, 42): "Libya shows itself to be surrounded by water, except so much of it as borders upon Asia. Neco, King of Egypt, was the first whom we know of that proved this; he, when he had ceased digging the canal leading from the Nile to the Arabian gulf, sent certain Phœnicians in ships with orders to sail back through the pillars of Hercules into the Northern Sea, and so to return to Egypt. The Phœnicians accordingly, setting out from the Red Sea, navigated the Southern Sea; when autumn came they went ashore, and sowed the land, by whatever part of Libya they happened to be sailing, and waited for harvest; then, having reaped the corn, they put to sea again. When two years had thus passed, in the third, having doubled the pillars of Hercules, they arrived in Egypt, and related what to me does not seem credible, but may to others, that as they sailed round Libya, they had the sun on the right hand." Again, Pliny tells us (Book ii. chap. lxvii, Translation by Bostock and Riley), "While the power of Carthage was at its height, Hanno published an account of a voyage which he made from Gades to the extremity of Arabia: besides, we learn from Cornelius Nepos, that one Eudoxus, a contemporary of his, when he was flying from King Lathyrus, set out from the Arabian Gulf, and was carried as far as Gades. And long

of America prior to Columbus by the Chinese in the fifth century, from the Asiatic side, and by the Norsemen under Leif Ericsson in the year 1001, from the European; and the anticipation of the so-called discoveries of Van Diemen and Tasman by the voyages of Arab and other navigators, from whose records El Edrisi,* in the twelfth century, was enabled to indicate the existence of New Guinea, and, I think, of the northern coast of Australia. For although the identity with Mexico of the country called Fu-sang, visited prior to A.D. 499

before him, Cœlius Antipater informs us, that he had seen a person who had sailed from Spain to Ethiopia for the purposes of trade. The same Cornelius Nepos, when speaking of the northern circumnavigation, tells us that Q. Metellus Celer, the colleague of L. Afranius in the consulship, but then proconsul in Gaul, had a present made to him by the King of the Suevi, of certain Indians, who, sailing from India for the purposes of commerce, had been driven by tempests into Germany."

Ptolemy Lathyrus commenced his reign 117 B.C. and reigned for thirty-six years. Cornelius Nepos is supposed to have lived in the century previous to the Christian era, and Cœlius Antipater to have been born in the middle of the second century B.C.

* Edrisi compiled, under the instruction of Roger, King of Sicily, Italy, Lombardy, and Calabria, an exhaustive geographical treatise comprising information derived from numerous preceding works, principally Arabic, and from the testimony of all the geographers of the day.

*Vide* the Translation into French by M. Amédée Jaubert, 2 vols. 4to, Paris, 1836, included in the *Recueil de Voyages et de Mémoires publié par la Société de Géographie.*

" Ce pays touch celui de Wac Wac où sont deux villes misérables et mal peuplées à cause de la rareté des subsistances et du peu de ressource en tout genre; l'une se nomme Derou et l'autre Nebhena; dans son voisinage est un grand bourg nommé Da'rgha. Les naturels sont noirs, de figure hideuse, de complexion difformé; leur langage est une espèce de sifflement. Ils sont absolument nus et sont peu visités (par les étrangers). Ils vivent de poissons, de coquillages, et de tortues. Ils sont (comme il vient d'être dit) voisins de l'ile de Wac Wac dont nous reparlerons, s'il plait à Dieu. Chacun de ces pays et de ces iles est situé sur un grand golfe, on n'y trouve ni or, ni commerce, ni navire, ni bêtes de somme."—*El Edrisi*, vol. i. p. 79.

by the Buddhist priest Hoei-shiu, has been disputed, yet the arguments in favour of it seem to preponderate. These were adduced primarily by Deguignes, and subsequently by C. F. Neumann, Leland and others, and are based on the facts stated in the short narrative in regard to distance, description of the Maguey plant, or great aloe,* the absence of iron, and abundance of copper, gold, and silver.

While there can be little question that the islands and land of Wák Wák are respectively some of the Sunda islands, New Guinea, and the adjacent portion of Australia, it does not appear to have struck any of the commentators on this question that the name " islands of Wák Wák " may be assumed to signify simply " Bird of Paradise islands." Wallace, in his *Malay Archipelago*, emphatically remarks that in the interior of the forests of New Guinea the most striking sound is the cry " Wok Wok " of the great Bird of Paradise, and we may therefore reasonably speculate on the bird having been known as the Wok Wok, and the islands as the Wok Wok islands, just as we ourselves use the imitative names of Cuckoo, Morepork, or Hoopoe for birds, or Snake islands, Ape Hill, &c. for places.

This view is to an extent strengthened by Wák Wák being the home of the lovely maiden captured by Hasan (in the charming story of Hasan of El Basrah in the *Arabian Nights*), after she had divested herself of her bird skin, and to which he had to make so weary a pilgrimage from island to island, and sea to sea, in search of her after her escape from him. It is evident that among the wonders related by navigators of islands so remote and unfrequented, not the least would be the superavian loveliness of the Birds of Paradise, and from the exaggerated narratives of travellers may have

---

* The *Agave Americane*, which substance has as many uses among the Mexicans as the bamboo (the iron of China) among the Chinese, or the camel among nomads.

arisen the beautiful fable incorporated in the *Arabian Nights*, as well as that other recorded by Eesa or Moosa the son of El Mubarak Es Serafee.\* "Here, too, is a tree that bears fruit like women with bodies, eyes, limbs, &c. like those of women; they have beautiful faces, and are suspended by the hair; they come forth from integuments like large leathern bags; and when they feel the air and the sun they cry out 'Wák Wák' until their hair is cut, and when it is cut they die; and the people of these islands understand their cry, and augur ill from it." This, after all, is not more absurd than the story of the origin of the barnacle duck, extant and believed in Europe until within the last century or so.

El Edrisi, who, in common with the geographers of the period, believed in a great antarctic continent, after describing Sofala with its mines of gold, abundance of iron, &c., jumps at once to the mainland of Wák Wák, which he describes as possessing two towns situated on a great gulf (Carpentaria ?), and a savage population.†

The two small towns may very well have been encampments of the aborigines, or trading stations of Malay merchants.

It may be noted that this identification of Wák Wák is in opposition to the view entertained by some commentators; for example, Professor de Goeje of Leyden has recently identified the Silà islands (which had previously been consi-

---

\* *The Thousand and One Nights*, vol. iii. chap. **xxv.** p. 480, Note 32, E. W. Lane, London, 1877.

A similar account is given by Quazvini. See *Scriptorum Arabum de Rebus Indicis*, J. Gildemeister, Bonn, 1838.

† The diggings are seventy to one hundred and fifty miles from Port Darwin. There is gold on Victoria River.

Jacks, in his report to the Queensland Government, published March or April of 1880, reports no paying gold in Yorke's peninsula.

One hundred miles from Port Darwin and twenty-six miles from the Adelaide River a new rush occurred in July 1880: nuggets from 70 to 80 oz. of common occurrence; one found weighed 187 oz.

dered as being Japan) with Corea, and Wák Wák with
Japan; but this does not agree with El Edrisi's account of
the people being black, unclothed, and living on fish, shell,
and tortoises (turtles), without gold, commerce, ships, or
beasts of burden.  Elsewhere El Edrisi says the women are
entirely naked, and only wear combs of ivory ornamented
with mother of pearl.

Lane thinks the Arabs applied the name of Wák Wák to
all the islands with which they were acquainted on the east
and south-east of Borneo.  Es Serafee, beside the details
given in a previous note, also says, "From one of these
islands of Wák Wák there issueth a great torrent like pitch,
which floweth into the sea, and the fish are burnt thereby,
and float upon the water."  And Hasan, in the story quoted
above, has, in order to reach the last of the seven islands of
Wák Wák, to pass over the third island, the land of the
Jinn, "where by reason of the vehemence of the cries of
the Jánn, and the rising of the flames about, of the sparks
and the smoke from their mouths, and the harsh sounds
from their throats, and their insolence, they will obstruct the
way before us," &c. &c.  I think that in each of these latter
instances, the volcanic islands of Java, and other of the
Sunda islands are indicated.

The information in our possession is as yet too meagre
to permit of our indulging in any profitable consideration of
the sources from which originated those nations which
peopled America during the very early pre-traditional ages,
of which geological evidence is accumulating daily.  In fact,
the theories on this point have advanced so little beyond the
limits of speculation that I feel it unnecessary to do more
than quote one of them, as summarized in the ensuing
extract.  "Professor Flowers, in remarking upon recent
palæontological investigations, which prove that an immense
number of forms of terrestrial animals that were formerly
supposed to be peculiar to the Old World are abundant in

the New; and that many, such as the horse, rhinoceros, and the camel, are more numerous in species and varieties in the latter, infers that the means of land communication must have been very different to what it is now, and that it is quite as likely that Asiatic man may have been derived from America as the reverse, or both may have had their source in a common centre, in some region of the earth now covered with sea."*

The most commonly accepted theory with regard to the origin of those who have peopled the American continent, within the limits of tradition, is that they are of Asiatic descent, and that the migration has been effected in comparatively recent times by way of Behring Straits, and supplemented by chance passages from Southern Asia by way of the Polynesian islands, or from the north of Africa, across the Atlantic. There are, however, some who elaborate Professor Flowers' suggestion, and contend, in opposition to the more generally received opinion, that the peopling of the present countries of the Old World has in fact been effected from the New.

For instance, a proficient Aztec scholar, Senor Altamirano† of Mexico, argues that the Aztecs were a race, originating in the unsubmerged parts of America, as old as the Asiatics themselves, and that Asia may in fact have been peopled from Mexico; while Mr. E. J. Elliott, in quoting him, says: " From the ruins recently found, the most northern of any yet discovered, the indications of improved architecture, the work of different ages, can be traced in a continual chain to Mexico, when they culminate in massive and imposing structures, thus giving some proof by circumstantial evidence to Altamirano's reasoning."

---

* *Scientific American*, Aug. 14, 1880.

† E. J. Elliott, " The Age of Cave Dwellers in America," *Pop. Sci. Monthly*, vol. xv. p. 488.

Again, "Dr. Rudolf Falb* discovers that the language spoken by the Indians in Peru and Bolivia, especially in Quichua and Aymara, exhibits the most astounding affinities with the Semitic languages, and particularly with the Arabic —in which tongue Dr. Falb himself has been skilled from his boyhood. Following up the links of this discovery, he has first found a connecting link with the Aryan roots, and, secondly, has arrived face to face with the surprising revelation that the Semitic roots are universally Aryan. The common stems of all the variants are found in their purest condition in Quichua and Aymara, from which fact Dr. Falb derives the conclusion that the high plains of Peru and Bolivia must be regarded as the point of exit of the present human race."

On the other hand, Mr. E. B. Tylor, in the course of an article upon Backgammon among the Aztecs,† which he argues must have reached them from Asia, and very likely through Mexico, points out that the myths and religion of the North American tribes contain many fancies well known to Asia, which they were hardly likely to have hit upon independently, and which they had not learned from white men : " Such as the quaint belief that the world is a monstrous tortoise floating on the waters ; and an idea which the Sioux have in common with the Tartars, that it is sinful to chop or poke with a sharp instrument the burning log on the fire." He quotes Alexander von Humboldt as having " argued years ago that the Mexicans did and believed things which were at once so fanciful and so like the fancies of the Asiatics that there must have been communication. Would two nations," he asks, " have taken independently to forming calendars of days and years by repeating and combining cycles of animals, such as tiger, dog, ape, hare, &c. ? Would they have deve-

---

* *Scientific American,* Jan. 24, 1880.
† *Macmillan's Magazine,* quoted in *Pop. Sci. Monthly,* No. 82.

loped independently similar astrological fancies about these
signs governing the periods they began, and being influential
each over a particular limb or organ of men's bodies ?
Would they, again, have evolved separately out of this con-
sciousness the myths of the world and its inhabitants having,
at the end of several successive periods, been destroyed by
elemental catastrophes ? "

He adds, " It may very well have been the same agency
which transported to Mexico the art of bronze-making, the
computation of time by periods of dogs and apes, the casting
of nativity, and the playing of backgammon."

Then, again, we have the theory of those, now indeed few
in number, who hold that the present Indian inhabitants of
America were a distinctly indigenous race.    Lord Kaimes, in
his *Sketches of the History of Man*, says, " I venture still
further, which is to conjecture that America has not been
peopled from any part of the Old World."    Voltaire had
preceded him in this line of argument, relying on ridicule
rather than on reason.    " The same persons that readily
admit that the beavers of Canada are of Canadian origin,
assert that the men must have come there in boats, and that
Mexico must have been peopled by some of the descendants
of Magog."*

Missionaries of various sects have endeavoured to identify
the Red man with the lost ten tribes.    Adair conceived the
language of the Southern Indians to be a corruption of
Hebrew, and the Jesuit Lafitan, in his history of the savages
of America, maintained that the Caribee language was radi-
cally Hebrew.

Mr. John Josselyn,† in an account of the Mohawks, states
that their language is a dialect of the Tartars, and Dr.
Williamson, in his history of North Carolina, considers it

---

* *Œuvres*, I. 7, pp. 197, 198.
† *Two Voyages to New England*, p. 124 ;  London, 1673.

can hardly be questioned that the Indians of South America
are descended from a class of the Hindoos in the southern
part of Asia.

Amongst others, Captain Don Antonio del Rio, who
described the ruins of an ancient city in Guatemala, believed
that they were the relics of a civilization founded by Phœnician colonists who had crossed the Atlantic ocean ; and yet
another theory is propounded by Mr. Knox,* who considers
the extinct Guanches, formerly inhabiting the Canary and
Cape de Verde islands, to have closely resembled the Egyptians in certain particulars.  He goes on to observe, " Now
cross the Atlantic, and in a nearly parallel zone of the earth,
or at least in one not far removed, we stumble all at once
upon the ruined cities of Copan and Central America.  To
our astonishment, notwithstanding the breadth of the
Atlantic, vestiges, of a nature not to be doubted, of a
thoroughly Egyptian character reappear — hieroglyphics,
monolithic temples, pyramids ; who erected these monuments
on the American continent ?  Perhaps at some remote period
the continents were not so far apart, they might have been
united, thus forming a zone or circle of the earth occupied
by a pyramid-building people."

It is not impossible that all of these theories may be
correct, and that numerous migrations may have been made
at various periods by different nations, the most facile would
of course be that from North-Eastern Asia by way of the
Aleutian islands, for, as the author of *Fu-sang* well remarks,
a sailor in an open boat might cross from Asia to America
by that route in summer time, and hardly ever be out of
sight of land ; and this in a part of the sea generally
abounding in fish, as is proved by the fishermen who inhabit
many of these islands, on which fresh water is always to be
found.  But it is more than likely that the direct route,

---

* Robert Knox, *The Races of Men* ; London, 1850.

from the islands of Japan to the coast of California or
Mexico, was also occasionally followed, voluntarily or in-
voluntarily, by mariners impelled by enterprise, religious
motives, or stress of weather.

Colonel B. Kennon, as an evidence of the possibility of
junks performing long ocean voyages, adduces the instance
of a Japanese junk picked up by an American whaler two
thousand three hundred miles south-east of Japan, and of
others which had drifted among the Aleutian islands nearly
half-way over to San Francisco ; and in noting the resemblance and probable co-origin of the Sandwich Islanders with
the Japanese, he adverts to the " ancient and confirmed
habit of both Japanese and Chinese of taking women to sea
with them, or of traders keeping their families on board,
which would fully account for the population of those
islands," or, to extend the argument, of points on the
American continent. The Jewish element might easily be
introduced through this channel, for the occasional admixture
of Jewish blood both among the Chinese and Japanese is
so strongly marked, as to have induced some authors to
contend for the absolute descent of the latter people at least
from Jewish parentage.

It must also be remembered that the waters of both the
North and South Pacific are peculiarly favourable to the
navigation of small craft, and that Captain Bligh, after
the mutiny on board the *Bounty*, was able to safely perform
a journey of two thousand miles in an open boat; while all
the islands both in North and South Polynesia must necessarily have been gradually peopled by the drifting over the
ocean of stray canoes.

Again, as the tradition of the existence of a large continent west of the African coast was extant amongst the
Egyptian priests long before the days of Solon, and, as I
shall show hereafter, among the Carthaginians and Tyrrhenians, it is, I think, more than probable that both Phœnician

and Egyptian mariners, either acting under a Royal Commission, or influenced by mercantile considerations, would endeavour to discover it, and, as in the case of Columbus, would have no difficulty in stretching across the Atlantic before a fair trade wind, though they might be less successful than him on their return.

The possibility of the existence of a large island or continent, midway between the Old and New World, within the traditional period, is included in the important question, which is still *sub judice* amongst geologists, whether the general disposition of land and water has or has not been variable during past ages. Sir Charles Lyell held the first view, and was of opinion* that complete alternations of the positions of continent and ocean had repeatedly occurred in geological time.

The opposite idea has been suggested at various dates by eminent authorities, suggested rather than sustained by elaborate arguments, until recently, when the question has been re-examined by Mr. Wallace and Dr. Carpenter.

The former, in that chapter of island life devoted to the permanence of continents, dwells forcibly upon Dr. Darwin's inference from the paucity of oceanic islands affording fragments of either Palæozoic or Secondary formations "that *perhaps* during the Palæozoic and Secondary periods neither continents nor continental islands existed where our oceans now extend ; for, had they existed, Palæozoic and Secondary formations would in all probability have been accumulated from sediment derived from their wear and tear ; and these would have been at least partially upheaved by the oscillations of level which must have intervened during these enormously long periods. If, then, we may infer anything from these facts, we may infer that, where our oceans now extend, oceans have extended from the remotest period of which we

---

* *Principles of Geology*, chap. xii.

have any record ; and, on the other hand, that where continents now exist, large tracts of land have existed, subjected
no doubt to great oscillations of level, since the Cambrian
period."

I am not aware whether Dr. Darwin has expressed himself
more authoritatively on this point in later works, or whether
the whole question has been discussed in detail otherwise
than by Mr. Wallace in the chapter referred to, in which he
quotes what must, I think, after all, only be taken in the
light of a suggestion as an auxiliary to the powerful arguments which he himself has enunciated in favour of a
similar conclusion. There is no doubt that the paucity of
any but volcanic or coralline islands throughout the greatest
extent of existing oceans has a certain but not absolute
significance, so far as recent geological epochs are concerned.

There is another line of reasoning, debated by Mr. Wallace, based on the formation of the Palæozoic and Secondary
strata from the waste of broken continents and islands occupying generally the site of the existing continents, and
separated by insignificant distances of inland sea or exten-
sions from the adjacent oceans. It is soundly based on their
lithological structure, as generally indicative of a littoral and
shallow water origin, but it seems to me to be only positive
so far as it shows that, throughout geological time, some land
has existed somewhere within the limits of the present upheaval, and simply negative as to what may or may not have
been the condition of what are now the great ocean spaces
of the world. Indeed, it would at first sight seem only
reasonable to infer, that the very depressions which caused
the inundations of Europe and Asia, during the deposition of
any important formation, would imply a corresponding elevation elsewhere, in order that the same relative areas of land
and water might be maintained.

This view has, however, been reduced in its proportions by
Dr. Carpenter, who has levelled the results of the recent

researches by the *Challenger* expedition against the advocates
of the intermutations of land and ocean, and, in pursuing
another line of reasoning from Mr. Wallace, has estimated
the solid contents of ocean and land above the sea-level
respectively, as bearing the proportion of thirty-six to one.
So that, supposing all the existing land of the globe to sink
down to the sea-level, this subsidence would be balanced by
the elevation of only one thirty-sixth part of the existing
ocean floor from its present depth to the same level.

It must be admitted that the balance of argument was
until lately considerably against the former existence of the
country of Atlantis, whose ghostly outlines, however, we
could almost imagine to be sketched out by faint contours in
the chart illustrative of the North Atlantic portion of the
*Challenger* investigations. But it was not so overwhelming as
to entitle us to ignore the story entirely as a fable. I do not
conceive it impossible that some centrally situated and
perhaps volcanic island may once have existed, sufficiently
important to have served as the basis of simple legends,
which, under the enchantment of distance and time became
metamorphosed and enriched.

Mr. A. R. Grote suggests that it is simply a myth founded
on the observation of low-lying clouds in a sun-flushed sky,
which gave the appearance like islands on a golden sea.

Mr. Donelly, on the other hand, in a very exhaustive and
able volume, contends first, that Atlantis actually existed, and
secondly, that it was the origin of our present civilization,
that its kings are represented by the gods of Greek mythology, and that its destruction originated our Deluge story.

The well-known story is contained in an epic of Plato, of
which two fragments only remain, found in two dialogues
(the Timæus and the Critias). Critias is represented as
telling an old-world story, handed down in his family from

---

* *Atlantis,* by Ignatius Donelly ; New York, 1882.

his great-grandfather Dropidas, who had heard it from Solon, who had it from the Egyptian priests of Sais.*

Ælian, again, contains an extract from Theophrastus, who wrote in the time of Alexander the Great, which can hardly imply anything else than an acquaintance with America. It is in the form of a dialogue between Midas the Phrygian and Silenus.

The latter informs Midas that Europe, Asia, and Africa were but islands surrounded on all sides by sea, but that there was a continent situated beyond these which was of immense dimensions, even without limits, and that it was so luxuriant as to produce animals of prodigious magnitude. That there men grew to double the size of themselves, and that they lived to a far greater age, that they had many cities, and their usages and laws were different from their own; that in one city there was more than a million of inhabitants, and that gold and silver were there in vast quantities.

Diodorus Siculus gives an account of what could only have been the mainland of America, or one of the West Indian islands; it is as follows.

" After cursorily mentioning the islands within the Pillars of Hercules, let us treat of those further ones in the open ocean, for towards Africa there is a very large island in the great ocean sea, situated many days' sail from Libya towards the west.

" Its soil is fruitful, a great part rising in mountains, but still with no scarcity of level expanse, which excels in pleasantness, for navigable rivers flow through and irrigate it. Gardens abound, stored with various trees and numerous orchards, intersected by pleasant streams.

" The towns are adorned with sumptuous edifices, and

---

* It is given in great detail by Mr. Donelly; want of space forbids my including it.

drinking taverns, beautifully situated in gardens, are everywhere met with ; as the convenient situation of these largely
invites to pleasure, they are frequented during the summer
season.

" The mountain region possesses numerous and large
forests, and various kinds of fruitful trees. It everywhere
presents deep valleys and springs suitable for mountain
recreations.

" Indeed the whole of this island is watered with springs
of sweet water, which gives rise not merely to the pleasure
of its inhabitants, but also to an accession of their health
and strength.

" Hunting furnishes all kinds of game, the abundance of
which in their banquets leaves nothing to be desired.

" Moreover, the sea which washes against this island
abounds with fish, since the ocean, from its nature everywhere, affords a variety of fish.

" Finally, the temperature is very genial, from which it
results that the trees bear fruit throughout the greater part
of the year.

" Lastly, it excels so much in felicity as to resemble the
habitations of the gods rather than of men.

" Formerly it was unknown, on account of the remoteness
of its situation from the rest of the world, but accident disclosed its position. The Phœnicians have been in the habit
of making frequent passages, for the sake of commerce, from
the very oldest dates, from whence it resulted that they were
the founders of many of the African colonies, and of not a
few of those European ones situated to the west ; and when
they had yielded to the idea which had entered their minds,
of enriching themselves greatly, they passed out beyond the
Pillars of Hercules into the sea which is called the Ocean,
and they first founded a city called Gades, on the European
peninsula, and near the straits of the Pillars [of Hercules]
in which, when others had flocked to it, they instituted a

sumptuous temple to Hercules. This temple has been held in the utmost veneration both in ancient times and during later periods up to the present day; therefore many Romans of illustrious nobility and reputation pronounce their vows to that god, and happily discharge their obligations.

" The Phœnicians for this reason continued their exploration beyond the Pillars, and when they were sailing along the African coast, being carried off by a tempest to a distant part of the ocean, were driven by the violence of the storm, after a period of many days, to the island of which I have spoken, and having first acquainted themselves with its nature and pleasing characters, introduced it to the notice of others. On that account, the Tyrrhenians, also obtaining the empire of the sea, determined on a colony there, but the Carthaginians prevented them, both because they feared lest many of their citizens, being allured by the advantages of the island, might migrate there, and because they wished to have a refuge prepared for themselves against a sudden stroke of fortune, if by chance the Carthaginian Republic should receive any deadly blow, for they contemplated that they would be able, while yet powerful at sea, to transport themselves and their families to the island unknown to the victors."*

Among the many proofs which may be cited of community of origin between the Asiatics and certainly a large proportion of the American population is the practice of scalping enemies, quoted by Herodotus as prevalent amongst the Scythians, and universally existing amongst all tribes of North American Indians; the discovery of jade ornaments amongst Mexican remains, and the general esteem in which that material is held by the Chinese; the use of the Quipos among the Peruvians, and the assertion in the *I-king*, or Book

---

* I use the text of the edition of Diodorus Siculus of L. Rhodomanus, Amsterdam, 1746.

of Change, one of the oldest of the Chinese Classics, that
" The ancients knotted cords to express their meaning, but
in the next age the sages renounced the custom and adopted
a system of written characters; "* the discovery of the
meander pattern among Peruvian relics, and the common use
of this ornamentation on Chinese vases and tripods, at dates
long preceding the Trojan era, in which it is commonly supposed to have originated; the similarity of the features of
Chinese, and other Mongols, with those of various Indian
tribes; the resemblance of masks and various other remains
to Chinese patterns discovered recently by Desirée de Charnay
in Central America; and the reserve and stolid demeanour
of both races.  A good illustration of this is afforded by the
story told of the celebrated statesman Sieh Ngan (A.D. 320–
385), in Mayer's *Chinese Reader's Manual*; it could be imagined
to apply to any Indian sachem.

It is related of Sieh Ngan that, at the time when the
capital was menaced by the advancing forces of Fukien, he
sat one day over a game of chess with a friend, when a
despatch was handed to him, which he calmly read and then
continued the game.  On being asked what the news was,
he replied : " It is merely an announcement that my young
people have beaten the enemy."  The intelligence was, in
fact, of the decisive rout of the invaders by the army under
his brother Sieh She and his nephew Sieh Hüan.  Only
when retired within the seclusion of his private apartments
did he give himself up to an outburst of joy.  The very expression " my young people " is the equivalent of " my
young men " which the Indian chief would have employed.

A singular custom prevails among the Petivaces, an Indian

---

† " Professor Virchow considers this an example how certain artistical
or technical forms are developed simultaneously, without any connection
or relation between the artists or craftsmen."—Preface to *Ilios*, Schliemann.  Murray, 1880.

tribe of Brazil.* "When they are delivered of a child, and ought to have all the ceremony and attendance proper to a lying-in woman, the husband presently lies down in his hammock (as if he had been brought to bed himself), and all his wives and neighbours come about and serve him. This is a pleasant fancy indeed, that the woman must take all the pains to bring the child into the world, and then the man lie down and gruntle upon it."

Compare with this the account given by Marco Polo of the same custom prevalent among the Miau-tze, or aborigines of China, as distinguished from their present occupants. Their reduction to submission is recorded in the early works on the country.

"Proceeding five days' journey, in a westerly direction from Karazan, you enter the province of Kardandan belonging to the dominion of the great Khan, and of which the principal city is named Vochang (probably Yung-chang in the western part of Yunnan). These people have the following singular usage. As soon as a woman has been delivered of a child, and rising from her bed, has washed and swathed the infant, her husband immediately takes the place she has left, has the child beside him, and nurses it for forty days. In the meantime the friends and relations of the family pay to him their visits of congratulation; whilst the woman attends to the business of the house, carries victuals and drink to the husband in his bed, and suckles the infant at his side."†

We find a reference in *Hudibras* to this grotesque practice, in which it is imputed, but erroneously, to the Chinese themselves, and it reappears on the western side of Europe, among those singular people the Basques, who have their

---

* Knivet's description of the West Indies, *Harris' Voyages*, vol. i. p. 705.

† T. Wright, *Marco Polo*, p. 267. Bohn, 1854.

own especial Deluge tradition, and use a language which, according to Humboldt, approaches some of the dialects of the North American Indians more nearly than any other. They profess to trace the custom up to Aïtor or Noah, whose wife bore a son to him when they were in exile, and, being afraid to stay by herself for fear of being discovered and murdered, bade her husband take care of the child, while she went out to search for food and firing.

The change of name which prevails among the Chinese and Japanese in both sexes, at different periods of life, is also found upon the other continent,* where males and females when they come to years of discretion do not retain the names they had when young, and, if they do any remarkable deed, assume a new name upon it.

Less importance is to be attached to the coincidence of sun worship, Deluge tradition, and the preservation of ancestral ashes.† These, though probably not, might have been indigenous; but we can hardly conceive this of serpent worship, which Mr. Fergusson suggests arose among a people of Turanian origin, from which it spread to every country or land of the Old World in which a Turanian settled. The coincidence between the serpent mounds of North America and such an one as is described by M. Phené in Argyllshire‡ is remarkable; and still more so is that between the Mexican myth of the fourfold destruction of the world by fire and water, with those current among the Egyptians and that of the four ages in the Hindu mythology.

Another coincidence, although perhaps of minor value, will be seen in the dresses of the soldiers of China and Mexico, as noted in the passages annexed. "Thus, in our

* *Harris' Voyages*, vol. i. p. 859.

† Dr. J. le Conte describes a ceremonial of cremation among the Cocopa Indians of California, and it is an ancient practice among the Chinese, dating back beyond the Greek and Roman historical periods.

‡ British Association, 1871.

own time, the Chinese soldiers wear a dress resembling the tiger skin, and the cap, which nearly covers the face, is formed to represent the head of a tiger " ;* while the Mexican warriors, according to Spanish historians, " wore enormous wooden helmets in the form of a tiger's head, the jaws of which were armed with the teeth of this animal."†

Mr. C. Wolcott-Brooks, in an address to the California Academy of Science, has pointed out that, according to Chinese annals, Tai Ko Fo Kee, the great stranger-king, ruled the kingdom of China, and that he is always represented in pictures with two small horns like those associated with the representation of Moses. He and his successors are said to have introduced into China " picture writing " like that in use in Central America at the time of the Spanish conquest. Now there has been found at Copan, in Central America, a figure strikingly like the Chinese symbol of Fo Kee, with his two horns. " Either," says Mr. Brooks, " one people learned from the other, or both acquired their forms from a common source."

In reviewing all these cases we cannot fail to perceive that early and frequent communication must have taken place between the two worlds, and that the myths of one have probably been carried with them by the migrants to the other.

---

* Staunton, *China*, vol. ii. p. 455.
† Humboldt, *Researches in America*, English Translation, vol. i. p. 133.

Fig. 32.—Mural Tablet, Temple of Longevity, Canton.

# CHAPTER VI.

### THE DRAGON.

FIG. 33.—*Draco,* or FLYING LIZARD FROM
SINGAPORE. (*After N. B. Dennys.*)

THE dragon is defined in the *Encyclopædia Britannica* for 1877 as " the name given by the ancients to a huge winged lizard or serpent (fabulous)."

The text also goes on to state that " they (the ancients) regarded it as the enemy of mankind, and its overthrow is made to figure among the greatest exploits of the gods and heroes of heathen mythology. A dragon watched the gardens of the Hesperides, and its destruction formed one of the seven labours of Hercules. Its existence does not seem to have been called in question by the older naturalists; figures of the dragon appearing in the works of Gesner and Aldrovandus, and even specimens of the monster, evidently formed artificially of portions of different animals, have been exhibited." A reference is also made to the genus Draco, comprising eighteen specimens of winged lizards, all small, and peculiar to India and the islands of the Malay archipelago.

Such is the meagre account of a creature which figures in the history and mythology of all nations, which in its different forms has been worshipped as a god, endowed with beneficent and malevolent attributes, combatted as a monster, or supposed to have possessed supernatural power, exercised alternately for the benefit or chastisement of mankind.

Its existence is inseparably wedded to the history, from the most remote antiquity, of a nation which possesses connected and authentic memoirs stretching uninterruptedly from the present day far into the remote past; on which the belief in its existence has been so strongly impressed, that it retains its emblem in its insignia of office, in its ornamentation of furniture, utensils, and dwellings, and commemorates it annually in the competition of dragon boats, and the processions of dragon images; which believes, or affects to believe, in its continued existence in the pools of the deep, and the clouds of the sky; which propitiates it with sacrifices and ceremonies, builds temples in its honour, and cultivates its worship; whose legends and traditions teem with anecdotes of its interposition in the affairs of man, and whose scientific works, of antiquity rivalling that of our oldest Western Classics, treat of its existence as a sober and accepted fact, and differentiate its species with some exactness. It is, moreover, though not very frequently, occasionally referred to in the Biblical history of that other ancient, and almost equally conservative branch of the human race, the Jews, not as a myth, or doubtfully existent supernatural monster, but as a tangible reality, an exact terrible creature.

Equally do we find it noticed in those other valuable records of the past which throw cross lights upon the Bible narrative, and confirm by collateral facts the value of its

Fig. 34.—Bronze Dragons supporting the Armillary Sphere, Observatory, Pekin.

historic truth; such as the fragments of Chaldæan history handed down by the reverent care of later historians, the careful narrative of Josephus, and the grand resurrection of Chaldæan and Assyrian lore effected by the marvellously well directed and fortunate labour of G. H. Smith and those who follow in his train.

Among the earliest classics of Europe, its existence is asserted as a scientific fact, and accepted by poets as a sound basis for analogies, comparisons, allegories, and fable; it appears in the mythology of the Goth, and is continued through the tradition and fable of every country of Europe; nor does it fail to appear even in the imperfect traditions of the New World,* where its presence may be considered as comparatively indigenous, and undetermined by the communications dependent on the so-called discovery of later days.

Turning to other popular accounts, we find equally limited and incredible versions of it. All consider it sufficiently disposed of by calling it fabulous,† and that a sufficient explanation of any possible belief in it is afforded by a reference‡ to the harmless genus of existing flying lizards referred to above.

---

* "In turning to the consideration of the primitive works of art of the American continent . . . when in the bronze work of the later iron period, imitative forms at length appear, they are chiefly the snake and dragon shapes and patterns, borrowed seemingly by Celtic and Teutonic wanderers, with the wild fancies of their mythology, from the far eastern land of their birth."—D. Wilson, *Prehistoric Man*, 1862.

"He had remarked that the Indians of the north-west coast frequently repeat in their well-known blackstone carvings the dragon, the lotus flower, and the alligator."—C. G. Leland, *Fusang*, London, 1875.

† "Dragon, an imaginary animal something like a crocodile."—Rev. Dr. Brewer, *Dictionary of Phrase and Fable*, p. 243.

‡ "In the woods of Java are certain flying snakes, or rather drakes; they have four legs, a long tail, and their skin speckled with many spots, their wings are not unlike those of a bat, which they move in flying, but otherwise keep them almost unperceived close to the body. They fly nimbly, but cannot hold it long, so that they fly from tree to

Some consider it an evolution of the fancy, typifying noxious principles; thus, Chambers* says, "The dragon appears in the mythical history and legendary poetry of almost every nation as the emblem of the destructive and anarchical principle; . . . as misdirected physical force and untamable animal passions. . . . The dragon proceeds openly to work, running on its feet with expanded wings, and head and tail erect, violently and ruthlessly outraging decency and propriety, spouting fire and fury both from mouth and tail, and wasting and devastating the whole land."

The point which strikes me as most interesting in this passage is the reference to the legendary theory of the mode of the dragon's progress, which curiously calls to mind the semi-erect attitude of the existing small Australian frilled lizard (*Chlamydosaurus*). This attitude is also ascribed to some of the extinct American Dinosaurs, such as the Stegosaurus.

No one, so far as I am aware, in late days has hitherto ventured to uphold the claims of this terrible monster to be accepted as a real contemporary of primitive man,† which

tree at about twenty or thirty paces' distance. On the outside of the throat are two bladders, which, being extended when they fly, serve them instead of a sail. They feed upon flies and other insects."—Mr. John Nieuhoff's Voyage and Travels to the East Indies, contained in a collection of *Voyages and Travels*, in 6 vols., vol. ii. p. 317; Churchill, London, 1732.

* *Chambers' Encyclopædia*, vol. iii. p. 635.

† The following is the nearest approach to such an assertion I have met with, but appears from the context to apply to geologic time prior to the advent of man. "When all those large and monstrous amphibia since regarded as fabulous still in reality existed, when the confines of the water and the land teemed with gigantic saurians, with lizards of dimensions much exceeding those of the largest crocodiles of the present day: who to the scaly bodies of fish, added the claws of beasts, and the neck and wings of birds: who to the faculty of swimming in water, added not only that of moving on the earth but that of sailing in air:

may even have been co-existent with him to a comparatively recent date, and but lately passed away into the cohort of extinct species, leaving behind it only the traditions of its ferocity and terrors, to stamp their impression on the tongues of all countries.

No one has endeavoured to collate the vast bulk of materials shrouded in the stories of all lands. If this were perfectly effected, a diagnosis of the real nature of the dragon might perhaps be made, and the chapter of its characteristics, alliances, and habits completed like that of any other well-established species.

The following sketch purposes only to initiate the task here propounded, the author's access to materials being limited, and only sufficient to enable him, as he thinks, to establish generally the proposition which it involves, to grasp as it were some of the broader and salient features of the investigation, while leaving a rich gleaning of corroborative information for the hand of any other who may please to continue and extend his observations.

At the outset it will be necessary to assign a much more extended signification to the word dragon than that which is contained in the definition at the head of this chapter. The popular mind of the present day doubtless associates it always with the idea of a creature possessing wings ; but the *Lung* of the Chinese, the δράκων of the Greeks, the

---

and who had all the characteristics of what we now call chimeras and dragons, and perhaps of such monsters the remains, found among the bones and skeletons of other animals more resembling those that still exist and propagate, in the grottos and caverns in which they sought shelter during the deluges that affected the infancy of the globe, gave first rise to the idea that these dens and caves were once retreats whence such monsters watched and in which they devoured other animals."— Thomas Hope, *On the Origin and Prospects of Man*, vol. ii. p. 346 ; London, 1831.

Southey, in his Commonplace Book, pityingly alludes to this passage, saying, "He believes in dragons and griffins as having heretofore existed."

*Draco* of the Romans, the Egyptian dragon, and the *Nâga* of the Sanscrit have no such limited signification, and appear to have been sometimes applied to any serpent, lacertian, or saurian, of extraordinary dimensions, nor is it always easy to determine from the passages in which these several terms occur what kind of monster is specially indicated.

Thus the dragon referred to by Propertius in the quotation annexed may have been a large python. "Lanuvium* is, of old, protected by an aged dragon; here, where the occasion of an amusement so seldom occurring is not lost, where is the abrupt descent into a dark and hollowed cave; where is let down—maiden, beware of every such journey—the honorary tribute to the fasting snake, when he demands his yearly food, and hisses and twists deep down in the earth. Maidens, let down for such a rite, grow pale, when their hand is unprotectedly trusted in the snake's mouth. He snatches at the delicacies if offered by a maid; the very baskets tremble in the virgin's hands; if they are chaste, they return and fall on the necks of their parents, and the farmers cry 'We shall have a fruitful year.'"†

To the same class may probably be ascribed the dragon referred to by Aristotle.‡ "The eagle and the dragon are enemies, for the eagle feeds on serpents"; and again,§ "the Glanis in shallow water is often destroyed by the dragon serpent." It might perhaps be supposed that the crocodile is here referred to, but this is specially spoken of in another passage, as follows‖: "But there are others which, though they live and feed in the water, do not take in water but air, and produce their young out of the water; many of these

---

* From the context, Lanuvium appears to have been on the Appian Road, in Latium, about twenty-fives miles from Rome.
† Propertius, *Elegy VIII.*; Bohn, 1854.
‡ *History of Animals*, Book ix., chap. ii. § 3; Bohn.
§ *Ibid.*, Book vi., chap. xx. § 12.
‖ *Ibid.*, Book i., § 6.

animals are furnished with feet, as the otter and crocodile, and others are without feet, as the water-serpent."

A somewhat inexplicable habit is ascribed to the dragon in Book ix.* : " When the draco has eaten much fruit, it seeks the juice of the bitter lettuce ; it has been seen to do this."

Pliny, probably quoting Aristotle,† also states that the dragon relieves the nausea which affects it in spring with the juices of the lettuce ; and Ælian‡ repeats the story.

It is also probable that some large serpent is intended by Pliny in the story which he relates,§ after Democritus, that a man called Thoas was preserved in Arcadia by a dragon. When a boy, he had become attached to it and had reared it very tenderly ; but his father, being alarmed at the nature and monstrous size of the reptile, had taken and left it in the desert. Thoas being here attacked by robbers who lay in ambush, he was delivered from them by the dragon, which recognized his voice and came to his assistance. It may be noted in regard to this that there are many authenticated instances of snakes evidencing considerable affection for those who have treated them with kindness.||

The impression that Pliny's dragon was intended to repre-

---

* *History of Animals*, Book ix., chap. vii. § 4.

† *Natural History of Pliny*, Book viii., chap. xli., translated by J. Bostock and H. T. Riley ; London, 1855.

‡ *Anim. Nat.*, Book vi., chap. iv.

§ *Natural History*, Book viii., chap. xxii.

|| " On the contrary, towards ourselves they were disappointingly undemonstrative, and only evinced their consciousness of the presence of strangers by entwining themselves about the members of the family as if soliciting their protection. . . . They were very jealous of each other, Mr. Mann said ; jealous also of other company, as if unwilling to lose their share of attention. . . . Two sweet little children were equally familiar with the other boas, that seemed quite to know who were their friends and playfellows, for the children handled them and petted them and talked to them as we talk to pet birds and cats."—Account of Snakes kept by Mr. and Mrs. Mann, of Cheyne Walk, Chelsea, in *Snakes*, by C. C. Hopley ; London, 1882.

sent some large boa or python is strengthened by his statement:* " The dragon is a serpent destitute of venom ; its head placed beneath the threshold of a door, the gods being duly propitiated by prayers, will ensure good fortune to the house, it is said."

It is remarkable that he attributes to the dragon the same desire and capacity to attack the elephant as is attributed to the Pa snake in Western China, and by the old Arabian voyagers to serpents in Borneo.

The *Shan-hai-king*, a Chinese work of extreme antiquity, of which special mention will be made hereafter, says : " The Pa snake swallows elephants, after three years it ejects the bones ; well-to-do people, eating it, are cured of consumption."

Diodorus Siculus, in speaking of the region of the Nile in Libya, says that, according to report, very large serpents are produced there and in great numbers, and that these attack elephants when they gather around the watering places, involve them in their folds till they fall exhausted, and then devour them.

Diodorus, in another passage referring to the crocodiles and hippopotami of Egypt, speaking of Ethiopia and Libya, mentions a variety of serpents as well as of other wild beasts, including dragons of unusual size and ferocity.

While El Edrisi says : " On peut encore citer le serpent de Zaledj dont parlent Ben Khordadébe, l'auteur du Livre des Merveilles, et divers autres écrivains qui s'accordent à dire qu'il existe dans les montagnes de l'ile de Zaledj une espèce de serpent qui attaque l'elephant et le buffle, et qui ne les abandonnent qu'après les avoir vaincu."†

---

* *Natural History*, Book xxix., chap. xx.

† " It is probable that the island of Zanig described by Qazvinius, in his geographical work (for extracts from which vide *Scriptorum Arabum de Rebus Indicis loci et opuscula inedita*, by I. Gildemeister, Bonnæ,

Artemidorus, also, according to Strabo,* "mentions serpents of thirty cubits in length, which can master elephants and bulls. In this he does not exaggerate; but the Indian and African serpents are of a more fabulous size, and are said to have grass growing on their backs."

Iphicrates, according to Bryant, "related that in Mauritania there were dragons of such extent that grass grew upon their backs."

It is doubtful whether large serpents, or real dragons, are referred to by Pliny in the following interesting passages which I give at length: the surprise which he expresses at Juba's believing that they had crests, leads me to suspect that there was possibly some confusion of species involved; that Juba might have been perfectly accurate so far as the crests are concerned, and that the beasts in question, in place of being pythons of magnitude, were rather some gigantic lizard-like creature, of great length and little bulk, corresponding with the Chinese idea of the dragon, and, therefore, naturally bearing horny crests, similar to those with which the monster is usually represented by the latter people.

It must be noticed here, that if we postulate the existence of the dragon, we are not bound to limit ourselves to a single species, or even two, as the same causes which effected the gradual destruction of one would be exceedingly likely to effect that of another; we must not, therefore, be too critical in comparing descriptions of different authors in different

---

1838), as the seat of the empire of the Mahraj, is identical with Zaledj. He says that it is a large island on the confines of China towards India, and that among other remarkable features is a mountain called Nacan (Kini Balu?), on which are serpents of such magnitude as to be able to swallow oxen, buffaloes, and even elephants. Masudi includes Zanig, Kalah, and Taprobana among the islands constituting the territory of the Mahraj."—P. Amédée Jaubert, *Géographie d'Edrisi*, vol. i. p. 104; Paris, 1836.

\* Book vi., chap. iv. § 16.

† *Serpent Worship*, p. 35; Welder, New York, 1877.

countries and epochs, since they may refer only to allied, but not identical, animals.

"Africa produces elephants, but it is India that produces the largest, as well as the *dragon*, who is perpetually at war with the elephant, and is itself of so enormous a size, as easily to envelop the elephants with its folds, and encircle them in its coils. The contest is equally fatal to both ; the elephant, vanquished, falls to the earth, and by its weight crushes the dragon which is entwined around it.*

"The sagacity which every animal exhibits in its own behalf is wonderful, but in these it is remarkably so. The dragon has much difficulty in climbing up to so great a height, and therefore, watching the road, which bears marks of their footsteps, when going to feed, it darts down upon them from a lofty tree. The elephant knows that it is quite unable to struggle against the folds of the serpent, and so seeks for trees or rocks against which to rub itself.

"The dragon is on its guard against this, and tries to prevent it, by first of all confining the legs of the elephant with the folds of its tail; while the elephant, on the other hand, tries to disengage itself with its trunk. The dragon, however, thrusts its head into its nostrils, and thus, at the same moment, stops the breath, and wounds the most tender parts. When it is met unexpectedly, the dragon raises itself up, faces its opponent, and flies more especially at the eyes ; this is the reason why elephants are so often found blind, and worn to a skeleton with hunger and misery.

"There is another story, too, told in relation to these combats. The blood of the elephant, it is said, is remarkably cold ; for which reason, in the parching heats of summer, it is sought by the dragon with remarkable avidity. It lies, therefore, coiled up and concealed in the river, in wait for

---

* *Pliny's Natural History*, Book viii., chap. xi., translated by J. Bostock and H. T. Riley ; Bohn, London, 1855.

the elephants when they come to drink; upon which it darts out, fastens itself around the trunk, and then fixes its teeth behind the ear, that being the only place which the elephant cannot protect with the trunk. The dragons, it is said, are of such vast size that they can swallow the whole of the blood; consequently the elephant, being drained of its blood, falls to the earth exhausted; while the dragon, intoxicated with the draught, is crushed beneath it, and so shares its fate.*

" Æthiopia produces dragons, not so large as those of India, but still twenty cubits in length. The only thing that surprises me is, how Juba came to believe that they have crests. The Æthiopians are known as the Asachæi, among whom they most abound; and we are told that on those coasts four or five of them are found twisted and interlaced together like so many osiers in a hurdle, and thus setting sail, with their heads erect, they are borne along upon the waves to find better sources of nourishment in Arabia."†

Pliny then goes on to describe, as *separate from dragons, large serpents in India,* as follows.

" Megasthenes‡ informs us that in India serpents grow to such an immense size as to swallow stags and bulls; while Metrodorus says that about the river Rhyndacus, in Pontus, they seize and swallow the birds that are flying above them, however high and however rapid their flight.

" It is a well-known fact that during the Punic war, at the river Bagrada, a serpent one hundred and twenty feet in length was taken by the Roman army under Regulus, being besieged, like a fortress, by means of balistæ and other engines of war. *Its skin and jaws* were preserved in a temple at Rome down to the time of the Numantine war.

" The serpents, which in Italy are known by the name of

---

* *Pliny's Natural History*, Book viii., chap. xii.
† *Ibid.*, Book viii., chap. xiii.
‡ *Ibid.*, Book viii., chap. xiv.

boa, render these accounts far from incredible, for they grow to such vast size that a child was found entire in the stomach of one of them which was killed on the Vaticanian Hill during the reign of Emperor Claudius."*

Aristotle tells us that "in Libya, the serpents, as it has been already remarked, are very large. For some persons say that as they sailed along the coast, they saw the bones of many oxen, and that it was evident to them that they had been devoured by serpents. And, as the ships passed on, the serpents attacked the triremes, and some of them threw themselves upon one of the triremes and overturned it."†

It is doubtful whether the dragons described by Benjamin of Tudela, who travelled through Europe and the East and returned to Castille in 1173,‡ as infesting the ruins of the palace of Nebuchodonosor at Babylon, so as to render them inaccessible, were creatures of the imagination such as the mediæval mind seems to have loved to dress up, or venomous serpents. But there is little doubt that the so-called dragons of later voyages were simply boas, pythons, or other large serpents, such as those described by John Leo, in his descrip-

---

* " At the present day the longest Italian serpents are the Æsculapian serpent (a harmless animal) and the *Colubes quadrilineatus*, neither of which exceeds ten feet in length."—*Nat. Hist.*, Book viii., chap. xiv.

† *Aristotle's History of Animals*, Book viii., chap. xxvii. § 6, by R. Cresswell, Bohn's Series ; Bell, London, 1878.

‡ An abridgment of these travels is contained in *Voyages par Pierre Bergeron*, à la Haye, 1735. They were originally written in Hebrew, translated into Latin by Benoit Arian Montare, and subsequently into French. [The introduction refers to his return to Castille in 1173, presumably after the termination of his voyages; but in the opening paragraph there is a marginal note giving the same date to his setting out from Sarragossa.] Sir John Mandeville gives a similar account in speaking of the tower of Babylon; he says, "but it is full long sithe that any man durste neyhe to the Tour: for it is all deserte and fulle of Dragouns and grete serpents, and fulle of dyverse venemous Bestes alle about he."—*The Voyages of Sir John Mandeville, Kt.*, p. 40 ; J. O. Halliwell, London, 1839.

tion of a voyage to Africa, as existing in the caverns of Atlas. He says, " There are many monstrous dragons which are thick about the middle, but have slender necks and tails, so that their motion is but slow.* They are so venomous, that whatever they bite or touch, certain death ensues." There is also the statement of Job Ludolphus that (in Æthiopia) " the dragons are of the largest size, very voracious, but not venomous."†

I fancy that at the present day the numbers, magnitude, and terrifying nature of serpents but feebly represent the power which they asserted in the early days of man's existence, or the terror which they then inspired. This subject has been so ably dealt with by a writer of the last century‡ that I feel no hesitation in transcribing his remarks at length.

" It is probable, in early times, when the arts were little known and mankind were but thinly scattered over the earth, that serpents, continuing undisturbed possessors of the forest, grew to an amazing magnitude, and every other tribe of animals fell before them. It then might have happened that the serpents reigned tyrants of the district for centuries together. To animals of this kind, grown by time and rapacity to one hundred or one hundred and fifty feet long, the lion, the tiger, and even the elephant itself were but feeble opponents. That horrible fetor, which even the commonest and the most harmless snakes are still found to diffuse, might in these larger ones become too powerful for any living being to withstand, and while they preyed without distinction, they might also have poisoned the atmosphere round them. In this manner, having for ages lived in the hidden and unpeopled forest, and finding, as their appetites were more powerful, the quantity of their prey decreasing, it is possible

---

* *Harris's Voyages*, vol. i. p. 360.

† *Ibid.*, vol. i. p. 392.

‡ *Encyclopædia of Arts and Sciences*, first American edition, Philadelphia, 1798.

they might venture boldly from their retreats into the more cultivated parts of the country, and carry consternation among mankind, as they had before desolation among the lower ranks of nature.

" We have many histories of antiquity presenting us such a picture, and exhibiting a whole nation sinking under the ravages of a single serpent. At that time man had not learned the art of uniting the efforts of many to effect one great purpose. Opposing multitudes only added new victims to the general calamity, and increased mutual embarrassment and terror. The animal, therefore, was to be singly opposed by him who had the greatest strength, the best armour, and the most undaunted courage. In such an encounter hundreds must have fallen, till one more lucky than the rest, by a fortunate blow, or by taking the monster in its torpid interval and surcharged with spoil, might kill and thus rid his country of the destroyer. Such was the original occupation of heroes.

" But as we descend into more enlightened antiquity we find these animals less formidable, as being attacked in a more successful manner.

" We are told that while Regulus led his army along the banks of the river Bagrada in Africa, an enormous serpent disputed his passage over. We are assured by Pliny that it was one hundred and twenty feet long, and that it had destroyed many of the army. At last, however, the battering engines were brought out against it, and then, assailing it at a distance, it was destroyed. Its spoils were carried to Rome, and the general was decreed an ovation for his success.

" There are, perhaps, few facts better ascertained in history than this : an ovation was a remarkable honour, and was only given for some signal exploit that did not deserve a triumph. No historian would offer to invent that part of the story, at least, without being subject to the most shameful detection.

" The skin was kept for several years after, in the Capitol, and Pliny says he saw it there.

" This tribe of animals, like that of fishes, seem to have no bounds put to their growth ; their bones are in a great measure cartilaginous, and they are consequently capable of great extension.

" The older, therefore, a serpent becomes, the larger it grows, and, as they live to a great age, they arrive at an enormous size.  Leguat assures us that he saw one in Java that was fifty feet long.*  Carli mentions their growing to above forty feet, and there is now in the British Museum one that measures thirty-two feet.

" Mr. Wentworth, who had large concerns in the Berbice in America, assures us that in that country they grow to an enormous length.  He describes an Indian mistaking one for a log, and proceeding to sit down on it, when it began to move.  A soldier with him shot the snake, but the Indian died of fright.  It measured thirty-six feet.  It was sent to the Hague.

" A life of savage hostility in the forest offers the imagination one of the most tremendous pictures in nature.  In those burning countries where the sun dries up every brook for hundreds of miles round : where what had the appearance of a great river in the rainy season becomes in summer one dreary bed of sand ; in those countries a lake that is never dry, or a brook that is perennial, is considered by every animal as the greatest convenience of nature.  When they have discovered this, no dangers can deter them from attempting to slake their thirst.  Thus the neighbourhood of a rivulet, in the heart of the tropical continents, is generally

* See *Voyage to the East Indies*, by Francis Leguat ; London, 1708. Leguat hardly makes the positive affirmation stated in the text.  In describing Batavia he says there is another sort of serpents which are at least fifty feet long.

the place where all the hostile tribes of nature draw up for the engagement.

"On the banks of this little envied spot, thousands of animals of various kinds are seen venturing to quench their thirst, or preparing to seize their prey. The elephants are perceived in a long line, marching from the darker parts of the forest. The buffaloes are there, depending upon numbers for security; the gazelles relying solely upon their swiftness; the lion and tiger waiting a proper opportunity to seize.

"But chiefly the larger serpents are upon guard there, and defend the accesses of the lake. Not an hour passes without some dreadful combat, but the serpent, defended by its scales, and naturally capable of sustaining a multitude of wounds, is of all others the most formidable. It is the most wakeful also, for the whole tribe sleep with their eyes open, and are consequently for ever upon the watch; so that, till their rapacity is satisfied, few other animals will venture to approach their station."

We read of a serpent exhibited in the time of Augustus at Rome, which, Suetonius tells us, "was fifty cubits in length."[*] But at the present day there are few authentic accounts of snakes exceeding thirty feet in length; and there are some people who discredit any which profess to speak of snakes of greater dimensions than this. There are some, however, among the annexed stories, which I think demand belief, and apparently we may conclude that the python and boa exceptionally attain as much as forty feet in length, or even more.

Wallace[†] merely reports by hearsay that the pythons in the Phillipines, which destroy young cattle, are said to reach more than forty feet.

Captain Sherard Osborn,[‡] in his description of Quedah in

[*] Broderip, *Leaves from the Note Book of a Naturalist*, p. 357.

[†] *Australasia*, p. 273.

[‡] *Quedah*; London, 1857.

the Malay peninsula, says, also, as a matter of popular belief : " The natives of Tamelan declared most of them to be of the boa-constrictor [species, but spoke of monsters in the deep forests, which might, if they came out, clear off the whole village. A pleasant feat, for which Jadie, with a wag of his sagacious head, assured me that an ' oular Bessar ' or big snake was quite competent.

" It was strange but interesting to find amongst all Malays a strong belief in the extraordinary size to which the boa-constrictors or pythons would grow ; they all maintained that in the secluded forests of Sumatra or Borneo, as well as on some of the smaller islands which were not inhabited, these snakes were occasionally found of forty or fifty feet in length."

Major McNair says* : " One of the keenest sportsmen in Singapore gives an account of a monster that he encountered. He had wounded a boar in the jungle, and was following its tracks with his dogs, when, in penetrating further into the forest, he found the dogs at bay, and, advancing cautiously, prepared for another shot at the boar ; to his surprise, however, he found that the dogs were baying a huge python, which had seized the boar, thrown its coils round the unfortunate beast, and was crushing it to death. A well-directed shot laid the reptile writhing on the ground, and it proved to be about thirty feet long. But such instances of extreme length are rare."

Unfortunately the exciting story of a serpent, between forty and fifty feet in length, which I extract from the *North China Daily News* of November 10th, 1880, the scene of which is also laid in the Malay peninsula, lacks the authenticity of the narrator's name. It is as follows :—

" The *Straits Times* tells the following exciting python story : ' A sportsman, who a few days ago penetrated into the

---

* *Perak and the Malays*, p. 77.

jungle lying between Buddoh and Sirangoon, came upon a lone hut in a district called Campong Batta, upon the roof of which the skin of an enormous boa or python (whichever may be the correct name) was spread out. The hut was occupied by a Malay and his wife, from whom our informant gathered the following extraordinary account. One night, about a week previously, the Malay was awakened by the cries of his wife for assistance. Being in perfect darkness, and supposing the alarm to be on account of thieves, he seized his sharp parang, and groped his way to her sleeping place, where his hand fell upon a slimy reptile. It was fully a minute before he could comprehend the entire situation, and when he did, he discovered that the whole of his wife's arm had been drawn down the monster's throat, whither the upper part of her body was slowly but surely following. Not daring to attack the monster at once for fear of causing his wife's death, the husband, with great presence of mind, seized two bags within reach, and commenced stuffing them into the corner of the snake's jaws, by means of which he succeeded in forcing them wider open and releasing his wife's arm. No sooner had the boa lost his prey than he attacked the husband, whom he began encircling in his fatal coils ; but holding out both arms, and watching his opportunity, he attacked the monster so vigorously with his parang that it suddenly unwound itself and vanished through an opening beneath the attap sides of the hut. His clothes were covered with blood, as was also the floor of the hut, and his wife's arm was blue with the squeezing it received between the boa's jaws. At daylight the husband discovered his patch of plaintain trees nearly ruined, where the boa, writhing in agony, had broken off the trees at the roots, and in the midst of the debris lay the monster itself, dead. The Malay assured our informant that he had received no less than sixty dollars from Chinese, who came from long distances to purchase pieces of the flesh on account of its supposed medical properties, and that he had refused six dollars for the skin, which he preferred to retain as a trophy. It was greatly decomposed, having been some days exposed in the open air, and useless for curing. There is no telling what may have been the measurement of this large reptile, but the skin, probably greatly stretched by unskilful removal, measured between seven and eight fathoms."

Bontius speaks of serpents in the Asiatic Isles. "The great ones," he says, "sometimes exceed thirty-six feet; and have such capacity of throat and stomach that they swallow whole boars."

Mr. McLeod, in the *Voyage of the Alceste*, states that during a captivity of some months at Whidah, on the coast of Africa, he had opportunities of observing serpents double this length.*

Broderip, in his *Leaves from the Note-book of a Naturalist* (Parker, 1852), speaks of a serpent thirty feet in length, which attacked the crew of a Malay proa anchored for the night close to the island of Celebes.

Mr. C. Collingwood in *Rambles of a Naturalist*, states that " Mr. Low assured me that he had seen one [python] killed measuring twenty-six feet, and I heard on good authority of one of twenty-nine feet having been killed there. In Borneo they were said to attain forty feet, but for this I cannot vouch."

That large pythons still exist in South and Western China, although of very reduced dimensions as compared with those described in ancient works, is affirmed by many writers, from whom I think it is sufficient to extract a notice by one of the early missionaries who explored that country.

"Pour ce qui est des serpens qu'on trouve dans Chine l'Atlas raconte que la Province de Quansi, en produit de si grands et d'une longueur si extrême, qu'il est presque incroyable ; et il nous assure, qu'il s'en est trouvé, qui étaient plus

---

* Figuier, *Reptiles and Birds*, p. 51.

longs que ne seraient pas dix perches attachées les unes avec les autres, c'est-à-dire, qu'ils avaient plus de trente pieds géométriques. Flore Sienois dit, ' Gento est le plus grand de tous ceux qui sont dans les provinces de Quansi, de Haynan, et de Quantun . . . il dévore les cerfs. . . . Il s'élève droit sur sa queue, et combat vigoureusement, en cette posture, contre les hommes et les bêtes farouches.' "*

We have unfortunately no clue to the actual length of the serpent Bomma, described by J. M. da Sorrento in *A Voyage to Congo in* 1682, contained in Churchill's collection of voyages published in 1732.† " The flesh they eat is generally that of wild creatures, and especially of a sort of serpent called Bomma. At a certain feast in Baia, I observed the windows, instead of tapestry and arras, adorned with the skin of these serpents as wide as that of a large ox, and long in proportion."

That harmless snakes of from twelve to fourteen feet in length occur abundantly in Northern Australia is generally known; but it is only of late years that I have been made acquainted with a firm belief, entertained by the natives in the interior, of the existence near the junction of the Darling and Murray, south of the centre of the continent, of a serpent of great magnitude.

I learn from Mr. G. R. Moffat that on the Lower Murray, between Swan Hill and the Darling junction—at the time of his acquaintance with the district (about 1857 to 1867)— the black fellows had numerous stories of the existence of a large serpent in the Mallee scrub. It was conspicuous for its size, thirty to forty feet in length, and especially for its great girth, swiftness, and intensely disgusting odour; this latter, in fact, constituted the great protection from it, insomuch

---

* *La Chine Illustré*, d'Athase Keichere, chap. x. p. 272. Amsterdam, cIɔ Iɔɔ LXX.

† Vol. i. p. 601.

as it would be impossible to approach without recognising its presence.

Mr. Moffatt learnt personally from a Mr. Beveridge, son of Mr. Peter Beveridge, of Swan Hill station, that he had actually seen one, and that his account quite tallied with those of the blacks. In answer to an inquiry which I addressed to Australia, I received the note attached below.*

Mr. Henry Liddell, who was resident on the Darling River in 1871-72, informs me that he has heard from stock-riders and ration-carriers similar accounts to that of Mr. Moffatt, with reference to the existence of large serpents of the boa species in an adjacent locality, viz. the tract of country lying to the east of Darling and Murray junction, in the back country belonging to Pooncaira station.

They described them as being numerous, in barren and rocky places, among big boulders; fully forty feet long; as thick as a man's thigh; and as having the same remarkable odour described by Mr. Moffatt. They spoke of them as quite common, and not at all phenomenal, between Wentworth and Pooncaira.

The Anaconda, in regard to which so much myth and superstition prevails among the Indians of Brazil, is thus spoken of by Condamine, in his *Travels in South America.* "The most rare and singular of all is a large amphibious serpent from twenty-five to thirty feet long and more than a foot thick, according to report. It is called Jacumama, or 'the mother of the waters,' by the Americans of Maynas,

---

* See *Proceedings* of Royal Society of Tasmania, September 13, 1880. Mr. C. M. Officer states—"With reference to the Mindi or Mallee snake, it has often been described to me as a formidable creature of at least thirty feet in length, which confined itself to the Mallee scrub. No one, however, has ever seen one, for the simple reason that to see it is to die, so fierce it is, and so great its power of destruction. Like the Bunyip, I believe the Mindi to be a myth, a mere tradition."

and commonly inhabits the large lakes formed by the river-water after flood." *

Ulloa, also, in his *Voyage to South America*,† says : " In the countries watered by that vast river (the Maranon) is bred a serpent of a frightful magnitude, and of a most deleterious nature. Some, in order to give an idea of its largeness, affirm that it will swallow any beast whole, and that this has been the miserable end of many a man. But what seems still a greater wonder is the attractive quality attributed to its breath,‡ which irresistibly draws any creature to it which happens to be within the sphere of its attraction. The Indians call it Jacumama, *i.e.* 'mother of water'; for, as it delights in lakes and marshy places, it may in some sense be considered as amphibious. I have taken a great deal of pains to inquire into this particular, and all I can say is that the reptile's magnitude is really surprising."

John Nieuhoff, in his *Voyages to Brazil*,§ speaking of the serpent Guaku or Liboya, says : " It is questionless the biggest of all serpents, some being eighteen, twenty-four, nay thirty feet long, and of the thickness of a man in his middle. The Portuguese call it Kobra Detrado, or the roebuck serpent, because it will swallow a whole roebuck, or any other deer it meets with ; after they have swallowed such a deer, they fall asleep, and so are catched. Such a one I saw at Paraiba, which was thirty feet long, and as big as a barrel. This serpent, being a very devouring creature, greedy of prey, leaps from amongst the hedges and woods, and standing upright upon its tail, wrestles both with men and wild

---

* Pinkerton's *Voyages*, vol. xiv. p. 247.

† *Ibid.*, vol. xiv. p. 514.

‡ It is interesting to compare this belief with stories given elsewhere, by Pliny, Book viii. chap. xiv., and Ælian, Book ii. chap. xxi., of the power of the serpents or dragons of the river Rhyndacus to attract birds by inhalation.

§ Pinkerton's *Voyages*, vol. xiv. p. 713.

beasts; sometimes it leaps from the trees upon the traveller, whom it fastens upon, and beats the breath out of his body with its tail."

The largest (water boa) ever met with by a European appears to be that described by a botanist, Dr. Gardiner, in his *Travels in Brazil.* It had devoured a horse, and was found dead, entangled in the branches of a tree overhanging a river, into which it had been carried by a flood; it was nearly forty feet long.

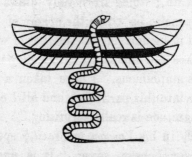

Fig. 35.—Egyptian Four-winged Serpent, Chanuphis, or Bait. (*From "Serpent Myths of Ancient Egypt," by W. R. Cooper.*)

## Winged Serpents.

The next section relates to winged serpents, a belief in which was prevalent in early ages, and is strongly supported by several independent works.

To my mind, Herodotus speaks without the slightest doubt upon the subject in the following passages. "Arabia* is the last of inhabited lands towards the south, and it is the only country which produces frankincense, myrrh, cassia, cinnamon, and ledanum." "The frankincense they procure by means of the gum styrax, which the Greeks get from the Phœnicians. This they burn, and thereby obtain the spice; for the trees which bear the frankincense are guarded by

---

* Herodotus, Book iii. chap. cvii., cviii.

winged serpents, small in size, and of various colours, whereof vast numbers hang about every tree. They are of the same kind as the serpents that invade Egypt, and there is nothing but the smoke of the styrax which will drive them from the trees."

Fig. 36.—The Symbolic Winged Serpent of the Goddess Mersokar or Melsokar. (*After W. R. Cooper.*)

Again,* " the Arabians say that the whole world would swarm with these serpents, if they were not kept in check, in the way in which I know that vipers are." "Now, with respect to the vipers and the winged snakes of Arabia, if they increased as fast as their nature would allow, impossible were it for man to maintain himself upon the earth. Accordingly, it is found that when the male and female come together, at the very moment of impregnation, the female seizes the male by the neck, and having once fastened cannot be brought to leave go till she has bit the neck entirely through, and so the male perishes; but after a while he is avenged upon the female by means of the young, which, while still unborn, gnaw a passage through the womb and then through the belly of their mother. Contrariwise, other snakes, which are harmless, lay eggs and hatch a vast number of young. Vipers are found in all parts of the world, but the winged serpents are nowhere seen except in Arabia, where they are all congregated together; this makes them appear so numerous."

* Herodotus, Book iii. chap. cviii.

Herodotus had so far interested himself in ascertaining the probability of their existence as to visit Arabia for the purpose of inquiry ; he says,* " I went once to a certain place in Arabia, almost exactly opposite the city of Buto, to make inquiries concerning the winged serpents. On my arrival I saw the back-bones and ribs of serpents in such numbers as it is impossible to describe ; of the ribs there were a multitude of heaps, some great, some small, some middle-sized. The place where the bones lie is at the entrance of a narrow gorge between steep mountains, which there open upon a spacious plain communicating with the great plains of Egypt. The story goes, that with the spring the snakes come flying from Arabia towards Egypt, but are met in this gorge by the birds called ibises, who forbid their entrance and destroy them all. The Arabians assert, and the Egyptians also admit, that it is on account of the service thus rendered that the Egyptians hold the ibis in so much reverence." He further† describes the winged serpent as being shaped like the water-snake, and states that its wings are not feathered, but resemble very closely those of the bat.

FIG. 37.—THE SYMBOLIC WINGED SERPENT OF THE GODDESS EILEITHYA.
(*After W. R. Cooper.*)

Aristotle briefly states, as a matter of common report, that there were in his time winged serpents in Ethiopia.‡ Both two and four winged snakes are depicted among the Egyptian

* Herodotus, Book ii., chap. lxxv.

† *Ibid.*, Book ii., chap. lxxvi.

‡ *Ibid.*, Book i., chap. v.

sculptures, considered by Mr. Cooper to be emblematic of
deities, and to signify that the four corners of the earth are
embraced and sheltered by the supreme Providence.

Josephus* unmistakably affirms his belief in the existence
of flying serpents, in his account of the stratagem which
Moses adopted in attacking the Ethiopians, who had invaded
Egypt and penetrated as far as Memphis. From this we
may infer that in his time flying serpents were by no means
peculiar to Arabia, but, as might have been expected, equally
infested the desert lands bordering the fertile strip of the Nile.

In Whiston's translation we read that "Moses prevented
the enemies, and took and led his army before those enemies were apprised of his attacking them; for he did not
march by the river, but by land, where he gave a wonderful
demonstration of his sagacity; for when the ground was
difficult to be passed over, because of the multitude of serpents (which it produces in vast numbers, and indeed is
singular in some of those productions, which other countries
do not breed, and yet such as are worse than others in power
and mischief, and an unusual fierceness of sight, some of
which ascend out of the ground unseen, and also fly in the
air, and so come upon men at unawares, and do them a
mischief), Moses invented a wonderful stratagem to preserve
the army safe and without hurt; for he made baskets, like
unto arks, of sedge, and filled them with ibes, and carried
them along with them; which animal is the greatest enemy
to serpents imaginable, for they fly from them when they
come near them; and as they fly they are caught and devoured by them, as if it were done by the harts; but the
ibes are tame creatures, and only enemies to the serpentine
kind; but about these ibes I say no more at present, since
the Greeks themselves are not unacquainted with this sort
of bird. As soon, therefore, as Moses was come to the land,

* *Antiquities of the Jews*, Book ii., chap. x.

which was the breeder of these serpents, he let loose the ibes, and by their means repelled the serpentine kind, and used them for his assistants before the army came upon that ground."

These statements of Herodotus and Josephus are both too precise to be explicable on the theory that they refer to the darting or jumping serpents which Nieuhoff describes, in his day, as infesting the palm trees of Arabia and springing from tree to tree; or to the jaculus of Pliny,* which darts from the branches of trees, and flies through the air as though it were hurled by an engine, and which is described by Ælian and graphically figured by Lucan† in the passage—"Behold! afar, around the trunk of a barren tree, a fierce serpent—Africa calls it the jaculus—wreathes itself, and then darts forth, and through the head and pierced temples of Paulus it takes its flight : nothing does venom there effect, death seizes him through the wound. It was then understood how slowly fly the stones which the sling hurls, how sluggishly whizzes the flight of the Scythian arrow."

Solinus, whose work, *Polyhistor*, is mainly a compilation from Pliny's Natural History, gives a similar account of the swarms of winged serpents about the Arabian marshes, and states that their bite was so deadly that death followed the bite before pain could be felt; he also refers to their destruction by the ibises, and is probably only quoting other authors rather than speaking of his own knowledge.

Cicero, again, speaks of the ibis as being a very large bird, with strong legs, and a horny long beak, which destroys a great number of serpents, and keeps Egypt free from pestilential diseases, by killing and devouring the flying serpents, brought from the deserts of Lybia by the south-west wind, and so preventing the mischief which might

---

* Book viii. chap. xxxv.
† *Pharsalia*, Book ix.

attend their biting while alive, or from any infection when dead.

There are not unfrequent allusions in ancient history to serpents having become so numerous as to constitute a perfect plague ; the dreadful mortality caused among the Israelites by the fiery serpents spoken of in Numbers is a case in point, and another * is the migration of the Neuri from their own country into that of the Budini, one generation before the attack of Darius, in consequence of the incursion of a huge multitude of serpents. It is stated that some of these were produced in their own country, but for the most part they came in from the deserts of the north. The home of the Neuri appears to have been to the northwest of the Pontus Euxinus, pretty much in the position of Poland, and I believe that at the present day the only harmful reptile occurring in it is the viper common to the rest of Europe. Diodorus Siculus† mentions a tradition that the Cerastes had once made an irruption into Egypt in such numbers as to have depopulated a great portion of the inhabited districts.

These stories are interesting as showing a migratory instinct occurring in certain serpents, either periodically or occasionally, and are thus to some extent corroborative of the account of the annual invasion of Egypt by serpents, referred to in a previous page. They also, I think, confirm the impression that serpents were more numerous in the days of early history, and had a larger area of distribution than they have now, and that possibly some species, such as the Arabian and flying serpents, which have since become extinct, then existed. Thus the boa is spoken of by Pliny as occurring commonly in Italy, and growing to such a vast size that a child was found entire in one of them, which was killed on the Vatican Hill during the reign of the

---

* Herodotus, Book iv. chap. cv.        † Book iii. chap. xx.

Emperor Claudius. Yet at the present day there are no snakes existing there at all corresponding to this description.

Parallel instances of invasions of animals materially affecting the prosperity of man are doubtless familiar to my readers, such as the occasional migration of lemmings, passage of rats, flights of locusts, or the ravages caused by the Colorado beetle; but many are perhaps quite unaware what a terrible plague can be established, in the course of a very few years, by the prolific unchecked multiplication of even so harmless, innocent, and useful an animal as the common rabbit. The descendants of a few imported pairs have laid waste extensive districts of Australia and New Zealand, necessitated an enormous expenditure for their extirpation, and have at the present day* caused such a widespread destruc-

---

* "It may be some comfort to graziers and selectors who are struggling, under many discouragements, to suppress the rabbit plague in Victoria, to learn that our condition, bad as it is, is certainly less serious than that of New Zealand. There, not only is an immense area of good country being abandoned in consequence of the inability of lessees to bear the great expense of clearing the land of rabbits, but, owing to the increase of the pest, the number of sheep depastured is decreasing at a serious rate. Three years ago the number exceeded thirteen millions; but it is estimated that they have since been diminished by two millions, while the exports of the colony have, in consequence, fallen off to the extent of £500,000 per annum. A Rabbit Nuisance Act has been in existence for some time, but it is obviously inefficient, and it is now proposed to make its provisions more stringent, and applicable alike to the Government as well as to private landowners. A select committee of both Houses of the Legislature, which has recently taken a large amount of evidence upon this subject, reports in the most emphatic terms its conviction that unless immediate and energetic action is taken to arrest the further extension of, and to suppress the plague, the result will be ruinous to the colony. A perusal of the evidence adduced decidedly supports this opinion. Many of the squatters cannot be accused of apathy. Some of them have employed scores of men, and spent thousands of pounds a year in ineffectual efforts to eradicate the rabbits from their runs. One firm last year is believed to have killed no less than 500,000; but the following spring their run was in as bad a state as if they had never put any poison down.

tion of property in the latter country, that large areas of ground have actually had to be abandoned and entirely surrendered to them.

It is interesting to find in the work of the Arabic geographer El Edrisi a tradition of an island in the Atlantic, called Laca, off the north-west coast of Africa, having been formerly inhabited, but abandoned on account of the excessive multiplication of serpents on it. According to Scaligerus, the mountains dividing the kingdom of Narsinga from Malabar produce many wild beasts, among which may be enumerated winged dragons, who are able to destroy any one approaching their breath.

Megasthenes (*tradente Æliano*) relates that winged serpents are found in India; where it is stated that they are noxious, fly only by night, and that contact with their urine destroys portions of animals.

---

Similar instances of failure could be easily multiplied. It is found, as with us, that one of the chief causes of non-success is the fact that the Government do not take sufficient steps to destroy the rabbits on unoccupied Crown lands. This foolish policy, of course, at once diminishes the letting value of the adjacent pastoral country—to such an extent, indeed, that instances have occurred in which 34,000 acres have been leased for £10 a year. Poison is regarded as the most destructive agent that can be employed, and it is especially effective when mixed with oats and wheat, a striking testimony to the value of Captain Raymond's discovery. Most of the witnesses examined were strongly of opinion that the Administration of the Rabbit Suppression Act should not be left to private and, perhaps, interested persons, as at present, but should be conducted by officers of the Government, probably the sheep inspectors, on a principle similar to that by which the scab was eradicated from the flocks of the colony. The joint committee adopted this view, and also recommended the Legislature to enact that all unoccupied Crown land, as well as all native, reserved, or private land, should bear a proportionate share of the cost of destroying the rabbits, and of administering the act. It is to be hoped that, in the midst of the party conflicts which have so impeded practical legislation this session, the Parliament will yet find time to give effect to the useful recommendations of the Rabbit Nuisance Committee."—*Australasian*, 10th September 1881.

Ammianus Marcellinus (who wrote about the fourth century A.D.) states that the ibis is one among the countless varieties of the birds of Egypt, sacred, amiable, and valuable as storing up the eggs of serpents in his nest for food and so diminishing their number. He also refers to their encountering flocks of winged snakes, coming laden with poison from the marshes of Arabia, and overcoming them in the air, and devouring them before they quit their own region. And Strabo,* in his geographical description of India, speaks of serpents of two cubits in length, with membraneous wings like bats : " They fly at night, and let fall drops of urine or sweat, which occasions the skins of persons who are not on their guard to putrefy." Isaiah speaks of fiery flying serpents, the term " fiery" being otherwise rendered in the Alexandrine edition of the Septuagint by θανατοῦντες " deadly," while the term " fiery" is explained by other authorities as referring to the burning sensation produced by the bite, and to the bright colour of the serpents.† Collateral evidence of the belief in winged serpents is afforded by incidental allusions to them in the classics. Thus Virgil alludes to snakes with strident wings in the line

Illa autem attolit stridentis anguibus alis.‡

Lucan§ refers to the winged serpents of Arabia as forming one of the ingredients of an incantation broth brewed by a Thessalian witch, Erictho, with the object of resuscitating a corpse, and procuring replies to the queries of Sextus, son of Pompey. There are other passages in Ovid and other poets, in which the words " winged serpents" are made use of, but

---

* Book xv. chap. i. § 37.

† See Smith's *Dictionary of the Bible,* p. 145–47.   Murray, 1863.

‡ *Æneid,* Book vii. 561.

§ Non Arabum volucer serpens, innataque rubris
Æquoribus custos pretiosæ vipera conchæ
Aut viventis adhuc Lybici membrana cerastæ.—

*Pharsalia,* Book vi. 677.

which I omit to render here, since from the context it seems doubtful whether they were not intended as poetic appellations of the monster to which, by popular consent, the term dragon has been generally restricted.

I feel bound to refer, although of course without attaching any very great weight of evidence to them, to the numerous stories popular in the East, in which flying serpents play a conspicuous part, the serpents always having something magical or supernatural in their nature. Such tales are found in the entrancing pages of the *Arabian Nights,* or in the very entertaining folk-lore of China, as given to us by Dr. N. P. Dennys of Singapore.*

The latest notice of the flying serpent that we find is in a work by P. Belon du Mans, published in 1557, entitled, *Portraits de quelques animaux, poissons, serpents, herbes et arbres, hommes et femmes d'Arabie, Egypte, et Asie, observés par P. Belon du Mans.* It contains a drawing of a biped winged dragon, with the notice "Portrait du serpent ailé" and the quatrain—

> Dangereuse est du serpent la nature
> Qu'on voit voler près le mont Sinai
> Qui ne serait, de la voir, esbahy,
> Si on a peur, voyant sa pourtraiture?

This is copied by Gesner, who repeats the story of its flying out of Arabia into Egypt.† I attach considerable importance to the short extract which I shall give in a future page from the celebrated Chinese work on geography and natural history, the *Shan Hai King,* or Mountain and Sea Classic. The *Shan Hai King* claims to be of great antiquity, and, as Mr. Wylie remarks, though long looked on with distrust, has been investigated recently by scholars of great

---

* The popular illustrations of the Story of the Black and White Snakes given by him, a favourite story among the Chinese, always represent them as winged. *Folk Lore of China,* N. P. Dennys, Ph.D.

† Broderip, *Zoological Recreations,* p. 333.

ability, who have come to the conclusion that it is at least as
old as the Chow dynasty, and probably older.  Now, as the
Chow dynasty commenced in 1122 B.C., it is, if this latter
supposition be correct, of a prior age to the works of Aristotle,
Herodotus, and all the other authors we have been quoting,
and therefore is the earliest work on natural history extant,
and the description of the flying serpent of the Sien mountains (*vide infrà*) the earliest record of the existence of such
creatures.

### Classical Dragon and Mediæval Dragon.

While the flying serpents of which we have just treated,
will, if we assent to the reality of their former existence,
assist greatly in the explanation of the belief in a winged
dragon so far as Egypt, Arabia, and adjacent countries are
concerned, it seems hardly probable that they are sufficient
to account for the wide-spread belief in it.  This we have
already glanced at ; but we now propose to examine it in
greater detail, with reference to countries so distant from
their habitat as to render it unlikely that their description
had penetrated there.

The poets of Greece and Rome introduce the dragon into
their fables, as an illustration, when the type of power and
ferocity is sought for.  Homer, in his description of the
shield of Hercules, speaks of " The scaly horror of a dragon
coiled full in the central field, unspeakable, with eyes oblique,
retorted, that askant shot gleaming fire."  So Hesiod* (750
to 700 B.C., Grote), describing the same object, says : " On
its centre was the unspeakable terror of a dragon glancing
backward with eyes gleaming with fire.  His mouth, too,
was filled with teeth running in a white line, dread and un-
approachable ; and above his terrible forehead, dread strife

---

* Compare Shakspeare, " Peace, Kent. Come not between the Dragon
and his wrath."

was hovering, as he raises the battle rout. On it likewise were heads of terrible serpents, unspeakable, twelve in number, who were wont to scare the race of men on earth, whosoever chanced to wage war against the son of Jove."

Here it is noteworthy that Hesiod distinguishes between the dragon and serpents.

Ovid* locates the dragon slain by Cadmus in Bœotia, near the river Cephisus. He speaks of it as being hid in a cavern, adorned with crests, and of a golden colour. He, like the other poets, makes special reference to the eyes sparkling with fire, and it may be noted that a similar brilliancy is mentioned by those who have observed pythons in their native condition. He speaks of the dragon as *blue*,† and terribly destructive owing to the possession of a sting, long constricting folds, and venomous breath.

The story of Ceres flying to heaven in a chariot drawn by two dragons, and of her subsequently lending it to Triptolemus, to enable him to travel all over the earth and distribute corn to its inhabitants, is detailed or alluded to by numerous poets, as well as the tale of Medea flying from Jason in a chariot drawn by winged dragons. Ceres‡ is

---

* *Metamorphoses*, Book iii. 35, translated by H. J. Riley ; London, 1872.

† In reference to colours so bright as to be inconsistent with our knowledge of the ordinary colours of reptiles, it may be of interest to compare the description by D'Argensola—who wrote the history of the successive conquests of the Moluccas, by the Spaniards, Portuguese and Dutch—of a blue and golden saurian existing upon a volcanic mountain in Tarnate. "Il y a aussi sur cette montagne un grand lac d'eau douce, entouré d'arbres, dans lequel on voit de crocodiles azurés et dorés qui ont plus d'un brasse de longueur, et qui se plongent dans l'eau lors qu'ils entendent des hommes."—D'Argensola, vol. iii. p. 4, translated from the Spanish, 3 vols. ; J. Desbordes, Amsterdam, 1706. And Pliny, *Nat. Hist.*, Book viii. chap. xxviii., speaks of lizards upon Nysa, a mountain of India, twenty-four feet long, their colour being either yellow, purple, or azure blue.

‡ Ovid, *Fasti*, Book iv. 501.

further made to skim the waves of the ocean, much after the
fashion of mythical personages depicted in the wood-cuts
illustrating passages in the *Shan Hai King*.* Ammianus
Marcellinus, whose history ends with the death of Valerius
in A.D. 378, refers, as a remarkable instance of credulity, to a
vulgar rumour that the chariot of Triptolemus was still
extant, and had enabled Julian, who had rendered himself
formidable both by sea and land, to pass over the walls of,
and enter into the city of Heraclea.  Though rational explanations are afforded by the theory of Bochart and Le Clerc,
that the story is based upon the equivocal meaning of a Phœnician word, signifying either a winged dragon or a ship
fastened with iron nails or bolts ; or by that of Philodorus,
as cited by Eusebius, who says that his ship was called a
flying dragon, from its carrying the figure of a dragon on its
prow ; yet either simply transposes into another phase the
current belief in a dragon, without prejudicing it.

Diodorus Siculus disposes of the Colchian dragon and
the golden-fleeced ram in a very summary manner, as
follows :—

"It is said that Phryxus, the son of Athamas and
Nephele, in order to escape the snares of his stepmother, fled
from Greece with his half-sister Hellen, and that whilst they
were being carried, under the advice of the gods, by the ram
with a golden fleece out of Europe into Asia, the girl acci-
dentally fell off into the sea, which on that account has
been called Hellespont. Phryxus, however, being carried
safely into Colchis, sacrificed the ram by the order of an
oracle, and hung up its skin in a shrine dedicated to
Mars.

"After this the king learnt from an oracle that he would
meet his death when strangers, arriving there by ship,
should have carried off the golden fleece.  On this account,

---

* These wood-cuts occur on pp. 239, 240.

as well as from innate cruelty, the man was induced to offer
sacrifice with the slaughter of his guests; in order that, the
report of such an atrocity being spread everywhere, no one
might dare to set foot within his dominions. He also surrounded the temple with a wall, and placed there a strong
guard of Taurian soldiery; which gave rise to a prodigious
fiction among the Greeks, for it was reported by them that
bulls, breathing fire from their nostrils, kept watch over the
shrine, and that a dragon guarded the skin, for by ambiguity
the name of the Taurians was twisted into that of bulls, and
the slaughter of guests furnished the fiction of the expiation
of fire. In like manner they translated the name of the
prefect Draco, to whom the custody of the temple had been
assigned, into that of the monstrous and horrible creature of
the poets.''

Nor do others fail to give a similar explanation of the
fable of Phryxus, for they say that Phryxus was conveyed in
a ship which bore on its prow the image of a ram, and that
Hellen, who was leaning over the side under the misery of
sea-sickness, tumbled into the water.

Among other subjects of poetry are the dragon which
guarded the golden apples of the Hesperides, and the two
which licked the eyes of Plutus at the temple of Æsculapius
with such happy effect that he began to see.

Philostratus* separates dragons into Mountain dragons and
Marsh dragons. The former had a moderate crest, which
increased as they grew older, when a beard of saffron colour
was appended to their chins; the marsh dragons had no
crests. He speaks of their attaining a size so enormous that
they easily killed elephants. Ælian describes their length
as being from thirty or forty to a hundred cubits; and Posidonius mentions one, a hundred and forty feet long, that
haunted the neighbourhood of Damascus; and another, whose

---

* Broderip, *Zoological Recreations*, p. 332.

lair was at Macra, near Jordan, was an acre in length, and
of such bulk that two men on horseback, with the monster
between them, could not see each other.

Ignatius states that there was in the library of Constantinople the intestine of a dragon one hundred and twenty feet
long, on which were written the *Iliad* and *Odyssey* in letters
of gold. There is no ambiguity in Lucan's* description of
the Æthiopian dragon : " You also, the dragon, shining
with golden brightness, who crawl in all (other) lands as
innoxious divinities, scorching Africa render deadly with
wings ; you move the air on high, and following whole herds,
you burst asunder vast bulls, embracing them with your
folds. Nor is the elephant safe through his size; everything
you devote to death, and no need have you of venom for a
deadly fate." Whereas the dragon referred to by Pliny
(*vide ante*, p. 169), as also combating the elephant, is evidently without wings, and may either have been a very
gigantic serpent, or a lacertian corresponding to the Chinese
idea of the dragon.

Descending to later periods, we learn from Marcellinus†
that in his day dragon standards were among the chief
insignia of the Roman army ; for, speaking of the triumphal
entry of Constantine into Rome after his triumph over Mag-
nentius, he mentions that numbers of the chief officers who
preceded him were surrounded by dragons embroidered on
various points of tissue, fastened to the golden or jewelled
points of spears ; the mouths of the dragons being open so
as to catch the wind, which made them hiss as though they
were inflamed with anger, while the coils of their tails were
also contrived to be agitated by the breeze. And again he
speaks of Silvanus‡ tearing the purple silk from the insignia

---

* Lucan, *Pharsalia*, Book ix. 726–32.
† Book xvi. chap. x.
‡ Book xv. chap. v.; A.D. 355.

of the dragons and standards, and so assuming the title of Emperor.

Several nations, as the Persians, Parthians, Scythians, &c., bore dragons on their standards : whence the standards themselves were called dracones or dragons.

It is probable that the Romans borrowed this custom from the Parthians, or, as Casaubon has it, from the Dacae, or Codin, from the Assyrians; but while the Roman dracones were, as we learn from Ammianus Marcellinus, figures of dragons painted in red on their flags, among the Persians and Parthians they were, like the Roman eagles, figures in relievo, so that the Romans were frequently deceived and took them for real dragons.

The dragon plays an important part in Celtic mythology. Among the Celts, as with the Romans, it was the national standard.

> While Cymri's dragon, from the Roman's hold
> Spread with calm wing o'er Carduel's domes of gold.*

The fables of Merllin, Nennius, and Geoffry describe it as red in colour, and so differing from the Saxon dragon which was white. The hero Arthur carried a dragon on his helm, and the tradition of it is moulded into imperishable form in the *Faerie Queen.* A dragon infested Lludd's dominion, and made every heath in England resound with shrieks on each May-day eve. A dragon of vast size and pestiferous breath lay hidden in a cavern in Wales, and destroyed two districts with its venom, before the holy St. Samson seized and threw it into the sea.

In Celtic chivalry, the word dragon came to be used for chief, a Pendragon being a sort of dictator created in times of danger; and as the knights who slew a chief in battle were said to slay a dragon, this doubtless helped to keep alive the popular tradition regarding the monster which had

---

* Lord Lytton, *King Arthur*, Book i. Stanza 4.

been carried with them westward in their migration from the common Aryan centre.

The Teutonic tribes who invaded and settled in England bore the effigies of dragons on their shields and banners, and these were also depicted on the ensigns of various German tribes.* We also find that Thor himself was a slayer of dragons,† and both Siegfried and Beowulf were similarly engaged in the Niebelungen-lied and the epic bearing the name of the latter.‡ The Berserkers not only named their boats after the dragon, but also had the prow ornamented with a dragon figure-head; a fashion which obtains to the present day among the Chinese, who have an annual *dragon-boat festival,* in which long snaky boats with a ferocious dragon prow run races for prizes, and paddle in processions.

So deeply associated was the dragon with the popular legends, that we find stories of encounters with it passing down into the literature of the Middle Ages; and, like the heroes of old, the Christian saints won their principal renown by dragon achievements. Thus among the dragon-slayers§ we find that—

1. St. Phillip the Apostle destroyed a huge dragon at Hierapolis in Phrygia.

2. St. Martha killed the terrible dragon called Tarasque at Aix (la Chapelle).

3. St. Florent killed a similar dragon which haunted the Loire.

4. St. Cado, St. Maudet, and St. Paul did similar feats in Brittany.

---

* *Chamber's Cyclopædia,* 1881.

† J. Grimm, *Deutsche Mythologie,* vol. ii. p. 653.

‡ A dragon without wings is called a lintworm or lindworm, which Grimm explains to mean a beautiful or shining worm (here again we have a corroboration of the idea of the gold and silver dragon given *ante.*)

§ Brewer's *Dictionary of Phrase and Fable.*

5. St. Keyne of Cornwall slew a dragon.

6. St. Michael, St. George, St. Margaret, Pope Sylvester, St. Samson, Archbishop of Dol, Donatus (fourth century), St. Clement of Metz, killed dragons.

7. St. Romain of Rouen destroyed the huge dragon called La Gargouille, which ravaged the Seine.

Moreover, the fossil remains of animals discovered from time to time, and now relegated to their true position in the zoological series, were supposed to be the genuine remains of either dragons or giants, according to the bent of the mind of the individual who stumbled on them : much as in the present day large fossil bones of extinct animals of all kinds are in China ascribed to dragons, and form an important item in the Chinese pharmacopœia. (*Vide* extract on

Fig. 38.—Skeleton of an Iguanodon.

Dragon bones from the *Pen-tsaou-kang-mu*, given on pp. 244 –246.)

The annexed wood-cut of the skeleton of an Iguanodon, found in a coal-mine at Bernissant, exactly illustrates the semi-erect position which the dragon of fable is reported to have assumed.

Among the latest surviving beliefs of this nature may be cited the dragon of Wantley (Wharncliffe, Yorkshire), who was slain by More of More Hall. He procured a suit of armour studded with spikes, and, proceeding to the well where the dragon had his lair, kicked him in the mouth, where alone he was vulnerable. The Lambton worm is another instance.

The explanations of these legends attempted by mythologists, based on the supposition that the dragons which are their subjects are simply symbolic of natural phenomena, are ingenious, and perhaps in many instances sufficient, but do not affect, as I have before remarked, the primitive and conserved belief in their previous existence as a reality.

Thus, the author of *British Goblins* suggests that for the prototype of the red dragon, which haunted caverns and guarded treasures in Wales, we must look in the lightning caverns of old Aryan fable, and deduces the fire-darting dragons of modern lore from the shining hammer of Thor, and the lightning spear of Odin.

The stories of ladies guarded by dragons are explained on the supposition* that the ladies were kept in the secured part of the feudal castles, round which the walls wound, and that an adventurer had to scale the walls to gain access to the ladies; when there were two walls, the authors of romance said that the assaulter overcame two dragons, and so on. St. Romain, when he delivered the city of Rouen from a dragon which lived in the river Seine, simply pro-

* Rev. Dr. Brewer, *Dictionary of Phrase and Fable*, London.

tected the city from an overflow, just as Apollo (the sun) is symbolically said to have destroyed the serpent Python, or, in other words, dried up an overflow. And the dragon of Wantley is supposed by Dr. Percy to have been an overgrown rascally attorney, who cheated some children of their estates, but was compelled to disgorge by a gentleman named More, who went against him armed with the " spikes of the law," whereupon the attorney died of vexation.

Furthermore, our dragoons were so denominated because they were armed with dragons, that is, with short muskets, which spouted fire like dragons, and had the head of a dragon wrought upon their muzzle.

This fanciful device occurs also among the Chinese, for a Jesuit, who accompanied the Emperor of China on a journey into Western Tartary in 1683, says, " This was the reason of his coming into their country with so great an army, and such vast military preparations; he having commanded several pieces of cannon to be brought, in order for them to be discharged from time to time in the valleys; purposely that the noise and fire, issuing from the mouths of the dragons, with which they were adorned, might spread terror around."

Though dragons have completely dropped out of all modern works on natural history, they were still retained and regarded as quite orthodox until a little before the time of Cuvier; specimens, doubtless fabricated like the ingeniously constructed mermaid of Mr. Barnum, were exhibited in the museums; and voyagers occasionally brought back, as authentic stories of their existence, fables which had percolated through time and nations until they had found a home in people so remote from their starting point as to cause a complete obliteration of their passage and origin.

For instance, Pigafetta, in a report of the kingdom of Congo,* " gathered out of the discourses of Mr. E. Lopes, a

---

* *The Harleian Collection of Travels*, vol. ii. p. 457.   1745.

Portuguese," speaking of the province of Bemba, which he
defines as " on the sea coast from the river Ambrize, until
the river Coanza towards the south," says of serpents,
" There are also certain other creatures which, being as big
as rams, have wings like dragons, with long tails, and long
chaps, and divers rows of teeth, and feed upon raw flesh.
Their colour is blue and green, their skin painted like scales,
and they have *two feet but no more.** The Pagan negroes
used to worship them as gods, and at this day you may see
divers of them that are kept for a marvel. And because they
are very rare, the chief lords there curiously preserve them,
and suffer the people to worship them, which tendeth greatly
to their profits by reason of the gifts and oblations which the
people offer unto them."

And John Barbot, Agent-General of the Royal Company of
Africa, in his description of the coasts of South Guinea,†
says : " Some blacks assuring me that they (*i.e.* snakes)
were thirty feet long. They also told me there are winged
serpents or dragons having a forked tail and a prodigious
wide mouth, full of sharp teeth, extremely mischievous to
mankind, and more particularly to small children. If we
may credit this account of the blacks, they are of the same
sort of winged serpents which some authors tell us are to be
found in Abyssinia, being very great enemies to the elephants.
Some such serpents have been seen about the river Senegal,
and they are adorned and worshipped as snakes are at Wida
or Fida, that is, in a most religious manner."

Ulysses Aldrovandus,‡ who published a large folio volume
on serpents and dragons, entirely believed in the existence of
the latter, and gives two wood engravings of a specimen

---

* The italics are mine.
† Churchill, *Collection of Voyages*, vol. v. p. 213 ; London, 1746.
‡ Ulyssis Aldrovandi *Serpentum et Draconum Historiæ*; Bononiæ,
1640.

which he professes to have received in the year 1551, of a true dried Æthiopian dragon.

He describes it as having two feet armed with claws, and two ears, with five prominent and conspicuous tubercles on the back. The whole was ornamented with green and dusky scales. Above, it bore wings fit for flight, and had a long and flexible tail, coloured with yellowish scales, such as shone on the belly and throat. The mouth was provided with sharp teeth, the inferior part of the head, towards the ears, was even, the pupil of the eye black, with a tawny surrounding, and the nostrils were two in number, and open.

He criticises Ammianus Marcellinus for his disbelief in winged dragons, and states in further justification of his censure that he had heard, from men worthy of confidence, that in that portion of Pistorian territory called Cotone, a great dragon was seen whose wings were interwoven with sinews a cubit in length, and were of considerable width; this beast also possessed two short feet provided with claws like those of an eagle. The whole animal was covered with scales. The gaping mouth was furnished with big teeth, it had ears, and was as big as a hairy bear. Aldrovandus sustains his argument by quotations from the classics and reference to more recent authors. He quotes Isidorus as stating that the winged Arabian serpents were called Sirens, while their venom was so effective that their bite was attended by death rather than pain; this confirms the account of Solinus.

He instances Gesner as saying that, in 1543, he understood that a kind of dragon appeared near Styria, within the confines of Germany, which had feet like lizards, and wings after the fashion of a bat, with an incurable bite, and says these statements are confirmed by Froschonerus in his work on Styria (*idque Froschonerus ex Bibliophila Stirio narrabat*). He classes dragons (which he considers as essentially winged animals) either as footless or possessing two or four feet.

He refers to a description by Scaliger* of a species of serpent four feet long, and as thick as a man's arm, with cartilaginous wings pendent from the sides. He also mentions an account by Brodeus, of a winged dragon which was brought to Francis, the invincible King of the Gauls, by a countryman who had killed it with a mattock near Sanctones, and which was stated to have been seen by many men of approved reputation, who thought it had migrated from transmarine regions by the assistance of the wind.

Cardan† states that whilst he resided in Paris he saw five winged dragons in the William Museum; these were biped, and possessed of wings so slender that it was hardly possible that they could fly with them. Cardan doubted their having been fabricated, since they had been sent in vessels at different times, and yet all presented the same remarkable form. Bellonius states that he had seen whole carcases of winged dragons, carefully prepared, which he considered to be of the same kind as those which fly out of Arabia into Egypt; they were thick about the belly, had two feet, and two wings, whole like those of a bat, and a snake's tail.

It would be useless to multiply examples of the stories, no doubt fables, current in mediæval times, and I shall therefore only add here two of those which, though little known, are probably fair samples of the whole. It is amusing to find the story of Sindbad's escape from the Valley of Diamonds reappearing in Europe during the Middle Ages, with a substitution of the dragon for the roc. Athanasius Kircher, in the *Mundus Subterraneus*, gives the story of a Lucerne man who, in wandering over Mount Pilate, tumbled into a cavern from which there was no exit, and, in searching round, discovered the lair of two dragons, who proved

* Scaliger, lib. iii. Miscell. cap. i. See *ante*, p. 182, " Winged Serpents."
† *De Naturâ Rerum*, lib. vii., cap. 29.

FIG. 39.—THE DRAGONS OF MOUNT PILATE. (*From the "Mundus Subterraneus" of Athanasius Kircher.*)

more tender than their reputation. Unharmed by them he remained for the six winter months, without any other sustenance than that which he derived from licking the moisture off the rock, in which he followed their example. Noticing the dragons preparing for flying out on the approach of spring, by stretching and unfolding their wings, he attached himself by his girdle to the tail of one of them, and so was restored to the upper world, where, unfortunately, the return to the diet to which he had been so long unaccustomed killed him. In memory, however, of the event, he left his goods to the Church, and a monument illustrative of his escape was erected in the Ecclesiastical College of St. Leodegaris at Lucerne. Kircher had himself seen this, and it was accepted as an irrefragable proof of the story.

Another story is an account also given by A. Kircher,[*] of the fight between a dragon and a knight named Gozione, in the island of Rhodes, in the year 1349 A.D. This monster is described as of the bulk of a horse or ox, with a long neck and serpent's head—tipped with mule's ears—the mouth widely gaping and furnished with sharp teeth, eyes sparkling as though they flashed fire, four feet provided with claws like a bear, and a tail like a crocodile, the whole body being coated with hard scales. It had two wings, blue above, but blood-coloured and yellow underneath; it was swifter than a horse, progressing partly by flight and partly by running. The knight, being solicited by the chief magistrate, retired into the country, when he constructed an imitation dragon of paper and tow, and purchased a charger and two courageous English dogs; he ordered slaves to snap the jaws and twist the tail about by means of cords, while he urged his horse and dogs on to the attack. After practising for two months, these latter could scarcely retain their frenzy at the mere sight of the image. He then proceeded to

---

[*] Athanasii Kircheri *Mundus Subterraneus*, Book viii. 27.

Rhodes, and after offering his vows in the Church of St.
Stephen, repaired to the fatal cave, instructing his slaves to
witness the combat from a lofty rock, and hasten to him
with remedies, if after slaying the dragon he should be over-
come by the poisonous exhalations, or to save themselves, in
the event of his being slain. Entering the lair he excited
the beast with shouts and cries, and then awaited it outside.
The dragon appearing, allured by the expectation of an easy
prey, rushed on him, both running and flying; the knight
shattered his spear at the first onset on the scaly carcase, and
leaping from his horse continued the contest with sword and
shield. The dragon, raising itself on its hind legs, endeavoured to grasp the knight with his fore ones, giving the

FIG. 40.—THE DRAGON OF THE DRACHENFELDT. (*Athanasius Kircher.*)

latter an opportunity of striking him in the softer parts of
the neck. At last both fell together, the knight being
exhausted by the fatigue of the conflict, or by mephitic exhalations. The slaves, according to instruction, rushed forward, dragged off the monster from their master, and fetched
water in their caps to restore him; after which he mounted
his horse and returned in triumph to the city, where he was
at first ungratefully received, but afterwards rewarded with

the highest ranks of the order, and created magistrate of the province.*

Kircher had a very pious belief in dragons. He says: "Since monstrous animals of this kind for the most part select their lairs and breeding-places in subterraneous caverns, I have considered it proper to include them under the head of subterraneous beasts. I am aware that two kinds of this animal have been distinguished by authors, the one with, the other without, wings. No one either can or ought to doubt concerning the latter kind of creature, unless perchance he dares to contradict the Holy Scripture, for it would be an impious thing to say it when Daniel makes mention of the divine worship accorded to the dragon Bel by the Babylonians, and after the mention of the dragon made in other parts of the sacred writings."

Harris, in his *Collection of Voyages,*† gives a singular *resumé*. He says:—"We have, in an ancient author, a very large and circumstantial account of the taking of a dragon on the frontiers of Ethiopia, which was one and twenty feet in length, and was carried to Ptolemy Philadelphus, who very bountifully rewarded such as ran the hazard of procuring him this beast.—Diodorus Siculus, lib. iii. . . . Yet terrible as these were they fall abundantly short of monsters of the same species in India, with respect to which St. Ambrose‡ tells us that there were dragons seen in the neighbourhood of the Ganges nearly seventy cubits in length. It was one of this size that Alexander and his army saw in a cave, where it was fed, either out of reverence or from curiosity, by the inhabitants; and the first lightning of its

---

* Probably many of my readers are acquainted with Schiller's poem based on this story, and with the beautiful designs by Retsch illustrating it.

† Harris, *Collection of Voyages*, vol. i. p. 474; London, 1764.

‡ *De Moribus Brachmanorum*, p. 63. Strabo, lib. 16, p. 75. Bochart Hieroz, p. 11, lib. 3, cap. 13.

eyes, together with its terrible hissing, made a strong impression on the Macedonians, who, with all their courage, could not help being frighted at so horrid a spectacle.* The dragon is nothing more than a serpent of enormous size; and they formerly distinguished three sorts of them in the Indies, viz. such as were found in the mountains, such as were bred in caves or in the flat country, and such as were found in fens and marshes.

" The first is the largest of all, and are covered with scales as resplendent as polished gold.† These have a kind of beard hanging from their lower jaw, their eyebrows large, and very exactly arched ; their aspect the most frightful that can be imagined, and their cry loud and shrill;‡ their crests of a bright yellow, and a protuberance on their heads of the colour of a burning coal.

" Those of the flat country differ from the former in nothing but in having their scales of a silver colour,§ and in their frequenting rivers, to which the former never come.

" Those that live in marshes and fens are of a dark colour, approaching to a black, move slowly, have no crest, or any rising upon their heads.‖ Strabo says that the painting them with wings is the effect of fancy, and directly contrary to truth, but other naturalists and travellers both ancient and modern affirm that there are some of these species winged.¶

---

* Ælian, *De Animal.*, lib. xv. cap. 21.

† Strabo, lib. xvi.

‡ Gosse tells us that it is still a common belief in Jamaica that crested snakes exist there which crow like a cock.

§ Strabo, lib. xvi.

‖ Jonston, *Theatr. Animal.*, tome ii. p. 34, " De Serpentibus." Note. —It is interesting to record that in China, to the present day, the tradition of the gold and silver scaled species of dragons remains alive. Two magnificent dragons, 200 feet and 150 feet long, representing respectively the gold and silver dragon, formed part of the processions in Hongkong in December 1881, in honour of the young princes.

¶ Strabo, lib. xvi.

Pliny says their bite is not venomous, other authors deny this. Pliny gives a long catalogue of medical and magical properties, which he ascribes to the skin, flesh, bones, eyes, and teeth of the dragon, also a valuable stone in its head. ' They hung before the mouth of the dragon den a piece of stuff flowered with gold, which attracted the eyes of the beast, till by the sound of soft music they lulled him to sleep, and then cut off his head.' "

I do not find Harris's statement in Diodorus Siculus, the author quoted, but there is the very circumstantial description of a serpent thirty cubits (say forty-five feet) in length, which was captured alive by stratagem, the first attempt by force having resulted in the death of several of the party. This was conveyed to Ptolemy II. at Alexandria, where it was placed in a den or chamber suitable for exhibition, and became an object of general admiration. Diodorus says: " When, therefore, so enormous a serpent was open for all to see, credence could no longer be refused the Ethiopians, or their statements be received as fables ; for they say that they have seen in their country serpents so vast that they can not only swallow cattle and other beasts of the same size, but that they also fight with the elephant, embracing his limbs so tightly in the fold of their coils that he is unable to move, and, raising their neck up underneath his trunk, direct their head against the elephant's eyes ; having destroyed his sight by fiery rays like lightning, they dash him to the ground, and, having done so, tear him to pieces."

In an account of the castle of Fahender, formerly one of the most considerable castles of *Fars*, it is stated—" Such is the historical foundation of an opinion generally prevalent, that the subterranean recesses of this deserted edifice are still replete with riches. The talisman has not been forgotten ; and tradition adds another guardian to the previous deposit, a dragon or winged serpent ; this sits for ever brooding over the treasure which it cannot enjoy."

I shall examine, on a future occasion, how far those figures correspond to the Persian ideas of dragons and serpents, the *azhdaha* (اژدها = dragon) and *már* (مار = snake), which, as various poets relate, are constant guardians of every subterraneous *ganj* (گنج = treasure).

The *már* at least may be supposed the same as that serpent which guards the golden fruit in the garden of the Hesperides.

# CHAPTER VII.

## THE CHINESE DRAGON.

WE now approach the consideration of a country in which the belief in the existence of the dragon is thoroughly woven into the life of the whole nation. Yet at the same time it has developed into such a medley of mythology and superstition as to materially strengthen our conviction of the reality of the basis upon which the belief has been founded, though it involves us in a mass of intricate perplexities in connection with the determination of its actual period of existence.

There is no country so conservative as China, no nation which can boast of such high antiquity, as a collective people permanently occupying the same regions, and preserving records of their polity, manners, and surroundings from the earliest date of their occupation of the territory which still remains the centre of their civilization ; and there is none in which dragon culture has been more persistently maintained down to the present day.

Its mythologies, histories, religions, popular stories, and proverbs, all teem with references to a mysterious being who has a physical nature and spiritual attributes. Gifted with an accepted form, which he has the supernatural power of casting off for the assumption of others, he has the power of influencing the weather, producing droughts or fertilizing rains at pleasure, of raising tempests and allaying them. Volumes could be compiled from the scattered legends which everywhere abound relating to this subject; but as they are, for the most part, like our mediæval legends, echoes of each other, no useful purpose would be served by doing so, and I therefore content myself with drawing, somewhat copiously, from one or two of the chief sources of information.

As, however, Chinese literature is but little known or valued in England, it is desirable that I should devote some space to the consideration of the authority which may be fairly claimed for the several works from which I shall make quotations, bearing on the Chinese testimony of the past existence, and date of existence, of the dragon and other so-called mythical animals.

Incidental comments on natural history form a usual part of every Chinese geographical work, but collective descriptions of animals are rare in the literature of the present, and almost unique in that of the past. We are, therefore, forced to rely on the side-lights occasionally afforded by the older classics, and on one or two works of more than doubtful authenticity which claim, equally with them, to be of high antiquity. The works to which I propose to refer more immediately are the *Yih King*, the *Bamboo Books*, the *Shu King*, the *'Rh Ya*, the *Shan Hai King*, the *Păn Ts'ao Kang Muh*, and the *Yuen Kien Léi Han*.

As it is well known that all the ancient books, with the exception of those on medicine, divination, and husbandry, were ordered to be destroyed in the year B.C. 212 by the Emperor Tsin Shi Hwang Ti, under the threatened penalty for non-compliance of branding and labour on the walls for four years, and that a persecution of the *literati* was commenced by him in the succeeding year, which resulted in the burying alive in pits of four hundred and sixty of their number, it may be reasonably objected that the claims to high antiquity which some of the Chinese classics put forth, are, to say the least, doubtful, and, in some instances, highly improbable.

This question has been well considered by Mr. Legge in his valuable translation of the Chinese Classics. He points out that the tyrant died within three years after the burning of the books, and that the Han dynasty was founded only eleven years after that date, in B.C. 201, shortly after which attempts were commenced to recover the ancient literature. He concludes that vigorous efforts to carry out the edict would not be continued longer than the life of its author— that is, not for more than three years—and that the materials from which the classics, as they come down to us, were compiled and edited in the two centuries preceding the Christian era, were genuine remains, going back to a still more remote period.

## THE "YIH KING" OR "YH KING."

The *Yih King* is one of those books specially excepted from the general destruction of the books. References in it to the dragon are not numerous, and will be found as quotations in the extracts from the large encyclopædia *Yuen Kien Léi Han,* given hereafter. This work has hitherto been very imperfectly understood even by the Chinese themselves, but the recent researches of M. Terrien de la Couperie lead us to suppose that our translations have been imperfect, from the fact that many symbols have different significations in the present day to those which they had in very ancient times, and that a special dictionary of archaic meanings must be prepared before an accurate translation can be arrived at, a consummation which may shortly be expected from his labours. I find in my notes, taken from the manuscript of a lecture given before the Ningpo Book Club in 1870, by the Rev. J. Butler, of the Presbyterian Mission, that " the way in which the dragon came to represent the Emperor and the Throne

of China* is accounted for in the *Yih King* as follows :—
The chief dragon has his abode in the sky, and all clouds
and vapours, winds and rains are under his control. He
can send rain or withhold it at his pleasure, and hence all
vegetable life is dependent on him. So the Emperor, from
his exalted throne, watches over the interests of his people,
and confers on them those temporal and spiritual blessings
without which they would perish." I abstain from dwelling
on this or any other passages in the *Yih King*, pending the
translation promised by M. De la Couperie, the nature of
whose views on it are condensed in the note† attached, being
extracts from his papers on the subject.

---

\* In China the dragon is peculiarly the emblem of imperial power,
as with us the lion is of the kingly. The Emperor is said to be seated
on the dragon throne. A five-clawed dragon is embroidered on the
Emperor's court-robes. It often surrounds his edicts, and the title-
pages of books published by his authority, and dragons are inscribed
on his banners. It is drawn stretched out at full length or curled up
with two legs pointing forwards and two backwards; sometimes holding
a pearl in one hand, and surrounded by clouds and fire.

† The *Yih King*—extracts from papers by Monsieur De la Couperie,
in the *Journal* of the Royal Asiatic Society.

"The *Yih King* is the oldest of the Chinese books, and is the
mysterious classic which requires '*a prolonged attention to make it reveal
its secrets*'; it has peculiarities of style, making it the most difficult of
all the Chinese classics to present in an intelligible version."

"We have multifarious proofs that the writing, first known in China,
was already an old one, partially decayed, but also much improved since
its primitive hieroglyphic stage. We have convincing proofs (*vide* my
'Early History of Chinese Civilization,' pp. 21–23, and the last section
of the present paper) that it had been borrowed, by the early leaders of
the Chinese Bak families [Poh Sing] in Western Asia, from an horizontal writing traced from left to right, the pre-cuneiform character,
which previously had itself undergone several important modifications.

"At that time the Ku-wen was really the phonetic expression of
speech. (By an analysis of the old inscriptions and fragments, and by
the help of the native works on palæography, some most valuable,
I have compiled a dictionary of this period.)

"If the *kwas*, which were a survival of the arrows of divination

THE ANNALS OF THE BAMBOO BOOKS.

These are annals from which a great part of Chinese
chronology is derived.    Mr. Legge gives the history of their

known to the ancestors of Chinese culture before their emigration
eastward," &c. &c.—Vol. xiv. part 4.

"This mysterious book is still avowedly not understood, and we
assist, now-a-days, at a most curious spectacle.    There are not a few
Chinese of education among those who have picked up some knowledge
in Europe or in translations of European works of our modern sciences,
who believe openly that all these may be found in their *Yih*.    Electricity,
steam power, astronomical laws, sphericity of the earth, &c., are all,
according to their views, to be found in the *Yih King*; they firmly
believe that these discoveries were not ignored by their sages, who have
embodied them in their mysterious classics, of which they will be able
to unveil the secrets when they themselves apply to its study a thorough
knowledge of the modern sciences.    It is unnecessary for any European mind to insist upon the childishness of such an opinion.    Even in
admitting, what seems probable, that the early leaders of the Bak people
(Poh Sing) were not without some astronomical and mathematical
principles, which have been long since forgotten, there is no possible
comparison between their rude notions and our sciences.

"It is not a mysterious book of fate and prognostics.    It contains a
valuable collection of documents of old antiquity, in which is embodied
much information on the ethnography, customs, language, and writing
of early China.

"Proofs of various kinds—similitude of institutions, traditions and
knowledge, affinities of words of culture; and, in what concerns the
writing, likenesses of shapes of characters, hieroglyphic and arbitrary,
with the same sounds (sometimes polyphons) and meanings attached to
them, the same morphology of written words, the same phonetic laws of
orthography—had led me, several years ago, to no other conclusion than
that (as the reverse is proved impossible by numerous reasons), at an
early period of their history, and before their emigration to the far
East, the Chinese Bak families had borrowed the pre-cuneiform writing
and elements of their knowledge and institutions from a region connected with the old focus of culture of south-western Asia.

"Numerous affinities of traditions, institutions, and customs, connect
the borrowing of script and culture by the Chinese Bak families with
the region of Elam, the confederation of states of which Susa was the
chief town, and the Kussi the principal population.

"What are the historical facts of this connection we do not know.

discovery, as related in the history of the Emperor Woo, the first of the sovereigns of Tsin, as follows :

" In the fifth year of his reign, under title of Hëen-ning* [=A.D. 279], some lawless parties, in the department of Keih, dug open the grave of King Sëang of Wei [died B.C. 295] and found a number of bamboo tablets, written over, in the small seal character, with more than one hundred thousand words, which were deposited in the imperial library."

Mr. Legge adds, "The Emperor referred them to the principal scholars in the service of the Government, to adjust the tables in order, having first transcribed them in modern characters. Among them were a copy of the *Yih King*, in two books, agreeing with that generally received, and a book of annals, in twelve or thirteen chapters, beginning with the reign of Hwang-te, and coming down to the sixteenth year of the last emperor of the Chow dynasty, B.C. 298."

" The reader will be conscious of a disposition to reject at once the account of the discovery of the Bamboo Books. He has read so much of the recovery of portions of the Shoo from the walls of houses that he must be tired of this

---

Has the break-up which happened in those states and resulted in the conquest of Babylonia by the Elamite king, Kudur Nakhunta, at the date, which is certain, of 2285 B.C., been also the cause of an eastern conquest and a settlement in Bactria ? and would this account for the old focus of culture coeval with the earlier period of Assyrian monarchy said to have existed in Central Asia ?

" The two ethnic names, which, as we have pointed out, were those of the Chinese invaders, Bak and Kutti or Kutta, are not altogether foreign to those regions. The Chinese Kutti and the Kussi, the Chinese Bak and Bakh, the ethnic of Bakhdi (Bactria), will be, most likely, one day proved to be the same ethnic names. Had not the Chinese, previous to my researches, and quite on different reasons, been traced back westerly to the regions of Yarkand and Khotan ? This is not far distant from the old focus of culture of Central Asia, and the connection cannot be objected to by geographical reasons."—Vol. xv. part 2.

* Dr. Williams, *Hien-ning*.

mode of finding lost treasures, and smiles when he is now called on to believe that an old tomb opened and yielded its literary stores long after the human remains that had been laid in it had mingled with the dust. From the death of King Sëang to A.D. 279 were 574 years."

Against this, however, which is not a very weighty objection, if we consider the length of time that Egyptian papyri have been entombed before their restoration to the light, Mr. Legge ranges preponderating evidence in favour of their authenticity, and concludes that " they had, no doubt, been lying for nearly six centuries in the tomb in which they had been first deposited when they were then brought anew to light."

The annals consist of two portions, one forming what is undoubtedly the original text, and consisting of short notices of occurrences, such as, " In his fiftieth year, in the autumn, in the seventh month, on the day Kang shin [fifty-seventh of cycle] phœnixes, male and female, arrived," &c. &c. It also records earthquakes, obituaries, accessions, and remarkable natural phenomena. The other portion is interspersed between these, in the form of rather diffuse, though not very numerous, notes, which by some are supposed to be a portion of the original text, by others, to have been added by the commentator Shin Yo [A.D. 502–557].

In the latter, frequent references are made to the appearance of phœnixes (the *fung wang*), *ki-lins* (unicorns), and dragons.

In the former we find only incidental references to either of these, such as, " XIV. The Emperor K'ung-kea. In his first year (B.C. 1611), when he came to the throne, he dwelt on the west of the Ho. He displaced the chief of Ch'e-wei,* and appointed Lew-luy† to feed the dragons."

---

* Williams, *Shi-Wéi.*
† Williams, *Liu-Léi.*

According to the latter, Hwang Ti (B.C. 2697) had a dragon-like countenance; while the mother of Yaou (B.C. 2356) conceived him by a dragon. The legend is : " After she was grown up, whenever she looked into any of the three Ho, there was a dragon following her. One morning the dragon came with a picture and writing. The substance of the writing was—the Red one has received the favour of Heaven. . . . The red dragon made K'ing-teo pregnant."

Again, when Yaou had been on the throne seventy years, a dragon-horse appeared bearing a scheme, which he laid on the table and went away.

The Emperor Shun (B.C. 2255) is said to have had a dragon countenance.

It is also said of Yu (the first emperor of the Hia dynasty) that when the fortunes of Hia were about to rise, all vegetation was luxuriant, and green dragons lay in the borders ; and that " on his way to the south, when crossing the Kiang, in the middle of the stream, two yellow dragons took the boat on their backs. The people were all afraid ; but Yu laughed, and said, ' I received my appointment from Heaven, and labour with all my strength to nourish men. To be born is the course of nature ; to die is by *Heaven's* decree. Why be troubled by the dragons?' On this the dragons went away, dragging their tails."

From these extracts it will be seen that the dragon, although universally believed in, was already mythical and legendary, so far as the Chinese were concerned.

### The "Shu King"* or "Shoo King"

is, according to Dr. Legge, simply a collection of historic memorials, extending over a space of one thousand seven hundred years, but on no connected method, and with great gaps between them.

---

* Williams, *Shu King.*

It opens with the reign of Yaou (B.C. 2357), and contains interesting details of the polity of those remote ages.

It contains a record of the great inundation occurring during his reign, which Mr. Legge does not identify with the Deluge of Genesis, but which Dr. Gutzlaff and other missionary Sinologues consider to be the same.

It is interesting to find in this work, claiming so high an antiquity, references to an antiquity which had preceded it— a bygone civilization, perhaps—as follows, in the book called *Yih and Ts'ih.** The emperor (Shun, B.C. 2255 to 2205) says, " I wish to see the emblematic figures of the ancients —the sun, the moon, the stars, the mountain, the dragon, and the flowery fowl, which are depicted *on the upper garment* ; the temple cup, the aquatic grass, the flames, the grains of rice, the hatchet, and the symbol of distinction, which are embroidered *on the lower garment.   I wish to see* all these dis- played with the five colours, so as to form the official robes ; it is yours to adjust them clearly." Here the dragon is chosen as an emblematic figure, in association with eleven others, which are objects of every-day knowledge, and this, I think, establishes a presumption that it itself was not at that date considered an object of doubtful credibility.

Similarly, we find the twelve symbolical animals, repre- senting the twelve branches of the Horary characters (dating, see Williams' Dictionary, from B.C. 2637), to be the rat, the ox, tiger, hare, dragon, serpent, horse, sheep, monkey, cock, dog, boar, where the dragon is the only one about whose existence a question can be raised. *From this latter we learn that there was no confusion of meaning then between dragons and serpents* ; the distinction of the two creatures was clearly recognized, just as it was many centuries after- wards by Mencius (4th century B.C.), who, in writing of these early periods, says, " In the time of Yaou, the waters,

---

* Williams, *Yih and Ts'ih.*

flowing out of their channels, inundated the Middle Kingdom. Snakes and dragons occupied it, and the people had
no place where they could settle themselves"; and again,
" Yu dug open their obstructed channels, and conducted
them to the sea. He drove away the snakes and dragons,*
and forced them into the grassy marshes."


### THE "'RH YA."

The *'Rh Ya* or *Urh Ya*,† also transliterated *Eul Ya* and
*Œl Ya*, a dictionary of terms used in the Chinese classics,
but more especially of those in the *Shi King*, or "Book of
Odes," a collection of ancient ballads compiled and arranged
by Confucius.

There is a tradition that it was commenced by the Duke
of Chow 1100 B.C., and completed or enlarged by Tsz Hia,
a disciple of Confucius.

Dr. Bretschneider suggests that each heading or phrase
in the original book merely represents the book names and
the popular names of the plants and animals.

The bulk of the work at present extant consists of the
commentary by Kwoh P'oh (about A.D. 300) and, in some
editions, of additional commentaries by other authors.

The illustrations selected from it for the present volume
are reduced from those in a very fine folio copy, for the loan

---

\* I am under the impression that the dragons to which Mencius
refers were probably alligators, of which one small species still exists,
though rare, in the Yang-tsze-kiang. So also we may regard as alligators
the dragons referred to above in the annals of the Bamboo Books on
the passage of the Kiang by Yu. Mr. Griffis, in his work on Corea,
says, "The creature called *a-ke*, or alligator, capable of devouring a
man, is sometimes found in the largest rivers."

† For a full account of this work, see an Article by E. C. Bridgman
in *Chinese Repository*, xviii. (1849), p. 169; and *Botanicon Sinicum*, by
Dr. E. Bretschneider, in the *Journal* of the North China Branch of the
Royal Asiatic Society, New Series, vol. xvi. 1881.

of which I am indebted to Mr. Thomas Kingsmill, of Shanghai.

These profess to date back so far as the Sung dynasty (A.D. 960 to A.D. 1127), and it is interesting to observe that

FIG. 41.—THE BANNER CALLED TSING K'I.  (*From the 'Rh Ya.*)

the representations of tools of husbandry then in use (Fig. 50, p. 232), and of the methods of hawking (Fig. 46, p. 225), fishing (Fig. 47, p. 227), and the like, are such as might be taken without alteration from those of the present day.

The drawings made by Kwoh P'oh appear to have been lost in the sixth century A.D.

Notices of the dragon only appear incidentally in the *'Rh Ya* as forming part of the decoration of banners, &c. ; but

FIG. 42.—THE K'I WITH BELLS. (*From the 'Rh Ya.*)

descriptions and figures of the Chinese unicorn are given; and of other remarkable animals, of which I shall eventually take notice.

These figures of dragons in the drawings of banners (Figs. 41–44) are especially interesting; as there is fair reason to suppose that they at least have been reproduced

time after time from pre-existing ones with tolerable accuracy; and that they give us a good notion of the general
character of the animal they purport to represent.

I have appended a few *fac-similes* of wood engravings from
the *'Rh Ya* on general subjects, in anticipation of others

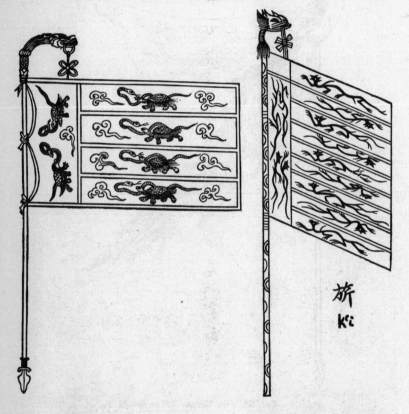

FIG. 43.—THE CHAO BANNER.          FIG. 44.—THE K'I OR KIAO LUNG
    (*From the 'Rh Ya.*)            STANDARD. (*From the San Li Tu.*)

dealing with specialities, which will be found in their
appropriate positions; they will serve to correct the notion
that the Chinese are entirely devoid of artistic power and
imagination (Figs. 46–49).

THE "SHAN HAI KING" OR CLASSIC OF MOUNTAIN AND SEAS.

Short notices of this remarkable work are given by Mr. Alexander Wylie* and Dr. Bretschneider,† and a more exhaustive one by M. Bazin.‡

FIG. 45.—ONE OF THE EAVE TILES FROM THE OLD IMPERIAL PALACE OF NANKIN, showing the Five-clawed or Imperial Dragon, an emblem which cannot be borne by any outside of the Imperial service, under the penalty of death. Commoners have to be satisfied with a four-clawed dragon.

FIG. 46.—RETURN FROM THE CHASE. (*From the 'Rh Ya.*)

* *Notes on Chinese Literature*, A. Wylie, Shanghai and London, 1867.
† "Bot. Sin." in *Journal* of N. China Branch R. A. S., 1881.
‡ *Journal Asiatique*, Extr. No. 17 (1839).

It is also largely quoted by Williams in his valuable Chinese dictionary. Otherwise Sinologues appear to have entirely ignored it.

Mr. Wylie remarks that "it has long been looked upon with distrust; but some scholars of great ability have recently investigated its contents, and come to the conclusion that it is at least as old as the Chow dynasty, and probably of a date even anterior to that period."

M. Bazin speaks of it as a fabulous description of the world, and attributes it to Taouist writers in the fourth century of our era, who forged the authority of the great Yü and Peh Yi. He thinks it would be useless to attempt the identification of the localities given in it, and offers a translation of a portion of the first chapter in support of his views.

The value of his translation is impaired by his making no distinction between the text and the commentary, and he appears to have possessed an inferior and incomplete version.

In an editorial article in the *North China Herald* of May 9, 1884 (presumably by Mr. Balfour, an excellent Sinologue), it is referred to the date of Ch'in Shih Huang, who connected the Heptarchy into a single kingdom, and conquered Cochin China about B.C. 222.

Kwoh Po'h* (A.D. 276–324), who prepared an edition which has descended to us, ascribes a date to it 3,000 years anterior to his time.

Liu Hsiu,* of the Han dynasty (B.C. 206 to A.D. 25), states that the Emperor Yü, the founder of the Hia dynasty (B.C. 2205), employed Yih and Peh Yi as geographers and natural historians, who produced the "Book of Wonders by Land and Sea." While Yang Sun,* of the Ming dynasty

---

* The three prefaces by these authors are given *in extenso* in the Appendix to this Chapter.

Fig. 47.—One Mode of Capturing Fish. (*From the Rh Ya.*)

夏為昊天

FIG. 48.—SUMMER.  (*From the 'Rh Ya.*)

(commencing A.D. 1368), states in his after-preface that the Emperor Yü had nine metal vases cast, on which all wonderful or rare animals were engraved, the commoner ones being recorded in the annals of Yü ; and that K'ung Kiah (of the Hia dynasty, B.C. 1879), included this varied information in the present work.

It is to be hoped that at no distant date some competent Sinologue will be induced to furnish a full translation of this remarkable work, with an adequate commentary.

There is no doubt that many would be deterred from doing so by an impression that a collection of fabulous stories, treating of supernatural beings and apparently impossible monsters, is unworthy the consideration of mature intellect, and only fit to be relegated to the domain of Jack the Giant Killer and other childish stories. After a close examination of the book, I apprehend that this view of it can hardly be maintained. That such stories or descriptions are interspersed throughout the work is not to be disputed ; but a large proportion of it consists of apparently authentic geographical records, including, as is customary with all works of a similar nature in China, descriptions of the most remarkable objects of natural history occurring in the different regions. I think it will be found possible to identify many of these at the present day, some may be conjectured at, and the residue are not more numerous in proportion than the similar fables or perverted accounts which figure in the western classic volumes of Ctesias, Aristotle, Pliny, and even much later writers. So far as the supernatural portions are concerned, it must be remembered that, even so late as the days of the childhood of Sir Humphrey Davy, pixies were still supposed by the lower classes to trace the fairy rings in Cornwall ; that quite lately, and perhaps among certain classes to the present day, the existence of the banshee in Ireland, of the kelpie in Scotland, and of persons gifted with the mysterious and awe-inspiring power of second sight,

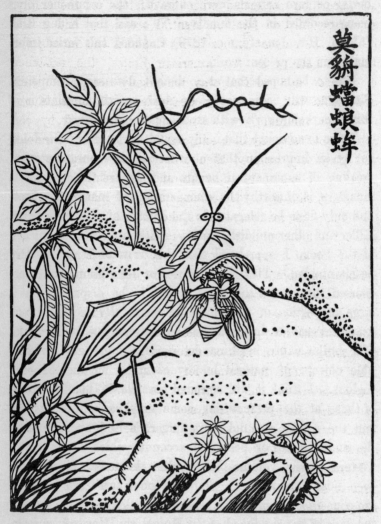

莫貒蟷蜋蛑

FIG. 49.—MANTIS (A VERY CHARACTERISTIC FIGURE).  (*From the 'Rh Ya.*)

was religiously believed in. There are few important
houses in England whose ancestral walls have not concealed
an apparition connected with the destinies of the family,
appearing only on fatal or eventful occasions ; and in the
days of the sapient James I. in England, and among the
Pilgrim Fathers in the American States, the existence
of wizards and witches was universally accepted as an
undeniable fact, proved by hundreds of instances of ex-
torted or voluntary confession, and supplemented by the
concurrent testimony of a still greater number of witnesses
who genuinely believed themselves to have been the spectators or victims of the supernatural powers of the accused.

An historian of these later times might well have described
such things as realities, and we should not be disposed, on
account of his having done so, to question the validity of his
description of other objects or creatures existing at the
period, presuming them to be more consistent with our
present notions of possibility.

No one, now-a-days, would discredit the veracity of Marco
Polo because he speaks of enormous serpents in Carajan,
possessing two feet, each armed with a single claw. That
there was a solid foundation for his story is admitted, and
commentators are only at variance as to whether the basis
was a large species of python, such as still exists in Southern
China, or a gigantic alligator, of which he might have seen
a mutilated specimen.

It must also be borne in mind that the existence of some
gigantic saurian, now extinct, possessing two limbs only, in
place of four, is not an impossibility ; as the small lizard,
Chirotes, is in that condition, and also the North American
genus *Siren*, belonging to the Newts.

I notice that Retzoch, in his designs to illustrate Schiller's
poem, " The Fight with the Dragon," makes the monster
have only two fore-legs, and this appears to have been a
common mediæval conception of it. Aldrovandus and Gesner

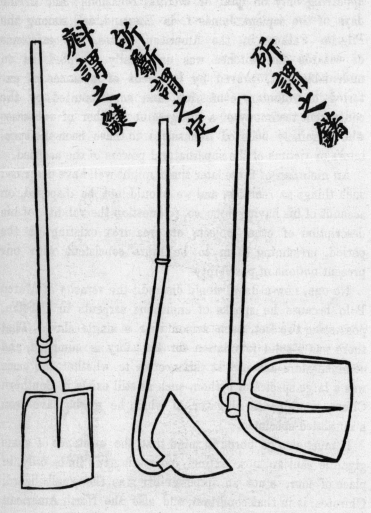

FIG. 50.—TOOLS OF HUSBANDRY. (*From the 'Rh Ya.*)

both give figures of biped dragons. There is also a curious drawing in the *Gentleman's Magazine* for 1749—which is transferred into the pages of the *Encyclopœdia of Philadelphia*, apparently a piracy of an English Cyclopædia, of what is styled a sea-dragon, four feet long, which stands bolt upright on two legs, and, like Barnum's mermaid, was probably a triumph of art.

Aldrovandus was probably imposed on by some waggish friend, in reference to the biped dragon without wings, two cubits long, which was said to have been killed by a countryman near Bonn in 1572 A.D., and which he first figured and

FIG. 51.—DRACO BIPES APTEROS CAPTUS IN AGRO BONONIENSI. (*Aldrovandus*).

then placed in his museum; and he evidently fully believed in the Ethiopian winged biped dragon, of which he gives two figures, but without quoting his authority.

FIG. 52.—DRACO ÆTHIOPICUS. (*Aldrovandus*.

Gesner gives a similar figure, after Belon, of the winged dragon of Mount Sinai; but Athanasius Kircher is more liberal, and gives his dragon not only wings but four legs.

FIG. 53.—THE FOUR-FOOTED WINGED DRAGON. (*Kircher.*)

In poetry we find Ashtaroth described as appearing to Faust in the form of a serpent with two little feet.

As to the mysterious powers imputed throughout the *Shan Hai King* to different creatures, of controlling drought, rain, and fire, or acting, when partaken of, as remedies for sundry ills and ailments, it may be asked whether we ourselves are free from analogous superstitious beliefs? Will a sailor view without uneasiness the destruction of a Mother Carey's chicken, or a Dutchman, of a stork? Or is the Chinese pharmacopœia of the present day much more trustworthy as to many of its items?

As to the human-visaged creatures, both snakes and four-footed beasts, may we not perhaps put them on a par with other fancied resemblances, which hold to the present day, of (for example) the hippopotamus, to a river-horse, of the pipe-fish, known as the hippocampus, to a sea-horse; of the manatee to a merman, and the like?

And, lastly, are the composite creatures, partly bird and partly reptilian, occasionally referred to, so entirely incredible? Is it not barely possible that some of those intervening types which we know from the teaching of Darwin, must have existed; which we know, from the researches of palæontology have existed; types intermediate to the *Struthionidæ*, the most reptilian of birds, and the *Chlamydæ*, the most avian of reptiles—is it not possible that some of these may have continued their existence down to a late date, and that the tradition of these existing as the descendants or the analogues of the Archæopteryx, and the toothed birds of America, may be embalmed in the pages in question? Is it impossible? Do not the Trigonias, the Terebratulas, the Marsupials, and, in part, the vegetation of Australia, form the spare surviving descendants of the forms which characterised the oolitic period on our own shores? Why, then, may not a few cretaceous and early tertiary forms have struggled on, through a happy combination of circumstances, to an aged and late existence in other lands.

After long, repeated, and careful examination of the *Shan Hai King*, I arrive at a very different conclusion from M. Bazin. I hold it to be an authentic and precious memorial which has been handed down to us from remote antiquity, the value of which has been unrecognised owing to the book being unfortunately a fusion of two and perhaps three distinct works.

Fig. 54.—THE PA SNAKE. (*From the Shan Hai King.*)

The oldest was the *Shan King*, and consists of five volumes, devoted respectively to the northern, southern, eastern, western, and central mountain ranges. This is devoid of all reference to persons and habited places. It is simply an abstract of the results of a topographical survey which may not impossibly have been, as it claims, the one conducted by Yü.

It contains lists of mountains and rivers, with valuable notes on their mineral productions, fauna and flora. It also gives lists of the divinities controlling or belonging to each mountain range, and the sacrifices suitable to them. There are few extravagances in this portion of the work.

The remainder is devoted to a history of the regions without and within the four *hai* or seas bounding the empire, and those constituting what is called the Great Desert. Here extravagant stories, myths, accounts of wonderful people, references to states, cities, and tribes are mingled with geographical notices which, from their repetition, show that this portion is itself resolvable into two distinct works of more modern date, whose origin was probably posterior to the wave of Taouist superstition which swept over China in the first six centuries of our era. I must add that the term, "within the four seas" does not imply the arrogant belief, as is generally supposed, that this Empire extended to the ocean on every side, the archaic meaning being the very different one of frontier or boundary region; while the word "desert" has a similar signification.

In that more credible portion of the work which I believe to have been the original *Shan King*, references to dragons are infrequent. In some instances the *kiao* (which I interpret as the gavial) is specifically referred to; in others the word *lung* is used; thus, it speaks of dragons and turtles abounding in the Ti River, flowing from one of the northern mountains east of the Ho. From the context, however, an aquatic creature, 'and probably an alligator, is indicated.

Fig. 55.—Flying Snakes from the Sien Mountains (Central Mountains).
(*Shan Hai King.*)

From the entire text I gather that the true terrestrial dragon was not an inmate of China, at all events after the period of Yü.  I further infer that it was a feared and much respected denizen of the more or less arid highlands, whence the early Chinese either migrated or were driven, and from which point the dragon traditions flowed pretty evenly east and west, beat against the Himalayan chain on the south, and only penetrated India in a later and modified form.

There is a short reference to the Ying Lung or winged dragon; it is as follows :—

" In the north-east corner of the Great Desert are mountains called Hiung-li and T'u K'iu.  The Ying Lung lives at the south extremity.

" [Commentary.—The Ying Lung is a dragon with wings.]

" He killed Tsz Yiu and Kwa Fu.

" [Commentary.—Tsz Yiu was a soldier.]

" He could not ascend to heaven.

" [Commentary.—The Ying Lung dwells beneath the earth.]

" So there is often drought.

" [Commentary.—Because no rain was made above.]

" When there is a drought, the form of the Ying dragon is made, and then there is much rain.

" [Commentary.—Now the false dragon is for this purpose, to influence (the heaven); men are not able to do it.]"

The better printed copies of this work are illustrated with a very truculent-looking dragon with outspread wings.  A stone delineation of a dragon with wings forms the ornamentation of the bridge at Nincheang Foo.  In the interior of China, it was observed by Mr. Cooper, and is given in his *Travels of a Pioneer of Commerce*.  These are the only cases in China in which I have come across illustrations of dragons with genuine wings.  As a rule, the dragon appears to be represented as having the power of translating itself without mechanical agency, sailing among the clouds, or rising from the sea at pleasure.

Fig. 65.—Ping I (Icy Exterminator), a River Divinity (?). From within the Sea and North. (*Shan Hai King.*)

FIG. 57.—THE EMPEROR K'I, OF THE HIA DYNASTY. From without the Sea and West. (*Shan Hai King.*)

The *Shan Hai King* contains valuable notices of winged snakes and gigantic serpents, as, for example, the so-called singing snakes. Speaking of the Sien mountain (one of the Central Mountains), it says : " Gold and jade abound. It is barren. The Sien river issues and flows north into the I river. On it are many singing snakes. They look like snakes, but have four wings. Their voice is like the beating of stones. When they appear there will be great drought in the city."

FIG. 58.—YÜ KIANG (A GOD). Without the Sea and North. (*Shan Hai King.*)

The Pa snake, already spoken of, is described as capable of gorging an elephant. The Ta Hien mountains were reputed uninhabitable on account of the presence of gigantic serpents (pythons ?), which were said to have been of the colour of mugwort, to have possessed hairs like pig's bristles projecting between the lines of their riband-like markings. Rumour had magnified their length to one hundred fathoms, and they made a noise like the beating of a drum or the striking of a watchman's wooden clapper. The Siong Jan mountains were infested by serpents, also gigantic, but of a different species.

The annexed wood-cuts (Figs. 56, 57) of Ping I (Icy exterminator), and the Emperor K'i (B.C. 2197), each in cars, driving two dragons, are interesting in connection

with the later fable of Medea and Triptolemus. The two
stories were probably derived from a common source; the
Chinese version, however, being much the older of the two.

FIG. 59.—THE TYPHOON DRAGON.
*(From a Chinese Painting.)*

The text as to K'i is :—
" K'i of the Hia dynasty
danced with Kiutai at the
Tayoh common. He drove
two dragons. The clouds
overhung in three layers.
In his left hand he
grasped a screen; in his
right hand he held ear ornaments; at his girdle
dangled jade crescents. It
is north of Tayun mount;
one author calls it Tai
common." The commen-
tator says Kiutai is the
name of a horse, and
" dance " means to dance
in a circle. [Probably this is the earliest reference extant
to a circus performance.]

Ping I is supposed to dwell in Tsung Ki pool near the
fairy region of Kwa-Sun, to have a human face, and to
drive two dragons.

Cursorily examined, the *Shan Hai King* is a farrago of falsehood; read with intelligence, it is a mine of historical wealth.

### THE PAN TSAO KANG MU.*

Descending to late times, we have the great Chinese
Materia Medica, in fifty-two volumes, entitled *Păn Tsao Kang*

---

* The reader is referred, for a careful *précis* of the contents of this
valuable work, to an exhaustive paper entitled " Botanicon Sinicum,"
in the *Journal* of North China Branch Royal Asiatic Society, 1881, by
E. Bretschneider, M.D.

*Mu,* made up of extracts from upwards of eight hundred preceding authors, and including three volumes of illustrations by Li Shechin, of the Ming dynasty (probably born early in the sixteenth century A.D.). It was first printed in the Wăn-leih period (1573 to 1620). I give its article upon the dragon *in extenso.*

" According to the dictionary of Hü Shăn, the character *lung* in the antique form of writing represents the shape of the animal. According to the *Shang Siao Lun,* the dragon is deaf, hence its name of *lung* (deaf). In Western books the dragon is called *nake* (*naga*). Shi-Chăn says that in the 'Rh Ya Yih of Lo-Yuen the dragon is described as the largest of scaled animals (literally, insects). Wang Fu says that the dragon has nine (characteristics) resemblances. Its head is like a camel's, its horns like a deer's, its eyes like a hare's,* its ears like a bull's, its neck like a snake's, its belly like an iguanodon's (?), its scales like a carp's, its claws like an eagle's, and its paws like a tiger's. Its scales number eighty-one, being nine by nine, the extreme (odd or) lucky number. Its voice resembles the beating of a gong. On each side of its mouth are whiskers, under its chin is a bright pearl, under its throat the scales are reversed, on the top of its head is the *poh shan,* which others call the wooden foot-rule. A dragon without a foot-rule cannot ascend the skies. When its breath escapes it forms clouds, sometimes changing into rain, at other times into fire. Luh Tien in the *P'i Ya* remarks, when dragon-breath meets with damp it becomes bright, when it gets wet it goes on fire. It is extinguished by ordinary fire.

" The dragon comes from an egg, it being desirable to keep it folded up. When the male calls out there is a breeze above, when the female calls out there is a breeze below, in

---

* The character for a hare is very like the character for a devil. The Japanese, in quoting this passage, have fallen into this error.

consequence of which there is conception. The *Shih Tien* states, when the dragons come together they are changed into two small serpents. In the *Siao Shwoh* it is said that the disposition of the dragon is very fierce, and it is fond of beautiful gems and jade (?). It is extremely fond of swallow's flesh; it dreads iron, the *mong* plant, the centipede, the leaves of the Pride of India, and silk dyed of different (five) colours. A man, therefore, who eats swallow's flesh should fear to cross the water. When rain is wanted a swallow should be offered (used); when floods are to be restrained, then iron ; to stir up the dragon, the *mong* plant should be employed; to sacrifice to *Küh Yuen*, the leaves of the Pride of India bound with coloured silk should be used (see Mayers, p. 107, § 326) and thrown into the river. Physicians who use dragons' bones ought to know the likes and dislikes of dragons as given above."

" *Dragons' Bones.*\*—In the *Pieh luh* it is said that these are found in the watercourses in Tsin (Southern Shansi) and in the earth-holes which exist along the banks of the streams running in the caves of the T'ai Shan (Great Hill), Shantung. For seeking dead dragons' graves there is no fixed time. Hung King says that now they are largely found in Leung-yih (in Shansi ?) and Pa-chung (in Sz-chuen). Of all the bones, dragon's spine is the best; the brains make the white earth *striæ*, which when applied to the tongue is of great virtue. The small teeth are hard, and of the usual appearance of teeth. The horns are hard and solid. All the dragons cast off their bodies without really dying. Han says the dragon-bones from Yea-cheu, Ts'ang-

---

\* The dragons' bones sold by apothecaries in China consist of the fossilized teeth and bones of a variety of species, generally in a fragmentary condition. The white earth striæ, or dragons' brains, here referred to, are probably asbestos. The asbestos sold in Chefoo market, under the name of Lung Ku or dragons' bones, is procured at O-tzu-kung.

cheu and T'ai-yuen (all in Shansi) are the best. The smaller bones marked with wider lines are the female dragon's; the rougher bones with narrower lines are those of the male dragon; those which are marked with variegated colours are esteemed the best. Those that are either yellow or white are of medium value; the black are inferior. If any of the bones are impure, or are gathered by women, they should not be used.

"P'u says dragons' bones of a light white colour possess great virtue. Kung says the bones found in Tsin (South Shansi) that are hard are not good; the variegated ones possess virtue. The light, the yellow, the flesh-coloured, the white, and the black, are efficacious in curing diseases in the internal organs having their respective colours, just as the five varieties of the *chi*\* plant, the five kinds of lime-stone, and the five kinds of mineral oil (literally, fat), which remain still for discussion in this work.

"Su-chung states: 'In the prefecture of Cheu kiün, to the "East of the River" (Shansi), dragons' bones are still found in large quantities.'

"Li-chao, in the *Kwoh-shi-pu*, says: 'In the spring floods the fish leap into the Dragon's Gate, and the number of cast-off bones there is very numerous. These men seek for medicinal purposes. They are of the five colours. This Dragon's Gate is in Tsin (Shansi), where this work (*Kwoh-shi-pu*) is published. Are not, then, these so-called dragons' bones the bones of fish?'

"Again, quoting from Sun Kwang-hien in the *Poh-mung Legends*: 'In the time of the five dynasties there was a contest between two dragons; when one was slain, a village hero, Kw'an, got both its horns. In the front of the horns was an object of a bluish colour, marked with confused lines,

---

\* The *boletus*, supposed to possess mystic efficacy.

which no one knew anything about, as the dragon was completely dead.'

" Tsung Shih says : ' All statements [concerning dragons' bones] disagree ; they are merely speculations, for when a mountain cavern has disclosed to view a skeleton head, horns and all, who is to know whether they are *exuviæ* or that the dragon has been killed ?  Those who say they are *exuviæ*, or that the dragon is dead, then have the form of the animal, but have never seen it alive.  Now, how can one see the thing (as it really is) when it is dead?  Some also say that it is a transformation, but how is it only in its appearance that it cannot be transformed ? '

" Ki, in the present work, says that they are really dead dragons' bones ; for one to say that they are *exuviæ* is a mere speculation.

" Shi Chǎn says : ' The present work considers that these are really dead dragons' bones, but To Shi thinks they are *exuviæ*.  Su and Kan doubt both these statements. They submit that dragons are divine beings, and resemble the principle of immortality (never-in-themselves-dying principle) ; but there is the statement of the dragon fighting and getting killed ; and further, in the *Tso-chw'en*, in which it is stated that there was a certain rearer of dragons who pickled dragons for food [for the imperial table ?].'

" The *I-ki* says : ' In the time of the Emperor Hwo, of the Han dynasty, during a heavy shower a dragon fell in the palace grounds, which the Emperor ordered to be made into soup and given to his Ministers.'

" The *Poh-wuh-chi* states that a certain Chang Hwa ' got dragon's flesh to dry, for it is said that when seasoning was applied the five colours appeared, &c.  These facts prove that the dragon does die, an opinion which is considered correct by [the writers of] the present work.' "

### The Yuen Kien Lei Han.

This is an encyclopædia in four hundred and fifty books or volumes, completed in 1710. More than eighty pages are devoted to the dragon. These, with all similar publications in China, consist entirely of extracts from old works, many of which have perished, and of which fragments alone remain preserved as above.

I have had the whole of this carefully translated, but think it unnecessary to trouble the reader, in the present volume, with more than the first chapter, which I give in the Appendix. There is also a description of the Kiao, of which I give extracts in the Appendix, together with others relating to the same creature, and to the T'o lung, from the *Păn Tsao Kang Mu.*

FIG. 60.—VIGNETTE. (*After Hokŭsai.*)

# CHAPTER VIII.

### THE JAPANESE DRAGON.

THERE is but little additional information as to the dragon to be gained from Japan, the traditions relating to it in that country having been obviously derived from China. In functions and qualities it is always represented as identical with the Chinese dragon. In Japan, however, it is invariably figured as possessing three claws, whereas in China it has four or five, according as it is an ordinary or an imperial emblem. The peasantry are still influenced by a belief in its supernatural powers, or in those of some large or multiple-headed snake, supposed to be a transformation of it, and to be the tenant of deep lakes or of springs issuing from mountains.

I give, as examples of dragon stories, two selected from the narratives of mythical history,* and one extracted from a native journal of the day.

---

* The first two stories are from the *Ko Ku Shi Riyăh*, a recent history of Japan, from the earliest periods down to the present time, by Matsunai, with a continuation by a later author. They are contained in

The first states that "Hi-koho-ho-da-mi no mikoto (a god) went out hunting, and his eldest brother Hono-sa-su-ri no mikoto went out fishing. They were very successful, and proposed to one another to change occupations. They did so.

"Hono-sa-su-ri no mikoto went out to the mountain hunting, but got nothing, therefore he gave back his bow and arrow; but Hi-ko-hoho-da-mi no mikoto lost his hook in the sea; he therefore tried to return a new one, but his brother would not receive it, and wanted the old one; and the mikoto was greatly grieved, and, wandering on the shore, met with an old man called Si-wo-tsu-chino-gi, and told him what had happened.

"The latter made a cage called mé-na-shi.kogo, enclosed him in it, and sank it to the bottom of the sea. The mikoto proceeded to the temple of the sea-god, who gave him a girl, Toyotama, in marriage. He remained there three years, and recovered the hook which he had lost, as well as receiving two pieces of precious jade called ' ebb ' and ' flood.' He then returned. After some years he died. His son, Hi-ko-na-gi-sa-ta-k'e-ouga-ya-fu-ki-ayā-dzu no mikoto, succeeded to the crown.

"When his father first proposed to return, his wife told him that she was *enciente*, and that she would come out to the shore during the rough weather and heavy sea, saying, ' I hope you will wait until you have completed a house for my confinement.' After some time Toyotama came there and begged him never to come to her bed when she was sleeping. He, however, crept up and peeped at her. He saw a dragon holding a child in the midst of its coils. It suddenly jumped up and darted into the sea."

the first chapter of the first volume. The third is given as an ordinary item of news in the journal called the *Chin-jei-Nippo*, April 30th, 1884.

Fig. 61.—Japanese Dragon (in Bronze).

The second legend is : " When the So-sa-no-o no mikoto went to the sources of the river Hi-no-ka-mi at Idzumo, he heard lamentations from a house; he therefore approached it and inquired the cause. He saw an old man and woman clasping a young girl. They told him that in that country there was a very large serpent, which had eight\* heads and eight tails, and came annually and swallowed one person. ' We had eight children, and we have already lost seven, and now have only one left, who will be swallowed; hence our grief.' The mikoto said, ' If you will give that girl to me, I will save her.' The old man and woman were rejoiced. The mikoto changed his form, and assumed that of the young girl. He divided the room into eight partitions, and in each placed one saki tub and waited its approach. The serpent arrived, drank the saki, got intoxicated, and fell asleep.

" Then the mikoto drew his sword and cut the serpent into small pieces. When he was cutting the tail his sword was a little broken; therefore he split open the tail to find the reason, and found in it a valuable sword, and offered it to the god O-mi-ka-mi, at Taka-maga-hara.

" He called the sword Ama no mourakoumo no tsurogi,† because there was a cloud up in the heaven where the serpent lies. Finally he married the girl, and built a house at Suga in Idzumo."

The third story runs as follows :—

### The White Dragon.

" There is a very large pond at the eastern part of Fu-si-mī-shi-ro-yama, at Yama-shiro (near Kioto); it is called

---

\* The idea of the eight heads probably originated in China; thus, in the caves in Shantung, near Chi-ning Chou, among carvings of mythological figures and divinities, dating from A.D. 147, we find a tiger's body with eight heads, all human.

† *Mourakoumo* means " clouds of clouds "; *ama* means " heaven "; *tsurogi* means " sword."

Ukisima. In the fine weather little waves rise up on account of its size. There are many turtles in it. In the summer-time many boys go to the pond to swim, but never go out into the middle or far from the shore. No one is aware how deep the centre of the pond is, and it is said that a white dragon lives in that pond, and can transform itself into a bird, which the people of the district call O-gon-cho, *i.e.* golden bird, because, when it becomes a bird, it has a yellow plumage. The bird flies once in fifty years, and its voice is like the howling of a wolf. In that year there is famine and pestilence, and many people die. Just one hundred years ago, when this bird flew and uttered its cry, there was a famine and drought and disease, and many people died. Again, at Tempo-go-nen (*i.e.* in the fifth year of Tempo), fifty years back from the present time, the bird flew as before, and there was once again disease and famine. Hence the people in that district were much alarmed, as it is now just fifty years again. They hoped, however, that the bird would not fly and cry. But at 2 A.M. of the 19th April it is said that it was seen to do so. The people, therefore, were surprised, and now are worshipping God in order to avert the famine and disease. The old farmers say, in the fine weather the white dragon may occasionally be seen floating on the water, but that if it sees people it sinks down beneath the surface." *

As a pendant to this I now quote a memorial from the *Pekin Gazette* of April 3rd, 1884, of which a translation is given in the *North China Herald* for May 16th, 1884.

" A Postscript Memorial of P'an Yü requests that an additional title of rank, and a tablet written by His Majesty's

---

* White snakes are occasionally, although rarely, seen in Japan. They are supposed to be messengers from the gods, and are never killed by the people, but always taken and carried to some temple. The white snake is worshipped in Nagasaki at a temple called Miyo-ken, at Nishi-yama, which is the northern part of the city of Nagasaki.

own hand, may be conferred on a dragon spirit, who has manifested himself and answered the prayers made to him.

" In the Ang-shan mountains, a hundred *li* from the town of Kuei-hai, there are three wells, of which one is on the mountain top, in a spot seldom visited. It has long been handed down that a dragon inhabits this well. If pieces of metal are thrown into the well they float, but light things, as silk or paper, will sink. If the offerings are accepted, fruits come floating up in exchange. Anything not perfectly pure and clean is rejected and sent whirling up again. The spirit dwells in the blackest depths of the water, in form like a strange fish, with golden scales and four paws, red eyes and long body. He ordinarily remains deep in the water without stirring. But in times of great drought, if the local authorities purify themselves, and sincerely worship him, he rises to the top. He is then solemnly conveyed to the city, and prayers for rain are offered to him, which are immediately answered. His temple is in the district city, on the To'ang-hai Ling. The provincial and local histories record that tablets to him have been erected from the times of the Mongol and the Ming dynasties. During the present dynasty, on several occasions, as, for instance, in the years 1845 and 1863, he has been carried into the city, and rain has fallen immediately. Last year a dreadful drought occurred, in which the ponds and tanks dried up, to the great terror of the people. On the 15th day of the eighth month, the magistrate conducted the spirit into the city, and, with the assembled multitude, prayed to him fervently ; thereupon a gentle rain, falling throughout the country, brought plenty in the place of scarcity, and gladdened the hearts of all. At about the same time, the people of a district in the vicinity, called Chin-yü, also had recourse to the spirit, with equally favourable results. These are well-known events, which have happened quite recently.

" It is the desire of the people of the district that some
mark of distinction should be conferred on the spirit ; and
the memorialist finds such a proceeding to be sanctioned both
by law and precedent ; he therefore humbly lays the wishes
of the people before His Majesty, who, perhaps, will be
pleased to confer a title and an autograph tablet as above
suggested.   The Rescript has already been recorded.

" No. 6 of Memorial."

The idea of the transformation of a sea-monster or dragon
into a bird is common both to China and Japan; for instance,
in *The Works of Chuang Tsze*, ch. i. p. 1, by F. H. Balfour,
F.R.G.S., we read that—

" In the Northern Sea there was a fish, whose name was
*kw'ên*.   It is not known how many thousand *li* this fish was
in length.   It was afterwards transformed into a bird called
*p'êng*, the size of whose back is uncertain by some thousands
of *li*.   Suddenly it would dart upwards with rapid flight, its

FIG. 62.—THE HAI RIYO.   (*Chi-on-in Monastery, Kioto.*)

wings overspreading the sky like clouds. When the waters were agitated [in the sixth moon] the bird moved its abode to the Southern Sea, the Pool of Heaven. In the book called *Ts'i Hieh*, which treats of strange and marvellous things, it is said that when the *p'êng* flew south, it first rushed over three thousand *li* of water, and then mounted to the height of ninety thousand *li*, riding upon the wind that blows in the sixth moon. The wild horses, *i.e.* the clouds and dust of heaven, were driven along by the zephyrs. The colour of the sky was blue; yet, is that the real colour of the sky, or only the appearance produced by infinite, illimitable depths? For the bird, as it looked downwards, the view was just the same as it is to us when we look upwards."

On the screens decorating the Chi-on-in monastery in Kioto, are depicted several composite creatures, half-dragon, half-bird, which appear to represent the Japanese rendering of the Chinese Ying Lung or winged dragon. They have dragons' heads, plumose wings, and birds' claws, and have been variously designated to me by Japanese as the *Hai Riyo* (Fig. 62), the *Tobi Tatsu*, and the *Schachi Hoko*.

FIG. 63.—JAPANESE DRAGON (BRONZE)

Fig. 64.

## Conclusion of Dragon Chapters.

The numerous quotations given in the above pages, or
in the Appendix, are merely a selection; and by no means
profess to be so extensive as they should be were this work
a monograph on the dragon alone. Having a special object
in view, I have forborne to diverge into those interesting
speculations which relate to its religious significance; these
I leave to those who deal specially with this portion of its
history. I therefore pass over the many traditions and
legends regarding it contained in the pages of the *Memoirs of
Hiouen-Thsang,** of *Foĕ Kouĕ Ki,*† and similar narratives, and

---

* *Mémoires sur les Contrées occidentales, traduits du Sanscrit en Chinois
en l'an 648 ; et du Chinois en Francais,* par M. Stanislas Julien. 2 vols.,
Paris, 1857.

† *Foĕ Kouĕ Ki, ou Relation des Royaumes Bouddhiques,* par Chĕ Fa

omit quoting folk-lore from the pages of Dennys, Eitel, and others who have written on the subject.

For my purpose it would be profitless to collate legends such as that given in the Apocrypha, in the story of Bel and the Dragon, and reappearing in the pages of El Edrisi as an Arab legend, with Alexander the Great as the hero, and the Canaries as the scene, or to dwell on the Corean and Japanese versions of dragon stories, which are merely borrowed, and corrupted in borrowing, from the Chinese. Nor shall I do more than allude to the fact that dragons are represented in the Brahminical caves at Ellora, and among the sculptures of Ancoar Wat in Cambodia.

FIG. 65.

The rude diagrams, Figs. 64, 65, 66, are facsimiles from a manuscript of folio size in the possession of J. Haas, Esq., Imperial Austro-Hungarian Vice-Consul for Shanghai, which he kindly placed at my disposal. This unique volume is at present, unfortunately, unintelligible. It comes from the western confines of China, and is believed to be an example of the written Lolo language, that is, of

---

*Hien.* Translated from the Chinese by M. Abel Remusat; Paris, 1836. This volume contains a number of very interesting dragon legends, and quaint conceits about them; but I find nothing in it to supplement my materialistic argument.

the language of the aboriginal tribes of China. They suffice
to show that the same respect for the dragon is shown among
these people as in China; but no opinion can be offered
as to whether this belief and respect is original or imported,
until their literature has been examined.

Fɪɢ. 66.

I regret that I am unable to give in this volume, as I had
wished, an account of the Persian dragon, which, I am
informed, is contained in a rare Persian work.

In conclusion, I must hope that the reader who has had
the patience to wade through the medley of extracts which I
have selected, and to analyse the suggestive reasoning of the
introductory chapters, will agree with me that there is
nothing impossible in the ordinary notion of the traditional
dragon; that such being the case, it is more likely to have
once had a real existence than to be a mere offspring of
fancy; and that from the accident of direct transmission of
delineations of it on robes and standards, we have probably

a not very incorrect notion of it in the depicted dragon of the Chinese.

We may infer that it was a long terrestrial lizard, hibernating, and carnivorous, with the power of constricting with its snake-like body and tail; possibly furnished with wing-like expansions of its integument, after the fashion of *Draco volans*, and capable of occasional progress on its hind legs alone, when excited in attack. It appears to have been protected by armour and projecting spikes, like those found in *Moloch horridus* and *Megalania prisca*, and was possibly more nearly allied to this last form than to any other which has yet come to our knowledge. Probably it preferred sandy, open country to forest land, its habitat was the highlands of Central Asia, and the time of its disappearance about that of the Biblical Deluge discussed in a previous chapter.

Although terrestrial, it probably, in common with most reptiles, enjoyed frequent bathing, and when not so engaged, or basking in the sun, secluded itself under some overhanging bank or cavern.

The idea of its fondness for swallows, and power of attracting them, mentioned in some traditions, may not impossibly have been derived from these birds hawking round and through its open jaws in the pursuit of the flies attracted by the viscid humours of its mouth. We know that at the present day a bird, the trochilus of the ancients, freely enters the open mouth of the crocodile, and rids it of the parasites affecting its teeth and jaws.

# CHAPTER IX.

### THE SEA-SERPENT.

> On the dark bottom of the great salt lake
> Imprisoned lay the giant snake,
> With naught his sullen sleep to break.
>
> *Poets of the North,* "Oelenschlæger." Translated by
> Longfellow.

THAT frank writer, Montaigne, says* :—

"Yet on the other side it is a sottish presumption to dis-
daine and condemne that for false, which unto us seemeth to
beare no show of likelihood or truth : which is an ordinarie
fault in those who perswade themselves to be of more sufficiencie than the vulgar sort.

"But reason hath taught me, that so resolutely to condemne a thing for false, and impossible, is to assume unto
himself the advantage, to have the bounds and limits of
God's will, and of the power of our common mother Nature
tied to his sleeve : and that there is no greater folly in the
world, than to reduce them to the measure of our capacitie,
and bounds of our sufficiencie.

"If we term those things monsters or miracles to which
our reason cannot attain, how many such doe daily present

---

* Montaigne, *Essays,* chap. xxvi.

themselves unto our sight? let us consider through what cloudes, and how blinde-folde we are led to the knowledge of most things, that passe our hands : verily we shall finde, it is rather custome, than Science that removeth the strangenesse of them from us : and that those things, were they newly presented unto us, wee should doubtless deeme them, as much, or more unlikely, and incredible, than any other."

Montaigne's remarks seem to me to apply as aptly to the much-vexed question of the existence or non-existence of the sea-serpent as though they had been specially written in reference to it.

The sea-serpent, at once the belief and the denied of scientific men; the accepted and ignored, according to their estimation of the evidence, of reasoners, not scientific perhaps, but intelligent and educated; the valued basis for items to the journalist, and the quintain for every self-sufficient gobemouche to tilt against; appearing mysteriously at long intervals and in distant places; the sea-serpent has as yet avoided capture and the honourable distinction of being catalogued and labelled in our museums.

Yet I do believe this weird creature to be a real solid fact, and not a fanciful hallucination. This assertion, however, has to be sustained under many difficulties. The dread of ridicule closes the mouths of many men who could speak upon the subject, while their dependent position forces them to submit to the half-bantering, half-warning expostulations of their employers. When, for example, an unimaginative shipowner breaks jests over his unfortunate shipmaster's head, and significantly hints his hope (as I know to have been the case) that on his next voyage he will see no more sea-serpents, or, in other words, that the great monster belongs to the same genus as the snakes seen in the boots of a western dram-drinker, we may be sure that an important barrier is put to any further communication on the subject

from that source, at least; * or when, again, some knot of
idle youngsters enliven the monotony of a long voyage by
preparing a deliberate hoax for publication on their arrival,
a certain amount of discredit necessarily attaches to the
monster on the ultimate exposure of the jest.

---

* " I fully believe in this great marine monster. I have as much
evidence as to its existence as of anything not seen. Some years ago,
Captain Austin Cooper and the officers and crew of the *Carlisle Castle*,
on a vogage to Melbourne, saw the 'varmint.' A description and sketch
of it were published in the *Argus*. This, when it arrived in London, it
being the 'silly season' in journalism, was seized and torn to pieces by
one of the young lions of the *Daily Telegraph*, in a leading article, in
which much fun was poked at the gallant sailor. ' I don't see any more
sea-serpents,' said my Irish friend to me. ' It is too much to be told
that one of Green's commanders can't tell the difference between a piece
of sea-weed and a live body in the water. If twenty serpents come on
the starboard, all hands shall be ordered to look to port. No London
penny-a-liner shall say again that Austin Cooper is a liar and a fool.'
After this we softened down over some Coleraine whiskey. Again,
some three years ago, the monster was plainly seen off the great reef of
New Caledonia by Commandant Villeneuve, and the officers of the
French man-of-war, the *Seudre*. Chassepots were procured to shoot it,
but before it came within easy range it disappeared. During my late
visit to Fiji, Major James Harding, who was an officer in Cakoban's
army when that chief, ' by the grace of God ' was king of Fiji, described
exactly the same creature as passing within a few yards of his canoe on
a clear moonlight night in the Bay of Suva. It swam towards a small
island outside the reef, which is known amongst Fijians as the ' Cave of
the Big Snake.' Major Harding is a cool, brave soldier, who saw much
hot work with Cakoban's men against the hill tribes of Vonua Levu.
He was once riddled by bullets, and left for dead. Accustomed for years
to travel about the reefs in canoes, every phase of the aspect of the
waters was known to him, and he was not likely to be frightened with
false fire. The extraordinary thing is, that the English sailor, the French
commander, and the Fijian soldier, all gave the same account of this
monster. It is something with a head slightly raised out of the water,
and with a sort of mane streaming behind it, whilst the back of a
long body is seen underneath the water. So, from these instances, in
which I know the witnesses, I fully believe in the sea-serpent. What
is there very wonderful in it, after all ? The whale is the largest living
thing. Why shouldn't the waters produce snakes of gigantic size."
THE VAGABOND, in Supplement to the *Australasian*, September 10, 1881.

Men also occasionally deceive themselves, and while honestly believing that they have seen his oceanic majesty, produce a story which, on analysis, crumbles into atoms and crowns him with disgrace as an impostor.

The hard logic of science, in the hand of one of our master minds, has also been arrayed against him, but fortunately weighs rather against special avatars than against his existence absolutely.

Finally, the narratives of different observers disagree so much in detail that we have a difficulty in reconciling them, except upon the supposition that they relate to several distinct creatures, a supposition which I shall hope to show is not improbable, as well as that the term sea-serpent is an unwarranted specific differentiation of that of sea-monster, the various creatures collectively so designated being neither serpents nor, indeed, always mutually related. In commencing my record, I must bear in mind Mrs. Glasse's proverbially excellent advice, and admit that it is simply a history of the various appearances of a creature or creatures too fugitive to admit of specific examination, and that until, by some remarkable stroke of fortune, specimens are secured, their zoological status must remain an unsolved, although closely guessed at, problem.

I have elsewhere stated my conviction that the serpent Midgard is only a corruption of accounts of the sea-serpent handed down from times when a supernatural existence was attributed to it; and we have in the Sagas probably the earliest references to it, unless, perhaps, the serpents mentioned by Aristotle, which attacked and overset the galleys off the Libyan coast, may have been of this species.

The coast of Norway, deeply indented by fjords, the channels of which, for a certain breadth, have a depth equal to that of the sea outside, seldom less than four hundred fathoms, and corresponding in some degree with the height of the precipitous cliffs which enclose them, abounding in

all kinds of fish, and in the season with whales, which at
one time used to number thousands in a shoal, appears,
until within the last thirty years, to have been peculiarly
the favourite haunt of the serpent. Paddle and screw are
probably answerable for his non-appearance on the surface
lately.

The west coast of the Isle of Skye is another locality from
which several reports of it have been received during this
century; less frequently it has been observed upon the
eastern American coast-line, upon the sea-board of China,
and in various portions of the broad ocean. It generally
follows the track of whales, and in two instances observers
affirm that it has been seen in combat with them.

I have no doubt but that the literature of Norway contains
frequent references to it of olden date, but the earliest notice
of it in that country which I have been able to procure is
one contained in *A Narrative of the North-East Frosty Seas*,
declared by the Duke of Mosconia his ambassadors to a
learned gentlemen of Italy, named Galeatius Butrigarius, as
follows* :—

"The lake called Mos, and the Island of Hoffusen in
myddest thereof is in the degree 45.30 and 61. In this
lake appeareth a strange monster, which is a serpent
of huge bigness; and as, to all other places of the world,
blazing stars do portend alteration, so doth this to Norway.
It was seen of late in the year of Christ 1522, appearing far above the water, rowling like a great pillar, and
was by conjecture far off esteemed to be of fifty cubits in
length."

Pontoppidan, the Bishop of Bergen, who published
his celebrated *Natural History of Norway* in 1755, and
who had at one time discredited its existence "till that
suspicion was removed by full and sufficient evidence from

---

* Contained in Eden's *Travels*.

creditable and experienced fishermen and sailors in Norway, of which there are hundreds, who can testify that they have annually seen them," states that the North traders, who came to Bergen every year with their merchandise, thought it a very strange question, when they were seriously asked whether there were any such creatures, as ridiculous, in fact, as if the question had been put to them whether there be such fish as eel or cod.

According to Pontoppidan, these creatures continually keep at the bottom of the sea, excepting in the months of July and August, which is their spawning time, and then they come to the surface in calm weather, but plunge into the water again so soon as the wind raises the least wave.

It was supposed by the Norway fishermen to have a great objection to castor, with which they provided themselves when going out to sea, shutting it up in a hole in the stern, and throwing a little overboard when apprehensive of meeting the sea-snake. The Faroe fisherman had the same idea with reference to the Tvold whale, which was supposed to have a great aversion to castor and to shavings of juniper wood.

Olaus Magnus, in his *Histor. Septentrion*, chap. xxvii., writing not from personal observation but from the relations of others, speaks of it as being two hundred feet in length and twenty feet round, having a mane two feet long, being covered with scales, having fiery eyes, disturbing ships, and raising itself up like a mast, and sometimes snapping some of the men from the deck.

Aldrovandus, quoting Olaus Magnus, says that about Norway there occasionally appears a serpent reaching to one hundred or two hundred feet in length, dangerous to ships in calm weather, as it sometimes snatches a man from the ship. It is said that merchant ships are involved by it and sunk.

Olaus Magnus also figures another serpent, which is said

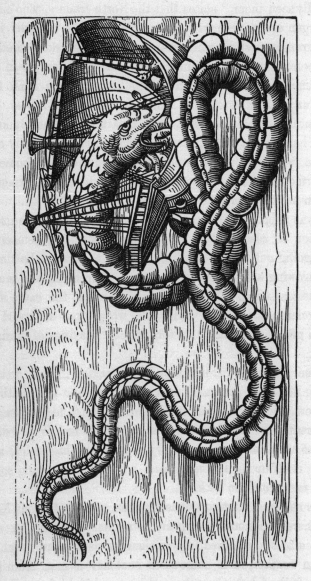

FIG. 67.—SEA-SERPENT ATTACKING A VESSEL. (*From Olaus Magnus.*)

to inhabit the Baltic or Swedish Sea; it is from thirty to forty feet in length, and will not hurt anyone unless provoked.

Arndt. Bernsen, in his account of the fertility of Denmark and Norway, says that the sea-snake, as well as the Tvold whale, often sinks both men and boats; and Pontoppidan was informed by the North traders that the sea-snake has frequently raised itself up and thrown itself across a boat, and even across a vessel of some hundred tons burthen, and by its weight sunk it to the bottom ; and that they would sometimes raise their frightful heads and snap a man out of a boat; but this Pontoppidan does not vouch for, and, indeed, says that if anything, however light, be thrown at and touch them they generally plunge into the water or take another course.

Hans (afterwards Bishop) Egede, in his *Full and Particular Relation of my Voyage to Greenland, as a Missionary, in the year* 1734, figures and describes a sea-monster which showed itself on his passage. He says : " On the 6th of July 1734, when off the south coast of Greenland, a sea-monster appeared to us, whose head, when raised, was on a level with our main-top. Its snout was long and sharp, and it blew water almost like a whale ; it had large broad paws; its body was covered with scales ; its skin was rough and uneven ; in other respects it was as a serpent ; and when it dived, its tail, which was raised in the air, appeared to be a whole ship's length from its body."

In another work, *The New Survey of Old Greenland*, Egede speaks of the same monster, with the addition that the body was full as thick and as big in circumference as the ship that he sailed in. The drawing (which I reproduce, Fig. 68) appears to have been taken by another missionary, Mr. Bing, who stated that the creature's eyes seemed red, and like burning fire. The paws mentioned by Egede were probably paddles like those of the Liassic Saurians.

FIG. 68.—SEA-SERPENT SEEN BY HANS EGEDE, IN 1734, OFF THE SOUTH COAST OF GREENLAND.

Pontoppidan considers this to be a different monster from the Norway sea-serpent, of which he gives a figure furnished him by the Rev. Hans Strom, made from descriptions of two of his neighbours at Herroe, who had been eye-witnesses of its appearance.

Lawrance de Ferry, a captain in the Norwegian Navy, and commander in Bergen in Pontoppidan's time, actually wounded one of the Norwegian serpents, and made two of his men, who were with him in the boat at the time, testify upon oath in court to the truth of the statement which he himself made, as follows :—

" The latter end of August, in the year 1746, as I was on a voyage, in my return from Trundheim, in a very calm and hot day, having a mind to put in at Molde, it happened that when we were arrived with my vessel within six English miles of the aforesaid Molde, being at a place called Jule-Næfs, as I was reading in a book, I heard a kind of murmuring voice from amongst the men at the oars, who were eight in number, and observed that the man at the helm kept off from the land. Upon this I inquired what was the matter ; and was informed that there was a sea-snake before us. I then ordered the man at the helm to keep to the land again, and to come up with this creature, of which I had heard so many stories. Though the fellows were under some apprehensions, they were obliged to obey my orders. In the meantime this sea-snake passed by us, and we were obliged to tack the vessel about, in order to get nearer to it. As the snake swam faster than we could row, I took my gun, that was ready charged, and fired at it ; on this he immediately plunged under the water. We rowed to the place where it sank down (which in the calm might be easily observed) and lay upon our oars, thinking it would come up again to the surface ; however, it did not. When the snake plunged down, the water appeared thick and red ; perhaps some of the shot might wound it, the distance being very little. The head of this snake, which it held more than two feet above the surface of the water, resembled that of a horse. It was of a greyish colour, and the mouth was quite black and very large. It had black eyes and a long white mane,* that hung down from the neck to the surface of the water. Besides the head and neck, we saw seven or eight folds or coils of this snake, which were very thick, and, as far as we could guess, there was about a fathom distance between each fold.—Bergen, 1751."

Pontoppidan remarks on the peculiarity of spouting water from the nostrils exhibited by the creature seen by Hans Egede, and states that he had not known it spoken of in any other instance.

FIG. 69.—THE NORWEGIAN SEA-SERPENT. (*According to Pontoppidan.*)

He also remarks that the Norway sea-snakes differ from the Greenland ones with regard to the skin, which in the former is as smooth as glass, and has not the least wrinkle, except about the neck, where there is a kind of mane, which looks like a parcel of sea-weeds hanging down to the water. Summarising the accounts which had reached him, he estimates the length at about one hundred fathoms or six hundred English feet. He states that it lies on the surface of the water (when it is very calm) in many folds, and that these are in a line with the head; some small parts of the back are to be seen above the surface of the water when it moves or bends, which at a distance appear like so many

---

* Connected with the breathing apparatus?

casks or hogsheads floating in a line, with a considerable distance between each of them.

" The creature does not, like the eel or land-snake, taper gradually to a point, but the body, which looks to be as big as two hogsheads, grows remarkably small at once just where the tail begins. The head in all the kinds has a high and broad forehead, but in some a pointed snout, though in others that is flat, like that of a cow or horse, with large nostrils, and several stiff hairs standing out on each side like whiskers."

" They add that the eyes of this creature are very large, and of a blue colour, and look like a couple of bright pewter plates. The whole animal is of a dark brown colour, but it is speckled and variegated with light streaks or spots that shine like tortoise-shell. It is of a darker hue about the eyes and mouth than elsewhere, and appears in that part a good deal like those horses which we call Moors-heads."

He mentions two places, one at Amunds Vaagen in Nordfiord, the other at the island of Karmen, where carcases of it had been left at high water. He supposes it to be viviparous.

In an account of the Laplanders of Finmark, by Knud Leems, with the notes of Gunner, Bishop of Drontheim, (Copenhagen, 1767, 4to., in Danish and Latin),* I find, " The Sea of Finmark also generates the snake or marine serpent, forty paces long, equalling in the size of the head the whale, in form the serpent. This monster has a maned neck, resembling a horse, a back of a grey colour, the belly inclining to white.

" On the canicular days, when the sea is calm, the marine serpent usually comes up, winding into various spirals, of which some are above, the others below, the water. The seamen very much dread this monster. Nor while he is

---

* Pinkerton, *Voyages and Travels*, vol. i. p. 376.

coming up do they easily entrust themselves to the dangers
of the deep."

Mr. J. Ramus records a large sea-snake which was seen in
1687 by many people in Dramsfiorden. It was in very calm
weather, and so soon as the sun appeared, and the wind
blew a little, it shot away just like a coiled cable that is suddenly thrown out by the sailors ; and they observed that it
was some time in stretching out its many folds.

Captain (afterwards Sir Arthur) de Capell Brooke* collected all accounts he could, during his journey to the
North Cape, respecting the sea-serpent, with the following
results :—

"As I had determined on arriving at the coast to make
every inquiry respecting the truth of the accounts which had
reached England the preceding year, of the sea-serpent having
recently been seen off this part of Norway, I shall simply
give the different reports I received during my voyage to the
North Cape, leaving others to their own conclusions, and
without expressing, at least for the present, my opinion
respecting them.

" The fisherman at Pêjerstad said a serpent was seen two
years ago in the Folden-Fjord, the length of which, as far as
it was visible, was sixty feet."

At Otersoen, the Postmaster, Captain Schielderup, who
had formerly been in the Norwegian sea service, and seemed
a quick intelligent man, stated that the serpent had actually
been off the island for a considerable length of time during
the preceding summer, in the narrow parts of the sound,
between this island and the continent, and the description he
gave was as follows :—

"It made its appearance for the first time in the month
of July 1849 off Otersoen. Previous to this he had often
heard of the existence of these creatures, but never before

* A. de Brooke, *Travels to the North Cape.*

believed it. During the whole of that month the weather was excessively sultry and calm ; and the serpent was seen every day nearly in the same part of the Sound.

"It continued there while the warm weather lasted, lying motionless, and as if dozing, in the sunbeams.

"The number of persons living on the island, he said, was about thirty; the whole of whom, from motives of curiosity, went to look at it while it remained. This was confirmed to me by subsequent inquiries among the inhabitants, who gave a similar account of it. The first time that he saw it he was in a boat, at the distance of two hundred yards. The length of it he supposes to have been about three hundred ells or six hundred feet. Of this he could not speak accurately; but it was of considerable length, and longer than it appeared, as it lay in large coils above the water to the height of many feet. Its colour was greyish. At the distance at which he was, he could not ascertain whether it were covered with scales; but when it moved it made a loud crackling noise, which he distinctly heard. Its head was shaped like that of a serpent; but he could not tell whether it had teeth or not. He said it emitted a very strong odour ; and that the boatmen were afraid to approach near it, and looked on its coming as a bad sign, as the fish left the coast in consequence! Such were the particulars he related to me.

"The merchant at Krogoën confirmed in every particular the account of Captain Schielderup, and that many of the people of Krogoën had witnessed it.

"On the island of Lekö I obtained from the son of Peter Greger, the merchant, a young man who employed himself in the fishery, still further information respecting the sea-serpent. It was in August of the preceding year, while fishing with others in the Viig or Veg-Fjord, that he saw it. At that time they were on shore hauling in their nets, and it appeared about sixty yards distant from them, at

which they were not a little alarmed, and immediately retreated. What was seen of it above water, he said, appeared
six times the length of their boat, of a grey colour, and
lying in coils a great height above the surface. Their fright
prevented them from attending more accurately to other
particulars. In fact, they all fairly took to their heels when
they found the monster so near to them.

"At Alstahoug I found the Bishop of the Nordlands. The
worthy prelate was a sensible and well-informed man, between
fifty and sixty years of age. To the testimony of others
respecting the existence of the sea-serpent, I shall now add
that of the Bishop himself, who was an eye-witness to the
appearance of two in the Bay of Shuresund or Sörsund, on
the Drontheim Fjord, about eight Norway miles from Drontheim. He was but a short distance from them, and
saw them plainly. They were swimming in large folds, part
of which were seen above the water, and the length of what
appeared of the largest he judged to be about one hundred
feet. They were of a darkish grey colour; the heads hardly
discernible, from their being almost under water, and they
were visible for only a short time. Before that period he
had treated the account of them as fabulous; but it was now
impossible, he said, to doubt their existence, as such numbers
of respectable people since that time had likewise seen them
on several occasions. He had never met with any person
who had seen the kraken, and was inclined to think it a
fable.

"During the time that I remained at Hundholm, a curious
circumstance occurred. One day, when at dinner at Mr.
Blackhall's house, and thinking little of the sea-serpent, concerning which I had heard nothing for some time, a young
man, the master of a small fishing-yacht, which had just
come in from Drontheim, joined our party. In the course of
conversation he mentioned that a few hours before, whilst
close to Hundholm, and previous to his entering the harbour,

two sea-snakes passed immediately under his yacht. When he saw them he was on the deck, and, seizing a handspike, he struck at them as they came up close to the vessel on the other side, upon which they disappeared. Their length was very great, and their colour greyish, but for the very short time they were visible he could not notice any further particulars.

" He had no doubt of their being snakes, as he called them, and the circumstance was related entirely of his own accord."

Captain Brooke sums up the reports he received with the following general observations :—

" Taking upon the whole a fair view of the different accounts related in the foregoing pages respecting the sea-serpent, no reasonable person can doubt the fact of some marine animal of extraordinary dimensions, and in all probability of the serpent tribe, having been repeatedly seen by various persons along the Norway and Finmark coasts. These accounts, for the most part, have been given verbally from the mouths of the fishermen, a honest and artless class of men, who, having no motive for misrepresentation, cannot be suspected of a wish to deceive ; could this idea, however, be entertained, the circumstance of their assertions having been so fully confirmed by others, in more distant parts, would be sufficient to free them from any imputation of this kind.

" The simple facts are these : In traversing a space of full seven hundred miles of coast, extending to the most northern point, accounts have been received from numerous persons respecting the appearance of an animal called by them a sea-serpent. This of itself would induce some degree of credit to be given to it ; but when these several relations as to the general appearance of the animal, its dimensions, the state of the weather when it was seen, and other particulars, are so fully confirmed, one by the other, at such considerable intervening distances, every reasonable man will feel satisfied of the truth of the main fact. Many of the informants, besides, were of superior rank and education; and the opinions of such men as the Amtmand (Governor) of Finmark, Mr. Steen, the clergyman of Carlsö, Prosten (Dean) Deinboll of Vadsö, and the Bishop of Nordland and Finmark, who was even an eye-witness, ought not to be disregarded.

"The Bishop of Nordland has seen two of them about eight miles from Drontheim, the largest being apparently one hundred feet, and, in 1822, one as bulky as an ox, and a quarter of a mile in length, appeared off the island of Sorö, near Finmark, and was seen by many people."

Not having the *Zoologist* at hand, I now quote a *resumé* of short notices extracted from it, contained in the *Illustrated London News* for October 28, 1848, as follows :—

" Our attention has been drawn to the *Zoologist* for the past year, wherein are several communications tending to authenticate the existence of the great sea-serpent. Thus, in the number for February 1847, we find paragraphs quoted from the Norse newspapers stating that in the neighbourhood of Christiansund and Molde, in the province of Romsdal, in Norway, several highly respectable and credible witnesses have attested the seeing of the serpent. In general, they state that it has been seen in the larger Norwegian fjords, seldom in the open sea. In the large bight of the sea at Christiansund it has been seen every year, though only in the warmest season, in the dog days, and then only in perfectly calm weather and unruffled water.

" Its length is stated at about forty-four feet, and twice as thick as a common snake, in proportion to the length. The front of the head was rather pointed, the eyes sharp, and from the back of the head commenced a mane like that of a horse. The colour of the animal was a blackish brown. It swam swiftly, with serpentine movements like a leech. One of the witnesses describes the body to be two feet in diameter, the head as long as a brandy anker (ten-gallon cask) and about the same thickness, not pointed, but round. It had no scales, but the body quite smooth. The witness acknowledged Pontoppidan's representation to be like the serpent he saw."

" The writer of this article received letters from Mr. Soren Knudtzon, stating that a sea-serpent had been seen in the neighbourhood of Christiansund by several people ; and from Dr. Hoffmann, a respectable surgeon in Molde, stating that, lying on a considerable fjord to the south of Christiansund, Rector Hammer, Mr. Krabt, curate, and several persons, very clearly saw, while on a journey, a sea-serpent of very considerable size.

"Four other persons saw a similar animal, July 28th, 1845.

" The next communication, dated Sund's Parsonage, August 31st, 1846, records the appearance of a supposed sea-serpent, on the 8th, in the course between the islands of Sartor Leer and Tös. Early on this day, just as the steamer *Biörgvin* passed through Rogne Fjord, towing a vessel to Bergen, Daniel Solomonson, a cotter, saw a sea-monster swimming from Rogne Fjord in a westerly direction towards his dwelling at Grönnevigskiæset, in the northern part of the parish of Sund. The head appeared like a Færing boat (about twenty feet long) keel uppermost; and from behind it raised itself forward in three, and sometimes four and five undulations, each apparently about twelve feet long. On the same morning a lad, out fishing in the Rogne Fjord, saw a serpent, which he describes to have been sixty feet long."

For further information on the Norwegian sea-serpent, I am indebted to the excellent chapter, devoted to the question generally, contained in Mr. Gosse's *Romance of Natural History*, First Series, from which I transfer, without abbre-

viation, a statement made by the Rev. W. Deinboll, Arch-
deacon of Molde :—

" On the 28th of July 1845, J. C. Lund, bookseller and
printer; G. S. Krogh, merchant; Christian Flang, Lund's
apprentice; and John Elgensen, labourer, were out on Romsdalfjord, fishing. The sea was, after a warm sunshiny day,
quite calm. About seven o'clock in the afternoon, a little
distance from shore, near the ballast place and Molde Hove,
they saw a large marine animal which slowly moved itself
forward, as it appeared to them, with the help of two fins on
the fore-part of the body nearest the head, which they judged
from the boiling of the water on both sides of it. The visible
part of the body appeared to be between forty and fifty feet in
length, and moved in undulations like a snake. The body
was round and of a dark colour, and seemed to be several
ells* in thickness. As they discerned a waving motion in
the water behind the animal, they concluded that part of the
body was concealed under water. That it was one connected
animal they saw plainly from its movement. When the
animal was about one hundred yards from the boat, they
noticed tolerably correctly its fore-part, which ended in a
sharp snout; its colossal head raised itself above the water
in the form of a semi-circle; the lower part was not visible.
The colour of the head was dark brown, and the skin smooth.
They did not notice the eyes, or any mane or bristles on the
throat. When the serpent came about a musket-shot near,
Lund fired at it, and was certain the shots hit it in the head.
After the shot he dived but came up immediately; he raised
his head like a snake preparing to dart on its prey. After
he had turned and got his body in a straight line, which he
appeared to do with great difficulty, he darted like an arrow
against the boat. They reached the shore, and the animal,
perceiving it had come into shallow water, dived immediately,
and disappeared in the deep."

---

* 1 ell=2 feet.

Mr. Gosse further quotes a statement made by an Englishman, writing under the signature of "Oxoniensis" in the *Times* of November 4th, 1848, to the effect that—

"A parish priest, residing on Romsdalfjord, about two days' journey south of Drontheim, an intelligent person, whose veracity I have no reason to doubt, gave me a circumstantial account of one which he had himself seen. It rose within thirty yards of the boat in which he was, and swam parallel with it for a considerable time. Its head he described as equalling a small cask in size, and its mouth, which it repeatedly opened and shut, was furnished with formidable teeth; its neck was smaller, but its body, of which he supposed that he saw about half on the surface of the water, was not less in girth than that of a moderate-sized horse. Another gentleman, in whose house I stayed, had also seen one, and gave a similar account of it; it also came near his boat upon the fjord, when it was fired at, upon which it turned and pursued them to the shore, which was luckily near, when it disappeared. They expressed great surprise at the general disbelief attached to the existence of these animals amongst naturalists, and assured me that there was scarcely a sailor accustomed to those inland lakes who had not seen them at one time or other."

The Rev. Alfred C. Smith, M.A., a naturalist, who visited Norway in 1850, summarises the result of his investigations in the words: "and I cannot withhold my belief in the existence of some huge inhabitant of those northern seas, when, to my mind, the fact of his existence has been so clearly proved by numerous eye-witnesses, many of whom were too intelligent to be deceived, and too honest to be doubted."

Passing from these numerous narratives, which are distinguished for a remarkable agreement in the main characteristic described, I will proceed to some of those whose scene lies on our own coast.

In 1809, Mr. McLean, the parish minister of Eigg, communicated to Dr. Neil, the Secretary of the Wernerian Society, the following statement :—*

" I saw the animal of which you inquire, in June 1808, on the coast of Coll. Rowing along that coast, I observed, at about the distance of half a mile, an object to windward, which gradually excited astonishment. At first view it appeared like a small rock ; but knowing that there was no rock in that situation, I fixed my eyes closely upon it. Then I saw it elevated considerably above the level of the sea, and, after a slow movement, distinctly perceived one of its eyes. Alarmed at the unusual appearance and magnitude of the animal, I steered so as to be at no great distance from the shore. When nearly in a line between it and the shore, the monster, directing its head, which still continued above water, towards us, plunged violently under water. Certain that he was in chase of us, we plied hard to get ashore. Just as we leapt out on a rock, and had taken a station as high as we conveniently could, we saw it coming rapidly under water towards the stern of our boat. When within a few yards of it, finding the water shallow, it raised its monstrous head above water, and, by a winding course, got, with apparent difficulty, clear of the creek where our boat lay, and where the monster seemed in danger of being embayed. It continued to move off, with its head above water and with the wind, for about half a mile before we lost sight of it. Its head was somewhat broad, and of form somewhat oval; its neck somewhat smaller ; its shoulders, if I can so term them, considerably broader, and thence it tapered towards the tail, which last it kept pretty low in the water, so that a view of it could not be taken so distinctly as I wished. It had no fins that I could perceive, and seemed to me to move progressively by undulation up and down. Its length I believed to be

* *Transactions* of the Wernerian Society, vol. i. p. 442.

between seventy and eighty feet. When nearest to me it did not raise its head wholly above water, so that, the neck being under water, I could perceive no shining filaments thereon, if it had any. Its progressive motion under water I took to be very rapid. About the time I saw it, it was seen near the Isle of Canna. The crews of thirteen fishing-boats, I am told, were so much terrified at its appearance, that they, in a body, fled from it to the nearest creek for safety. On the passage from Rum to Canna, the crew of one boat saw it coming towards them, with the wind, and its head high above water. One of the crew pronounced the head as large as a little boat, and its eye as large as a plate. The men were much terrified, but the monster offered them no molestation."

I next extract, from the pages of the *Inverness Courier,* some very pertinent remarks upon a description of the sea-monster seen by the Rev. Messrs. McRae and Twopeny, contained in the *Zoologist,* and I add the article there referred to. I had the advantage of hearing from a gentleman related to Mr. McRae that he could substantiate his statement, having himself about the same time, and in that locality, observed the same appearance, though at a greater distance off.

The following is the article in the *Inverness Courier* :—

"We are glad to see that the two gentlemen who favoured us last autumn with an account of what they believed to be a strange animal seen off the west coast, Inverness-shire, have published in the *Zoologist,* a monthly journal of natural history, a careful description of the creature which they saw, and which seems to resemble the engravings of what is called the Norwegian sea-serpent. We subjoin the magazine article entire. There is such a dread of ridicule in appearing publicly in company with this mysterious and disreputable monster, that we must commend the boldness of the two clergymen in putting their names to the narrative ; especially as we observe that other observers have not been so

courageous, and that they have been obliged to give some of
their information anonymously.

" The huge serpent, if serpent it may be called, invariably appears in still warm weather, and in no other.
There are certain Norwegian fjords and narrow seas which it
frequents, and it is scarcely ever seen in the open sea.   In
the present case, the limit in which the animal has been seen
on our coast, is Lochduich to the north and the Sound of
Mull to the south, only about a fifth of the space between
Cape Wrath and the Mull of Kintyre ; and it is in that part
it should be most looked for.   We beg to draw the attention
of our readers on the West Coast to the fact, now established
on indubitable evidence, of the supposed animal having been
seen there last year, and to the possibility of its appearing
again in similar weather this year.   If it chances to turn up
once more, some full and accurate account of the phenomenon would certainly be most desirable."

The following is the article in the *Zoologist** :—

Appearance of an animal, believed to be that which is called the Norwegian Sea-serpent, on the Western Coast of Scotland, in August
1872, by the Rev. John McRae, Minister of Glenelg, Inverness-
shire, and the Rev. David Twopeny, Vicar of Stockbury, Kent.

On the 20th of August 1872 we started from Glenelg in a small
cutter, the *Leda*, for an excursion to Lochourn.   Our party consisted,
besides ourselves, of two ladies, F. and K., a gentleman, G. B., and a
Highland lad.   Our course lay down the Sound of Sleat, which on that
side divides the Isle of Skye from the mainland, the average breadth
of the channel in that part being two miles.

It was calm and sunshiny, not a breath of air, and the sea perfectly
smooth.   As we were getting the cutter along with oars we perceived a
dark mass about two hundred yards astern of us, to the north.   While
we were looking at it with our glasses (we had three on board) another
similar black lump rose to the left of the first, leaving an interval
between ; then another and another followed, all in regular order.   We
did not doubt its being one living creature : it moved slowly across
our wake, and disappeared.   Presently the first mass, which was

* No. 92, May 1873; London, Van Voorst.

evidently the head, reappeared, and was followed by the rising of the other black lumps, as before. Sometimes three appeared, sometimes four, five, or six, and then sank again. When they rose, the head appeared first, if it had been down, and the lumps rose after it in regular order, beginning always with that next the head, and rising gently; but when they sank, they sank altogether rather abruptly, sometimes leaving the head visible.

It gave the impression of a creature crooking up its back to sun itself. There was no appearance of undulation; when the lumps sank, other lumps did not rise in the intervals between them. The greatest number we counted was seven, making eight with head, as shown in sketch No. 1 [two engravings are given]. The parts were separated from each other by intervals of about their own length, the head being rather smaller and flatter than the rest, and the nose being very slightly visible above the water; but we did not see the head raised above the surface either this or the next day, nor could we see the eye. We had no means of measuring the length with any accuracy; but taking the distance from the centre of one lump to the centre of the next to be six feet, and it could scarcely be less, the whole length of the portion visible, including the intervals submerged, would be forty-five feet.

Presently, as we were watching the creature, it began to approach us rapidly, causing a great agitation in the sea. Nearly the whole of the body, if not all of it, had now disappeared, and the head advanced at a great rate in the midst of a shower of fine spray, which was evidently raised in some way by the quick movement of the animal—it did not appear how—and not by spouting. F. was alarmed and retreated to the cabin, crying out that the creature was coming down upon us. When within about a hundred yards of us it sank and moved away in the direction of Syke, just under the surface of the water, for we could trace its course by the waves it raised on the still sea to the distance of a mile or more. After this it continued at intervals to show itself, careering about at a distance, as long as we were in that part of the Sound; the head and a small part only of the body being visible on the surface; but we did not again, on that day, see it so near nor so well as at first.

At one time F. and K. and G. B. saw a fin sticking up at a little distance back from the head, but neither of us were then observing. On our return the next day we were again becalmed on the north side of the opening of Lochourn, where it is about three miles wide, the day warm and sunshiny as before. As we were dragging slowly along in the afternoon the creature again appeared over towards the south side, at a greater distance than we saw it the first day. It now showed itself in three or four rather long lines, as in the sketch No. 2, and looked considerably longer than it did the day before; as nearly as we could compute, it looked at least sixty feet in length. Soon it began careering about, showing but a small part of itself, as on the day before, and appeared to be going up Lochourn. Later in the afternoon, when we were still becalmed in the mouth of Lochourn, and by using the oars had nearly reached the island of Sandaig, it came rushing past us about a hundred and fifty yards to the south, on its return from Lochourn. It went with great rapidity, its black head only being visible through the clear sea, followed by a long trail of agitated water. As it shot along, the noise of its rush through the water could be distinctly heard on board. There were no organs of motion to be seen, nor was there any shower of spray as on the day before, but merely such a commotion in the sea as its quick passage might be expected to make. Its progress was equable and smooth, like that of a log towed rapidly. For the rest of the day, as we worked our way home northwards through the Sound of Sleat, it was occasionally within sight of us until nightfall, rushing about at a distance, as before, and showing only its head, and a small part of its body on the surface. It seemed on each day to keep about us, and as we were always then rowing, we were inclined to think it perhaps might be attracted by the measured sound of the oars. Its only exit in this direction to the north was by the narrow Strait of Kylerhea, dividing Skye from the mainland, and only a third of a mile wide, and we left our boat, wondering whether this strange creature had gone that way or turned back again to the south. We have only to add to this narrative of what we saw ourselves, the following instances of its being seen by other people, of the correctness of which we have no doubt. The ferrymen on each side of Kylerhea saw it pass rapidly through on the evening of the 21st, and heard the rush of the water; they were surprised, and thought it might be a shoal of porpoises, but could not comprehend their going so quickly.

Finlay McRae, of Bundaloch, in the parish of Kintail, was within the mouth of Lochourn on the 21st, with other men in his boat, and saw the creature at about the distance of one hundred and fifty yards. Two days after we saw it, Alexander Macmillan, boat-builder at Dornie, was fishing in a boat in the entrance of Lochduich, half-way between Druidag and Castledonan, when he saw the animal, near enough to hear the noise, and see the ripple it made in rushing along in the sea. He says that what seemed its head was followed by four or more lumps, or "half-rounds," as he calls them, and that they sometimes rose and sometimes sank altogether. He estimated its length at not less than between sixty and eighty feet. He saw it also on two subsequent days in Lochduich. On all these occasions his brother, Farquhar, was with him in the boat, and they were both much alarmed, and pulled to the shore in great haste.

A lady at Duisdale, in Skye, a place overlooking the part of the Sound which is opposite the opening of Lochourn, said that she was looking out with a glass when she saw a strange object on the sea, which appeared like eight seals in a row. This was just about the time that we saw it. We were also informed that about the same time it was seen from the island of Eigg, between Eigg and the mainland, about twenty miles to the south-west of the opening of Lochourn. We have not permission to mention the names in these two last instances.

JOHN McRAE.
DAVID TWOPENY.

*P.S.*—The writers of the above account scarcely expect the public to believe in the existence of the creature which they saw. Rather than that, they look for the disbelief and ridicule to which the subject always gives rise, partly on account of the animal having been pronounced to be a snake, without any sufficient evidence, but principally because of the exaggerations and fables with which the whole subject is beset. Nevertheless, they consider themselves bound to leave a record of what they saw, in order that naturalists may receive it as a piece of evidence, or not, according to what they think it is worth. The animal will very likely turn up on those coasts again, and it will be always in that "dead season," so convenient to editors of newspapers, for it is never seen but in the still warm days of summer or early autumn. There is a considerable probability that it has visited the same coasts before.

In the summer of 1871, some large creature was seen for some time rushing about in Lochduich, but it did not show itself sufficiently for anyone to ascertain what it was. Also, some years back, a well-known gentleman of the West Coast, now living, was crossing the Sound of Mull, from Mull to the mainland, " on a very calm afternoon, when," as he writes, " our attention was attracted to a monster which had come to the surface, not more than fifty yards from our boat. It rose without causing the slightest disturbance of the sea, or making the slightest noise, and floated for some time on the surface, but without exhibiting its head or tail, showing only the ridge of the back, which was not that of a whale or any other sea animal that I had ever seen. The back appeared sharp and ridge-like, and in colour very dark, indeed black, or almost so. It rested quietly for a few minutes, and then dropped quietly down into the deep, without causing the slightest agitation. I should say that about forty feet of it, certainly not less, appeared on the surface."

It should be noticed that the inhabitants of that Western Coast are quite familiar with the appearance of whales, seals, and porpoises, and when they see them they recognise them at once. Whether the creature which pursued Mr. McLean's boat off the island of Coll in 1808, and of which there is an account in the *Transactions* of the Wernerian Society (vol. i. p. 442), was one of these Norwegian animals, it is not

easy to say. Survivors who knew Mr. McLean, say that he could quite
be relied upon for truth.

The public are not likely to believe in the creature till it is caught,
and that does not seem likely to happen just yet, for a variety of
reasons, one reason being that it has, from all the accounts given of it,
the power of moving very rapidly. On the 20th, while we were becalmed in the mouth of Lochourn, a steam-launch slowly passed us,
and, as we watched it, we reckoned its rate at five or six miles an hour.
When the animal rushed past us on the next day at about the same
distance, and when we were again becalmed nearly in the same place,
we agreed that it went twice as fast as the steamer, and we thought
that its rate could not be less than ten or twelve miles an hour. It
might be shot, but would probably sink. There are three accounts of its
being shot at in Norway ; in one instance it sank, and in the other two
it pursued the boats, which were near the shore, but disappeared when
it found itself getting into shallow water.

It should be mentioned that when we saw this creature, and made our
sketches of it, we had never seen either Pontoppidan's *Natural History*
or his print of the Norwegian sea-serpent, which has a most striking
resemblance to the first of our own sketches. Considering the great
body of reasonable Norwegian evidence, extending through a number of
years, which remains after setting aside fables and exaggerations, it
seems surprising that no naturalist of that country has ever applied
himself to make out something about the animal. In the meantime, as
the public will most probably be dubious about quickly giving credit to
our account, the following explanations are open to them, all of which
have been proposed to me, viz. :—porpoises, lumps of sea-weed, empty
herring-barrels, bladders, logs of wood, waves of the sea, and inflated
pig-skins! but as all these theories present to our mind greater difficulties than the existence of the animal itself, we feel obliged to decline
them.

The editor of the *Zoologist* adds :—

I have long since expressed my firm conviction that there exists a
large marine animal unknown to us naturalists ; I maintain this belief
as firmly as ever.

I totally reject the evidence of published representations ; but I do
not allow these imaginary figures to interfere with a firm conviction.

Here, again, we have the same general resemblances,
observed under the same conditions of weather, as in the case
of the Norwegian serpent. As to the pursuit, which may
either have been urged from motives of curiosity or of anger,
it is curious to find a remarkable account of a similar incident

in *Kotzebue's Vogages*, where it is stated that M. Kriukoff, while in a boat at Beering's Island, was pursued by an animal like a red serpent, and immensely long, with a head like that of a sea-lion, but the eyes disproportionately large. "It was fortunate," observed M. Kriukoff, " we were so near land, or the monster would have swallowed us; he raised his head far above the surface, and the sea-lions were so terrified, that some rushed into the water, and others concealed themselves on the shore ! "

The last notice of its appearance in British waters is extracted from *Nature*, as follows :—

Believing it to be desirable that every well-authenticated observation indicating the existence of large sea-serpents should be permanently registered, I send you the following particulars :—

About three P.M. on Sunday, September 3, 1882, a party of gentlemen and ladies were standing at the northern extremity of Llandudno pier, looking towards the open sea, when an unusual object was observed in the water near to the Little Orme's Head, travelling rapidly westwards towards the Great Orme. It appeared to be just outside the mouth of the bay, and would therefore be about a mile distant from the observers. It was watched for about two minutes, and in that interval it traversed about half the width of the bay, and then suddenly disappeared. The bay is two miles wide, and therefore the object, whatever it was, must have travelled at the rate of thirty miles an hour. It is estimated to have been fully as long as a large steamer, say two hundred feet; the rapidity of its motion was particularly remarked as being greater than that of any ordinary vessel. The colour appeared to be black, and the motion either corkscrew-like or snake-like, with vertical undulations. Three of the observers have since made sketches from memory, quite independently, of the impression left on their minds, and on comparing these sketches, which slightly varied, they have agreed to sanction the accompanying outline as representing as nearly as possible the object which they saw. The party consisted of W. Barfoot, J.P., of Leicester, F. J. Marlow, solicitor, of Manchester, Mrs. Marlow, and several others. They discard the theories of birds or porpoises as not accounting for this particular phenomenon.

F. T. MOTT.

Birstall Hill, Leicester,
        January 16th, 1883.

It must also be mentioned that Dr. Hibbert* states that the sea-serpent has been seen in the Shetland seas, and instances one seen off the Isle Stonness, Valley Island, and Dunvossness.

The first that we hear of the appearance of the sea-serpent in American waters is of one which appeared on the coast of Maine, in Penobscot Bay, at intervals, during the thirty years preceding 1809. The Rev. Abraham Cummings, who reports this, saw it himself at a distance of about eighty yards, and considered it to be seventy feet long; it was seen by the British in their expedition to Bagaduse, during the first American war, and supposed to be three hundred feet long. The next record relates to one appearing in August 1817, which was frequently seen in the harbour of Gloucester, Cape Aure, about thirty miles from Boston. It is the subject of a report, published by a committee appointed by the Linnæan Society of New England. Dr. Hamilton summarises the results as follows :—

" The affidavits of a great many individuals of unblemished character are collected, which leaves no room to apprehend anything like deceit. They do not agree in every minute particular, but in regard to its great length and snake-like form, they are harmonious."

Eleven depositions were taken, in which the length was variously estimated at from fifty to one hundred feet. It was either seen lying perfectly still, extended upon the surface of the water, or progressing rapidly at the rate of a mile in two, or at the most three, minutes; the mode of progression is generally spoken of as vertical undulation. The tenth deposition states : " On the 20th of June 1815, my boy informed me of an unusual appearance on the surface of the sea in the Cove. When I viewed it through the glass, I was in a moment satisfied that it was some aquatic animal, with

* *Shetland Islands*, p. 565.

the form, motions, and appearance of which I was not previously acquainted. It was about a quarter of a mile from the shore, and was moving with great rapidity to the southward ; it appeared about thirty feet in length. Presently it turned about, and then displayed a greater length, I suppose at least one hundred feet. It then came towards me very rapidly, and lay entirely still on the surface of the water. His appearance then was like a string of buoys. I saw thirty or forty of these protuberances, or bunches, which were about the size of a barrel. The head appeared six or eight feet long, and tapered off to the size of a horse's head. He then appeared about one hundred and twenty feet long ; the body appeared of a uniform size ; the colour deep brown. I could not discover any eye, mane, gills, or breathing holes. I did not see any fins or lips."

One of the Committee of the Linnæan Society was himself an eye-witness, and Colonel Perkins, of Boston, published in 1848 a communication which was a copy of a letter he had written in 1820, detailing his personal experience in confirmation of the Society's Report, as follows :—" In a few moments after my exclamation, I saw, on the opposite side of the harbour, at about two miles from where I had first seen, or thought I saw, the snake, the same object, moving with a rapid motion up the harbour, on the western shore. As he approached us, it was easy to see that his motion was not that of the common snake, either on the land or in the water, but evidently the vertical movement of the caterpillar. As nearly as I could judge, there was visible at a time about forty feet of his body. It was not, to be sure, a continuity of body, as the form from head to tail (except as the apparent bunches appeared as he moved through the water) was seen only at three or four feet asunder. It was very evident, however, that his length must be much greater than what appeared, as in his movement he left a considerable wake in his rear. I had a fine glass, and was within from one-third to half a mile of him. The head was flat in the water, and the animal was, as far as I could distinguish, of a chocolate colour. I was struck with an appearance in front of the head like a single horn, about nine inches to a foot in length, and of the form of a marline-spike. There were a great many people collected by this time, many of whom had before seen the same object, and the same appearance. From the time I first saw him until he passed by the place where I stood, and soon after disappeared, was not more than fifteen or twenty minutes.

" Subsequent to the period of which I have been speaking, the snake was seen by several of the crews of our coasting vessels, and in some instances within a few yards. Captain Tappan, a person well known to me, saw him with his head above the water two or three feet, at times moving with great rapidity, and at others slowly. He also saw what explained the appearance, which I have described, of a horn on the front of the head. This was doubtless what was observed by Captain Tappan to be the tongue, thrown in an upright position from the mouth, and having the appearance which I have given to it.

" One of the revenue cutters, whilst in the neighbourhood of Cape Ann, had an excellent view of him at a few yards' distance. He moved slowly ; and upon the approach of the vessel, sank and was seen no more."

Dr. Hamilton* states that an animal of similar appearance was again seen, in August 1819, off Nahant, Boston, and remained in the neighbourhood for some weeks. Two hundred persons witnessed it, thirteen folds were counted, and the head, which was serpent-shaped, was elevated two feet above the surface. Its eye was remarkably brilliant and glistening. The water was smooth, and the weather calm and serene. When it disappeared, its motion was undulatory,

* Jardine's *Naturalist's Library*, vol. xxv.

making curves perpendicular to the surface of the water, and giving the appearance of a long moving string of corks. It appeared again off Nahant in July 1833. "It was first seen on Saturday afternoon, passing between Egg Rock and the Promontory, winding his way into Lynn Harbour; and again on Sunday morning, heading for South Shores. It was seen by forty or fifty ladies and gentlemen, who insist that they could not have been deceived."

The *Zoologist* for May 1847 contains an account of a sea-serpent seen in Mahone Bay, about forty miles east of Halifax, by five officers of the garrison, when on a fishing excursion :—" We were surprised by the sight of an immense shoal of grampuses, which appeared in an unusual state of excitement, and which in their gambols approached so close to our little craft that some of the party amused themselves by firing at them with rifles. At this time we were jogging at about five miles an hour, and must have been crossing Margaret's Bay, 'when suddenly,' at a distance of from a hundred and fifty to two hundred yards on our starboard bow, we saw the head and neck of some denizen of the deep, precisely like those of a common snake, in the act of swimming, the head so far elevated and thrown forward by the curve of the neck, as to enable us to see the water under and beyond it. The creature rapidly passed, leaving a regular wake, from the commencement of which to the fore part, which was out of water, we judged in length to be about eighty feet, and this within rather than beyond the mark. It is most difficult to give correctly the dimensions of any object in the water. The head of the creature we set down at about six feet in length, and that portion of the neck which we saw the same; the extreme length, as before stated, at between eighty and one hundred feet. The neck in thickness equalled the bole of a moderate-sized tree. The head and neck of a dark brown or nearly black colour, streaked with white in irregular streaks. I do not recollect seeing any part of the body."

Considerable interest was excited in 1848 by the account of a sea-serpent seen by the captain and officers of Her Majesty's ship *Dædalus* while on her passage from the Cape of Good Hope to St. Helena, in lat. 24° 44′ S. and long. 9° 22′ E. In this case the usual concomitants of calm weather and absence of swell are wanting. The official report to the Admiralty is as follows :—

FIG. 70.—SEA-SERPENT SEEN BY THE CREW OF H.M.S. "DÆDALUS," IN 1848.

H.M.S. *Dædalus*,
Hamoaze, Oct. 11.

SIR,—In reply to your letter of this day's date, requiring information as to the truth of a statement published in the *Times* newspaper, of a sea-serpent of extraordinary dimensions having been seen from Her Majesty's ship *Dædalus*, under my command, on her passage from the East Indies, I have the honour to acquaint you, for the information of my Lords Commissioners of the Admiralty, that at 5 o'clock P.M. on the 6th of August last, in latitude 24° 44′ S. and longitude 9° 22′ E., the weather dark and cloudy, wind fresh from the N.W., with a long ocean swell from the S.W., the ship on the port tack, heading N.E. by N., something very unusual was seen by Mr. Sartoris, midshipman, rapidly approaching the ship from before the beam. The circumstance was immediately reported by him to the officer of the watch, Lieutenant

Edgar Drummond, with whom and Mr. William Barrett, the master, I was at the time walking the quarter-deck. The ship's company were at supper.

On our attention being called to the object, it was discovered to be an enormous serpent, with head and shoulders kept about four feet constantly above the surface of the sea; and as nearly as we could approximate by comparing it with the length of what our main topsail-yard would show in the water, there was at the very least sixty feet of the animal *à fleur d'eau*, no portion of which was, in our perception, used in propelling it through the water, either by vertical or horizontal undulation. It passed rapidly, but so close under our lee quarter that had it been a man of my acquaintance I should have easily recognized his features with the naked eye; and it did not, either in approaching the ship or after it had passed our wake, deviate in the slightest degree from its course to the S.W., which it held on at the pace of from twelve to fifteen miles per hour, apparently on some determined purpose. The diameter of the serpent was about fifteen or sixteen inches behind the head, which was, without any doubt, that of a snake; and it was never, during the twenty minutes that it continued in sight of our glasses, once below the surface of the water; its colour, a dark brown with yellowish white about the throat. It had no fins, but something like the mane of a horse, or rather a bunch of sea-weed, washed about its back. It was seen by the quarter-master, the boatswain's mate, and the man at the wheel, in addition to myself and officers above mentioned.

I am having a drawing of the serpent made from a sketch taken immediately after it was seen, which I hope to have ready for transmission to my Lords Commissioners of the Admiralty by to-morrow's post.

I have, &c.,

PETER M'QUHŒ, *Capt.*

To Admiral Sir W. H. Gage, G.C.B.,
   Devonport.

This drawing was figured in the *Illustrated London News* in illustration of a short but very valuable memoir, and is reproduced upon a smaller scale here.

A similar, perhaps the same, monster was fallen in with at a slightly later date, 20° further south, as described in a letter addressed to the editor of the *Globe*.

*Mary Ann of Glasgow.*
Glasgow, Oct. 19, 1848.

SIR,—I have just reached this port, on a voyage from Malta to Lisbon, and my attention having been called to a report relative to an animal seen by the master and crew of Her Majesty's ship *Dædalus*, I take the liberty of communicating the following circumstance:—

" When clearing out of the port of Lisbon, upon the 30th of September last, we spoke the American brig *Daphne*, of Boston, Mark Trelawny master; she signalled for us to heave to, which we did, and standing close round her counter lay to while the mate boarded us with the jolly boat, and handed a packet of letters, to be despatched per first steamer for Boston on our arrival in England. The mate told me that when in lat. 4° 11′ S., long. 10° 15′ E., wind dead north, upon the 20th of September, a most extraordinary animal had been seen. From his description, it had the appearance of a huge serpent or snake, with a dragon's head.

" Immediately upon its being seen, one of the deck guns was brought to bear upon it, which, having been charged with spike-nails and whatever other pieces of iron could be got at the moment, was discharged at the animal, then only distant about forty yards from the ship. It immediately reared its head in the air, and plunged violently with its body, showing evidently that the charge had taken effect. The *Daphne* was to leeward at the time, but was put about on the starboard tack, and stood towards the brute, which was seen foaming and lashing the water at a fearful rate. Upon the brig nearing, however, it disappeared, and, though evidently wounded, made rapidly off at the rate of fifteen or sixteen knots an hour, as was judged from its appearing several times upon the surface. The *Daphne* pursued for some time; but the night coming on, the master was obliged to put about and continue his voyage.

From the description given by the mate, the brute must have been nearly a hundred feet long, and his account of it agrees in every respect with that lately forwarded to the Admiralty by the master of the *Dædalus*.

JAMES HENDERSON, Master.

The account of the creature seen by the officers and crew of the *Dædalus* excited more than the usual attention given to these stories; for the professional status of the observers guaranteed at once the veracity of their statement, and the probability of their judgment being accurate. Considerable correspondence ensued, including a very masterly attack upon the identification of the creature by Professor Owen, which will be again referred to further on. It also elicited another sea-serpent story which appeared in the *Bombay Bi-monthly Times* for January 1849.

I see, in your paper of the 30th of December, a paragraph in which a doubt is expressed of the authenticity of the account given by

Captain M'Quhœ of the great "sea-serpent." When returning to India, in the year 1829, I was standing on the poop of the *Royal Saxon,* in conversation with Captain Petrie, the commander of that ship. We were at a considerable distance south-west of the Cape of Good Hope, in the usual track of vessels to this country, going rapidly along (seven or eight knots) in fine smooth water. It was in the middle of the day, and the other passengers were at luncheon, the man at the wheel, a steerage passenger, and ourselves being the only persons on the poop. Captain Petrie and myself, at the same instant, were literally fixed in astonishment by the appearance, a short distance ahead, of an animal of which no more generally correct description could be given than that by Captain M'Quhœ. It passed within thirty-five yards of the ship without altering its course in the least; but as it came right abreast of us, it slowly turned its head towards us. Apparently about one-third of the upper part of its body was above water, in nearly its whole length ; and we could see the water curling up on its breast as it moved along, but by what means it moved we could not perceive. . . . We saw this apparently similar creature in its whole length, with the exception of a small portion of the tail, which was under water ; and by comparing its length with that of the *Royal Saxon* (about six hundred feet) when exactly alongside in passing, we calculated it to be in that, as well as its other dimensions, greater than the animal described by Captain M'Quhœ. I am not quite sure of our latitude and longitude at the time, nor do I exactly remember the date, but it was about the end of July.

R. Davidson,
*Superintending Surgeon,*
*Nagpore Subsidiary Force.*

Kamptu,
3rd January 1849.

Again, Lieutenant-Colonel Thomas Steele, of the Coldstream Guards, wrote to the *Zoologist* : " I have lately received the following account from my brother, Captain Steele, 9th Lancers, who, on his way out to India in the *Barham,* saw the sea-serpent. Thinking it might be interesting to you, as corroborating the account of the *Dædalus,* I have taken the liberty of sending you the extract from my brother's letter :—' On the 28th of August, in long. 40° E., lat. 37° 16' S., about half-past two, we had all gone down below to get ready for dinner, when the first mate called us on deck to see a most extraordinary sight. About five hundred yards from the ship there was the head and neck of an

enormous snake; we saw about sixteen or twenty feet out of
the water, and he *spouted* a long way from his head; down
his back he had a crest like a cock's comb,* and was going
very slowly through the water, but left a wake of about fifty
or sixty feet, as if dragging a long body after him. The
captain put the ship off her course to run down to him, but
as we approached him he went down. His colour was green,
with light spots. *He was seen by everyone on board.'* My
brother is no naturalist; and I think this is the first time
the monster has ever been seen to spout."

One of the officers of the ship wrote: " On looking over
the side of the vessel I saw a most wonderful sight, which I
shall recollect as long as I live. His head appeared to be
about sixteen feet above the water, and he kept moving it up
and down, sometimes showing his enormous neck, which was
surmounted with a huge crest in the shape of a saw. It
was surrounded by hundreds of birds, and we at first thought
it was a dead whale. He left a track in the water like the
wake of a boat, and from what we could see of his head and
part of his body, we were led to think he must be about
sixty feet in length, but he might be more. The captain
kept the vessel away to get nearer to him; and when we
were within a hundred yards he slowly sank into the depths
of the sea. While we were at dinner he was seen again."

The *Times*, of Feb. 5, 1858, contains a statement made
by Captain Harrington, of the ship *Castilian*, and certified to
by his chief and second officers, as follows :—

"Ship *Castilian*, Dec. 12, 1857; N.E. end of St. Helena,
distant ten miles. At 6.30 P.M., strong breezes and cloudy,
ship sailing about twelve miles per hour. While myself and
officers were standing on the leeside of the poop, looking
towards the island, we were startled by the sight of a huge
marine animal, which reared its head out of the water within

* How this reminds one of the Chinese dragon.

twenty yards of the ship, when it suddenly disappeared for about half a minute, and then made its appearance in the same manner again, showing us distinctly its neck and head about ten or twelve feet out of the water. Its head was shaped like a long nun-buoy, and I suppose the diameter to have been seven or eight feet in the largest part, with a kind of scroll, or tuft of loose skin, encircling it about two feet from the top ; the water was discoloured for several hundred feet from its head, so much so that, on its first appearance, my impression was that the ship was in broken water, produced, as I supposed, by some volcanic agency since the last time I had passed the island ; but the second appearance completely dispelled those fears, and assured us that it was a monster of extraordinary length, which appeared to be moving slowly towards the land. The ship was going too fast to enable us to reach the masthead in time to form a correct estimate of its extreme length ; but from what we saw from the deck, we conclude that it must have been over two hundred feet long. The boatswain and several of the crew who observed it from the topgallant forecastle, state that it was more than double the length of the ship, in which case it must have been five hundred feet. Be that as it may, I am convinced that it belonged to the serpent tribe ; it was of a dark colour about the head, and was covered with several white spots."

A writer in the *New York Sun* (I have the clipping, but, unfortunately, not the date), discussing the best authenticated stories, says : " The Lynn sea-serpent appears to be the most authentic, the writer having seen several persons who saw it from the beach, and knowing others personally or by reputation. The first animal of this kind seen about Lynn was in 1638, and was seen by Dr. John Josselyn ; and again another was observed, in 1819, by Mr. Cabot. Amos Lawrance, one of the pillars of old Boston, said : ' I have never had any doubt of the existence of the sea-serpent since the morning he was seen off Nahant by old Marshal Prince through his famous masthead spy-glass. For within the next two hours I conversed with Samuel Cabot and Daniel P. Parker, I think, and one or more persons besides, who had spent a part of that morning in witnessing its movements. In addition, Colonel Harris, the commander at Fort Independence, told me that the creature had been seen by a number of his soldiers while standing sentry at early dawn, some time before this show at Nahant ; and Colonel Harris believed it as firmly as though the creature were drawn up before us in State Street, where we then were.' Such is the history of the Lynn sea-serpent ; and the following is an extract from the report of the Linnæan Society of Boston, made by Dr. Bigelow and F. C. Gray : ' The monster was from eighty to ninety feet long ; his head usually carried about two feet above the water ; the body of a dark brown colour, with thirty or forty more protuberances, compared by some to four-gallon kegs, by others to a string of buoys, and called, by some, bunches on the back. Motions very rapid—faster than those of a whale ; swimming a mile in three minutes, and sometimes more, leaving a wake behind him ; chasing mackerel, herrings, and other fish, which were seen jumping out of the water fifty at a time as he approached. He only came to the surface of the sea in calm and bright weather. A skilful gunner fired at him from our boat, and, having taken good aim, felt sure he must have hit him on the head. The creature turned towards him, then dived under the boat, and reappeared a hundred yards on the other side.' In February of 1846 a letter was printed in the various newspapers, signed by Captain Lawson, giving a description of a monstrous snake seen by him from his vessel off Capes Charles and Henry. The length was stated at one hundred feet, and on the back were seen sharp projections. The head was small in proportion to the length."

I next append a few short statements which have appeared at various dates in the public prints.

The *News of the World*, Sept. 28, 1879, states that Captain J. F. Cox, master of the British ship *Privateer*, which arrived at Delaware breakwater on Sept. 9, from London, says : " On August 5, one hundred miles west of Brest (France), weather fine and clear, at 5 P.M., as I was walking the quarter-deck, I saw something black rise out of the water, about twenty feet, in shape like an immense snake of three feet diameter. It was about three hundred yards from the ship, coming towards us. It turned its head partly from us, and went down with a great splash, after staying up about five seconds, but rose again three times at intervals of ten seconds, until it had turned completely from us, and was going from us at a great speed, and making the water boil all round it. I could see its eyes and shape perfectly. It was like a great eel or snake, but as black as coal tar, and appeared to be making great exertions to get away from the ship. I have seen many kinds of fish, in five different oceans, but was never favoured with a sight of the great sea-snake before."

The *Singapore Daily News*, April 6, 1878, in its Australian news quotes from Wellington (New Zealand), Feb. 26 (this month corresponds with August north of the Line): " The captain of the steamship *Durham* reports having seen a monster serpent off Nerowas Island. Thirty feet of the monster was visible out of the water. The crew and passengers corroborate the report."

The *Australian Sketcher* for November 24, 1877, states: " Captain W. H. Nelson, of the American ship *Sacramento*, which arrived in this port from New York on October 20, reported that he saw the sea-serpent on his voyage. The *Argus* paragraph on the subject stated : ' The date on which the creature was seen was on July 30, the ship then being in lat. 31° 59′ N. and long. 37° W. The man at the wheel was the first to observe the monster, and he at once called Captain

Nelson, telling him what he saw; but the latter, having the same feeling of incredulity with regard to the sea-serpent as most other people, did not hurry from below. On coming on deck, however, he was rewarded with a distant glimpse of the supposed sea-serpent, which the helmsman, for his part,

Fig. 71.—Sea-Serpent seen from the Ship "Sacramento," July 30, 1877. (*From the " Australian Sketcher.*")

declared he saw quite plainly. Some forty feet of the monster was alleged to be observable. It appeared to be about the size of a flour-barrel in girth, and its colour was yellowish; the head is described as being flat. The eyes were plainly visible. Captain Nelson is convinced that what he saw was some extraordinary marine monster.' We have obtained from John Hart, the man at the wheel, a pencil sketch of the creature, of which we give an engraving. The sketch is accompanied with a further description, in which the writer says : ' This is a correct sketch of the sea-serpent seen by me while on board the ship *Sacramento*, on her passage from New York to Melbourne, I being at the wheel at the time. It had the body of a very large snake ; its length appeared to me to be about fifty feet or sixty feet. Its head was like an alligator's, with a pair of flippers about ten feet from its head. The colour was of a reddish brown. At the time seen it was lying perfectly still, with its head raised about three feet above the surface of the sea, and as it got thirty or forty feet astern, it dropped its head.' "

I confess that I do not attach much weight to this last example, from the suspicious resemblance which the illustration given in the *Sketcher* bears to an alligator, suggesting that possibly such a creature may have been blown by winds or carried by currents to the position where it was seen. It is true that Mr. Gosse quotes the size of the largest alligator on record as only seventeen feet and a half, whereas the estimated length of the supposed sea-serpent in this instance was from forty to sixty. But against that may be argued the difficulty of estimating lengths or heights when you have but a short inspection, and no object immediately near with which to institute a comparison* ; while I am by no means certain that Mr. Gosse's maximum is correct. Dr. Dennys, of Singapore, has assured me that some years back an alligator, approaching thirty feet in length, haunted for some

---

\* Within a few days of writing these lines I made one of a party of four to visit the waterfalls of Taki-kwannon, near Nagasaki. I asked for estimates of the height of the fall, which was variously guessed, by different members of the party, at from forty-three to one hundred and fifty feet.

days the small tidal creek which runs through, and for some miles above, that town ; while I very well remember Mr. Gregory, the Surveyor-General of Queensland, informing me that in the rivers in the north of that colony there were alligators equalling in length a whale-boat, say twenty-eight feet.

The *Graphic* of April 19th, 1879, contains a drawing of " a marine monster seen from S.S. *City of Baltimore*, in the Gulf of Aden, January 28th." The descriptive letter-press is as follows : —

" The following is an abstract of the account given by our correspondent, Major H. W. I. Senior, of the Bengal Staff Corps, to whom we are indebted for the sketch from which

Fig. 72.—Sea-Serpent seen from the S.S. "City of Baltimore," in the Gulf of Aden, Jan. 28, 1879. (*From the " Graphic" of April* 19, 1879.)

our engraving is taken: ' On the 28th January 1879, at about 10 A.M., I was on the poop deck of the steamship *City of Baltimore*, in latitude 12° 28′ N., longitude 43° 52′ E. I observed a long black object a-beam of the ship's stern on the starboard side, at a distance of about three-quarters of a mile, darting rapidly out of the water and splashing in again with a noise distinctly audible, and advancing nearer and nearer at a rapid pace. In a minute it had advanced to within half-a-mile, and was distinctly recognisable as the " veritable sea-serpent." I shouted out " Sea-serpent ! sea-serpent ! Call the captain ! " Dr. C. Hall, the ship's surgeon, who was reading on deck, jumped up in time to see the monster, as did also Miss Greenfield, one of the passengers on board. By this time it was only about five hundred yards off, and a little in the rear, owing to the vessel then steaming at the rate of about ten knots an hour in a westerly direction. On approaching the wake of the ship, the serpent turned its course a little way, and was soon lost to view in the blaze of sunlight reflected on the waves of the sea. So rapid were its movements, that when it approached the ship's wake, I seized a telescope, but could not catch a view, as it darted rapidly out of the field of the glass before I could see it. I was thus prevented from ascertaining whether it had scales or not ; but the best view of the monster obtainable, when it was about three cables' length, that is, about five hundred yards, distant, seemed to show that it was without scales. I cannot, however, speak with certainty. The head and neck, about two feet in diameter, rose out of the water to a height of about twenty or thirty feet, and the monster opened its jaws wide as it rose, and closed them again as it lowered its head and darted forward for a dive, reappearing almost immediately some hundred yards ahead. The body was not visible at all, and must have been some depth under water, as the disturbance on the surface was too slight to attract notice, although occasionally a splash was seen at some distance behind the head. The shape of the head was not unlike pictures of the dragon I have often seen, with a bull-dog appearance of the forehead and eye-brow. When the monster had drawn its head sufficiently out of the water, it let itself drop, as it were, like a huge log of wood, prior to darting forward under the water.' "

Major Senior's statement is countersigned by the two persons whom he mentions as co-witnesses.

When in Singapore, in 1880, I received the personal testimony of Captain Anderson, at that time chief officer of the *Pluto* (property of the Straits Government) and formerly a commander in the P. and O. Company's service.

Captain Anderson assured me that he had twice seen large sea-serpents. Once off Ushant, when he was chief officer of the *Delta* in 1861. No account was entered in the log nor any notice sent to the newspapers, for fear of ridicule. On that occasion the whole ship's company saw it ; it was five (?) miles distant, and showed fifteen feet of its body out of the water. It resembled a snake with a large fringe round the neck. It appeared to be travelling, and moved its head to and fro like a snake. It never spouted, and was observed for a quarter of an hour.

The second occasion was in the Red Sea, when he was in command of the *Sumatra,* on the outward trip in October or November 1877. Off Mocha he saw an animal, five miles distant, that lifted the body high out of the water like a snake. All exclaimed, "There is the sea-serpent!" but no entry was made in the log, or report made of it. The same creature was, however, seen shortly after by a man-of-war close to Suez and reported.

In 1881 I once more had the personal testimony of an eye-witness.

Mr. J. H. Hoar, of the pilot station, Shanghai, China, informed me that he saw a sea-serpent some years previously, when he was stationed at Ningpo, on the China coast-line, a little south of the embouchure of the Yangtse-kiang. He was at the time on the look-out for a vessel, from the top of the bank of Lowchew Island, Chinsang, on the southern side of the island fronting the six-mile passage. This island lies east of Worth Point. The hill he was on was about one hundred and fifty feet high, the snake distant about two hundred and fifty yards, the depth of water seven fathoms. His attention was directed to it by a group of Chinamen calling out " Shê," which means " snake." He saw it lying on the surface of the water, resembling two masts of a junk end to end, but with a slight interval. Presently it rose slightly, and then appeared all in one, extended flat upon the surface of the water. He examined it with his glass, and noticed the eye, which appeared to be as big as a coffee saucer, and slate-coloured. The head was flat on the top. He estimated the length at from one hundred and twenty to one hundred and forty feet.

He learned that it was the third occasion of its being seen in that place within eight years. An account was published in one of the local journals, by Mr. Sloman, from the statements of the Chinese observers. Mr. Hoar was prevented from doing the same by the fear of being ridiculed. I may note that there is a bay, not far from this spot, among the Chusan islands, which has long been credited with being the abode of a great sea-dragon, and in passing over which junks take certain superstitious precautions.

I have little doubt of the identity of the sea-serpent with the sea-dragon of the Chinese. Dr. Dennys* says : " Of course our old friend, the sea-serpent, turns up on the coasts of China, and the description of him does not greatly differ from that recorded elsewhere. According to a popular legend, the Chien Tang river was at one time infested by a great *kiau* or sea-serpent, and in 1129 A.D., a district graduate is said to have heroically thrown himself into the flood to encounter and destroy the monster. It has been already noted that most of the river gods are supposed to appear in the form of water-snakes, and that the sea-serpents noticed in Chinese records have always infested the mouths of rivers."

The Rev. Mr. Butler, of the Presbyterian Mission in Ningpo,

---

* *Folklore of China*, p. 113.

informed me that a dragon which threatened boats was supposed by the Chinese to infest a narrow passage called Quo
Mung, outside of Chinaye.   Formerly there were two of them
in the neighbourhood, which were very furious, and frequently
upset boats.   They had to be appeased by a yearly offering
of a girl of fair appearance and perfect body.   At last, one of
the *literati* determined to stop this.   He armed himself, and
jumped into the water; blood rose to the surface.   He had
killed one of the dragons.   The other retired to the narrow
place.   A temple was erected to the hero at Peach Blossom
ferry.

It may be noted that both the Malays and the Chinese
attribute the origin of ambergris to either a sea-dragon or a
sea-serpent.   Thus, in the description of Ambergris Island or
Dragon Spittle Island, contained in the *History of the Ming
Dynasty*, Book 325, from which an extract is given (in translation) by Mr. W. P. Groeneveldt, in his *Notes on the Malay
Archipelago and Malacca*, compiled from Chinese sources,*
we find it stated that " this island has the appearance of a
single mountain, and is situated in the Sea of Lambri, at a
distance of one day and one night from Sumatra.   It rises
abruptly out of the sea, which breaks on it with high waves."

" Every spring numerous dragons come together to play
on this island, and they leave behind their spittle.   The
natives afterwards go in canoes to the spot and collect this
spittle, which they take with them.

" The dragon-spittle is at first like fat, of a black and
yellow colour, and with a fishy smell; by length of time it
contracts into large lumps; and these are also found in the
belly of a large fish, of the size of the Chinese peck, and
also with a fishy smell.   When burnt it has a pure and
delicious fragrance.

---

* *Vide Verhandelingen van Het Bataviaasch Genootschap van Kunsten
en Weten Schappen*, Deel xxxix., 1ere Stuk., Batavia, 1877.

"It is sold in the market of Sumatra, one tael, official weight, costing twelve golden coins of that country, and one cati,* one hundred and ninety-two of such pieces, equal to about nine thousand Chinese copper cash ; and so it is not very cheap."

Dr. F. Porter Smith† states that there can be no doubt that the costly, odorous, light yellow, gummy substance, found floating on the sea, or procured from the belly of some large fish in the Indian Ocean, and known by the Chinese of the present day as *lung sin,* or dragon's spittle, is actually ambergris.   The dragon is said to cough it up.

"A similar substance, called *kih-tiau-chi,* brought from Canton and Foochow in former days, is said to be the egg of the dragon or a kind of sea-serpent named *kih tiau.* The name *kih tiau* is singularly like the Greek name for a sea-monster."

One of the most remarkable accounts of sea-monsters, which I believe to be thoroughly trustworthy, is of an animal seen in the Malacca Straits in 1876.

The first notice of it appeared in the *Straits Times Overland Journal* for September 18th, 1876, in the form of a short editorial.

"Our friend Mr. Henry Lee, of *Land and Water,* who in his late work has taken so much trouble to enter into and describe the habits and peculiarities of the sea-serpent,‡ will

---

* About 1⅓ lb. avoirdupois.

† *Contributions to Materia Medica and Natural History of China,* by F. P. Smith, M.B., London ; Shanghai and London, 1871.

I give, in the appendix to this chapter, some accounts of a reputed monster, the Shan, the description of which by Chinese authors, although vague, appears to me to point to the sea-serpent.   I only insert a portion of the latter part of the legends regarding it which I find in my authority, as they are perfectly valueless.   The sample given may, however, be interesting as an example of how the Taouists compiled their absurd miraculous stories.

‡ For *sea-serpent* read *octopus.*

be glad to hear that the passengers and officers of the S.S. *Nestor,* which arrived here this morning, are unanimous in the conclusion, and vouch for the fact, that an extraordinary sea-monster was seen by them between Malacca and Penang on their voyage to this port, on Monday, about noon. It was about two hundred and fifty feet long, about fifty feet broad, square-headed, with black and yellow stripes, closely resembling a salamander."

This was followed, on the succeeding day, by a letter from the captain.

SIR,—In reference to your paragraph in your yesterday's issue, relating to our having seen a sea-monster answering to the popular notion of a sea-serpent, I am prepared to vouch for the correctness of the statement already made to you by the doctor and a passenger by my ship.

Being on the bridge at the time (about 10 A.M.) with the first and third officers, we were surprised by the appearance of an extraordinary monster going in our course, and at an equal speed with the vessel, at a distance from us of about six hundred feet. It had a square head and a dragon black and white striped tail, and an immense body, which was quite fifty feet broad when the monster raised it. The head was about twelve feet broad, and appeared to be occasionally, at the extreme, about six feet above the water. When the head was placed on a level with the water, the body was extended to its utmost limit to all appearance, and then the body rose out of the water about two feet, and seemed quite fifty feet broad at those times. The long dragon tail with black and white scales afterwards rose in an undulating motion, in which at one time the head, at another the body, and eventually the tail, formed each in its turn a prominent object above the water.

The animal, or whatever it may be called, appeared careless of our proximity, and went our course for about six minutes on our starboard side, and then finally worked round to our port side, and remained in view, to the delight of all on board, for about half an hour. His length was reckoned to be over two hundred feet.

JOHN W. WEBSTER,

Singapore,                                      Commander, S.S. *Nestor.*

18th Sepember 1876.

Mr. Cameron, proprietor of the journal, subsequently informed me that he had specially warned Captain Webster of the certain doubt that would be cast upon his statement, but he still insisted on its publication. It was confirmed by Mr. H. R. Beaver, a merchant of Singapore, and other persons who were passengers by the boat.

The same newspaper (*Straits Times Overland Journal*), on November 2, 1876, had the following extract from the *China Mail*:—

"It is more than probable that Captain Webster, of the steamer *Nestor*, will be ' interviewed ' very extensively when he reaches a berth in London Docks. A genuine sea-serpent is not met with every day, and as the observations made by the officers of the ship have, we understand, been set down in some formal way before Consul Medhurst at Shanghai, to be forwarded to the *Field*, the naturalists will be in a position to pursue their researches when the captain arrives. Competent authorities are now of opinion that the part of the monster formerly supposed to have been its head, must have been a hump; and that its head's being under water would account for the supreme contempt with which it treated the passage of the steamer. The undulating motion of the huge animal would explain the statement that this knob or hump rose occasionally about six feet out of the water. The alternate yellow and black stripes which covered all that could be seen of the body, appear to have conveyed the impression that the tail was like that of a dragon covered with scales, although that conclusion need not necessarily be looked upon as certain. If the head of this unknown ' shape ' was actually under water, then the length becomes proportionately greater. It was over two hundred feet long before, it must now be regarded as measuring, say, two hundred and fifty feet, which, with forty-five or fifty feet beam, gives a leviathan of something like the dimensions of an old-fashioned frigate."

A correspondent of the *Celestial Empire*, of Shanghai, wrote thus to the journal :—

Sir,—If it is true that one of those who observed the marine monster from the *Nestor* is still here, it is very desirable that he should give some fuller account of what he saw. Only a sciolist will deny the possibility of such a beast, and Professor Owen himself has remarked that the only absolutely incredible part of the accounts of those who have seen it, is the statement of its vertical sinuosity, which is impossible to any of the serpent tribe.

The monster seen by the *Nestor*, however, was probably one of the Chelonidæ, "the father of all the turtles," as he is fitly called by the natives of Sumatra, who fully believe in his existence, and to whom he occasionally appears. Indeed, Baumgarten, in his *Malaysien*, published at Amsterdam in 1829, describes the monster, and estimates its length and breadth at one hundred and twenty and thirty cubits respectively, measurements which agree very nearly with those given by Captain Webster. Baumgarten* adds that it is a general belief in Sumatra (vol. ii. p. 321, Ed. 1820), that whosoever sees him will die within the year. "This," he says naively enough, "I have not been able to prove."

Mr. David Aitken, of Singapore, wrote to the *Daily Times* as follows :—

DEAR SIR,—Like many others, I have been astonished at the dimensions given by you of the sea-serpent. They are certainly enormous, and they far surpass anything I have ever seen or heard of. The largest snake ever I authentically heard about was one which passed between the surveying brigs *Krishna* and *Menx* when under the command of Lieutenant Ward, of the Indian Navy, when surveying off the coast of Sumatra, about the years 1858 and 1859. This monster passed by the brigs one Sunday morning when they were moored somewhere opposite Malacca. Its length was variously estimated at from the length of the *Krishna* to one hundred feet. Sixty feet was the moderate length set down for its frame.

In or near the same place, another monster had been seen by a previous surveying party.

Mr. Stephen Cave, M.P. for Shoreham, in 1861, communicated to Mr. Gosse a short statement, which throws some light upon the food of the monster. It is in the form of an

* I must also add, on the information of Mr. H. C. Syers, of Selangor, that Captain Douglas, late Resident of Perak, had a large sea-serpent rise close to him, somewhere off Perak, when in a boat manned by Malays. Mr. Syers had the account both from Captain Douglas and from the crew; and he tells me that there is a universal belief in the existence of some large sea-monster among the Malays of the western coast of the Peninsula.

extract from his journal written during a voyage to the West Indies, in 1846, as follows :—

"Thursday, December 10, off Madeira, on board R.M.S. *Thomas*, made acquaintance with a Captain Christmas, of the Danish Navy, a proprietor in Santa Cruz, and holding some office about the Danish court. He told me he once saw a sea-serpent between Iceland and the Faroe islands. He was lying-to in a gale of wind, in a frigate of which he had the command, when an immense shoal of porpoises rushed by the ship as if pursued ; and, lo and behold, a creature with a neck moving like that of a swan, about the thickness of a man's waist, with a head like a horse, raised itself slowly and gracefully from the deep, and, seeing the ship, it immediately disappeared again, head foremost, like a duck diving. He only saw it for a few seconds. The part above the water seemed about eighteen feet in length. He is a singularly intelligent man, and by no means one to allow his imagination to run away with him."

Witty journalists had a good time over the publication of the story of the serpent seen by Captain Drevar, with which I shall wind up my list of apparitions. As will be seen, however, the captain stuck manfully to his guns, and I, for one, am of the belief that he really saw the incident which he narrates. I have not met the captain himself, but I did, in Singapore, meet with many who had heard the whole story from his own lips, and whose impression was that he was a truthful man.

### The Barque "Pauline" Sea-serpent.

#### To the Editor of the *Calcutta Englishman.*

SIR,—As I am not sure that my statement respecting the sea-serpent reached the *Shipping Gazette* in London, I enclose a copy that may be interesting to your numerous readers. I have been sent plenty of extracts from English papers, nearly all of them ridiculing my statement. I can laugh and joke on the subject as well as anyone, but I can't see why, if people can't fairly refute my statement, they should use falsehood to do so. The *Daily Telegraph* says, "The ribs of the ill-

fated fish were distinctly heard cracking one after the other, with a
report like that of a small cannon; its bellowings ceased, &c.  To use
the eloquent words of the principal spectator, it ' struck us all aghast
with terror.'"  If the writer knew anything of sailors, he would not write
such bosh.  Fear and terror are not in Jack's composition; and such
eloquent words he leaves to such correspondents as described the ever-
doubtful " man-and-dog-fight."  I am just as certain of seeing what I
described, as that I met the advertisement that the *Telegraph* has
the largest circulation in the world staring me at every street corner in
London.  It is easy for such a paper to make any man, good, great, or
interesting, look ridiculous.  Little wonder is it that my relatives write
saying that they would have seen a hundred sea-serpents and never
reported it; and a lady also wrote that she pitied anyone that was
related to anyone that had seen the sea-serpent.  It is quite true that it
is a sad thing for any man to see more, to feel more, and to know
more, than his fellows; but I have some of the philosophy that made
O'Connell rejoice in being the most abused man in the United Kingdom,
for he also had the power of giving a person a lick with the rough side
of his tongue.  If I had any such power I would not use it, for contempt
is the sharpest reproof; and this letter is the only notice I have taken
of the many absurd statements, &c. &c. &c.

GEORGE DREVAR,
Master of the *Pauline*.

Barque *Pauline*,
    Chittagong, January 15, 1876.

FIG. 73.—SEA-SERPENT ATTACKING WHALE, AS SEEN BY CAPT. DREVAR,
OF THE BARQUE "PAULINE," IN 1876.

Barque *Pauline*, January 8th, 1875, lat. 5° 13′ S., long. 35° W., Cape
    Roque, north-east corner of Brazil distant twenty miles, at
    11 A.M.

The weather fine and clear, the wind and sea moderate.  Observed
some black spots on the water, and a whitish pillar, about thirty-five
feet high, above them  At the first glance I took all to be breakers, as
the sea was splashing up fountain-like about them, and the pillar, a

pinnacle rock bleached with the sun; but the pillar fell with a splash, and a similar one rose. They rose and fell alternately in quick succession, and good glasses showed me it was a monster sea-serpent coiled twice round a large sperm whale. The head and tail parts, each about thirty feet long, were acting as levers, twisting itself and victim around with great velocity. They sank out of sight about every two minutes, coming to the surface still revolving, and the struggles of the whale and two other whales that were near, frantic with excitement, made the sea in this vicinity like a boiling cauldron; and a loud and confused noise was distinctly heard. This strange occurrence lasted some fifteen

FIG. 74.—SEA-SERPENT ATTACKING WHALE.—THE END OF THE STRUGGLE.

minutes, and finished with the tail portion of the whale being elevated straight in the air, then waving backwards and forwards, and laving [lashing?] the water furiously in the last death-struggle, when the whole body disappeared from our view, going down head-foremost towards the bottom, where, no doubt, it was gorged at the serpent's leisure; and that monster of monsters may have been many months in a state of coma, digesting the huge mouthful. Then two of the largest sperm whales that I have ever seen moved slowly thence towards the vessel, their bodies more than usually elevated out of the water, and not spouting or making the least noise, but seeming quite paralysed with fear; indeed, a cold shiver went through my own frame on beholding the last agonising struggle of the poor whale that had seemed as helpless in the coils of the vicious monster as a small bird in the talons of a hawk. Allowing for two coils round the whale, I think the serpent was about one hundred and sixty or one hundred and seventy feet long, and seven or eight in girth. It was in colour much like a conger eel, and the head, from the mouth being always open, appeared the largest part of the body. . . . . I think Cape San Roque is a landmark for whales leaving the south for the North Atlantic. . . . . I wrote thus far, little thinking I would ever see the serpent again; but at 7 A.M., July 13th, in the same latitude, and some eighty miles east of San Roque, I was astonished to see the same or a similar monster. It was throwing its head and about forty feet of its body in a horizontal position out of the water as it passed onwards by the stern of our vessel. I began musing why we were so much favoured with such a strange visitor, and concluded that the band of white paint, two feet wide above the copper, might have looked like a fellow-serpent to it, and, no doubt, attracted its attention. . . . . While thus thinking, I was startled by the cry of "There it is again," and a short distance to leeward, elevated some sixty feet in the air, was the great leviathan, grimly looking towards the vessel. As I was not sure it was only our free board it was viewing, we had all our axes ready, and were fully determined, should the brute embrace the *Pauline*, to chop away for its backbone with all our might, and the wretch might have found for once in its life that it had caught a Tartar. This statement is strictly true, and the occurrence was witnessed by my officers, half the crew, and myself; and we are ready, at any time, to testify on oath that it is so, and that we are not in the least mistaken. . . . . A vessel, about three years ago, was dragged over by some sea-monster in the Indian Ocean.

GEORGE DREVAR,
Master of the *Pauline*.

Chittagong, January 15, 1876.

Captain George Drevar, of the barque *Pauline*, appeared on Wednesday morning at the Police-court, Dale-street, before Mr. Raffles, stipendiary magistrate, accompanied by some of his officers and part of the crew of the barque, when they made the following declaration :—

"We, the undersigned, captain, officers, and crew of the barque *Pauline*, of London, do solemnly and sincerely declare that on July 8th, 1875, in latitude 5° 13′, longitude 35° W., we observed three large sperm whales, and one of them was gripped round the body with two turns of what appeared to be a large serpent. The head and tail appeared to have a length beyond the coils of about thirty feet, and its girth eight or nine feet. The serpent whirled its victim round and round for about fifteen minutes, and then suddenly dragged the whale to the bottom, head first.

" GEORGE DREVAR, *Master*,
" HORATIO THOMPSON,
" HENDERSON LANDELLO,
" OWEN BAKER,
" WILLIAM LEWAN.

"Again, on July 13th, a similar serpent was seen about two hundred yards off, shooting itself along the surface, head and neck being out of the water several feet. This was seen only by the captain and one ordinary seaman.

" GEORGE DREVAR, *Master*.

" A few moments after, it was seen elevated some sixty feet perpen-
dicularly in the air by the chief officer and the following able seamen,
Horatio Thompson, Owen Baker, William Lewan. And we make this
solemn declaration, conscientiously believing the same to be true.

" GEORGE DREVAR, *Master.*
" WILLIAM LEWAN, *Steward.*
" HORATIO THOMPSON, *Chief Officer,*
" JOHN HENDERSON LANDELLO, 2nd *Officer,*
" OWEN BAKER."

Some confirmation of Captain Drevar's story is afforded by
one quoted by the Rev. Henry T. Cheeves, in *The Whale
and his Captors.* The author says :—

" From a statement made by a Kinebeck shipmaster in
1818, and sworn to before a justice of the peace in Kinebeck
county, Maine, it would seem that the notable sea-serpent
and whale are sometimes found in conflict. At six o'clock
in the afternoon of June 21st, in the packet *Delia,* plying
between Boston and Hallowell, when Cape Ann bore west-
south-west about two miles, steering north-north-east,
Captain Shuback West and fifteen others on board with him
saw an object directly ahead, which he had no doubt was
the sea-serpent, or the creature so often described under that
name, engaged in fight with a large whale. . . . .

" The serpent threw up its tail from twenty-five to thirty
feet in a perpendicular direction, striking the whale by it with
tremendous blows, rapidly repeated, which were distinctly
heard, and very loud, for two or three minutes ; they then
both disappeared, moving in a south-west direction ; but after
a few minutes reappeared in-shore of the packet, and about
under the sun, the reflection of which was so strong as to
prevent their seeing so distinctly as at first, when the serpent's fearful blows with his tail were repeated and clearly
heard as before. They again went down for a short time,
and then came up to the surface under the packet's larboard
quarter, the whale appearing first, and the serpent in pursuit, who was again seen to shoot up his tail as before, which

he held out of water for some time, waving it in the air
before striking, and at the same time his head fifteen or
twenty feet, as if taking a view of the surface of the sea.
After being seen in this position a few minutes, the serpent
and whale again disappeared, and neither was seen after by
any on board.   It was Captain West's opinion that the

Fig. 75.—Sea-Serpent attacking Whale.   (*From Sketches by Capt. Davidson,*
*S.S. " Kiushiu-maru.*")

whale was trying to escape, as he spouted but once at a time
on coming to the surface, and the last time he appeared he
went down before the serpent came up."

A remarkable and independent corroboration of modern
date comes from the Japan seas.   It was reported both in

local papers and in the *San Francisco Californian Mail-Bag*
for 1879, from which I extract the notice and the illustrative
cuts (Fig. 75).

" The accompanying engravings are *fac-similes* of a sketch
sent to us by Captain Davidson, of the steamship *Kiushiu-
maru*,* and is inserted as a specimen of the curious drawings
which are frequently forwarded to us for insertion.   Captain
Davidson's statement, which is countersigned by his chief
officer, Mr. McKechnie, is as follows :—

" ' Saturday, April 5th, at 11.15 A.M., Cape Satano distant
about nine miles, the chief officer and myself observed a
whale jump clear out of the sea, about a quarter of a mile
away.

" ' Shortly after it leaped out again, when I saw there
was something attached to it.   Got glasses, and on the next
leap distinctly saw something holding on to the belly of the
whale.   The latter gave one more spring clear of the water,
and myself and chief officer then observed what appeared to
be a creature of the snake species rear itself about thirty feet
out of the water.   It appeared to be about the thickness of a
junk's mast, and after standing about ten seconds in an
erect position, it descended into the water, the upper end
going first.   With my glasses I made out the colour of the
beast to resemble that of a pilot fish.''

There is an interesting story† of a fight between a water-
snake and a trout, by Mr. A. W. Chase, Assistant United
States Coast Survey, which, *magnis componere parva*, may be
accepted as an illustration of how a creature of serpentine
form would have to deal with a whale ; only, as on the surface or in mid-water it would be prevented from grasping any
rocks by which to anchor itself, we may readily conceive it

---

* This is one of the fleet of the important Japanese Mitsu Bish
Company, the equivalent of the P. and O. Company in Japan.

† *Pop. Sci. Monthly*, No. 56, December 1876, p. 234.

holding on with a tenacious grip of its extended jaws, and drawing itself up to the enemy until it could either embrace it in its coils or stun it with violent blows of the tail.*

"The trout, at first sight, was lying in mid-water, heading up stream. It was, as afterwards appeared, fully nine inches in length. . . . . This new enemy of the trout was a large water-snake of the common variety, striped black and yellow. He swam up the pool on the surface until over the trout, when he made a dive, and by a dexterous movement seized the trout in such a fashion that the jaws of the snake closed its mouth. The fight then commenced. The trout had the use of its tail and fins, and could drag the snake from the surface; when near the bottom, however, the snake made use of its tail by winding it round every stone or root that it could reach. After securing this tail-hold, it could drag the trout towards the bank, but on letting go the trout would have a new advantage. This battle was continued for full twenty minutes, when the snake managed to get its tail out of the water and clasped around the root of one of the willows mentioned as overhanging the pool. The battle was then up, for the snake gradually put coil after coil around the root, with each one dragging the fish toward the land. When half its body was coiled it unloosed the first hold, and stretched the end of its tail out in every direction, and finding another root, made fast; and now, using both, dragged the trout on the gravel bank. It now had it under control, and, uncoiling, the snake dragged the fish fully ten feet up on the bank, and, I suppose would have gorged him," &c. &c.

---

* It must be remembered that it is with a blow of its powerful tail that the alligator stuns its prey and knocks it into the water (when any stray animal approaches the bank), and it is with the tail that the dragon, in the fable related by Ælian, chastises, although gently, its mistress, and constricts, according to Pliny, the elephant in its folds.

Captain Drevar follows Pontoppidan (probably unwittingly) in identifying the sea-serpent with the leviathan of Scripture, quoting Isaiah xxvii. 1, "In that day the Lord with his sore and great and strong sword shall punish leviathan, the piercing serpent, even leviathan that crooked serpent; and he shall slay the dragon that is in the sea." As I read the above passage, it is the dragon that is in the sea, and not the leviathan, which should be identified with the sea-serpent, unless the two, dragon and leviathan, are in apposition, which does not seem to be the case.

These various narratives which I have collected are, for the most part, well attested by the signature, or declaration on oath, of well-known and responsible people. Captain Drevar, in the small pamphlet which he had printed for private circulation, says: "Does any thinking person imagine I could keep command over men with a deliberate lie in our mouths?" and a similar question may be asked, with, I think, the possibility of only one reply, in the case of the narratives of Captain M'Quhœ and other officers and commanders in various navies and merchant vessels, and of the numerous other reputable witnesses who have affirmed, either as a simple statement or on oath, that they have seen sundry remarkable sea-monsters. I used the expression, "I think," because, of course, there is the possibility of scepticism.

"Authority, in matters of opinion, divides itself (say) into three principal classes: there is the authority of witnesses; they testify to matters of fact. The judgment upon these is commonly, though not always, easy; but this testimony is always the substitution of the faculties of others for our own, which, taken largely, constitutes the essence of authority.

"This is the kind which we justly admit with the smallest jealousy. Yet not always; one man admits, another refuses, the authority of a sea-captain and a sailor or two on the existence of a sea-serpent." *

I, for my part, belong to the former of these two categories. I believe in the statements that I have recorded, and in the following reasoning address only those who do likewise.

That mistakes have occasionally occurred is undoubted. Mr. Gosse records two instances in which long patches of sea-weed so far excited the imagination of captains of vessels as to cause them to lower boats and proceed to the attack.

The credibility of ghost stories generally is much affected when supposed apparitions are investigated and traced to some simple cause; and the hypersceptical may argue on parallel grounds that the transformation, in some few instances, of a supposed sea-serpent into sea-weed, or the admission of the plausible suggestion that it has been simulated by a seal, a string of porpoises, or some other very ordinary animals, largely affects the whole question.

And this would undoubtedly be the case if the conditions of the several examples were at all similar. But the hesitation or temporary misapprehension of captains or crews, in a thousand instances, as to the nature of a string of weed, supine on the surface, and lashed into fantastic motion by the surge of the ocean waves, has absolutely no bearing on the positive stories of a creature which is seen in calm fjords and bays to roll itself coil after coil, uplift its head high above the water, exhibit capacious jaws armed with teeth, conspicuous eyes, and paws or paddles, which pursues and menaces boats, presents a tangible object to a marksman, and when struck disappears with a mighty splash.

The probability of a gigantic seal, or of a string of por-

---

* *Nineteenth Century*, March 1877, p. 20. Article on " Authority in Matters of Opinion," by G. Cornewall Lewis. Reviewed by W. E. Gladstone.

poises, being mistaken for a sea-serpent by post-captains and their officers in the Navy is small, but becomes almost, if not quite, impossible when the observers are fishermen on coasts like those of Norway, who have been in the habit of seeing seals and porpoises almost every day of their lives. We may, therefore, freely grant that occasional mistakes have arisen, just as we have admitted that undoubtedly many hoaxes have been indulged in.

A rational and commonplace explanation is quite possible in some cases, as, for example, in that of a creature of abnormal appearance seen by the crew of Her Majesty's yacht, the *Osborne*, in the Mediterranean, which was suggested, with great probability, to have been, if I remember correctly, some species of shark; while the supposed sea-serpent, washed up on the Isle of Stronsa, in 1808, proved, on scientific examination, to be a shark of the genus Selache, probably belonging to the species known as "the barking shark."

The great oceanic bone shark, known to few except whalers, which has been stated to reach as much as sixty feet in length, may also occasionally have originated a misconception; and there must be still remaining in the depths of the ocean undescribed species of fish, of bizarre form, and probably gigantic size, the occasional appearance of which would puzzle an observer.

For example, in November 1879, an illustration was given in the *Graphic* of "another marine monster," professing to be a sketch in the Gulf of Suez from H.M.S. *Philomel*, accompanied by the following descriptive letter-press :—

"This strange monster," says Mr. W. J. Andrews, Assistant Paymaster, H.M.S. *Philomel*, "was seen by the officers and ship's company of this ship at about 5.30 P.M. on October 14, when in the gulf of Suez, Cape Zafarana bearing at the time N.W. seventeen miles, lat. 28° 56′ N., long. 32° 54′ E.

"When first observed it was rather more than a mile distant on the port bow, its snout projecting from the surface of the water, and strongly marked ripples showing the position of the body. It then opened its jaws, as shown in the sketch, and shut them again several times, forcing the water from between them as it did so in all directions in large jets. From time to time a portion of the back and dorsal fin appeared at some distance from the head. After remaining some little time in the above-described position, it dis-

FIG. 76.—ANOTHER MARINE MONSTER. A Sketch in the Gulf of Suez, from H.M.S. "Philomel," Oct. 14, 1879. (*From the "Graphic," Nov. 1879.*)

appeared, and on coming to the surface again it repeated the action of elevating the head and opening the jaws several times, turning slowly from side to side as it did so.

"On the approach of the ship the monster swam swiftly away, leaving a broad track like the wake of a ship, and disappeared beneath the waves.

"The colour of that portion of the body that was seen was black, as was also the upper jaw. The lower jaw was grey round the mouth, but of a bright salmon colour underneath, like the belly of some kinds of lizard, becoming redder as it approached the throat. The inside of the mouth appeared to be grey with white stripes, parallel to the edges of the jaw, very distinctly marked. These might have been rows of teeth or of some substance resembling whalebone. The height the snout was elevated above the surface of the water was at least fifteen feet, and the spread of the jaws quite twenty-five feet."

Strangely enough, a proximate counterpart of this fish, but of mimic size, was made known to science in 1882. My attention was called by Mr. Streich, of the German Consulate in Shanghai, to a description of this in the *Daheim*, an illustrated family paper, published in Leipzig, with an illustrative figure, from which I inferred that the monster seen by the crew of the *Philomel* was only a gigantic and adult specimen of a species belonging to the same order, perhaps to the same genus, as the Eurypharynx, adapted to live in the depths of the ocean, and only appearing upon the surface rarely and as the result of some abnormal conditions. I give *fac-similes* of both engravings, in order that my readers may draw their own comparison. The letter-press of the *Daheim* is as follows :—

### " *A New Fish.**

" The deep-sea explorations of last year, which extended over eight thousand metres in depth, brought to light some very extraordinary animals, of which, up to the present date, we have no idea. The most curious one was found by the French steamer *Le Travailleur*, on which there was a staff of naturalists, and of the number was M. Milne Edwards. They were entirely devoted to deep-sea dredging.

" Between Morocco and the Canary Islands, at two thousand three hundred metres depth, the dredge caught a most wonderful animal, which at the first glance nobody thought

* From the *Daheim*, No. 17, Supplement. January 27th, 1883. Leipzig.

to be a fish. This fish, of which we give here a picture,
dwells on the bottom of the sea where the water is +5°
Celsius,* in a kind of red slime composed of the shells of
small Globigerinæ. On account of its curious mouth it has
been called *Eurypharynx Pelicanoides, i.e.* the Pelican-like
Broad-jaws. This creature is distinguished from all its class
by the peculiar construction of its mouth, its under jaw being
of a structure different from that of any other fish, possessing only two small teeth and a big pouch of most expansible

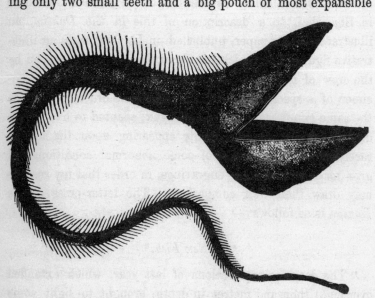

FIG. 77.—EURYPHARYNX PELICANOIDES. (*From the Daheim.*)

skin, similar to the sac which a pelican has on its under jaw.
In this sac it (the Broad-jaw) collects its food, and as its
stomach is of very small dimensions, we may, from analogy
with other fishes, conclude that it digests partly in this
sac.

"The swimming apparatus of this fish is not much developed, and reduced to a number of spines erect from the back
and the belly.

* 41 Fahrenheit.

" The pectoral fins, which are immediately behind the eye, are also very small, so that we may conclude from this that this fish does not move much, and is not a good swimmer.

" It only inhabits the bottom of the sea. Its body decreases gradually backwards till it finishes in a string-like tail. The organs for breathing are not much developed. Six slits (gill apertures?) allow the water to enter.

" The colour of the fish (the size of which we do not find in our authority) is velvet black."

Before proceeding further I must point out that we may dismiss from our minds the possibility of the so-called sea-serpent being merely a large example of those marine serpents of which several species and numerous individuals are known to exist on the coast of many tropical countries, for these are rarely more than from four to six feet in length, although Dampier\* mentions one which he saw on the northern coast of Australia, which was long (but the length is not specified) and as big as a man's leg. He gives a curious instance of these biters being bit, which he observed not far from Scoutens Island, off New Guinea :—

" On the 23rd we saw two snakes, and the next morning another passing by us, which was furiously assaulted by two fishes that had kept in company five or six days. They were shaped like mackerel, and were about that bigness and length, and of a yellow-greenish colour. The snake swam away from them very fast, keeping his head above water. The fish snapped at his tail ; but when he turned himself that fish would withdraw and another would snap ; so that by turns they kept him employed. Yet he still defended himself, and swam away at a great pace, till they were out of sight."

---

\* *A Collection of Voyages,* in 4 volumes.   J. J. Knapton, London, 1729.

Leguat* speaks of a marine serpent, over sixty pounds in weight, which he and his comrades in misfortune captured and tasted, when marooned by order of the Governor of the Mauritius on some small island off the harbour, about six miles from the shore.   He says :—

" It was a frightful sea-serpent, which we in our great simplicity took for a large lamprey or eel.   This animal seemed to us very extraordinary, for it had fins, and we knew not that there were any such  creatures as sea-serpents. Moreover, we had been  so accustomed to discover creatures that were new to us, both at land and at sea, that we did not think this to be any other than an odd sort of eel that we never had  seen before, yet which we could  not but think more resembled a snake than an eel.   In a word, the monster had a serpent or crocodile's head, and a mouth full of hooked, long and sharp teeth. . . . . When our purveyors came we related to them what had happened to us, and showed them the eel's head, but they only said they had never seen the like."

In spite of Leguat's impression, I think it was only some species of conger eel.

Marine serpents are abundant on the Malay coast, and particularly so in the Indian Ocean.   Niebuhr says :—

" In the Indian Ocean, at a certain distance from land, a great many water-serpents, from twelve to fifteen inches in length, are to be seen rising above the surface of the water. When these serpents are seen they are an indication that the coast is exactly two degrees distant.   We saw some of these serpents, for the first time, on the evening of the 9th of September ;  on  the  11th we landed  in  the  harbour of Bombay." †

---

* *A Voyage to the East Indies*, by Francis Leguat.   London, 1708.

† I find the following note in *Maclean's Guide to Bombay*, for 1883 : " Since the first edition of this Gazette was published, Captain Dundas, of the P. and O. Company's steamer *Cathay*, has informed me that the

These sea-snakes are reputed to be mostly, if not entirely, venomous. Their motion in the water is by undulation in a horizontal, not in a vertical, direction; they breathe with lungs; their home is on the surface, and they would perish if confined for any considerable period beneath it.

Fig. 78.—Scoliophis atlanticus. Killed on the Sea-shore near Boston, in 1817, and at that time supposed to be the young of the Sea-Serpent.

It is an open question whether conger eels may not exist, in the ocean depths, of far greater dimensions than those of the largest individuals with which we are acquainted. Major Wolf, who was stationed at Singapore while I was there in 1880, gave me information which seems to corroborate this idea. He stated that when dining some years before with a retired captain of the 39th Regiment, then resident at Wicklow, the latter informed him that, having upon one occasion gone to the coast with his servant in attendance on him, the latter asked permission to cease continuing on with the captain in order that he might bathe. Having received permission, he proceeded to do so, and swam out beyond the edge of the shallow water into the deep. A coastguards-man, who was watching him from the cliff above, was horrified to see something like a huge fish pursuing the man after he had turned round towards the shore. He was afraid to call out lest the man should be perplexed. The man,

statements of old travellers regarding these serpents are quite accurate. The serpents are not seen excepting during the south-west monsoon the season in which alone voyages used to be made to India. In Horsburgh's *Sailing Directions*, shipmasters are warned to look out for the serpents, whose presence is a sign that the ship is close to land. Captain Dundas says that the serpents are yellow or copper-coloured. The largest ones are farthest out to sea. They lie on the surface of the water, and appear too lazy even to get out of a steamer's way.

however, heard some splash or noise behind him, and looked round and saw a large head, like a bull-dog's head, projecting out of the water as if to seize him.  He made a frantic rush shoreways, and striking the shallow ground, clambered out as quickly as possible, but broke one of his toes from the violence with which he struck the ground.  This story was confirmed by a Mr. Burbidge, a farmer, who stated that on one occasion when he himself was bathing within a mile or so of the same spot, the water commenced swirling around him, and that, being alarmed, he swam rapidly in, and was pursued by something perfectly corresponding with that described by the other narrator, and which he supposed to be a large conger eel.  In each case the length was estimated at twenty feet.  Mr. Gosse gives the greatest length recorded at ten feet.

Were we only acquainted with a small and certain proportion of the sea-serpent stories, we might readily imagine that they had been originated by a sight of some monstrous conger, but there are details exhibited by them, taken as a whole, which forbid that idea.  We must therefore search elsewhere for the affinities of the sea-serpent.

And first as to those authorities who believe and who disbelieve in its existence.

Professor Owen, in 1848, attacked the *Dædalus* story in a very masterly manner, and extended his arguments so as to embrace the general non-probability of other stories which had previously affirmed it.  He was, in fact, its main scientific opponent.

Sir Charles Lyell, upon the other hand, was, I believe, persuaded of its existence from the numerous accounts which he accumulated on the occasion of his second visit to America, especially evidence procured for him by Mr. J. W. Dawson, of Pictou, as to one seen, in 1844, at Arisaig, near the north-east end of Nova Scotia, and as to another, in August 1845, at Merigomish, in the Gulf of St. Lawrence.

Agassiz also gave in his adhesion to it. " I have asked myself, in connection with this subject, whether there is not such an animal as the sea-serpent. There are many who will doubt the existence of such a creature until it can be brought under the dissecting knife ; but it has been seen by so many on whom we may rely, that it is wrong to doubt any longer. The truth is, however, that if a naturalist had to sketch the outlines of an icthyosaurus or plesiosaurus from the remains we have of them, he would make a drawing very similar to the sea-serpent as it has been described. There is reason to think that the parts are soft and perishable, but I still consider it probable that it will be the good fortune of some person on the coast of Norway or North America to find a living representative of this type of reptile, which is thought to have died out."

Mr. Z. Newman was the first scientific man to absolutely affirm his belief in its existence, and to indicate its probable zoological affinities ; and he was ably followed by Mr. Gosse, who, in the charming work* already frequently quoted, exhaustively discusses the whole question.

Mr. Gosse, however, to my mind, forgoes a great portion of the advantage of his argument by a too limited acceptance of authorities, and leaves untouched, as have all who preceded him, the question of the breathing apparatus of the creature, and also omits insisting, as he might well have done, on the remarkable coincidence of the seasons and climatic conditions at and under which the creature ordinarily exhibits itself, which may be quoted first as an argument in favour of the reality of the different stories, and, secondly, as affording indica-

* The *Romance of Natural History*, P. H. Gosse, F.R.S., First Series, London, 1880, 12th edition ; Second Series, 1875, 5th edition.

tions of the nature and habits of the creature to which they relate.

Both Mr. Newman and Mr. Gosse, moreover, laboured under the disadvantage of being unacquainted with some of the later stories, such as that of the *Nestor* sea-serpent seen in the Straits of Malacca, which appears to amply substantiate the general conclusion at which they had already, happily, as I conceive, arrived.

In nearly all the cases quoted, and in all of those where the creature has appeared in the deep fjords of Norway or in the bays of other coasts, the date of its appearance has been some time during the months of July and August, and the weather calm and hot. These last summer conditions, in high latitudes, do not obtain for long together, so that the auspices favourable to the appearance of the creature would probably not exist for more than a few weeks in each season, and during the remainder of the year it would rest secluded in the depths of the fjords, presuming those to be its permanent habitation, or in some oceanic home, if, as would seem more likely to be the case, its appearance in the bays and fjords was simply due to a temporary visit, made possibly in connection with its reproduction; for, were its habitation in the fjords constant, we should expect it to make its appearance annually, instead of at irregular and distant intervals.

We must also infer that it is a non-air-breathing creature.

Professor Owen, in his very able discussion of the *Dædalus* story, bases his main argument against the serpentine character of the creature seen in this and other instances on there being either no undulation at all of the body, or a vertical one, which is not a characteristic of serpents, and on the fact of no remains having ever been discovered washed up on the Norway coasts. He says :—

" Now, a serpent, being an air-breathing animal, with long vesicular and receptacular lungs, dives with an effort, and commonly floats when dead, and so would the sea-serpent, until decomposition or accident had opened the tough integument and let out the imprisoned gases. . . . . During life the exigencies of the respiration of the great sea-serpent would always compel him frequently to the surface; and, when dead and swollen, it would

> Prone on the flood, extended long and large,
> Lie floating many a rood.

Such a spectacle, demonstrative of the species if it existed, has not hitherto met the gaze of any of the countless voyagers who have traversed the seas in so many directions."

But, assuming it to be neither a serpent nor an air-breathing creature, the very cogent arguments which he applied so powerfully fall to the ground, and I may at once state that a review of the whole of the reported cases of its appearance entirely favours the first assumption, while a little reflection will show the necessity of the latter. No air-breathing creature, or rather a creature furnished with lungs, could possibly exist, even for a season only, in the inland bays of populous countries like Norway and Scotland without continually exposing itself to observation; but this is not the case. Whereas there is no difficulty in conceiving that a creature adapted to live in the depths of the ocean could breathe readily enough at the surface, even for considerable periods; for we know that fish of many kinds, and notably carp, can retain life for days, and even weeks, when removed from the water, provided they happen to be in a moist situation.

Again, a power of constriction, a characteristic of boas and pythons, and therefore implying an alliance with them, is not necessarily indicated, as might be supposed, even by the action affirmed in Captain Drevar's story; for a creature of serpentine form, attacking another, might coil itself round for the mere purpose of maintaining a hold while it tore its

victim open with its powerful jaws and teeth.   This action is
simply that of an eel which, on being hooked, grasps weeds
at the bottom to resist capture.

Nor are we bound to accept in any way the captain's
suggestion that the monster gorged its victim after the fashion
of a land-serpent.   It may as readily have torn it open and
fed on it as an eel might ; and it is, indeed, not unreasonable
to suppose that so powerful a monster would find its prey
among large creatures, such as seals, porpoises, and the
smaller cetaceæ.

That the sea-serpent was formerly more frequently seen
on the Norwegian coasts than now I consider probable, as
also that its visits were connected with its breeding season,
and discontinued in consequence of the greater number and
larger size of vessels, and especially of the introduction of
steam.   As a parallel instance, I may mention that, in the
early days of the settlement of Australia, sperm whales
resorted to the harbours along its coasts for calving purposes, and were sufficiently numerous to cause the mainte-
nance of what were called " bay whaling stations " at Hobart
Town, Spring Bay, and many other harbours of Tasmania
and South Australia.   At the present time, the sperm whale
rarely approaches within ten miles of the coast, and the small
whaling fleet finds scanty occupation in the ocean extending
south from the great Australian bight to the south cape
of Tasmania.   Mr. Gosse eliminates from his concluding
analysis of sea-serpent stories all those recorded by Norwegian and American observers, and argues only upon a selected
number resting on British evidence.

By this contraction he loses as a basis of argument a
number of accounts which I consider as credible as those he
quotes, and from which positive deductions might be drawn,
more weighty than those of similar, but merely inferential,
character which he employs.

The account of the monster seen by Hans Egede, for

example, where the creature exhibited itself more completely than it did in any of the instances selected by Mr. Gosse, specifically indicated the possession of paws, flippers, fins or paddles, while this can only be surmised at, in the latter cases to which I refer, from the progressive steady motion of the creature, with the head and neck elevated above the surface, and apparently unaffected by any undulatory motion of the body. This at once removes it from the serpent class, without any necessity for the additional confirmation which the enlarged proportions of the body in comparison with those of the neck, as given in Egede's amended version, afford us.

The creature seen in the Straits of Malacca, and one quoted by Mr. Newman, in the *Zoologist*, exhibit characters which confirm Egede's story. In the latter instance, " Captain the Hon. George Hope states that, when in H.M.S. *Fly*, in the Gulf of California, the sea being perfectly calm and transparent, he saw at the moment a large marine animal, with the head and general figure of an alligator, except that the neck was much longer, and that instead of legs the creature had four large flappers, somewhat like those of turtles, the anterior pair being larger than those of the posterior. The creature was distinctly visible, and all its movements could be observed with ease. It appeared to be pursuing its prey at the bottom of the sea. Its movements were somewhat serpentine, and an appearance of annulations or ring-like divisions of the body were distinctly perceptible." Mr. Gosse, commenting on this story, says: " Now, unless this officer was egregiously deceived, he saw an animal which could have been no other than an Enaliosaur, a marine reptile of large size, of sauroid figure, with turtle-like paddles."

In the former case the creature was far more gigantic and robust, in contradistinction to the slender and serpentine form more usually observed, and we must consequently infer that there is not merely one but several distinct species of marine monster, unknown and rarely exhibiting themselves, belonging to different genera, and perhaps orders, but all popularly included under the title of " sea-serpent."

The attempt to classify these presents difficulties. Mr. Gosse, however, has very ably reviewed the somewhat scanty materials at his command, and, agreeing with the suggestion made originally by Mr. Newman, has elaborated the argument that one of the old Enaliosaurs exists to the present day. This form, Palæontology tells us, commenced in the Carboniferous, attained its maximum specific development in the Jurassic, and continued to the close of the Cretaceous periods. This rational suggestion is supported by the collateral argument that some few Ganoid fishes and species of Terebratula, have continuously existed to the present time ; that certain Placoid fishes, of which we have no trace, and which consequently must have been very scarce during Tertiary periods, reappear abundantly as recent species; that the Iguanodon is represented by the Iguana of the American tropics, and that the Trionychidæ, or river tortoises, which commenced during the Wealden, and disappeared from thence until the present period, are now abundantly represented in the rivers of the Old and the New World.

The points of resemblance between the northern and most often seen form of the sea-serpent and certain genera of the Enaliosaurs, such as Plesiosaurus, are a long swan-like neck, a flattened lizard-like head and progress by means of paddles. A difficulty in this connection arises, however, in respect to the breathing apparatus. Palæontologists favour the idea that the Plesiosaurus and its allies were air-breathing creatures with long necks, adapted to habitual projection above the surface. Such a construction and habit is, as I have before said, to my mind, impossible in the case of an animal of so scarce an appearance as the sea-serpent; and I am incapable of estimating how far the theory is inflexible in regard to the old forms that I have mentioned. May there not be some large marine form combining some of the characters of the salamander and the saurians; may not the pigmy newt of Europe, the large salamander tenanting the depths of Lake Biwa in Japan, and the famous fossil form, the *Homo Diluvii Testis* of Sheuzberg, have a marine cousin linking them with the gigantic forms which battled in the Oolitic seas? May not the tuft of loose skin or scroll encircling its head have some connection with a branchial apparatus analagous to that of the Amphibia; and was not the large fringe round the neck, like a beard, noticed on the one seen by Captain Anderson when in the Delta in 1861, of a similar nature?

In conclusion, I must strongly express my own conviction, which I hope, after the perusal of the evidence contained in the foregoing pages, will be shared by my readers, that, let the relations of the sea-serpent be what they may; let it be serpent, saurian, or fish, or some form intermediate to them; and even granting that those relations may never be determined, or only at some very distant date; yet, nevertheless, the creature must now be removed from the regions of myth, and credited with having a real existence, and that its name includes not one only, but probably several very distinct gigantic species, allied more or less closely, and constructed to dwell in the depths of the ocean, and which only occasionally exhibit themselves to a fortune-favoured wonder-gazing crew.

### NOTE.

It is with great pleasure that I add the following testimony of a belief in the existence of the sea-serpent, from a country which has not hitherto been supposed to have any traditions relating to it. My inquiries in Burmah, as to a belief among its inhabitants in sundry so-called mythical beings, led me unexpectedly on the track of the following information, for which I am indebted to the scholarship and courtesy of F. Ripley, Esq., Government Translator in the Secretariat Department, Rangoon.

EXTRACT from the *Kavilakhana dépani*, pp. 132–133.

[Author—Mingyi Thiri Mahazeyathu, the Myaunghla Myoza, Nanig-ngan-gya Wundauk, or Sub-Minister for Foreign Affairs to His Majesty the late King of Burmah.]

"The creature Nyan is called in the Mágadha language *Tanti-gáha*, in the Bengáli *Gara*; in the Sakkata, *Gráha* or *Avagráh*; and in the Burmese, *Nyan*.

"Hence are to be found the following passages, viz. :—

"'*Tanti-gáha*—The creature Nyan, of the immense length of one or two hundred fathoms,' in the *Shri Sariputtara Apadan*.

"'*Graho* or *Avagraho*—a predatory monster, in shape like an earthworm,' in the *Amarakosha Abhidhan*;

and

"'*Dvagar samudda maha nady sanga mela táká yazantu vigera itichate*,' in the commentary of the *Amarakosha Abhidhan*.

"From these works, which contain definitions of two words designative of the creature Nyan, it will be gathered that there does exist a predatory monster in the form of an earthworm, which inhabits estuaries and the mouths of great rivers.

"Regarding the predatory instincts of this creature, it should be understood that it attacks even such animals as elephants. Hence the *Dhammathats*, in dealing with the decision of cases of hire of live-stock, wishing to point out that no fault lies through losses owing to natural accidents, make the following remarks :—

"'There shall be no fault held if oxen die by reason of a snake gliding under them.'

"'There shall be no fault held, if buffaloes die by reason of a dove resting on their horns.'

"'There shall be no fault held if oxen and buffaloes die of their having eaten a grasshopper.'

"'There shall be no fault held if elephants die by reason of their having been encoiled in the folds of a Nyan.'

"'There shall be no fault held if horses die by reason of their having been sucked by bilas.'

"The Poetical Version of the *Pokinnaka Dhammathat*, which is a compilation of several Dhammathats, in the same strain, says :—

[Here follows a verse, the same in effect as the above.]

"From such passages it will be seen that there is a frightful monster of extraordinary strength, which is capable of capturing even such animals as elephants."

"In the form of oath of fealty administered by successive kings to their feudatories and vassals, the following imprecation is to be found :—

" ' May I die through being seized by alligators and Nyans.' "

[Here follows an explanatory note respecting the four species of danger to be found in the ocean.]

"In the reign of King Alaung-mindara-gyé, the founder of the city of Ratana Singha—when he went on an expedition against Ayudhara or Yodhaya (Siam) and was crossing the Martaban river, he lost some two or three elephants, which were destroyed as soon as they had entered the water. The King ascertained from the lower country inhabitants that they had been captured and bitten by the creature Nyan. Two or three elephants were similarly lost in Ava, when it was also ascertained that they had been captured by the Nyan. There goes a saying that the Nyan is some one to two hundred fathoms long. The form of oath of fealty contains an imprecation in which the Nyan is to fulfil a part. And there are writings which make mention of its existence."

## CHAPTER X.

### THE UNICORN.

A BELIEF in the unicorn, like that in the dragon, appears to have obtained among both Eastern and Western authors, at a very early period. In this case, however, it has survived the revulsion from a fatuous confidence in the fables and concocted specimens of the Middle Ages, and even now the existence or non-existence of this remarkable animal remains a debateable question.

Until within a late period occasional correspondents of the South African journals continued to assert its existence, basing their communications on the reports of hunters from the interior, while but a few hundred years since travellers spoke of actually seeing it or of passing through countries in which its existence was absolutely affirmed to them. Horns, generally those of the narwhal, but occasionally of one species of rhinoceros, were brought home and deposited in museums as those of the veritable unicorn, or sold, under the same pretext, for large sums, on account of their reputed valuable medicinal properties.* The animal is variously described as resembling a horse or some kind of deer; this description

---

* " At length, in the sixteenth and seventeenth centuries, they were thrown open for examination by the desire which then existed in Germany to possess the *ebur fossile,* or 'unicorn's horn,' a supposed infallible specific for the cure of many diseases. The unicorn horn was to be found in the caves, and the search for it revealed the remains of lions, hyænas, elephants, and many other tropical and strange animals." *Pop. Sci. Monthly,* No. 32.

may possibly refer to some animal of a type intermediate to them, now almost, if not quite, extinct. In some instances it is supposed that a species of rhinoceros is indicated.

There has been much discussion as to the identity of the animal referred to in many passages of the Bible, the Hebrew name of which, *Reem*, has been translated "unicorn." Mr. W. Smith considers that a species of rhinoceros could not have been indicated, as it is spoken of in one passage as a sacrificial animal, whereas the ceremonial ritual of the Jews forbade the use of any animal not possessing the double qualifications of chewing the cud and being cloven-footed. The qualities attributed to it are great strength, an indomitable disposition, fierce nature, and an active and playful disposition when young. He considers that the passage, Deut. xxxiii. 17, should be rendered "his horns are like the horns of a unicorn," and not, as it is given, "horns of unicorns"; and is of opinion that some species of wild ox is intended.

Among profane Western authors we first find the unicorn referred to by Ctesias, who describes it as having one horn, a cubit long. Herodotus also mentions it in the passage,* "For the eastern side of Libya, where the wanderers dwell, is low and sandy, as far as the river Triton; but westward of that, the land of the husbandmen is very hilly and abounds with forests and wild beasts, for this is the tract in which the huge serpents are found, and the lions, the elephants, the bears, the aspicks, and the horned asses"; and again, "Among the wanderers are none of these, but quite other animals, as antelopes, &c. &c., and asses, not of the horned sort, but of a kind which does not need to drink."

Aristotle† mentions two unicorn animals. "There are only a few [animals] that have a solid hoof and one horn, as the Indian ass and the oryx."

---

* Book iv. ch. cxci. and cxcii.
† Book ii. ch. ii. § 8.

Pliny* tells us that the Orsæan Indians hunt down a very
fierce animal called the monoceros, which has the head of
the stag, the feet of the elephant, and the tail of the boar,
while the rest of the body is like that of the horse. It makes
a deep lowing noise, and has a single black horn, projecting
from the middle of its forehead, and two cubits in length.
This animal, it is said, cannot be taken alive. In speaking
of the Indian ass, he says,† " the Indian ass is only a one-
horned animal "; and of the oryx of Africa,‡ "the oryx is
both one-horned and cloven-footed."

Ælian§ transfers the locality back again from Africa to
Asia, and it may be presumed, in the following quotation,
that he indicates the country north of the Himalaya, Thibet,
and Tartary, which still has the reputation of being one of
the homes of the unicorn.

" They say that there are mountains in the innermost
regions of India inaccessible to men, and full of wild beasts ;
where those creatures which with us are domesticated,
such as sheep, dogs, goats, and cattle, range about at their
own free will, free from any charge by a shepherd or herds-
man.

" Both historians, and the more learned of the Indians,
among whom the Brahmins may be specified, declare that
there is a countless number of these beasts. Among them
they enumerate the unicorn, which they call cartazonon, and
say that it reaches the size of a horse of mature age, possesses a mane and reddish yellow hair, and that it excels in
swiftness through the excellence of its feet and of its whole
body. Like the elephant, it has inarticulate feet, and it has
a boar's tail ; one black horn projects between the eyebrows,

---

* Book viii. ch. xxxii.
† Book xi. ch. cvi.
‡ *Ibid.*
§ Ælian, *De Naturâ Animalium*, Book xvi. ch. xx.

not awkwardly, but with a certain natural twist, and terminating in a sharp point.

" It has, of all animals, the harshest and most contentious voice. It is said to be gentle to other beasts approaching it, but to fight with its fellows. Not only are the males at variance in natural contention amongst themselves, but they also fight with the females, and carry their combats to the length of killing the conquered; for not only are their bodies generally indued with great strength, but also they are armed with an invincible horn. It frequents desert regions and wanders alone and solitary. In the breeding season it is of gentle demeanour towards the female, and they feed together; when this has passed and the female has become gravid, it again becomes fierce and wanders alone.

" They say that the young, while still of tender age, are carried to the King of the Prasians for exhibition of their strength, and exposed in combats on festivals; for no one remembers them to have been captured of mature age."

Cæsar* records the reputed existence in his day, within the bounds of the great Hercynian Forest, of a bull, shaped like a stag, with one horn projecting from the middle of its forehead and between the ears.

Cosmas,† surnamed Indicopleustes, a merchant of Alexandria, who lived in the sixth century, and made a voyage to India, and subsequently wrote works on cosmography, gives a figure of the unicorn, not, as he says, from actual sight of it, but reproduced from four figures of it in brass contained in the palace of the King of Ethiopia. He states, from report, that " it is impossible to take this ferocious beast alive; and that all its strength lies in its horn. When it finds itself pursued and in danger of capture, it throws

---

* *De Bello Gallico*, ch. ii. p. 26.
† *Vide* Charton's *Voyageurs du Moyen Ages*, vol. ii. p. 25.

itself from a precipice, and turns so aptly in falling, that it receives all the shock upon the horn, and so escapes safe and sound." It is noteworthy that this mode of escape is attributed, at the present day, to both the musk ox and the Ovis Ammon.

Marco Polo may or may not indicate a rhinoceros in the passage, " Après avoir descendu ces deux journées et demie, on trouve une province au midi qui est sur les confins de l'Inde, on l'appelle Amien—on marche quinze journées par des lieux desertes et par de grands bois où il y a beaucoup d'éléphants et de licornes et d'autres bêtes sauvages. Il n'y a ni hommes ni habitations aussi, nous laisserons ce lieu."

But no such inference can be attached to the descriptions of the Ethiopian unicorn by Leo and Ludolphus.

The first says :*

" The unicorn is found in the mountains of high Ethiopia. It is of an ash colour and resembles a colt of two years old, excepting that it has the head of a goat, and in the middle of its ¦forehead a horn three feet long, which is smooth and white like ivory, and has yellow streaks running along from top to bottom.

" This horn is an antidote against poison, and it is reported that other animals delay drinking till it has soaked its horn in the water to purify it. This animal is so nimble that it can neither be killed nor taken. But it casts its horn like a stag, and the hunters find it in the deserts. But the truth of this is called in question by some authors."

Ludolphus† says :

" Here is also another beast, called arucharis, with one horn, fierce and strong, of which unicorn several have been seen feeding in the woods."

---

* Harris' *Voyages*, vol. i. p. 362; "Africa," by John Leo.

† Pinkerton's *Voyages*, vol. i. p. 392; "Ethiopia," by Jobus Ludolphus.

Coming down to later days we find the unicorn described by Lewes Vertomannus*—he who, having visited, among other places, the site of the legend of St. George and the Dragon,† and undergone a variety of adventures, visits, in the course of them, the temple of Mecca, and, as follows, gives a description " of the unicorns of the Temple of Mecha, which are not seen in any other place."

" On the other part of the temple are parks or places enclosed, where are seen two unicorns, named of the Greeks monocerotæ, and are there showed to the people for a miracle, and not without good reason, for the seldomness and strange nature. The one of them, which is much higher than the other, yet not much unlike to a colt of thirty months of age; in the forehead groweth only one horn, in manner right foorth, of the length of three cubits. The other is much younger, of the age of one year, and like a young colt; the horn of this is of the length of four handfulls.

" This beast is of the colour of a horse of weesell colour, and hath the head like a hart, but no long neck, a thynne mane hanging only on the one side. Their leggs are thin and slender like a fawn or hind. The hoofs of the fore-feet are divided in two, much like the feet of a goat. The outer part of the hinder feet is very full of hair.

" This beast doubtless seemeth wild and fierce, yet tempereth that fierceness with a certain comeliness.

"These unicorns one gave to the Sultan of Mecha as a most precious and rare gift. They were sent him out of Ethiope by a king of that country who desired by that present to gratify the Sultan of Mecha."

Visiting the interior of Arabia from Aden, and afterwards

---

* *The Navigation and Voyage of Lewes Vertomannus, of Rome, into Arabia, Egypt, &c., in* 1503, contained in *" The History of Travayle in the East and West Indies,"* done into English by Richard Eden. London, 1577.

† Berynto, a city on the seacoast of Syria, Phœnicia.

starting for Persia, Vertomannus was driven back by a contrary wind to Zeila (in Africa), which he describes as being an important city with much merchandise—when again he says, "I saw there also certain kyne, having only one horn in the middle of the forehead, as hath the unicorn, and about a span in length, but the horn bendeth backwards. They are of bright shining red colour."

In an account of the travels of Johann Grueber, Jesuit (about 1661), contained in Astley's collection of voyages, we find :—

"Sining* is a great and populous city, built at the vast wall of China, through the gate of which the merchants from India enter Katay or China. There are stairs to go a-top of the wall, and many travel on it from the gate at Sining to the next at Soochew, which is eighteen days' journey, having a delightful prospect all the way, from the wall, of the innumerable habitations on one side, and the various wild beasts which range the desert on the other side.

"Besides wild bulls, here are tigers, lions, elephants, rhinoceroses, and monoceroses, which are a kind of horned asses.

"Thus the merchants view the beasts free from danger, especially from that part of the wall which, running southward, approaches Quang-si, Yunnan, and Tibet; for at certain times of the year they betake themselves to the Yellow River, and parts near the wall which abound with thickets, in order to get pasture and seek their prey."

Father Jerome Lobo, a Portuguese Jesuit, who embarked for Abyssinia in the year 1622,† states that—

"In the province of Agaus has been seen the unicorn; that beast so much talked of and so little known. The prodigious swiftness with which the creature runs from one

---

* Sining is on the western frontier of Kansuh, towards Kokonor.

† Pinkerton's *Vogages*, vol. xv. p. 23.

wood into another has given me no opportunity of examining it particularly; yet I have had so near a sight of it as to be able to give some description of it.

"The shape is the same with that of a beautiful horse, exact and nicely proportioned, of a bay colour, with a black tail, which in some provinces is long, in others very short; some have long manes hanging to the ground. They are so timorous that they never feed but surrounded with other beasts that defend them.

"Deer and other defenceless animals often herd about the elephant, which, contenting himself with roots and leaves, preserves the beasts that place themselves, as it were, under his protection, from the others that would devour them."

There is a somewhat doubtful story contained in the *Narrative of a Journey from St. Petersburg, in Russia, to Peking, in China, in* 1719,* to the effect that between Tobolsky and Tomski—

"Our baggage having waited at Tara till our arrival, we left that place on the 18th, and next came to a large Russian village sixty versts from Tara, and the last inhabited by Russians till you pass the Baraba and come to the river Oby. . . . . One of these hunters told me the following story, which was confirmed by several of his neighbours, that in the year 1713, in the month of March, being out a-hunting, he discovered the track of a stag, which he pursued. At overtaking the animal he was somewhat startled on observing it had only one horn, stuck in the middle of its forehead. Being near this village, he drove it home, and showed it, to the great admiration of the spectators. He afterwards killed it, and ate the flesh, and sold the horn to a comb-maker in the town of Tara, for ten alteens, about fifteen pence sterling.

"I inquired carefully about the shape and size of this

* Pinkerton's *Voyages*, vol. vii. p. 333.

unicorn, as I shall call it, and was told that it exactly resembled a stag.

"The horn was of a brownish colour, about one archæon or twenty-eight inches long, and twisted from the root till within a finger's length of the tip, where it was divided, like a fork, into two points, very sharp."

One of the most trustworthy of observers, the Abbé Huc, speaks very positively on the subject of the unicorn.* He says: "The unicorn really exists in Thibet. . . . We had for a long time a small Mongol Treatise on Natural History, for the use of children, in which a unicorn formed one of the pictorial illustrations. . . . The Chinese Itinerary says, on the subject of the lake you see before your arrival at Atzder (going from east to west), 'The unicorn, a very curious animal, is found in the vicinity of this lake, which is forty *li* long.'"

The unicorn is known in Thibet by the name of *serou*; in Mongolia, by that of *kere*; while in a Thibetan manuscript examined by the late Major Lattre, it is called the one-horned *tsopo*.

Mr. Hazlitt, in his notes appended to the statement by Huc as to the unicorn, states that Mr. Hodgson, of Nepaul, sent to Calcutta the skin and horn of a unicorn that died in the menagerie of the Rajah of Nepaul.

It was described as being very fierce, and abundant in the plains of Tingri, in the southern part of the Thibetan province of Tsang, watered by the Arroun; it assembled round salt beds. The form is graceful, colour reddish, two tufts of hair project from the exterior of each nostril, and there is much down round the hair and mouth. The hair is rough and seems hollow. Doctor Able designated it *Antelope Hodgsonii*.

Baron von Müller described,† through the medium of M.

---

* *Travels in Tartary, Thibet, and China.* Huc and Gabet. Translated by W. Hazlitt, vol. ii. p. 245.

† Gosse, *Romance of Natural History*.

Antoine d'Abbadie, a unicorn animal which he had received
when at Melpes in Kordofan :—

" I met, on the 17th of April 1848, a man who was in the
habit of selling to me specimens of animals. One day he
asked me if I wished also for an *a'nasa*, which he described
thus : ' It is the size of a small donkey, has a thick body and
thin bones, coarse hair, and tail like a boar. It has a long
horn on its forehead, and lets it hang when alone, but erects
it immediately on seeing an enemy. It is a formidable
weapon, but I do not know its exact length. The *a'nasa* is
found not far from here (Melpes), towards the south-south-
west. I have seen it often in the wild grounds, where the
negroes kill it, and carry it home to make shields from its
skin.' *N.B.*—This man was well acquainted with the rhinoceros, which he distinguished, under the name of *fetit*, from
the *a'nasa*.

" On June the 14th I was at Kursi, also in Kordofan, and
met there a slave merchant who was not acquainted with
my first informer, and gave me spontaneously the same
description of the *a'nasa*, adding that he had killed and eaten
one long ago, and that its flesh was well flavoured."

This creature is mentioned by Rupell, under the name of
*Nillekma* or *Arase*, as indigenous to Kordofan, and, by
Cavassi, as known in Congo under that of *Abada*.

Mr. Freeman, in the *South African Christian Recorder*
(vol. i.), gives the native account of an animal not uncommon
in Makooa, and called the *Ndzoodzoo*, described as being
about the size of a horse, extremely fleet and strong, with a
single horn from two feet to two and a half feet in length,
projecting from its forehead, which is said to be flexible
when the animal is asleep, and capable of being curled up at
pleasure, but becoming stiff and hard under the excitement of
rage. It is extremely fierce, and invariably attacks a man
when it discerns him. The female is without a horn.

Our latest information as to this species comes from Prejevalski,* who, speaking of it as the orongo, says that it has elegant black horns standing vertically above the head; the back is dun-coloured; the middle of the breast, stomach, and rump, white; seen at a distance it appears white; it is very numerous in Northern Thibet. He adds: " Another prevalent superstition is that the orongo has only one horn growing vertically from the centre of the head. In Kansu and Kokonor we were told that unicorns were rare, one or two in a thousand. The Mongols in Tsaidan deny it, but say it may be so in south-west Thibet."

Turning to the Chinese classics and books of antiquity, we find references, sometimes vague and mythical, sometimes exact, to several distinct unicorn animals. These may be enumerated as :—

† 1. The Ki-Lin, represented in Japan by the Kirin.
2. The King.
3. The Kioh Twan.
4. The Poh.
5. The Hiai Chai.
6. The Too Jon Sheu.

Besides these there are clear descriptions of the rhinoceros, which cannot in any way be confounded with the above. The only one of these popularly familiar is the Ki-Lin, the history of which is interwoven with that of remote ages. The first mention of it is made in the Bamboo Books—only in that part, however, of them which is apparently a commentary, note, or subsequent addition, though some authorities hold it to be a portion of the actual text. The work states that, during the reign of Hwang-Ti (B.C. 2697), Ki-Lins appeared in the parks.

Their appearance was generally supposed to signalise the reign of an upright monarch, and Confucius considered that

---

* Prejevalski's *Mongolia*, vol. ii. p. 207; London, 1876.
† See *'Rh Ya* and *Yuen Keen Luy Han*, vol. ccccxxix. p. 1.

the appearance of one during his epoch was a bad omen, as it did not harmonise with the troubled state of the times. The name Ki-Lin is a generic or dual word, composed of those of the Ki and the Lin, the respective male and female of the creature.

FIG. 79.—THE KI-LIN. (*After a modern Chinese painting.*)

This peculiar species of word formation is adopted in other instances in reference to birds and animals; thus we have the male Fung and the female Hwang united in the Fung Hwang, or so-called Chinese phœnix, and the Yuen and Yang in the Yuen Yang, or mandarin duck.

Sometimes the word Lin alone is used with the same generic meaning.

The 'Rh Ya, in the original text, defines the Lin as having a Kiun's body (the Kiun is a kind of muntjack or deer), an ox's tail, and one horn. The commentary states that the tip of the horn is fleshy, and that the King Yang chapter of the " Spring and Autumn Annals " of Confucius defines it as a horned Kiun.

FIG. 80.—THE LIN (FEMALE OF THE CHINESE UNICORN). (*From the 'Rh Ya.*)

The preface to the *Shi Shu* quotes Li Siün to the effect that the Lin is an auspicious and perfect beast.

Sun Yen says it is a spiritual beast.　The *Shwoh Wan* says

the Lin is the female of the K'i and the K'i is a beast endowed with goodness, possessing a Kiun's body, an ox's tail, and one horn. According to the *Shwoh Wan*, the Lin may be considered as a large female deer. Now the *Shu King* considers that many of these beasts are comprised under the Ki-Lin, only the characters, though retaining the sound, have become altered in form.

Cheu Nau calls it Lin-che-chi and Man Chw'en says that the Lin is truthful, and reducible to rule.

The *Li Yuen* says: " If the unicorn can once be tamed, then the other beasts will not show terror."

Ta Tai, in the *Li Ki*, quoting the *Yih* [*King*], says there are 360 kinds of hairy creatures, and the Ki-Lin is the chief of them.

The *Li Ki*, commenting on the *King Fang I Chw'en*, says: " The Lin has a Kiun's body, an ox's tail, a horse's hoof, and is of five colours. It is twelve feet high." *

Again, in commenting on Fuh Kien's *Ho Chwen*, it says: " The Lin springs from the earth's central regions. It is a beast of superior integrity, is attached to its mother, and reducible to rule. The *Shu King*, quoting Luh Li, says the Lin has a Kiun's body, an ox's tail, a horse's feet, and a yellow colour, round hoofs, and one horn ; the tip of the horn is erect and fleshy.

" Its call in the middle part thereof is like a monastery bell. Its pace is regular ; it rambles only on selected grounds and after it has examined the locality. It will not live in herds, or be accompanied in its movements. It cannot be beguiled into pitfalls, or captured in snares. When the monarch is virtuous, this beast appears."

At present there are Lin existing on the frontiers of Ping

---

* This height will have to be reduced in accordance with the difference between the magnitude of old and new standards of measurement.

Cheu. Even the large or small Lin are always like deer, so that this species is not the auspicious Ying Lin ; although Tsz Ma Siang Su,* in his odes on the shooting of the Mi and trapping Lin, says that it is.

The top of the horn being fleshy is a characteristic of the Lin, and Mao Chw'en says that the Lin's horn is an emblem of goodness. Ching Tsien says that the horn has a fleshy termination, indicating the peaceful character of the beast, and that it has no use for it.

The " Book of Rites," quoting the *Kwang Ya*, says that on account of its elegant style it takes place, *par excellence*, among the large-horned beasts ; the existing edition of the *Kwang Ya* omits this.

The *Kung Yang Chw'en* says the Kiun also has horns.

Kung Ssun Tsz, in the annals of the fourteenth year of the Duke Ngai (State of Lu), says that the Kiun has fleshy horns.

Kwoh, in his preface, proves the Lin to have a Kiun's body.

The *'Rh Ya* gives the drawing of a unicorn animal called the Ki ; but no reference to the horn is given in the text, which simply describes it as a large Kiun with a yak's tail and dog's feet.

The Ki is not defined in the *'Rh Ya*, and the only information I have as to it is derived from Williams' dictionary, where it is stated to be " a fabulous auspicious animal, which appears when sages are born ; the male of the Chinese unicorn. It is drawn like a piebald scaly horse, with one horn and a cow's tail, and may have had a living original in some extinct equine animal." But there is a very full account of an animal called the King. It is not impossible that it is identical with the King which, in the usual brief

---

* A poet, native of Hang Cheu.

style of the original text of the *'Rh Ya*, is epitomised as a large Biao (a kind of stag), with an ox's tail and one horn; and the several commentaries on it are as follows :—

FIG. 81.—THE KI.

"In the time of the Emperor Wu, of the Han dynasty, during the worship of heaven and earth at the solstices at Yung, there was captured a unicorn beast like a Piao; it

was at that time designated the Lin; it was, however, a Piao
related to the Chang (a kind of deer)."

The *Shwoh Wan* says: "The King is a large stag with an

FIG. 82.—THE KING. (*From the Rh Ya.*)

ox's tail and one horn." It may be a large form of the
Piao. The Wang Hwu Analects say that the Piao is an
object of the chase, and that it is as swift as a stag.

Kwan Tsz, in the *Ti Yuen* volume, says that as there are Mi and Piao and many species of deer, so also the Piao is a species of deer.

The " Shi Ki," in the book *Fung Shen*, says that during the worship at the solstices at Yung, there was captured a one-horned beast like a Piao, and that the local authorities assert that as His Majesty was making reverential invocations on the country altar to the Supreme Being, he was recompensed for the sacrifice by a beast which was a unicorn.

Wu Chao's preface to the *Loh Yiu* says: " The body is like that of a muntjack, and it has one horn "; while the Spring and Autumn (Annals) allude to this animal in speaking of the horned Kiun.

The inhabitants of Ch'u say the Kiun is a Piao. Kwoh, in his preface, says that the capture made in the time of Wu, of the Han dynasty, was actually a Piao, as demonstrated by the Han books. The *Chung Kiun* narrative states that in Shang Yung was captured a white Lin bearing one horn, of which the tip was fleshy. At the present day nothing has been heard of a Piao with a fleshy tip, therefore these must be different beasts.

Kwoh also says that the Piao is identical with the Chang, and the Chang with the Kiun. This corresponds with what Wei Chao So had already stated, that the people of Ch'u assert that the Kiun is a Piao, and that the Piao is certainly a kind of deer.

Its meat is eminently savoury.

Luh Ki says that of all four-footed creatures, the Piao is the most excellent.

Yeu Shi states in the *Kiao Sz* annals ("Sacrifices to Heaven and Earth "), that the Piao is a kind of deer. Its body exactly resembles that of the Chang.

Finally, the explanatory prefaces of many classical works, when commenting on the *'Rh Ya*, say that the Piao is

FIG. 83.—THE KI-RIN. (*From a Japanese Drawing in a Temple at Kioto.*)

identical with the Chang and of a black colour; and they confirm Kwoh's opinion, although the *'Rh Ya* forgets to allude to the three characters denoting the black colour.

It was probably some unicorn animal which is referred to in the General History of China, called the *Tong Kien Kang Mu* (*vide* Père de Mailla's translation), as having been presented to the Emperor Yung Loh of the Ming dynasty, in A.D. 1415, by envoys from Bengal. De Mailla says it was called a Ki-Lin by the Chinese out of flattery.

Again, the same History says that in the succeeding year the kingdom of Malin sent as tribute a Ki-Lin similar to that from Bengal.

The Ki-Rin, a Japanese version of the Ki-Lin, is simply borrowed from Chinese sources. It is figured in the illustrated edition of the great Japanese Encyclopædia *Kasira gaki zou vo Sin mou dzu wi tai sei*,\* and represented, as in the Chinese drawings, as covered with scales; but it must be noted that nothing in any of the texts of either country warrants this furniture of the body.†

The same encyclopædia figures another unicorn beast under the name of the Kai Tsi, and describes it as being an animal of foreign countries, resembling a lion, and having a single horn. It is also called the Sin You or divine sheep. It is able to distinguish between right and wrong. When Kau You exercised criminal jurisdiction, he handed over those whose crime was doubtful to the Kai Tsu, and it is said that this animal destroyed the guilty and spared the innocent.

---

\* *Vide* the translation into French by L. Serrurier, Leyden, 1875.

† "The Chinese have a tradition that this animal skips, and is so holy or harmless that it won't even tread upon an insect, and that it is to come in the shape of an incomparable man, a revealer of mysteries, supernatural and divine, and a great lover of all mankind, who is expected to come, about the time of a particular constellation in the heavens, on a special mission for their benefit. The Japanese unicorn answers the description of the animal bearing that name, and supposed to be still extant in Ethiopia, and which is equal to the size of a small

This is described in the Chinese work *Yuen Kien Léi Han*,[*] under the name of the Hiai Chai, and similar powers of discrimination are there attributed to it.

兄
似
牛
。

FIG. 84.—THE SZ, OR MALAYAN RHINOCEROS. (*From the 'Rh Ya.*)

horse, reddish in colour, and slender as a gazelle, the male having one horn. The unicorn is the ancient crest of the kings of Israel, and is still retained by the Mikado." *Epitome of the Ancient History of Japan*, p. 116; N. McLeod, Nagasaki, 1875.

[*] Vol. ccccxxx. p. 18.

A synonym for it was the Chiai Tung. It states that, according to the *Si Yang Y Shu*, a one-horned spiritual lamb was born in the Ping Shen district, and in the twenty-first year of Kai Yuen. The horn was fleshy, and the top of the head covered with white hair. The second chapter on the same subject says that, in ancient times, if parties were at law, the judge brought this animal out, and it would gore at the guilty one.

The Kioh Twan is yet another unicorn animal described in the *Yuen Kien Léi Han*,* which is said to have the appearance of a deer with the tail of a horse, but to be of a greenish colour, with one horn above the nose, and to be capable of traversing eighteen thousand *li* in one day.

The *Li Kau Sing Sha Shao* says that the Emperor Yuen Ti Su sent his ambassadors to the western part of India, who procured animals several tens of feet in height,† unicorn, like the rhinoceros. The rumour went that these were inauspicious for the Emperor, and they were immediately returned.

### The Poh.

The *Shan Hai King* describes an animal as existing among the plains of Mongolia, having the appearance of a horse, with a white body, black tail, one horn, teeth and claws like a tiger, which howls like the roll of a drum, devours tigers and leopards, and is capable of being used instead of soldiers; it is called Poh.

The *'Rh Ya* describes the same animal as like a horse, with saw teeth, existing on tigers and leopards.

The " History of the North " says that in the Kingdom of Peh Chi (?) a magistrate named Chung Wa held office,

---

* Vol. ccccxxxii. p. 38.

† This will have to be reduced by nearly one-half, to equate it with the present measures of length.

who was very equitable in his rule. His district was invaded
by some ferocious animals. Suddenly six of the Poh came
and killed and devoured them as a reward for his good rule.

The Sung History says that a man named Leu Chang,
an ambassador, arrived at a district called Shen Su, where
the mountains contained a strange animal, in appearance
like a horse, but capable of eating tigers and leopards.
The people were unacquainted with it, and asked Leu Chang
what it was, who said it was called the Poh, and referred
them to the *Shan Hai King* for a description of it.

中 樹 皮

FIG. 85.—TARGET IN THE FORM OF A SPHYNX. (*From the San Li T'u.*).
The arrows were discharged upwards and fell into the cylinder behind the figure.

Among other remarkable and interesting drawings which
have come down from antiquity in the *San Li T'u,** or
illustrated edition of the three (ceremonial) rituals, are some
representing the various targets used by officials of different

---

* *San Li T'u*, vol. viii. p. 3. The *San Li T'u* is an illustrated,
modern, edition by Nieh Tsung I. of the old *San Li*; it was written
during the reign of the great patron of literature, Kang Hi (A.D. 1661
to 1723).

ranks in the military examinations, in which the arrows had
to be lodged by shooting upwards from a distance. These
are fashioned in the form of animals, one realising the idea

Fig. 86.—The Lu Target. (*From the San Li T'u.*)

of the sphinx, and two representing unicorn animals, called
respectively the Lu—which, according to some, is like an ass
with one horn, but, according to others, differing from a
donkey in having a cleft hoof—and the Sz, which is said to
be like an ox with one horn.

Fig. 87.—The Sz Target. (*From the San Li T'u.*)

FIG. 88.—THE TOO JOU SHEN. (*From the Ming Tombs.*)

The Too Jou Shen is the name of an animal with a lion-like body and head, cloven hoofs, and a blunt short horn

FIG. 89.—THE TOO JOU
SHEN.
(*From the Ming Tombs.*)

projecting from the centre of the forehead. Two pairs of these form a portion of the avenue of stone figures of animals leading up to the Ming tombs, about eighty miles north of Pekin. I have not found it described in any book.

A writer in the *China Review** endeavours to prove that the Ki-Lin is a reminiscence of the giraffe, which he supposes may once have spread over Asia, and, in addition to various passages included among those which I have quoted above, adduces one from the *Wu Tsah Tsu,* which states that, "In the period Yung Loh of the Ming dynasty (1403–1425) a Ki-Lin was caught, and a painter was ordered to make a sketch and hand it up to the high magistrates. According to the picture, the body was perfectly shaped like that of a

* Vol. vii. No. 1, p. 72.

deer, *but the neck was very long, perhaps three or four feet.*" I must admit that I cannot agree with him in his conclusions. Harris* has given much better arguments in favour of the unicorn being merely a species of oryx. He appears to me, however, to speak too absolutely, to make his facts too pliant, and to base his main belief on the untenable theory that the myth, tradition, or theory is based on the profile drawing of an oryx, exhibiting one horn only. We might

---

* Harris, *Game and Wild Animals of Southern Africa*. The Oryx Capensis—The Gemsbock.

"The figure of the renowned unicorn can be traced in all the ancient ear-rings, coins, and Latin heraldic insignia, to some one of the members of the oryxine family; of all the whimsies of antiquity, whether emanating from the unbridled and fertile fancies of the people of Egypt and Persia, or devised by the more chaste and classic taste which distinguished Greece and Rome, the unicorn—unquestionably the most celebrated—is the chimera which has in modern ages engrossed the largest portion of attention from the curious.

"The rhinoceros is supposed to be the animal so often alluded to in Scripture under the name of *reem* or unicorn, yet the combination presented in the oryx of the antelopine and equine characters, the horns and cloven hoof of the one, blended with the erect mane, general contour and long switch tail of the other, corresponds in all essential particulars with the extant delineations and descriptions of the heraldic unicorn, which is universally represented to have been possessed of a straight slender horn, ringed at the base, and to have the hoof divided; to have worn a mane reversed, a black flowing tail, and a turkey-like tuft on the larynx, whilst both the size and ground colour were said to be those of the ass, with the addition of sundry black markings, imparting to the face and forehead a piebald appearance.

"The alterations required to reduce the African oryx to the standard of this model, are slight and simple, nor can it be doubted that they have been gradually introduced by successive copyists; the idea of the single horn having been derived in the first instance from profile representations of that animal given in bas-relief on the sculptured monuments of ancient Egypt and Nubia. . . . . They have in their aspect a certain bovine expression; and Arabs and other natives never consider them as antelopes but as a species of buffalo . . . . . The oryx boldly defends itself when pressed by the hunters, is quarrelsome during the rutting season, and it is said that even the lion dreads an encounter with it."

just as soon expect people to start stories of two-legged cows or horses, or one-legged races of men, if so slender a basis for forging a species were sufficient. What the zoological status of the unicorn may be I am not prepared to show, but I find it impossible to believe that a creature whose existence has been affirmed by so many authors, at so many different dates, and from so many different countries, can be, as mythologists demand, merely the symbol of a myth. There is a possible solution, which does not appear to have struck previous writers on the subject, viz., that the unicorn may be merely a hybrid produced occasionally and at more or less rare intervals.

By accepting this view we could explain the extraordinary combinations of character assigned to it, and the discrepancy which exists between the qualities of courage and gentleness ascribed to it by Western and Chinese authors. A valuable chapter remains to be written by naturalists and progression- ists on the limits within which hybridization exists in a state of nature among the higher animals; its prevalence among the lower and among plants is, of course, well known. A cross between some equine and cervine species might readily result in a unicorn offspring, and either the courageous qualities of the sire* or the gentleness of the dam might preponderate, according to the relations of the species in each of the instances.

As an alternative, we may speculate on the unicorn being a generic name for several distinct species of (probably) now extinct animals; missing links between the three families, the Equidæ, Cervidæ, and Bovidæ; creatures which were the contemporaries of prehistoric man, and which, before they

---

* Even the patient ass, in a state of nature, is endowed with great courage. Baharan, one of the early Persian monarchs, received the surname Baharan Guz from his transfixing, with one arrow, a wild ass and a lion engaged in active combat.

finally expired, attracted the attention of his descendants, during early historic times, by the rare appearance of a few surviving individuals.

The supernatural qualities ascribed to these by various nations must be considered merely the embroidery of fancy, designed to enrich and adorn an article esteemed rare and valuable.

## CHAPTER XI.

FROM the date of the earliest examination of the literature of China, it has been customary among Sinologues to trace a fancied resemblance between a somewhat remarkable bird, which occupies an important position in the early traditions of that Empire, and the phœnix of Western authors. Some mythologists have even subsequently concluded that the Fung Hwang of the Chinese, the phœnix of the Greeks, the Roc of the Arabs, and the Garuda of the Hindoos, are merely national modifications of the same myth. I do not hold this opinion, and, in opposing it, purpose, in the future, to discuss each of these birds in detail, although in the present volume I treat only of the Fung Hwang.

The earliest notice of it is contained in the *'Rh Ya*, which, with its usual brevity, simply informs us that the male is called Fung and the female Hwang; the commentator, Kwoh P'oh, adding that the Shui Ying bird (felicitous and perfect —a synonym for it) has a cock's head, a snake's neck, a swallow's beak, a tortoise's back, is of five different colours, and more than six feet high. The *'Rh Ya Chen I*, a later and supplementary edition of the former work, quotes the *Shwoh Wan* to the effect that the united name of the male and female bird is Fung Hwang, and that Tso's commentary on the 17th year of the Chao, says one appeared in the time of the Emperor Che (dynastic title, Shaou Haou). The

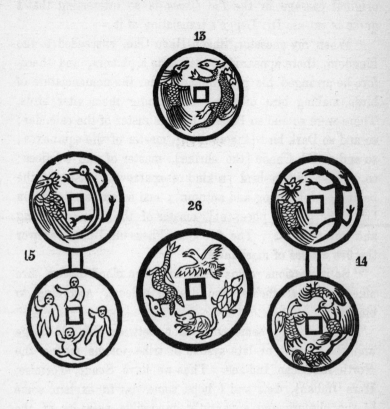

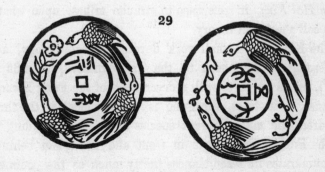

FIG. 90.—TEMPLE MEDALS FROM CHINA: DRAGON AND PHŒNIX.

original passage in the *Tso Chuen* is so interesting that I
quote *in extenso* Dr. Legge's translation of it :—

" When my ancestor, Shaou-Haou Che, succeeded to the
kingdom, there appeared at that time a phœnix, and therefore he arranged his government under the nomenclature of
birds, making bird officers, and naming them after birds.
There were so and so Phœnix bird, minister of the calendar ;
so and so Dark bird [the swallow], master of the equinoxes ;
so and so Pih Chaou [the shrike], master of the solstices ;
so and so Green bird [a kind of sparrow], master of the
beginning (of spring and autumn) ; and so and so Carnation
bird [the golden pheasant], master of the close (of spring
and autumn). . . . The five Che [Pheasants] presided over
the five classes of mechanics.

" So in previous reigns there had been cloud officers, fire
officers, water officers, and dragon officers, according to
omens."

I think there is some connection between this old usage
and the present or late system of tribe totems among the
North American Indians. Thus we have Snake, Tortoise,
Hare Indians, &c., and I hope some day to explain some
of the obscure and apparently impossible passages of the
*Shan Hai King*, in reference to strange tribes, upon what I
may call the totem theory.

The *Kin King*, a small work devoted to ornithology, and
professing to date back to the Tsin dynasty [A.D. 265 to
317], opens its pages with a description of the Fung Hwang,
because, as it states, the Fung is the principal of the three
hundred and sixty different species of birds. According to
it, the Fung is like a swan in front and like a Lin behind ;
it enumerates its resemblances pretty much as the commentator in the '*Rh Ya* gives them ; but we now find a commencement of extraordinary attributes. Thus the head is
supposed to have impressed on it the Chinese character
expressing virtue, the poll that for uprightness, the back

that for humanity; the heart is supposed to contain that of
sincerity, and the wings to enfold in their clasp that of
integrity; its foot imprints integrity; its low notes are
like a bell, its high notes are like a drum. It is said that
it will not peck living grass, and that it contains all the five
colours.*

When it flies crowds of birds follow. When it appears,
the monarch is an equitable ruler, and the kingdom has
moral principles. It has a synonym, "the felicitous *yen*."
According to the *King Shun* commentary upon the '*Rh Ya*, it
is about six feet in height. The young are called Yoh Shoh,
and it is said that the markings of the five colours only
appear when it is three years of age.†

There appears to have been another bird closely related
to it, which is called the Lwan Shui. This, when first
hatched, resembles the young Fung, but when of mature age
it changes the five colours.

The *Shăng Li Teu Wei I* says of this, that when the world
is peaceful its notes will be heard like the tolling of a bell, Pien
Lwan [answering to our " ding-dong "]. During the Chao
dynasty it was customary to hang a bell on the tops of
vehicles, with a sound like that of the Lwan.‡ From another
passage we learn that it was supposed to have different names
according to a difference in colour. Thus, when the head

---

* Black, red, azure (green, blue, or black), white, yellow.

† Many species of bird do not attain their mature plumage until long
after they have attained adult size, as some among the gulls and birds
of prey. I think I am right in saying that some of these latter only
become perfect in their third year. We all know the story of the ugly
duckling, and the little promise which it gave of its future beauty.

‡ According to Dr. Williams, the Lwan was a fabulous bird described
as the essence of divine influence, and regarded as the embodiment of
every grace and beauty, and that the argus pheasant was the type
of it.

Dr. Williams says that it was customary to hang little bells from the
phœnix that marked the royal cars.

and wings were red it was called the red Fung; when blue, the Yu Siang; when white, the Hwa Yih; when black, the Yin Chu; when yellow, the To Fu. Another quotation is to the effect that, when the Fung soars and the Lwan flies upwards, one hundred birds follow them. It is also stated that when either the Lwan or the Fung dies, one hundred birds peck up the earth and bury them.

Another author amplifies the fancied resemblances of the Fung, for in the *Lun Yü Tseh Shwai Shing* we find it stated that it has six resemblances and nine qualities. The former are: 1st, the head is like heaven; 2nd, the eye like the sun; 3rd, the back is like the moon; 4th, the wings like the wind; 5th, the foot is like the ground; 6th, the tail is like the woof. The latter are: 1st, the mouth contains commands; 2nd, the heart is conformable to regulations; 3rd, the ear is thoroughly acute in hearing; 4th, the tongue utters sincerity; 5th, the colour is luminous; 6th, the comb resembles uprightness; 7th, the spur is sharp and curved; 8th, the voice is sonorous; 9th, the belly is the treasure of literature.

When it crows, in walking, it utters " Quai she " [returning joyously]; when it stops crowing, " T'i fee " [I carry assistance?]; when it crows at night it exclaims " Sin " [goodness]; when in the morning, " Ho si " [I congratulate the world]; when during its flight, "Long Tu che wo" [Long Tu knows me] and " Hwang che chu sz si " [truly Hwang has come with the Bamboos].* Hence it was that Confucius wished to live among the nine I [barbarian frontier countries] following the Fung's pleasure.

The Fung appears to have been fond of music, for, according to the *Shu King*, when you play the flute, in nine cases out of ten the Fung Wang comes to bear you company; while, according to the *Odes*, or Classic of Poetry, the Fung,

---

* In reference to Hwang Ti (?) writing the Bamboo Books ?

in flying, makes the sound *hwui hwui*, and its wings carry it up to the heavens ; and when it sings on the lofty mountain called Kwang, the Wu Tung tree flourishes,\* and its fame spreads over the world.

The presence of the Fung was always an auspicious augury, and it was supposed that when heaven showed its displeasure at the conduct of the people during times of drought, of destruction of crops by insects (locusts), of disastrous famines, and of pestilence, the Fung Wang retired from the civilised country into the desert and forest regions.

It was classed with the dragon, the tortoise, and the unicorn as a spiritual creature, and its appearance in the gardens and groves denoted that the princes and monarch were equitable, and the people submissive and obedient.

Its indigenous home is variously indicated. Thus, in the *Shan Hai King*, it is stated to dwell in the Ta Hueh mountains, a range included in the third list of the southern mountains; it is also, in the third portion of the same work (treating of the Great Desert), placed in the south and in the west of the Great Desert, and more specifically as west of Kwan Lun.

There is also a tradition that it came from Corea ; and the celebrated Chinese general, Sieh Jan Kwéi, who invaded and conquered that country in A.D. 668, is said to have ascended the Fung Hwang mountain there and seen the phœnix.

According to the Annals of the Bamboo Books phœnixes, male and female, arrived in the autumn, in the seventh month, in the fiftieth year of the reign of Hwang Ti (B.C. 2647), and the commentary states that some of them abode

---

\* The Wu Tung is the *Eleococca verrucosa*, according to Dr. Williams ; others identify it with the *Sterculia platanifolia*. There is a Chinese proverb to the effect that without having Wu Tung trees you cannot expect to see phœnixes in your garden,

in the Emperor's eastern garden; some built their nests
about the corniced galleries (of the palaces), and some sung
in the courtyard, the females gambolling to the notes of the
males.

The commentary of the same work adds that (among a
variety of prodigies) the phœnix appeared in the seventieth
year of the reign of Yaou (B.C. 2286), and again in the first
year of Shun (B.C. 2255).

Kwoh P'oh states that, during the times of the Han
dynasty (commencing B.C. 206 and lasting until A.D. 23),
the phœnixes appeared constantly.

In these later passages I have adopted the word phœnix,
after Legge and other Sinologues, as a conventional admission; but, as will be seen from all the extracts given, there
are but few grounds for identifying it, whether fabulous or
not, with the phœnix of Greek mythology. It reappears in
Japanese tradition under the name of the Ho and O (male
and female), and, according to Kempfer, who calls it the
Foo, " it is a chimerical but beautiful large bird of paradise,
of near akin to the phœnix of the ancients. It dwells in
the high regions of the air, and it hath this in common with
the Ki-Rin (the equivalent of the Chinese Ki-Lin), that it
never comes down from thence but upon the birth of a *sesin*
(a man of incomparable understanding, penetration, and
benevolence) or that of a great emperor, or upon some
such other extraordinary occasion."

It is a common ornamentation in the Japanese temples;
and I select, as an example, figures from some very beautiful
panels in the Nichi-hong-wanji temple in Kioto. They
depart widely from the original (Chinese) tradition, every
individual presenting a different combination of gorgeous
colours; they only agree in having two long central tail
feathers projecting from a plumose, bird-of-paradise-like
arrangement.

These can only be accepted as the evolution of an artist's

fancy; nor can any opinion be arrived at from the figure of it illustrating the 'Rh Ya, of which I reproduce a *fac-simile*. I have already stated that Kwoh P'oh's illustrations have been lost.

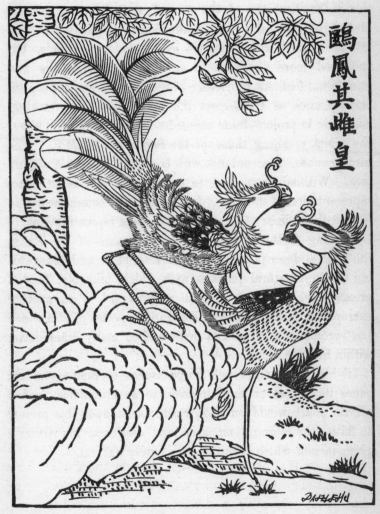

FIG. 91.—THE FUNG HWANG.  (*From the 'Rh Ya.*)

The frontispiece to this volume is reduced from a large and very beautiful painting on silk, which I was fortunate enough to procure in Shanghai, by an artist named Fang

Heng, otherwise styled Sien Tang; it professes to be made according to the designs of ancient books. The original is, I believe, of some antiquity.

In this case the delineation of the bird shows a combination of the characters of the peacock, the pheasant, and the bird of paradise; the comb is like that of a pheasant. The tail is adorned with gorgeous eyes, like a peacock's, but fashioned more like that of an argus pheasant, the two middle tail feathers projecting beyond the others, while stiffened plumes, as I interpret the intention of the drawing, are made to project from the sides of the back, and above the wings, recalling those of the *Semioptera Wallacii*. The bird perches, in accordance with tradition, on the Wu-Tung tree. Without pretending to assert that this is an exact representation of the Tung, I fancy that it comes nearer to it than the ordinary Chinese and Japanese representations.

Looking to the history of the appearance of the Fung, the general description of its characteristics, and disregarding the supernatural qualities with which, probably, Taouist priests have invested it, I can only regard it as another example of an interesting and beautiful species of bird which has become extinct, as the dodo and so many others have, within historic times.

Its rare appearance and gorgeousness of plumage would cause its advent on any occasion to be chronicled, and a servile court would only too readily seize upon this pretext to flatter the reigning monarch and ascribe to his virtues a phenomenon which, after all, was purely natural.

# APPENDICES.

## APPENDIX I.

### THE DELUGE TRADITION ACCORDING TO BEROSUS.*

"Obartés Elbaratutu being dead, his son Xisuthros (Khasisatra) reigned eighteen sares (64,800 years). It was under him that the great Deluge took place, the history of which is told in the sacred documents as follows: Cronos (Ea) appeared to him in his sleep, and announced that on the fifteenth of the month of Daisios—the Assyrian month Sivan—a little before the summer (solstice) all men should perish by a flood. He therefore commanded him to take the beginning, the middle, and the end of whatever was consigned to writing, and to bury it in the city of the Sun, at Sippara; then to build a vessel and to enter it with his family and dearest friends; to place in this vessel provisions to eat and drink, and to cause animals, birds, and quadrupeds to enter it; lastly, to prepare everything for navigation. And when Xisuthros inquired in what direction he should steer his bark, he was answered 'Toward the gods,' and enjoined to pray that good might come of it for men.

"Xisuthros obeyed, and constructed a vessel five stadia long and five broad; he collected all that had been prescribed to him, and embarked his wife, his children, and his intimate friends.

"The Deluge having come, and soon going down, Xisuthros loosed some of the birds. These, finding no food nor place to alight on, returned to the ship. A few days later Xisuthros again let them free, but they returned again to the vessel, their feet full of mud. Finally, loosed the third time, the birds came no more back.

"Then Xisuthros understood that the earth was bare. He made an

---

* Berosus lived in the time of Alexander the Great, or about B.C. 330-260, or 300 years after the Jews were carried captive to Babylon.

opening in the roof of the ship, and saw that it had grounded on the top of a mountain. He then descended with his wife, his daughter, and his pilot, who worshipped the earth, raised an altar, and there sacrificed to the gods ; at the same moment he vanished with those who accompanied him.

"Meanwhile those who had remained in the vessel, not seeing Xisuthros return, descended too, and began to seek him, calling him by his name. They saw Xisuthros no more ; but a voice from heaven was heard commanding them piety towards the gods ; that he, indeed, was receiving the reward of his piety in being carried away to dwell thenceforth in the midst of the gods, and that his wife, his daughter, and the pilot of the ship shared the same honour. The voice further said that they were to return to Babylon, and, conformably to the decrees of fate, disinter the writings buried at Sippara, in order to transmit them to men. It added that the country in which they found themselves was Armenia. These, then, having heard the voice, sacrificed to the gods and returned on foot to Babylon. Of the vessel of Xisuthros, which had finally landed in Armenia, a portion is still to be found in the Gordyan mountains in Armenia, and pilgrims bring thence asphalte that they have scraped from its fragments. It is used to keep off the influence of witchcraft. As to the companions of Xisuthros, they came to Babylon, disinterred the writings left at Sippara, founded numerous cities, built temples, and restored Babylon."

The large amount of work done by the few followers of Xisuthros, seems very surprising, but easily accounted for if we take the version of the Deluge given by Nicolaus Damascenus (a philosopher and historian of the age of Augustus, and a friend of Herod the Great).

"He mentions that there is a large mountain in Armenia, which stands above the country of the Minyæ, called Baris. To this it was said that many people betook themselves in the time of the Deluge, and were saved. And there is a tradition of one person in particular floating in an ark, and arriving at the summit of the mountain."*

* *Encyclopædia Britannica.*

# APPENDIX II.

## THE DRAGON.

### ÆLIANUS DE NATURÂ ANIMALIUM.

#### Book II. ch. 26.

The dragon [which is perfectly fearless of beasts], when it hears the noise of the wings of an eagle, immediately conceals itself in hiding-places.

#### Book II. ch. 21.

Æthiopia generates dragons reaching thirty paces long; they have no proper name, but they merely call them slayers of elephants, and they attain a great age. So far do the Æthiopian accounts narrate. The Phrygian history also states that dragons are born which reach ten paces in length; which daily in midsummer, at the hour when the forum is full of men in assembly, are wont to proceed from their caverns, and [near the river Rhyndacus], with part of the body on the ground, and the rest erect, with the neck gently stretched out, and gaping mouth, attract birds, either by their inspiration, or by some fascination, and that those which are drawn down by the inhalation of their breath glide down into their stomach—[and that they continue this until sunset,] but that after that, concealing themselves, they lay in ambush for the herds returning from the pasture to the stable, and inflict much injury, often killing the herdsmen and gorging themselves with food.

#### Book VI. ch. 4.

When dragons are about to eat fruit they suck the juice of the wild chicory, because this affords them a sovereign remedy against inflation. When they purpose lying in wait for a man or a beast, they eat deadly roots and herbs; a thing not unknown to Homer, for he makes mention of the dragon, who, lingering and twisting himself in front of his den, devoured noxious herbs.

## Book VI. ch. 21.

In India, as I am told, there is great enmity between the dragon and elephant. Wherefore the dragons, aware that elephants are accustomed to pluck off boughs from trees for food, coil themselves beforehand in these trees, folding the tail half of their body round the limbs, and leaving the front half hanging like a rope. When an elephant approaches for the purpose of browsing on the young branches, the dragon leaping on him, tears out his eyes, and then squeezing his neck with his front part and lashing him with his tail, strangles him in this strange kind of noose.

## Book VI. ch. 22.

The elephant has a great horror of the dragon.

## Book VI. ch. 17.

In Idumea, or Judæa, during Herod's power, according to the statement of the natives of the country, a very beautiful, and just adolescent, woman, was beloved by a dragon of exceptional magnitude; who visited her betimes and slept with her as a lover. She, indeed, although her lover crept towards her as gently and quietly as lay in his power, yet utterly alarmed, withdrew herself from him; and to the end that a forgetfulness of his passion might result from the absence of his mistress, absented herself for the space of a month.

But the desire of the absent one was increased in him, and his amatory disposition was daily so far aggravated that he frequently came both by day and night to that spot, where he had been wont to be with the maiden, and when unable to meet with his inamorata, was afflicted with a terrible grief. After the girl returned, angry at being, as it were spurned, he coiled himself round her body, and softly and gently chastised her on the legs.

## Book VI. ch. 63.

A dragon whelp, born in Arcadia, was brought up with an Arcadian child; and in process of time, when both were older, they entertained a mutual affection for one another. The friends of the boy, seeing how the dragon had increased in magnitude in so short a time, carried him, while sleeping with the boy in the same bed, to a remote spot, and, leaving him there, brought the boy back. The dragon thereon remained in the wood [feeding on growing plants and poisons], preferring a solitary life to one in towns and [human] habitations. Time having rolled on, and the boy having attained youth, and the dragon maturity, the former, while travelling upon one occasion through the wilds in the neighbourhood of his friend, fell among robbers, who attacked him with drawn swords, and being struck, either from pain, or in the hopes of assistance, cried out. The dragon being a beast of acute hearing and sharp vision, as soon as he heard the lad with whom he had been brought up, gave a hiss in expression of his anger, and so struck them with fear, that the trembling robbers dispersed in different directions, whom having caught, he destroyed by a terrible death. Afterwards, having cared for the wounds of his ancient friend, and escorted him through the places infested with serpents, he returned to the spot where he himself had been exposed—not showing any anger towards him on account of his having been expelled into solitude, nor because ill-feeling men had abandoned an old friend in danger.

## Book VIII. ch. 11.

Hegemon, in his Dardanic verses, among other things mentions, concerning the Thessalian Alevus, that a dragon conceived an affection for him. Alevus possessed, as Hegemon states, golden hair, which I should call yellow, and pastured cattle upon Ossa near the Thessalian spring called Hæmonium [as Anchises formerly did on Ida]. A dragon of great size fell violently in love with him, and used to crawl up gently to him, kiss his hair, cleanse his face by licking it with his tongue, and bring him various spoils from the chase.

## Book X. ch. 25.

Beyond the Oasis of Egypt there is a great desert which extends for seven days' journey, succeeded by a region inhabited by the Cynoprosopi, on the way to Æthiopia. These live by the chase of goats and antelopes. They are black, with the head and teeth of a dog, of which animal, in this connection, the mention is not to be looked upon as absurd, for they lack the power of speech, and utter a shrill hissing sound, and have a beard above and below the mouth like a dragon; their hands are armed with strong and sharp nails, and the body is equally hairy with that of dogs.

## Book X. ch. 48.

Lycaonus, King of Emathia, had a son named Macedon, from whom eventually the country was called, the old name becoming obsolete. Now, one of Macedon's sons, named Pindus, was indued both with strength of mind and innate probity, as well as a handsome person, whereas his other children were constituted with mean minds and less vigorous bodies.

When, therefore, these latter perceived Pindus's virtue and other gifts, they not only oppressed him, but in the end ruined themselves in punishment for so great a crime.

Pindus, perceiving that plots were laid for him by his brothers, abandoning the kingdom which he had received from his father, and being robust and taking pleasure in hunting, not only took to it himself, but led the others to follow his example.

Upon one occasion he was pursuing some young mules, and, spurring his horse to the top of its powers, drew away a long distance from those who were hunting with him. The mules passing into a deep cavern, escaped the sight of their pursuer, and preserved themselves from danger. He leaped down from the horse, which he tied to the nearest tree, and whilst he was seeking with his utmost ability to discover the mules, and probing the dens with his hands, heard a voice warning him not to touch the mules. Wherefore, when he had long and carefully looked about, and could see no one, he feared that the voice was the result of some greater cause, and, mounting his horse, left the place. On the next day he returned to the spot, but, deterred by the remembrance of the voice he had heard, he did not enter the place where they had concealed themselves.

When, therefore, he was cogitating as to who had warned him from following his prey, and, as it appeared, was looking out for mountain shepherds, or hunters, or some cottage—a dragon of unusual magnitude appeared to him, creeping softly with a great part of its body, but raising up its neck and head a little way, as if stretching himself—but his neck and head were of such height as to equal that of the tallest man.

Although Pindus was alarmed at the sight, he did not take to flight, but, rallying himself from his great terror, wisely endeavoured to appease the beast by giving him to eat the birds he had caught, as the price of his redemption.

He, cajoled by the gifts and baits, or, as I may say, touched, left the spot. This was so pleasing to Pindus, that, as an honourable man, and grateful for his escape, he carried to the dragon, as a thank-offering, whatever he could procure from his mountain chases, or by fowling.

Nor were these gifts from his booty without return, for fortune became immediately more favourable to him, and he achieved success in all his hunting, whether he pursued ground or winged game.

Wherefore he achieved a great reputation, both for finding and quickly catching game.

Now, he was so tall that he caused terror from his bulk, while from his excellent constitution and beautiful countenance he inflamed women with so violent an affection for him, that the unmarried, as if they were furious and bacchantes, joined his hunting expeditions; and married women, under the guardianship of husbands, preferred passing their time with him, to being reported among the number of goddesses. And, for the most part, men also esteemed him highly, as his virtue and appearance attracted universal admiration. His brothers only held a hostile and inimical feeling towards him. Wherefore upon a certain occasion they attacked him from an ambush, when he was hunting alone, and having driven him into the defiles of a river close by, when he was removed from all help, attacked him with drawn swords and slew him.

When the dragon heard its friend's outcries (for it is an animal with as sharp a sense of hearing as it has quickness of vision), it issued from its lair, and at once, casting its coils round the impious wretches, suffocated them.

It did not desist from watching over its slain [friend] with the utmost care, until those nearest related to the deceased came to him, as he was lying on the ground; but nevertheless, although clad in proper mourning, they were prevented through fear of the custodian from approaching and interring the dead with proper rites, until it, understanding from its profound and wonderful nature, that it was keeping them at a distance, quietly departed from its guard and station near the body, in order that it might receive the last tokens of esteem from the bystanders without any interruption.

Splendid obsequies were performed, and the river where the murder was effected received its name from the dead man.

It is therefore a peculiarity of these beasts to be grateful to those from whom they may have received favours.

### Book XI. ch. 2.—*Dragon Sacred to Apollo.*

The Epirotes, both at home and abroad, sacrifice to Apollo, and solemnise with extreme magnificence a feast yearly in his honour, There is a grove among them sacred to the god, and inclosed with a wall, within which are dragons, pleasing to the god. Hither a sacred virgin comes alone, naked, and presents food to the dragons. The Epirotes say that these are descended from the Delphic python. If they regarded the virgin ministering to them with favour, and took the food promptly, they were believed to portend a fertile and healthful year; if they were rude towards her, and would not accept the proffered food, some predicted, or at least expected, the contrary for the coming year.

### Book II. ch. 16.—*Dragon in Lavinium.*

There is a peculiar divination of the dragon, for in Lavinium, a town of the Latins but in Lavinium, there is a large and dense sacred grove, and near it the shrine of the Argolic Juno. Within the grove is a cave and deep den, the lair of a dragon.

Sacred virgins enter this grove on stated days, who carry a barley cake in their hands, with bandaged eyes. A certain divine afflatus leads them accurately to the den, and gently, and step by step, they proceed without hindrance, and as if their eyes were uncovered. If they are virgins, the dragon admits the food as pure and fit for a deity.

If otherwise, it does not touch it, perceiving and divining them to be impure.

Ants, for the sake of cleansing the place, carry from the grove the cake left by the vitiated virgin, broken into little pieces, so that they may easily carry it. When this happens, it is perceived by the inhabitants, and those who have entered are pointed out and examined, and whoever proves to have forfeited her virginity is punished with the penalties appointed by the laws.

"The masculine sex also seems to be privileged by nature among brutes, inasmuch as the male dragon is distinguished by a crest and hairs, with a beard."

## Book XVI. ch. 39.

Onesicritus Astypalæus writes that there were two dragons in India [nurtured by an Indian dancer], one of forty-six and the other of eighty cubits, and that Alexander (Philip's son) earnestly endeavoured to see them. It is affirmed in Egyptian books that, during the reign of Philadelphus, two dragons were brought from Æthiopia into Philadelphia alive, one forty, the other thirty cubits in magnitude.

Three were also brought in the time of King Evergetis, one nine and another seven cubits. The Egyptians say that the third was preserved with great care in the temple of Æsculapius.

It is also said that there are asps of four cubits in length. Those who write the history of the affairs of Chios say that a dragon of extreme magnitude was produced in a valley, densely crowded and gloomy with tall trees, of the Mount Pelienæus in that island, whose hissing struck the Chians with horror.

As none either of the husbandmen or shepherds dare, by approaching near, estimate its magnitude, but from its hissing judged it to be a large and formidable beast, at length its size became known by a remarkable accident. For the trees of the valley being struck by a very strong wind, and the branches ignited by the friction, a great fire thence arising, embraced the whole spot, and surrounded the beast, which, being unable to escape, was consumed by the ardour of the flame. By these means all things were rendered visible in the denuded place, and the Chians freed, from their alarms, came to investigate, and lighted on bones of unusual magnitude, and an immense head, from which they were enabled to conjecture its dimensions when living.

## Book XI. ch. 17.

Homer was not rash in his line,

> Terrible are the gods when they manifest themselves.

For the dragon, while sacred and to be worshipped, has within himself something still more of the divine nature of which it is better to remain in ignorance.

Indeed, a dragon received divine honours in a certain tower in Melita in Egypt. He had his priests and ministers, his table and bowl. Every day they filled the bowl with flour kneaded with honey, and went away; returning on the following day, they found the bowl empty.

Upon one occasion, a man of illustrious birth, who entertained an intense desire of seeing the dragon, having entered alone, and placed the food, went out; and when the dragon commenced to feed at the table, he opened suddenly and noisily the doors, which according to custom he had closed.

The dragon indignantly left; but he who had desired to see him, to his own destruction, being seized with an affliction of the mind, and having confessed his crime, presently lost his speech, and shortly after died.

Book XII. ch. 39.

When Halia, the daughter of Sybasis, had entered the grove of Diana in Phrygia, a certain sacred dragon of large size appeared and copulated with her; whence the Ophiogenæ deduce the origin of their race.

Book XV. ch. 21.—*Concerning the Indian Dragon.*

Alexander (while he attacked or devastated some portions of India, and also seized others), lighted on, among other numerous animals, a dragon, which the Indians, because they considered it to be sacred, and worshipped it with great reverence, in a certain cave, besought him with many entreaties to let alone, which he agreed to. However, when the dragon heard the noise made by the passing army (for it is an animal endowed with a very acute sense of hearing as well as of vision), it frightened and alarmed them all with a great hissing and blowing. It was said to be seventy cubits long.

It did not, however, show the whole of itself, but only exposed its head from the cave. Its eyes were said to have been of the size (and rotundity) of a Macedonian shield.

# APPENDIX III.

## ORIGINAL PREFACE TO "WONDERS BY LAND AND SEA" ("SHAN HAI KING").

The Classic containing "Wonders by Land and Sea" has been praised by all who have read it, for its depth, greatness, far sightedness and completeness; since the narratives therein contained are all wonderful and different from ordinary things. Moreover, the truth or veracity of the book is a matter of doubt to nearly all men, and I therefore think it fit that I should give my opinion on the subject. It has been said by the philosopher Chuang that "the things that men do know can in no way be compared, numerically speaking, to the things that are unknown," thus in reading "Wonders by Land and Sea," the force of his remark becomes apparent to me.

Now, since heaven and earth are vast, it follows that the beings which inhabit them must reasonably be numerous. The positive and negative elements being heated by vernal warmth, produce myriads of living beings of classes innumerable. When the essence of ether combines, motion becomes apparent and generates into wondrous and roving spirits, which, floating about and coming into contact with anything, enter into it and thus create wonderful beings, whether they be inhabitants of mountain or sea, or wood or stone; yea, so numerous are they, that it is an impossible task for me to give them in detail.

The evolution of the essence of the elements generates sound, which by development produces a certain image. When we call a thing wonderful, it is because we do not know the reasons attending its origin, and what we do not call wonderful, we still are unaware why it is not so. And why? A thing is, *per se*, not wonderful, it is because we wish to consider it so; the wonder is in ourselves and not in the thing. For instance, when a savage looks at the cotton cloth we wear, he calls it hemp; and when an inhabitant of Yüch (Soochow and vicinity) sees a rug, he calls it fur or hair. The reason may be found in this: we believe only those things to which we have been educated, and anything which might not be perfectly understood by us we deem wonderful. Hence the shortsightedness of human nature. I will now give a passing remark of what is known amongst us. A place called Ping Shui (?) produces fire, while the Yen mountain produces rats. Now all men know these facts, and !yet when we read and speak of the classic treating of the "Wonders by Land and Sea," we call it wonderful! When a thing is really wonderful, we do not consider it so; and what is not wonderful, we persist in considering it to be so. Such being the case, if, what should be wondered at, we do not call it so, then there cannot be a single wonder in the whole Universe; and if we call a thing wonderful which in truth is not so, then up to the present time there can be nothing wonderful. Moreover, if what is unknowable appears clear to our minds, it follows that all things on earth should be understood by us.

According to the Bamboo Annals of Chi Chuen, and the records of King Müh, it is said that when that King went to visit the Fairy Queen of the West, he took with him as gifts to her, beautiful jade stones, and the best of raw and embroidered silks; while, on the other hand, the Fairy Queen gave a banquet in honour of the King, on the banks of the lake formed by white jade stones. During the banquet they composed and spoke their thoughts in verse, and the sentiments embodied therein were beautiful. Then the royal pair repaired to the hillock adjoining the Küen Lun mountain, and roamed over the palaces of King Hsüen Yüan, which were situated there, and thence to the artificial terraces of the Chung hill, and gazed on the precious and wonderful things collected by that king. Returning to the residence of the Fairy Queen, King Müh had a stone tablet engraved recording the event, and erected it in the Queen's magic garden. On King Müh's return home, he brought with him to the Middle Kingdom beautiful wood and magnificent flowers, precious stones and elegant jades, golden oils and silver candles. In his travels, King Müh rode in a chariot drawn by eight splendid horses; the right-hand horses were of a dark colour, while those on the left hand were greenish. Tsao Fu was the charioteer, and Pen Yung, who stood on the King's right, was the body-guard. Myriads of *lis* could thus be traversed. They went over barren wastes and over celebrated mountains and large rivers, yet none of them barred their onward course. To the east they came across the Halls of the Giants; to the west they arrived at the mansions of the Fairy Queen; to the south they crossed over a bridge composed of immense tortoises; and to the north they drove over streets made of layers of feathers. Traversing these, then, King Müh commenced his journey homeward full of joy. History informs us that " King Müh, riding in a chariot drawn by eight magnificent horses, with Tsao Fu as charioteer, made a journey to the west, in search of adventures in hunting, and, coming to the Fairy Queen of the West, was so happy, that he almost forgot to return home." These words are similar to those recorded in the "Bamboo Annals" of Chi Chuen. The classic called "Spring and Autumn," says that "King Müh was a man of vast ambition, and desired that the whole world should bear the tracks of his cart-wheels, and receive the imprints of his horse's hoof," and the "Bamboo Annals" illustrate this ambition.

The disciples of Ts'ian Chow were all eminent scholars of famous attainments, but they were all sceptical as to the veracity of the adventures of King Müh, and say that in looking over history they are convinced of their fallacy. Sz Ma Tseen also, in writing the preface to the "Records of Ta Wan," says that when Chang Ch'ien went on his mission to Ta Hsia, he traversed the whole length of the Huang Ho up to its very source, but never came across the Küen Lun mountain. Moreover, Sz Ma Tsëen in his own history also says, in referring to the "Book of Wonders by Land and Sea," that, "As to the wonders described in that work, I, for my part, dare not vouch for their truth." In the face, therefore, of all these authorities, is it not a hard task for me to prove the contrary? If the "Bamboo Annals" of a thousand years ago be not taken at the present day as a truthful record of the past, then, indeed, most of the narratives contained in the "Book of Wonders by Land and Sea" must be false. Now, Tung Fang Shun knew of Pe Fang; Lin Tsz Chen proved satisfactorily the existence of Tao Chea by a corpse from that kingdom. Wang Ch'i had an interview with men having two distinct faces on their heads, and a man from the sea coast picked up a dress having two very long sleeves. In carefully studying, therefore, these books, I am convinced that their stories mainly coincide with the tales in the "Book of Wonders by Land and Sea." Behold these evidences then, ye who doubt, and place some credence in the narrations contained in this book.

The Sage King made exhaustive researches into these wondrous beings, and then drew their images. It is indeed impossible to hide the existence of these wonders! The "Book of Wonders by Land and Sea" was compiled seven dynasties ago (up to the Tsin dynasty), a space of 3,000 years. During the Han dynasty this book received the closest attention, and was elucidated for the benefit of its readers; but shortly after it again fell into neglect. Moreover, since then, the names of some mountains and rivers have undergone changes. At the present day, teachers and expounders are unable to explain these wonders, and hence through disuse their reasons given at an earlier age have almost sunk into oblivion. Alas, for the loss of Reason! Fearing, therefore, that it will be entirely lost, I have written the accompanying work, making lucid the points that are obscure, and erasing those that are useless; pointing out what would not be noticeable, and explaining the parts that are deep. I shall endeavour to reclaim what has almost become obsolete, that it may stand for thousand of ages, and the wonders herein recorded shall not, from the present day, be lost. Thus the works of the Emperor Yü of the Hsia dynasty will not be lost in the future, and the records of the Barren Wastes beyond the boundaries of this Empire will be transmitted to posterity. Will not this be a laudable object?

Insects that spring from grassy ground cannot soar as high as the birds of the air, nor can the living beings that inhabit the sea rise up heavenwards like the dragon. A man of medium abilities in music can never be a member of the Orchestra in the Halls of Chuen Tien, nor can the water-buffalo traverse the watery deeps to which even ships dare not venture. Hence, unless a person be of the highest understanding, it would be a hard task to converse with him intelligently of the "Wonders by Land and Sea." And I sigh because it is only the learned and intelligent man that can read understandingly the tales in this work.

KWOH P'OH,
Assistant Secretary and an Official of the 6th Rank,
of the Tsin Dynasty.

# APPENDIX IV.

## A MEMORIAL PRESENTED BY LIU HSIU, BY ORDER OF HIS IMPERIAL MAJESTY THE EMPEROR, ON THE "BOOK OF WONDERS BY LAND AND SEA."

The Memorialist, an officer of the Fourth Rank and Charioteer to His Majesty the Emperor, having received commands to comment upon and make right wonderful books, now reports that an officer named Wang, a subordinate in the Board of Civil Office, had already made comments and set right thirty-two chapters of the "Book of Wonders by Land and Sea," but which the memorialist has reduced to eighteen chapters. This book was compiled during the time of the three Emperors (Yao, Shun, and Yü). At that time there was a great flood, insomuch that the people had no places to live, but only in caves and holes in the rocks, and upon the tops of trees.

The father of Yü, by name K'un, being ordered by the Emperor to assuage the floods, was unable to do so; the Emperor Yao therefore ordered Yü, the son, to do so. Yü used four things in his journey around to make the floods flow away. He first cut away the trees on high mountains to obtain a view of the surrounding country; and having settled as to which was the highest mountain, and which the largest river, Yih and Peh Ye undertook to drive away the wild beasts and birds abounding in the country, and named the mountains and rivers, and classified the fauna of the country, and pointed out which was water and which was land. The feudal lords assisted Yü in his work, and thus he traversed the four quarters of the Empire, where footprint of man seldom could be found, and where boats and carts scarcely reached. He named the five mountain divisions of the Empire and eight seas that bound it. He noted where each kind of precious stone could be found, and the wonderful things he had seen. The abode of animals of land and sea, flora of the country, birds of the air, and beasts of the field, worms, the unicorn, and the phœnix, all these he fixed, and also made known their hiding-places; also the furthest removed kingdom of the earth, and men who were different from human beings. Yü divided the Empire into nine divisions, and determined upon the tribute to be given by each division, and Yih and his comrade noted which was hurtful and which was harmless for the "Book of Wonders by Land and Sea."

All the deeds handed down to us of the sages are clearly noted in the Maxims of the Ancients. The work therein expressed is a matter that can be believed in. During the reign of Shiao Wu there was commonly seen a rare bird, which would eat nothing. Tung Fang Suh saw this bird, and gave its name; he also told what it would eat. His words being attended to, the bird ate what was given it. Someone asked Suh how he knew of it; he said he had read of the bird in the "Book of Wonders by Land and Sea." During the reign of Shiao Hsüen, a large stone was broken in Shang Chuen, which then sank into the ground and displayed a house of stone; in the house was a man of Tao Chia, with his arms tied. At that time the memorialist's father, named Hsiang, was a Censor, and he said that this Tao Chia man was a traitor to his king. Being questioned by the Emperor how he could know it, he said that he had read of it in the "Book of Wonders by Land and Sea," which says, "A traitor having killed his king in Tao Yü, he was chained and confined in a mountain, his right leg was cut off, and both his arms tied behind his back." The Emperor was much surprised at this. All scholars acknowledge that this book is perfectly wonderful, and all intelligent men should read it, and be able to speak upon these wonderful beings and things, and learn the customs of far-off kingdoms and their inhabitants. Hence the Yi King says, "In speaking of the products of the empire, care should be taken to avoid confusion," and learned men, therefore, may not be doubtful.

A memorial presented to the Throne by

LIU HSIU.

# APPENDIX V.

## AFTER PREFACE TO THE "BOOK OF WONDERS BY LAND AND SEA."

In the sayings of the philosopher Tso, the following remarks may be found : " Virtue existed during the times of the Hsia dynasty ; drawings of all animals far and wide were made, and the metal from which the urn was made, for the purpose of engraving thereon the images of these animals, was presented as tribute by the feudal lords of the Nine Kingdoms.  This urn contained the images of all manner and kinds of animals.  This was for the purpose of letting the people know about their existence, so that they might avoid them in entering the mountains and forests, and the genii of the mountains and rivers. Hence the object of the classic treating on the ' Wonders by Land and Sea.' "  When Yü assuaged the floods, the Emperor presented him with a red-coloured wand made of jadestones, and then abdicated his throne in his favour ; on this account he ordered a tribute of metals from the feudal lords of the Nine Kingdoms, wherewith to cast the urn, on which were engraved all kinds of animals from far and wide, such as the wonderful animals and beings of mountains, rivers, grass, and wood, as well as the wonders to be found among walking animals and inhabitants of the air.  Yü, when Emperor, caused the forms of these wonders to be described, how produced, and their natures ; he also had them classified.  When he had described those wonders, whether seen or heard of, or common or uncommon, or rarely heard of, all these he had described minutely, whereby, when the people heard of them, an exceeding fear fell on them.  All animals and beings that were common in those days were described in the Annals of Yü, but such as were wonderful and rare were engraved on the nine urns.  These urns when completed were placed in those parts of the empire where these wonders originally came from, in order that the people of that age might learn and see daily the things that were either heard of or seen by others.

The things brought by tribute-bearers from afar were also added unto the nine urns. Indeed, this made wonders an ordinary matter. That the people might learn these things was the idea of the sage King Yü. Hence, even though at that time all things were described honestly, still the works of that period are far deeper than those of the Chow dynasty. At the time of the last Emperor of the Hsia dynasty, the historiographer Chung Ku, fearing that that Emperor might destroy the books treating of the ancient and present time, carried them in flight to Yin. History also says that K'ung Kiah compiled into a book all the things that were engraved on the vases and dishes from the time of Hwang Ti and his ministers, Yao and Sz. And the Annals treating on the animals described on the nine urns were due to such men as Chung Ku and K'ung Kiah. These Annals are now known as the classic treating on "Wonders by Land and Sea." The nine urns were extinct at the time of Tsing, but the pictures and classic still existed. During the Tsin dynasty, T'ao Chang and his school of poets gazed upon the pictures of the "Wonders of Land and Sea." In the "Seven Commentaries" of the Yuen family, there is observed a case of Chang Sun Yao's pictures of these wonders. These cases may be cited as proofs of the authenticity of the wonders. At the present time, the classic treating on these wonders still exists, but the pictures have become extinct. This classic has been treated upon and commented on and made intelligent by the people that have come after it, insomuch that the names of different districts of the Tsing and Han dynasties have been made to correspond with some of the names mentioned in the "Book of Wonders by Land and Sea." Hence the readers of this book are divided into the believing and the doubting. The believers base their belief upon the fact that it was the Emperor Yü who compiled it and explained its origin. The doubtful base their doubt on the probable fact of the book having been written by people who existed after Yü, and therefore unreasonable. This is indeed a base calumny. Liu Hsiu of the Han dynasty makes mention of the book in his seven chapters treating on it. And his style of composition might be said to be very ancient. Kwoh P'oh of the Tsin dynasty in his preface and notes on this book, states these wonders. The honour of transmitting this book to posterity is due to Liu Hsiu and Kwoh P'oh; but, to prevent learners from considering that the notes made by the two scholars are of no importance, I have therefore written this preface.

YANG SUN,
Of the Ming Dynasty.

# APPENDIX VI.

## EXTRACTS FROM "SOCIAL LIFE OF THE CHINESE,"

BY JUSTUS DOOLITTLE.

Ch. II., p. 264.

" The dragon holds a remarkable position in the history and government of China. It also enjoys an ominous eminence in the affections of the Chinese people. It is frequently represented as the great benefactor of mankind. It is the dragon which causes the clouds to form and the rain to fall. The Chinese delight in praising its wonderful properties and powers. It is the venerated symbol of good.

" The Emperor appropriates to himself the use of the *true* dragon, the one which has five claws on each of its four feet. On his dress of state is embroidered a likeness of the dragon. His throne is styled 'the dragon's seat.' His bedstead is the 'dragon's bedstead.' His countenance is 'the dragon's face.' His eyes are 'the dragon's eyes.' His beard is 'the dragon's beard.'

" The true dragon, it is affirmed, never renders itself visible to mortal vision wholly at once. If its head is seen, its tail is obscured or hidden. If it exposes its tail to the eyes of man, it is careful to keep its head out of sight. It is always accompanied by or enshrouded in, clouds, when it becomes visible in any of its parts. Water-spouts are believed by some Chinese to be occasioned by the ascent and descent of the dragon. Fishermen and residents on the border of the ocean are reported to catch occasional glimpses of the dragon ascending from the water and descending to it.

" It is represented as having scales, and without ears; from its forehead two horns project upwards. Its organ of hearing seems to be located in these horns, for it is asserted that it hears through them. It is regarded as the king of fishes.

Proclamations emanating directly from the Emperor, and published on yellow paper, sometimes have the likenesses of two dragons facing each other, and grasping or playing with a pearl, of which the dragon is believed to be very fond.

## Ch. II. p. 338.

" The sagacious geomancer is also careful to observe the mountain or hill on the right and left sides of the spot for a lucky grave. The left-hand side is called the black dragon; the right-hand side is called the white tiger. The lucky prospects, in a Chinese sense, on the hills situated to the left, should clearly surpass the prospects of the hills on the right. And the reason for this is manifest, for the *black dragon* is naturally weaker than the *white tiger*.

## Ch. I. p. 275.

" The common belief is that the dragon and the tiger always fight when they meet; and that when the dragon moves, the clouds will ascend and rain will soon fall.

" Hence, in a time of drought, if the bones of a tiger should be let down into this well called the ' dragon's well,' and kept there for three days at the most, there will, it is sagely affirmed, most likely be rain soon.

" The tiger's bones are used to stir up or excite the dragon."

# APPENDIX VII.

## EXTRACTS FROM THE "PAN TSAOU KANG MU."

THE KIAO-LUNG. (The four-footed coiled Dragon.　The Iguanodon.
　　　　　　—*Eitel.*)

This animal, according to Shi Chan, belongs to the dragon family.
Its eye-brows are crossed, hence its name signifies "the crossed reptile."
The scaled variety is called the *Kiao-Lung,* the winged the *Ying-Lung.*
The horned kind are called *K'iu,* the hornless kind *Li.*　In Indian
books it is called *Kwan-P'i-Lo.*

Shi Chan, quoting from the *Kwan Cheu Ki,* says : "The Iguanodon (?)
is more than twelve feet long; it resembles a snake, it has four feet,
and is broad like a shield.　It has a small head and a slender neck, the
latter being covered with numerous protuberances.　The front of its
breast is of a red colour, its back is variegated with green, and its sides
as if embroidered.　Its tail is composed of fleshy rings; the larger ones
are several.　Its eggs are also large.　It can induce fish to fly, but if a
turtle is present they will not do so.

"The Emperor Chao, of the Han, when fishing in the river Wéi,
caught a white Iguanodon.　It resembled a snake, but was without
scales.　Its head was composed of soft flesh, and tusks issued from the
mouth.　The Emperor ordered his ministers to get it preserved.　Its
flesh is delicious ; bones green, flesh red."

From the above it may be seen the Iguanodon is edible.

## THE CROCODILE.

"The *T'o* Fish, we call it the Earth Dragon, and have correctly
written the character.　It resembles the dragon, its voice is terrible,

and its length is a *ch'ang* (a hundred and forty-one English inches).
When it breathes it forms clouds, which condense into rain. Being
a dragon, the term 'fish' should be done away with."

Shi Chan says the *T'o* character in appearance resembles the head,
the belly, and the tail. One author says that an animal, which is
identified with the crocodile, is found in the lagoons and marshes of
the Southern Sea, at no fixed time. Its skin is made into drums. It
is very tenacious of life. Before it can be flayed quantities of boiling
water have to be poured down its throat. Another author states that
the crocodile is of a sleepy disposition, with the eyes (nearly) always
shut. It is of immense strength. It frequently dashes itself against
the river bank. Men dig them out of their caves. If a hundred men
dig them out, a hundred men will be required to pull them out; but if
one man dig, one man may pull them out; but the event in either case
is very uncertain. Another author states that recently there were found
in the lakes and estuaries many animals resembling lizards and pango-
lins in appearance, which utter dreadful cries during the night, to the
great terror of sailors. Shi Chan says crocodiles' dens are very deep,
and that bamboo ropes are baited in order to catch him; after he has
swallowed the bait he is gradually pulled out. He flies zigzag, but
cannot fly upwards. His roar is like a drum's, and he responds to the
striking of the watches of the night, which is called the crocodile drum,
or the crocodile watch. The common people, when they hear it, predict
rain. The nape of the neck is bright and glistening, more brilliant
than those of fish. It lays a large number of eggs, as many as a
hundred, which it sometimes eats. The people of the South appreciate
the flesh, and use it at marriage festivities. One author states that the
crocodile has twelve different varieties of delicious flesh; but the tail,
like serpent's flesh, is very poisonous. The crocodile's flesh cures quite
a host of diseases.

THE JĂN SHĒ, or SOUTHERN SNAKE. (*Mai-Teu-Shê*=closed up
(concealed) head snake.)

Shi Chan says: "This snake is a reptile (having a wriggling motion).
Its body is immense, and its motion is wrig-wriggling (*jăn-jăn*)* and
slow; hence its name, *Jăn-Shê*. Another author says its scales have
hair like moustaches (*jăn*). It lives in Kwangtung and Kwangsi
(literally, South of the Hills). Those that do not lift their head are
the true kind; in this way they were called the 'Concealed Head
Snake.'"

---

* *Jăn-jăn* means a gradual but imperceptible advance.

Sung quotes T'ao Hung King to the effect that its habitat is in Tsin-ngan (Fukien), and also Su Kung, who says that it is found in Kwéicheu and Kwangcheu, towards the south, at Kaocheu and Hoün. At several places in the south of the Hills they are still found. Hung King says the large ones (in their coils?) are several fathoms in circumference. Those that walk without raising their heads are the genuine ones. Those that conceal their heads are not genuine. Its fat and gall can be mixed together. The large ones are more than a foot in diameter and more than twelve feet long. It is a snake, but it is short and bulky. Su Kung remarks that its form resembles a mullet's and its head a crocodile's. Its tail is round and without scales. It is very tenacious of life. The natives cut up its flesh into slices, and esteem it as a great delicacy. Another says: When steeped in vinegar the slices curl round the chop-sticks, and cannot be released; but when the chop-sticks are made of grass stems (*mong'tso*), then it is practicable.

Another says: "This snake is a hundred and forty-four feet long; it often swallows a deer. When the deer is completely digested, then it coils round a tree, when the bones of the deer in the stomach protrude through the interstices of the scales. . . . If a woman's dress is thrown towards it, it will coil round and will not stir."

Shi Chan, quoting "The Wonderful Records," says: "The boa is sixty to seventy feet long, and four to five feet in circumference; the smaller ones from thirty-six to forty-eight feet long. Their bodies are striped like a piece of embroidery. In spring and summer it frequents the recesses of forests, waiting for the deer, to devour them. When the deer is digested the boa becomes fat. Someone says that it will eat a deer every year."

Another author says: "The boa, when it devours a deer or wild boar, begins with the hind legs. The poisonous breath of the boa comes in contact with the horns; these fall off. The galls, the smaller they are the better they are." Another says: "Boas abound in Wang Cheu (Kwangsi). The large ones are more than a hundred and forty feet long. They devour deer, reducing the horns and bones to a pulp. The natives use the dolishos and rattans to fill up the entrance to its den. The snake, when it smells them, becomes torpid. They then dig him out. Its flesh is a great delicacy. Its skin may be made into a drum, and for ornamenting swords, and for making musical instruments."

The *Yü Häng Chi* says: "Rustic soldiers in Kwangsi, when capturing boas, stick flowers in their heads, which when the snake observes it, cannot move. They then come up to it and cut off its head. They then wait till it exhausts itself by its jumping about and dies. They then take it home and feast on it." Compare Ælian [*De Naturâ Animalium*, lib. vi. chap. xxi.]: "They hung before the mouth of the Dragon's den a piece of stuff flowered with gold, which attracted the eyes of the beast, till by the sound of soft music they lulled him to sleep, and then cut off his head."

The *Shan Hai King* says : "The *Pa* snake can eat an elephant, the bones of which, after three years, are got rid of. Gentlemen that eat of this snake will be proof against consumption." Kwoh P'oh, in his commentary, says the boa of to-day is identical with the *Pa* snake.

# APPENDIX VIII.

## EXTRACT FROM THE "YUEN KEEN LEI HAN."

### The Dragon.—Chap. I.

The *Shwoh Wăn* says: "The dragon is the chief of scaly reptiles : in the spring he mounts the heavens, in the autumn he frequents the streams.　This is favourable."　Again, "When the dragon walks he is called *sah*, when he flies he is a *yao*."

The *Kwang Ya* says : "When he has scales he is a *Kiao*,\* when he has wings a *Ying-Lung*,† when horns a *Kiu-Lung*,‡ without horns a *Chih-Lung*.

The *Ming Wuh Kiai* of the *Odes* says the dragon has horns at five hundred years, at one thousand years he is a *Ying-Lung*.

The *P'i Ya Kwang Yao* says : "The dragon has eighty-one scales.　This is nine times nine, nine is the *yang* (male principle).　The dragon is produced from an egg, in which he is enfolded."　Again, it says that the *Néi Tien* says : "Dragon-fire comes in contact with moisture and there is smoke, with water and it is consumed (*i.e.* a man may extinguish it with water)."

The *Fang Yen* says : "Before the dragon has ascended to heaven he is a *P'an*§ *Lung*."　The *Yih King* says : "When his clouds move the rain falls, and the various things put forth their forms at the time he rides upon the six dragons and ascends the heavens."　"The first nine : The hidden dragon is inactive.　The diagram indicates that the subtile ether is below.　The second nine : When the dragon is seen in the

---

\* Defined by Williams "as the dragon of morasses and thickets, which has scales and no horn, corresponding very nearly to the fossil iguanodon."　*Vide* the description (ante) from the *Pan-Tsaou-Kang-mu*, &c.

† *Ying*—correct, true.

‡ According to Williams, this is a young dragon without a horn, although others, as in the text, say with one.

§ *P'an*—to curl up, to coil.

fields it is profitable to meet the great man. The diagram indicates that virtue is extended. Fifth nine: The flying dragon appears in the heavens: The diagram indicates the great man creates." Again, "The dragons contend in the wilds, their blood is azure and yellow." Again, "Thunder is a dragon."

The Yuen-Ming-Pao section of the *Ch'un ts'iu* says: "The dragons begin to speak, *yin* and *yang*\* are commingled"; thence, it is said, the dragon ascends and clouds are multiplied. The *Yih King*, in all the diagrams, clearly says: "The summer winds arise and the dragon mounts the skies."

In the *Yuen-Shăn-K'i* of the *Hiao King* it is said: "Virtue approaches the fountains and the yellow dragon appears. It is the Prince's image."

In the "*Tso-K'i*" of the *Hiao King* it is said: "The Emperor is filial, the heavenly dragon bears the plans and the earthly tortoise issues a book." The *Ho-t'u* says: "Yellow gold after one thousand years produces a yellow dragon, azure gold after one thousand years, the azure dragon; red and white dragon is also thus. Black gold after one thousand years produces the black dragon."

The *Twan-ying-t'u* says: "The yellow dragon is the chief of the four dragons, the true beauty of the four regions. He can be large or small, obscure or manifest, short or long, alive or dead; the king cannot drain the pool and catch him. His intelligence and virtue are unfathomable; moreover he ensures the peaceful air, and sports in the pools." Again, it says: "The yellow dragon does not go in company, and does not live in herds. He certainly waits for the wind and rain, and disports himself in the azure air. He wanders in the wilds beyond the heavens. He goes and comes, fulfilling the decree; at the proper seasons if there is perfection he comes forth, if not he remains (unseen)."

The *Shi Ki* says: "The bright moon pearl is concealed in the oyster, the dragon is there."

Books of the after Wei dynasty say, "Persia has three pools." They narrate that a dragon lives in the largest, his wife in the second, and his child in the third. If travellers sacrifice, they can pass; if they do not sacrifice they encounter many storms of wind and rain.

Lü-lan asserts that Confucius said, "The dragon feeds in the pure (water) and disports in the clear (water)."

Sun-k'ing-tsz says: "The accumulated waters form the streams, the *Kiao-Lung* is brought forth." Han-Féi-shwoh-nan says: "Now as the dragon is a reptile he can be brought under control and ridden.† But below his throat are tremendous scales, projecting a foot. If a man should come in contact with them he would be killed."

---

\* The male and female principle.
† See the notices in the body of the work from the *Shan Hai King*.

Kwan-tsz says: "The dragon's skin has five colours, and he moves like a spirit; he wishes to be small and he becomes like a silkworm; great, and he fills all below heaven; he desires to rise, and he reaches the ether; he desires to sink, and he enters the deep fountains. The times of his changing are not fixed, his rising and descending are undetermined; he is called a god (or spirit)."

Hwai-nan-tsz says: "The dragon ascends and the brilliant clouds follow." Again, he says: "This *Kiao-Lung* is hidden in the streams, and his eggs are opened at the mound. The male cries above and the female cries below, and he changes; his form and essence are of the most exalted (kind). Man cannot see the dragon when he flies aloft. He ascends, and wind and rain escort him."

The *Tihing P'ien* says: "Wings beautiful grow for the flying dragon; hair soft like that of a calf on the *ying* dragon; scales only for the *Kiao-Lung*. Only in pools is found the *Sien-Lung*." Chang-hang said: "How the *Ts'ang-Lung* meets the summer and aspires to the clouds, and shakes his scales, accomplishing the season. He passes the winter in the muddy water, and, concealed, he escapes harm." Pan-ku, answering Pin-hi, said: "The *Ying-Lung* hides in the lakes and pools. Fish and turtle contemn him, and he does not observe it. He can exert his skill and intelligence, and suddenly the clear sky appears. For this reason the *Ying-Lung*, now crouching in the mud, now flying in the heavens, appears to be divine."

Lun-hang says, "When the dragon is small, all the fish are small; this is divine."

Pao-pòh-tz says: "There are self-existent dragons and there are worms which are changed into dragons." Again, he says: "Among the hills the *Ch'ün day*, called the rain master, is a dragon." Hwai-nan-tsz said: "The *Chuh-Lung* is north of the goose gate concealed in the Wei-Ü mountain." The *Shan-hai-king* says the god of the Chung-shan is called *Chuh-Lung*. When he opens his eyes it is day, when he shuts his eyes it is night. His body is three thousand *li* long.

The *Shui-king-chu* says: "The *Yulung* considers the autumn days as night. But the dragon descends in the autumn and hibernates in the deep pools; how then can he say that autumn is night?" It also says: "There is a divine dragon in the vermilion pools at Kiao-chew. Whenever there was a drought, the village people obstructed the upper tributaries of the pool, and many fish died; the dragon became enraged at such times, and caused much rain."

The *Kwah-ti-t'u* says: "At the dragon pool there is a hill with four lofty sides, and within them is a pool seven hundred *li* square; a herd of dragons live there, and feed upon the many different kinds of trees.

---

\* See the description of the dragon from the *P'au-Tsaou-Kang-mu*

It is beyond Hwui-ki forty-five thousand *li.*" Again, it says: "If you do not ride on a dragon you cannot reach the weak waters* of the Kwan-lun hill."

The *Poh-Wuh-Chi* says: "If you soak the dragon's flesh in an acid (and eat it), you can write essays." Again, it says: "The Tiao-sheh is in form like a dragon, but smaller. It likes danger; hence it is appointed to guard decayed timber." Again, it says: "The dragon lays three eggs. The first is *Ki-tiao.* He goes ashore and cohabits with the deer or deposits his semen at the water's edge, where it becomes attached to passing boats or floating wood and branches. It appears like a walnut, it is called *Tsz-chao* flower, and constitutes what is mentioned in the *Tao-ch'u* as dragon-salt." Again, it says: "Below the dragon-gate every year in the third month of spring, yellow carps, two† fish, come from the sea, and all the streams, with speed to the contest. But seventy-one can ascend the dragon-gate in a year; when the first one ascends the dragon-gate there is wind and rain. It is followed by fire which burns his tail, and then he is a dragon."

The *Shih-I-Ki* says: "East of the hills 'of Fang-chang there is a dragon plain where there are dragon skins and bones like a mountain: spread out they would cover one thousand five hundred acres. To meet him when he sloughs his bones is like the birth of a dragon. Or it is said the dragons constantly wrangle at this place. It is enriched with blood like flowing water."

The *Shuh-I-Ki* says: "In the P'uning district there are the isles where the dragons are buried. Fu-loo says the dragons shed their bones at these isles, the water now contains many dragon-bones, in these mountains, hills, peaks, and gorges. The dragons make the wind and rain. There are dragons' bones everywhere, whether in the deep or shallow places; there are many in the ground. Teeth, horns, vertebral columns, feet, it seems as though they are everywhere. The largest measure one hundred feet or exceed one hundred feet. The smallest are two feet or three or four inches. The bones are everywhere. Constantly when looking for anything they are seen." Again, it says: "It is told of the Kuh mountains in Ki-cheu that when the dragon is a thousand years old, he enters the mountains and casts his bones. Now there is a dragon hill, from the midst of the hill issues the dragon's brains."

The *K'ié-Lan Records at Loh-yang‡* say: "You cannot trust the hills in the west. They are too cold. There is snow both winter and summer. In the hills there is a pool where a bad dragon lives; long ago some merchants rested near the pool, until the dragon became enraged, abused, and killed them. A priest,§ Pan-T'o, heard of it, and, leaving his seat to the pupils, went to the kingdom of Wuchang to

* Waters of such specific gravity that even a feather would sink.
† Probably a pair from each stream.
‡ In Foh-kien.
§ Probably equivalent to "abbot."

learn the Po-lo-man incantations ; he mastered them in four years, and returned to his seat. He went to the pool and invoked the dragon. The dragon was transformed into a man, repented, and followed the king. The king then removed." Again, it says : "To the west of the kingdom of Wuchang there is a pool in which the dragon prince dwells. There is a monastery on the banks of the pool, in which there are more than fifty priests. Whenever the dragon prince does anything marvellous, the king comes and beseeches him, using gold, precious stones, pearls, and valuables, throwing them into the pool. Afterwards they are cast up and the priests gather them. This monastery relies upon the dragon for food and clothing and the means to assist people. Its name is ' Dragon Prince Monastery.' "

The *Ts'i-ti* records say there is a well in the city of Ch'áng-ping at the brambles ; when the water is disturbed a spiritual dragon comes and goes. So the city is called the dragon city.

The *Shi-San-Tsin* records say Ho-li has also the name Dragon Gate. Great fish collect below it, in number one thousand. They cannot ascend. If one ascends it is a dragon. Those which do not ascend are fish. Hence it is called the " Pao-sai-lung-man. (Great carp ascend the dragon gate and become dragons ; those which do not ascend prick the forehead and strike the cheek.) Again, it says : " The Lung-sheu mountains are sixty *li* long ; the head enters the Wei waters, the tail extends to the Fan streams. This head is two hundred feet high ; his tail descends gradually to a height of fifty or sixty feet. It is said that long ago a strange dragon came out from south of the mountains to drink the Wei waters. The road he travelled became mountain. Hence the name."

The *Kiao-Cheu-Ki* says : " In Kiao-chi at Fung-ki-hien there is a dyke with a dragon gate ; the water is one hundred fathoms deep. Great fish ascend this gate and become dragons. Those which cannot pass, strike the cheek and puncture the forehead, until the blood flows. This water is continually like the Vermilion pool."

The annals of Hwa-yang say : " Only at Wu-ch'ing district does the earth meet the gate of heaven ; the dragon which mounts to heaven and does not reach it, falls dead to this place, hence when excavating you find dragon-bones."

The *I-Tung-Chi* says : "Twenty *li* west of Lin-fung-hien is a stone dragon, among the cliffs is a rock like a dragon. In a year of drought wash it, and it rains." Again, it says : " At Yen-T'ang there is a pond called Smoky Pond ; it is north-east of the city ten *li*. Its depth has never been ascertained. It is reported that long ago a man caught a white eel, and was about to cook it, when an old man said, ' This is the dragon of the river Siang ; I fear calamity will follow.' The man was angry, and, regarding the words as vain, proceeded. The next day the whole village was submerged."

The *Kwoh-Shi-Pu* says : " At the time of the spring rains the carp springs through the dragon gate and becomes transformed. At the present time, in Fan-cheu of Shansi, there is a cave in the mountains; in it are many cast bones and horns of dragons. They are collected for medicine, and are of five colours. It is recorded in the *Chw'en* that north of the Wu-t'ai hills, below the terrace, is Azure Dragon Pool, about one-third of an acre in extent. The Buddhist books say five hundred evil dragons are confined (here). Whenever it is mid-day a thick mist gradually arises. A pure priest and candidates for the priesthood may see it. If a nun or females approach then there is great thunder, lightning, and tempest. If they come near the pool, he certainly will belch forth poisonous breath and they will die at once. Foreigners say that in Piolosz there is a spiritual dragon which goes and comes among the granaries. When a servant comes for rice the dragon vanishes. If the servant comes constantly for rice the dragon does not suffer it. If there is no rice in the granaries, the servant worships the dragon, and the granaries are filled."

*Yuin-Chu-Tsih* records : " If one sees a dragon's egg in the lake or river there will certainly be a flood."

The *Nan-Pu-Sin-Shu* says : " The dragon's disposition is ferocious, and he fears bees'-wax, loves jade, and the King-ts'ing delight to eat the flesh of cooked sparrows. For this reason men who eat sparrows do not cross the sea."

The *Pah-mung-so-yen* says : " The perverse dragon, when rain is wanted, sneaks away into old trees or into the beams of houses. The thunder god pulls him out."

*Wu-ch'ăn-tsah-ch'ao* says : " There is a great dragon which sloughed his skin on the brink of the Great Lake. Insects come out from his scaly armour. Instantly they are transformed into dragon-flies of a red colour. If men gather them they get fever and ague. If men now-a-days see these red dragon-flies they call them dragon-armour, also dragons' grandsons, and are unwilling to hurt them."

*Pi-shu-suh-hwa* says : " In Suh-chan and Hang-cheu the twentieth day of the fifth month is called the day of the separation of the dragons. Therefore, in the fifth and sixth months, whenever there is thunder, and the clouds crowd together, if they see a tail bent down, and stretching to earth from among the clouds, moving like a serpent, they say, ' The dragon is suspended.' "

*Tsu-tz* say : " The spiritual dragon leaves the water and dwells in the dry place, and the mole, crickets, and ants annoy him."

Kung Sun Hung replied to Tung Fang Shoh, saying : " Before the dragon has ascended he is of a sort with fish and turtles ; after he has ascended the heavens his scales cannot be seen."

Siu Tsung Yuen answered an inquirer, saying : " The *Kiao-Lung* ascends to the heavenly fountain. He pervades the six regions (North,

South, East, West, Above, Below). He moistens all things. Shrimps and the leech cannot depart one foot from the water."

The *Shwoh-Wan* says: " The *Kiao* belongs to the dragon species. When a fish attains three thousand six hundred [years?] it becomes a *Kiao*; on attaining this much the dragon flies away." Again, it says: "[Dragons] without horns are *Kiao*."

The *P'i-Ya* says: "The *Kiao's* bones are green, and they can bring their heads and tails together and constrict anything; hence they are called *Kiao*. A popular name for them is 'the horse's lasso.'" Another author says the *Kiao's* tail has fleshy rings; they are able to compress any creature, and then tear it with the head.

The *Shuh-I-Ki* says the eye-brows of a *Kiao* unite, and their uniting is a proof that it is a *Kiao*.

The *Siang-Shu* (Book of Physiognomy) says that when the eye-brows unite the epithet *Kiao* is applied, because the *Kiao Shǎn* has crossed eye-brows.

The *Yueh-kiu* (Divisions of Seasons) says that the season of autumn is unfavourable to the *Kiao*.

The *Kia-Yü* (Family Discourses) says that if a stream contains fish, then no *Kiao* will stay in it.

Hwai-nan-tsze says that no two *Kiao* will dwell in one pool.

The *Shan-Hai-King* says the *Kiao* is like a dragon and snake, with a small head and fine neck. The neck has white ornamentations on it. The girth (?) is five cubits; the eggs of the capacity of three catties; and it can swallow a man.

# APPENDIX IX.

## APPENDIX TO THE CHAPTER ON THE SEA-SERPENT.

### THE SHAN.*

" The *Shăn* belongs to the snake species."

" The *Tsah Ping Shu* (Work on Military Science) says: 'In drilling an army,† when you arrange it like the *Shăn* expelling its breath, its appearance is like that of a snake, but the waist is large; below there are scales, running backwards.'

" One says that its form is like that of the Ch'i-lung, which has ears and horns and a mane of a red colour. When it exhales its breath, it forms a cloud just like a palace or tower, looking as if its walls are moving in a cloud of mist, or like a weary bird flying above. This makes everyone feel very happy until the exhalation or snorting of the breath is finished.

" There is a popular saying about building a *Shăn* tower. When the sky appears to rain you can see a resemblance of it.

" The *Shi-Ki* (Book of Odes or Classical Poetry) uses the expression, The *Shăn's* breath forms a tower '; it is in allusion to this.

" At the present day it is said that the *Chi* (a pheasant or francolin‡) and the snake copulate and produce the *Shăn*.

" The oily substance of *Shăn* combined with wax makes the Chinese wax candles, the fragrance of which, when burning, can be recognized for one hundred feet in all directions; and the smoke emitted from the flame forms the appearance of a tower."

" The *Pih T'an* (Familiar Stories) says that at Tang-cheu (in Shan-tung), in the midst of the sea, there are often clouds arise and appear

---

* Extract from the *Yuen Keen Lei Han*, vol. ccccxxxviii., p. 23.
† In drilling an army there are names for all positions of the army. Thus, the general says: "Arrange yourselves like a snake, or like a dragon, or any other imaginable shape."
‡ Williams gives this translation only, but I think there must be another meaning; probably some sort of reptile is indicated.

like the imperial palace, or towers of the city walls, and there is also an appearance of people, carriages, and horses busily engaged [mirage?]. They call this phenomenon 'the market of the sea,' while others say it is but the breath of the *Shăn Kiao.*

"The *Wu Léi Siang Kan Chi* says the *Shăn* is but another sort of dragon, and can be found in some of the ponds and wells. They throw out the air, forming rain as in the locality of Wu San Yin.

"The *P'i Ya Kwang Yao* says, when a snake transforms it becomes a *shăn*, in the likeness of the *Kiao*, but without paws."

## SECTION II.

"The twelfth chapter of *Ching Kiün Chw'en* says that Hü Ching Kiün, author of the above book, met a youth, quite handsome in his apparel. The youth pretended to be very modest, Hu Kiün knowing all the time that he was a *Kiao* in another form. So he told his followers, 'I regret to think that the province of Kiang-si will often meet with the misfortune of inundation if we do not exterminate that *Kiau Shăn*, and are not careful to prevent its escape.' But the *Shăn* knew what Hu Kiün was saying, and gradually slipped away to a place called Sung-sha-cheu, where he transformed himself into a yellow ox. But at the same time Ching Kiün also transformed himself into a black ox, tying a handkerchief over his neck to distinguish him from the other ox, and ordered his disciple, Shi Tai Yu, to use his sword, and thrust at the left thigh, because he had entered within the city wall, in the western part of which there is a well. By jumping this well he found a road to Tau-cheu, and once more transformed himself into a handsome youth, and by so doing got married to the daughter of a magistrate called Ku Yu, with plenty of jewels and gold. Then Ching came to see Ku Yu and said, 'I hear that you have a very noble son-in-law. May I see him?' Ku answered 'Yes,' and told him to come out. But he excused himself upon account of sickness, and hid himself. Then Ching Kiün, saying, 'The dangerous things of the rivers and the lake are old devils, and they dare to transform themselves into human beings,' ordered the son-in-law to transform himself into his original form, and hid himself beneath the table. Then the magistrate said, 'Kill this,' and they did so. Then Kiün sprinkled water on the two sons, and they were immediately transformed into *Shăn*. [There must be children born from the marriage.—*Translator.*] He advised Ku Yu that he must put them away immediately, or the whole house would be in danger of breaking."

"The *Tai Ping Kwang Ki* says that the lake of Wan Tun, at Fì Chi, contains a *Shăn* which often fought with the *Shăn* of Lake Su. Near this lake is a place called Yao, where there lived a man called Ch'ang Sing Shan, of great bravery, and an expert archer. He once dreamed that a *Shăn* snake was transformed into a Taouist, and then it said to him : ' I am endangered by the *Shăn* of the lake of Lu. Can your honour assist me? if so I will reward you heavily. The tight white chain is me.' Next day Sing Shan went with a youth of Yao to the shore of the lake and dreamed. He waited until the waves rose and the surf struck the shore, making a noise like thunder. He saw two oxen coming, one with a white belly and legs ; then Sing Shan discharged an arrow at it, and it turned out to be a *Shăn*. The water immediately turned into blood, and the *Shăn*, after receiving the wound, tried to return to the lake of Lu, but died before it reached there."

### *Kang Hi Dictionary.*

" The *Shăn Kiao* belongs to the *Kiao* species, and also has the appearance of a snake. It has horns like a dragon ; the mane is red below the waist ; all the scales are projecting. It eats swallows, and can emit an air which appears like a tower.

" Again, any turtle when old enough may be called a *Shăn*."